Y0-BGD-239

LENCHO

A Tale of Decent Vagabonds

By

L.L. KELLERMAN

James
Lenda
Future Love
Happy Trails
Lendell

A BIOGRAPHICAL NOVEL

1st Edition
Copyright© 2014 by L. L. Kellerman
All rights reserved. Printed in the United States of America. No Part of this book may be used or reproduced in any manner whatsoever without written permission except in the case of brief quotations embodied in critical articles and reviews.

www.lenchoweedman.com
www.facebook.com/LLKellerman

Books are available at special discounts for bulk purchases in the United States by corporations, institutions, and other organizations. For more information, visit our website.

Excerpt from 'East of Eden', John Steinbeck by permission Penguin Group and the Steinbeck Family Foundation.

Songs released by Waymore (Waylon) Jennings used by permission given by Waylon (Shooter) Albright Jennings

DEDICATION

Callie B 1976—2009
I delivered you into this world. You brought joy and much
laughter into so many of us. I miss you.

Father 1919—2011
I know you loved me. I love you, too. We never found the middle
ground. The warden wouldn't let me come to the funeral.

Waylon Jennings 1937—2002
My guru. You sang my life. Thank you.

TABLE OF CONTENTS

And this I believe: that the free, exploring mind of the individual human is the most valuable thing in the world. And this I would fight for: the freedom of the mind to take any direction it wishes, undirected. And this I must fight against: any idea, religion, or government which limits or destroys the individual. This is what I am and what I am about. I can understand why a system built on a pattern must try to destroy the free mind, for that is one thing which can by inspection destroy such a system. Surely I can understand this, and I hate it and I will fight against it to preserve the one thing that separates us from the uncreative beasts. If the glory can be killed, we are lost.

—John Steinbeck, East of Eden 1952

ACKNOWLEDGEMENTS

Lencho wishes to express thanks to all the guys at Federal Prison Camp Lompoc and a couple others in the free world that contributed to the writing of this book.

Special thanks to Cindy, Jessica, Lew Stieger, Crystal Reed, Christina Kraker, Liz, Connica for editorial input. And thanks to Jim McClain for print production editing.

My five typists: John (Yanni) Pappas, M.C. Kelley, Ray Appleton, Chuka, and Jeff Kilbride. Yanni changed my text, Ray and Chuka both went to the hole and vanished, Jeff picked up from around chapter eight and saw it through to the end (including these acknowledgments). I thank them all for the valiant effort.

Armando gave us insight into the history of the infamous Mexican cartels as did Richard Pinion and Jorge Torres.

Alex Nguyen contributed on Asia and Chinese / Viet Namise organized crime history, locals, food, and general background as needed.

Tab Broome is an expert pilot and was invaluable in explaining how to land, takeoff, and crash at various airports and in muddy fields.

Harry Washborne, camp baker and master of the one liner, provided several memorable colloquialisms.

Michael Bell and Dee helped with the history of downtown L.A. and the hood, as well as colorful crack dealers of the 1980s who are either still in prison or dead. (The exception being Freeway Ricky Ross who left the low here at Lompoc recently after a dozen years). Dee is at seventeen years on a twenty five year sentence.

Scott Iguichi, Gordon Shuster, Larry Siedenfeld, Doug Hanft, and Reed Slatkin all contributed general data when we needed it on one subject or another.

Dr. Bob Jones DDS (retired) and Christine Beems both long suffering and very close friends that have always stuck by us and were there to go online and Google all sorts of subjects when we got stuck.

The artwork was done by Jason, Jr., Eddie, Sam, Steve Ferchaud, Gary Quiring (gqphoto@comcast.net) and Lisa.

INTRODUCTION

January 21, 2012, Federal Prison Camp, Lompoc, California, 8:30 a.m. I've just finished having my morning coffee and watching Good Morning America, which is my normal morning routine. I returned to my bunk to do a little reading and catch a short nap. I've been down now for 52 months of an 80 month sentence I received for a drug trafficking conspiracy. With good time credit plus one year off for completing the drug program, I have 6 months of the sentence left. I'm due to be released from custody tomorrow morning at 7:30 a.m. My wife will be picking me up and driving me to a half-way house in Fresno, California, where I don't expect to stay for more than a couple of days. Then, I will be sent to home confinement where I will finish off the balance of the 6 months.

I am a weed dealer. I have been for 45 years. I buy, sell, smuggle, transport, grow, cultivate, harvest, package, and personally use marijuana. Most of the money I've made over the years I've spend on alcohol, drugs, and wild women; the rest of it I wasted. It is my personal choice. You may or may not understand me.

It's not my first rodeo. I'm stretched out on my bunk when the inmate clerk steps up to inform me that I am wanted over at the officer's station immediately. Thinking that it may have something to do with my release, I get over there to see what's up. "What have you got for me, boss?" I ask.

He replies, "They want you over at the big house, Lencho, something about some x-rays they gotta get before you leave."

"Nothing like waiting until the last minute, aye, boss? It amazes me that you people can keep this place going at all!" I muse.

"Just go out front, and the Lieutenant will pick you up in a few minutes," he finished. The big house is a medium security prison that houses 1,700 inmates. It's a real prison with all the bells and whistles. Not a fun place to hangout.

The Lieutenant pulls up in his jeep and I get in to take the short drive over to the entrance of the prison. Getting into the prison is a major process, which begins with a metal detector, and then a pat down search. Afterwards, I am led to a bull pen area with two gates. I pass through the first gate and wait until it closes; then the second gate opens and I walk through it. Now I'm in a courtyard, which leads into the front entrance of the main building. Here I must now enter yet another bull pen where I have to go through the same process one more time. Finally, I am now inside the main lobby, which in turn leads to the administration offices and medical services area. I have been here before for x-rays, so when the two guards flanking me steer me to the left instead of the right, where I know that the x-ray room is, I ask, "Where am I going?"

"Hands against the wall and spread 'em," is all the goon says to me. He gives me a quick shakedown, running his hands around my collar, up and down my arms, around my chest, and then down each of my legs to see what's hanging between them.

"A little to the left there, big fella," I say. The guards make some grunting noises that I cannot understand, but that they seem to. We then march down a big hall; you can feel the suffering and death that's been going on here for the last 60 to 70 years. Some guys spend their entire lives here. We pass some offices, but I don't see anyone milling about. They open a door, and I step inside of what is obviously an interrogation room. It has the standard table and chairs already set up and waiting for me. I'm told to take a seat. The goons leave.

Before I can get myself comfortable, a cheap suit with an asshole in it comes waltzing through the door. Another young, dumb-assed Federal clone with a buzzed haircut and shiny Government Issue shoes. They must order these clowns right out of a catalog of Federal dorks.

"Sit down, Lencho. I'll try not to take up too much of your time cause I'm sure you must still have some more packing to do," he said.

"You're too kind," I reply. "Can I see some I.D.?"

"The fact that I am in this building is all of the I.D. you need. You can call me Sam."

"That seems to be a real popular name with you guys, Sam. What can I do for you?"

"It's like this, Lencho: You're going to do something for me, and I'm going to do something for you—or not something, as the case may be," he explains.

"Oh boy, this should be good," I say.

He opens his briefcase and takes out a stack of papers that I recognize as a copy of the manuscript I've been working on for the last four years. "I'm sure that you are familiar with this, Lencho, and now so am I. You see, when you went to your counselor to mail a copy of this to your niece for correction and editing, the counselor red flagged it. Before it cleared the mail room security, they ran their own copy just to see what you were up to. As you know, this is our legal right. The B.O.P. can open and read all correspondence coming to or from the prisons. It seems as though they found your work interesting enough to send a copy to the Department of Justice, and that is how it finally ended up on my desk. We like to investigate anything that could be considered subversive or a matter of National Security," he informed me.

"I had a feeling something like that had taken place when it took a month to get delivered," I replied.

"Be that as it may, I've read your story in its entirety, and then spent some time doing a background check on your criminal career. It's all a matter of public record, at least most of it is. You have been a menace to society for a long time now, Lencho. My question to you is: Why would a man spend his entire life in a world such as you have been living in?"

"It's called freedom, Sam. A concept that guys like you just don't understand. It's you and your kind who are the menaces to society, Sam. Not me. You, and the parasites like you, create this so called drug war and suck the blood out of the American taxpayers. You guys have been doing this for the last 50 years, so don't get me started. You are all just a bunch of scum bags, and you know it as well as I do. So, let's finish this conversation, cause I got shit to do."

"Okay, Lencho, here it is. If you publish this book as a true story—naming the people you have named, the places you describe, and the dates relating to these events—we're coming after you. Let me explain to you exactly what that means. You've got five years of probation to complete after your time in the halfway house. I promise you, you will never make it. All it takes is for you to be found with or anywhere near drugs, guns, or a large amount of money and you will be put away for life. If that is not enough, you'll also never be able to cross an international border again without raising a Red Flag, after which you will be immediately detained for questioning. We know that you enjoy traveling, and we also know where you usually go. Did I forget to mention the IRS? You will not be able to fart without them crawling up your ass for the rest of your life, Lencho."

"Did you read that part in my book where I said you are all a bunch of no good motherfuckers?" I sneered.

"Hey, it's like this, Lencho, it's not all bad news. I told you I would do something in return for you. Go ahead and print the book, sell a million copies, we don't really give a shit, but on the copyright page this is what we want it to read." He slides a sheet of paper to me in bold print that says:

This is a work of fiction. Names, characters, and incidents are the product of the author's imagination or are used fictitiously. Any resemblance to actual events or people, living or dead, is entirely coincidental.

"Well, I've finally seen it all. They have me down and are now going to start kicking me. Sam, you are interrupting my nap time. Are we done, yet?" I said.

"Yeah, we're done. Better think about it carefully, Lencho," he intoned.

"Sure, Sam, and fuck you very much," I replied.

Chapter One

"Good Hearted Woman"
Released 1972
Waylon Jennings

He likes the bright light, the night life
And good-timin' friends
When the party's all over
She'll welcome him back home again
She don't understand him,
But she does the best that she can
This good-hearted woman
Lovin' a good-timin' man

ORIGINS

The Mexicans called him Lencho, and for reasons that will become obvious, we will leave it at that.

In 1959, his dad moved his large family from Hardin, Illinois, to Prescott, Arizona. Out of eleven brothers and sisters, he was number seven. The 1960s were around the corner, and great upheaval was at hand. Was it foretold? He was to become Prescott, Arizona's, oracle of consciousness expansion and a pot smuggling major domo; he'd eventually find himself at the forefront of common sense and an enemy of obfuscation. But before all of that, he was a young redneck boy that liked to fight and chase girls.

As a boy he learned to ride horses. He worked in feedlots and meat packing plants. In the life of the southwest, he became acquainted with all things ranching. He identified with Arizona, and loved its dry heat and frontier with Mexico.

In 1964, he was arrested for the first time for cattle rustling. He learned at a young age that the law had a penchant for exaggeration. He and a few pals drove madly after some bovines drinking, laughing, and yelling, dangling from the front fender of an old Plymouth sedan with lazos in hand. They didn't notice the game warden sitting on a hill watching them with his binoculars. Judge Ogg intoned from the bench, "You boys got two choices: prison for one year or join the military and go fight the communists in Asia. What'll it be?"

So Lencho joined the Navy, and in 1964 found himself in boot camp, NTC San Diego, California. He hated it, and decided that when he finished the initial training he was going AWOL. How bad could it be after all?

Back in Prescott, Officer Allan Wing spotted him sauntering down Whiskey Row, and pulled up. "Hey, Lencho, how ya doing? Guess you didn't like the Navy too much? They're looking for ya. Better go back, son." Lencho heeded his advice, and he went back and got a room at the YMCA in downtown San Diego. From the pay phone he called up the shore patrol.

"I'm willing to turn myself in, but you guys gotta promise no rough stuff. This is just a little misunderstanding. Okay?"

"Sure," the shore patrol replied. "Not a problem. Happens all the time. Where are you?" Five minutes later they showed up at his door to drag his sorry ass to the brig on 32nd Street. When he arrived at the brig, the jarheads that ran the place bruised his ribs and busted his knuckles.

After two weeks, he got orders to present himself to the watch on the afterdeck of the USS Galveston, where he respectfully reported for duty. The XO was remarkably kind, and told him these were difficult days for America and American youth. Lencho understood, and also realized that things were going to heat up overseas in the coming years. There was a draft: If you didn't enlist, you were forced to join. Either way, it was about the same thing. Now he had a second opportunity to make amends and learn to be a good citizen and a good sailor.

"How about it, son?"

But the young man was aghast at the waste and theft he found all around him. The military buildup was in full swing, and so was the corruption that always accompanied war. About half of the provisions brought aboard seemed to leave just as fast down the bow and into the trunks of officers and enlisted cars. He was a fighter for sure, not some peace nick, but this just sucked eggs. As more provisions arrived aboard the Galveston, they vanished before they ever made it to their enlisted destinations. What a racket.

His continuing dissatisfaction was so apparent that he stood before the XO once again a short time later. Truly, this gentleman must have been the rarity of second in command and head of discipline because he said, "I don't want the unmotivated on my ship, son. A big war is coming, and as I told you last time we talked, I believe there will be protests from those who are forced to be here. Therefore, I am recommending a general discharge under honorable conditions. You're very lucky not to get a BCD."

The big chicken dinner, Lencho pondered. Lucky indeed, and he walked off the Galveston a few months later, discharge in hand and now a veteran. It was back to Prescott and the rodeo.

*****

Lencho hadn't graduated from high school because of the military, so he got his GED and sought employment. The baby boom generation was crowding the job market, so his dad did what he had always done with his brood and farmed them out to the neighbors for odd jobs. One such job was to hand dig a basement. Tunneling skills would come in handy down the road, but at that time it was backbreaking labor that netted a buck an hour, less the ten percent he had to pay to his dad for room and board. It did engender a work ethic, but he cast about for better remuneration and found a job at his brother-in-law's family feed store/meat market. Art and his sister, Susie, were kinder than the old man, and he was up to $2.00 an hour in no time, a big improvement to be sure.

Then one day trouble walked into town. Four fellows from the west coast were spotted at the Texaco station. Bill Kasner, John Lay, and Steve Skurja stopped by and told Lencho of the menace. Their hair was long, for God's sake, so they must've been queers.

"I think we should kick their asses," Skurja suggested.

"Long hair you say?" Lencho replied. "I think we should give them all haircuts."

With scissors and a sharp knife, they cornered the first hippies they had ever seen, and did indeed shear their locks. Crying and whimpering, the now balder iconoclasts fled. With a shopping bag of locks as their prize, the boys went whooping and laughing over to Lencho's place for a coke and to show his dad their trophy. After hearing their story, the old man put his hand on Lencho's shoulder in what was a very rare show of affection, and told them all, "I'm proud of you boys. This town don't need no beatniks."

Lencho went down to the local print shop and got the owner to make them up a batch of bumper stickers: "Come to Prescott, get your ass kicked." Heady times indeed.

After work, he'd drink beer and look for trouble. Trouble took many forms, but cowboys were always ready. As most do in Arizona, he lived alongside the Mexican population, ate their food, and ogled their women. He always liked the Mexican people; he admired their forbearance in a prejudiced land and their willingness to do the hard jobs whites wouldn't do. Even so, he could get mean when he was drunk with his buddies, which now and then added to the racial strife that surrounded him.

One Saturday night at the local dance a black fellow walked in and the rednecks decided they better put this nigger in his place. Really, Lencho had nothing against black people. He didn't even actually know any black people, but between the beer and peer pressure, he decided to confront the man anyway. Just before he took a swing, in walked Tony Yesquez, a Marine who was to be killed in action a year later. Tony was a popular young Hispanic, and not as prejudiced as the whites. He knocked Lencho on his ass with one blow.

"What's the matter with you, Lencho?" he scolded. "What did this man ever do to you?" Not a damn thing. Lencho took the lesson to heart, and forever after forswore ignorance in the matter of race.

*****

On a warm summer day in 1967, twins Jimmy and Bob Smith asked Lencho if he wanted to go for a swim with the gang over at the quarry. He had the day off, so they went in a battered old Ford. Out on Willow Creek road, Jimmy looked slyly at his brother Bob and they both glanced conspiratorially at Lencho. "What?" Lencho asked, sensing something was up.

"You ever smoke marijuana?" Bob asked.

"Naw. Well, I heard about it. Sorta like heroin, ain't it?"

"Naw," they replied. "Want to join us?" he said as he pulled out a corncob pipe that was stuffed with green plant material.

"Sure," Lencho agreed uneasily. Can't look like a pussy, he thought.

The boys staggered out of the car fifteen minutes later in a cloud of smoke.

Lencho had an epiphany. The world shimmered, the water in the quarry below sparkled as never before, the girls that lined the cliff edges were never lovelier, and he couldn't stop grinning. When it was his turn to swing out over the fifteen foot drop on the rope, he was both terrified and giddy with euphoria. When he let go, it must have taken a half hour to hit the cold water. He couldn't believe it. What exhilaration. Was this the same world? Well, no—it was suddenly a new one.

And there, looking down from on high, was Prescott's first domestic hippie, Bill Hunter. He even had longish hair. "Hey Bill," Lencho called to him, "what's the good word?"

"God bless the Jefferson Airplane, Lencho," Bill replied. That said it all. Nothing was ever the same. His words rang in Lencho's mind as if etched there by the finger of God, and he didn't even have a clue who or what a Jefferson Airplane even was.

*****

A couple of Lencho's pals, G.G. Harris and Walter Coughran, moved to Phoenix for better employment, so Lencho followed. The bright lights and the big city.

For companionship, he traveled back on the weekends to visit his high school sweetheart, Karen. He would sneak into her room through a window and spend the night. That worked out well until her dad charged in one morning and found him hiding under the bed. It looked like he would be shot at that point, so his mom counseled him to marry. "But Mom," he protested, "I'm barely twenty-one. I don't want to get married."

"Honorable men marry their girls, Lencho," she chided, "and then they have children." A week later he and Karen drove to Las Vegas and lived in sin no more.

They moved into a little flat in Phoenix, where she began her career in dental hygiene and he shoveled shit at stockyards alongside his buddies. It was a union job that paid $3.75 an hour. The world was his oyster. Big bucks, and his own man. Between the two of them, they earned enough money to party on the weekends, go out to nice restaurants, and smoke the best pot they could find. The booze slackened off, and marijuana took center stage in the intoxicants. A lot of giggling and munchies, but no hangovers. In order to keep getting the pot, he asked Walt Coughran if he had any sources. "I do, man," Walt told him. "I'll get us a can."

A few days later the can appeared, and it was literally a can previously full of Sir Walter Raleigh tobacco. Now it had about twenty joints of pot in it. Walt took a quarter, and charged him the ten bucks it cost.

"Whoa," Lencho protested. "I don't mind the ten dollars, Walt, but how come you're taking such a big pinch?"

"Pot's illegal, ain't it?" he replied. "Well, when a guy goes out and breaks the law, he runs the risk of going to jail. For that risk, I get compensated. It's a fundamental rule of business."

Well, that did make sense, but regardless of the expense, Lencho gave away most of his product week after week anyway. Then, all the people he generously shared with started to bug him to supply them. So, he looked up the local celebrity and country music star Richie Albright. Albright was drumming for the now legendary Waylon Jennings, who had the good fortune of not taking the airplane that crashed in the Iowa cornfield and killed Buddy Holly, the Big Bopper, and Richie Valens.

"What we'll do man," Albright told him, "is I'll front you ten baggies of weed. In a week, you pay me 80 bucks. Go sell them to your friends, and then pay me."

One week later, Lencho was back with the 80 dollars. Richie said, "Far out, here's ten more," and the process was repeated. After a month of this, and with demand ever increasing, Lencho had a surplus of marijuana. When he went to see Richie as usual, he pointed this out.

"I guess you ain't clear on the concept, Lencho," Richie Albright told him. "All the extra bags are yours. It's called 'profits.' Now go out and sell those bags, and that will turn them into cash. Understand?" A light went on, and an entrepreneur was born. With $150 a week from his job at the stockyards, Karen's pay check, and now all the extra dough, the cowboy was really rolling.

*****

The two went on a vacation to Ocean Beach, California, because that's where Karen's sister lived. Fun and sun and the mighty pacific. He had been down that way a few times during his short Naval career, and all the pretty girls had blown him away. Nothing had changed. Situated on the other side of Point Loma, OB was very hip. Besides the surfer dudes and pretty girls, it was a well-educated, well-heeled, and urbane area, located near the colleges of San Diego. And, it was awash in marijuana and LSD.

Lencho's brother-in-law, Powder, put them up in a converted bread truck that sat adjacent to his rented house. Lencho and Powder became fast friends. Powder was a young man of many accomplishments, dabbling in music and theology. He had a degree in anthropology, and was currently working on his Master's. They both shared a zeal for the herb.

In short order, Lencho and Karen decided the deserts of Arizona were no longer for them, and they quit their jobs and moved to OB. Living at first on unemployment benefits, it was no time at all until Lencho scored a good connection via a guy named Mitch McIntyre. Borrowing $125 from a girl named Cuba, he bought his first 'kilo' from Mitch. They were euphemistically called kilos, but were seldom a true one thousand grams. More like a block of mediocre sticks and stems. The Mexicans had a long way to go at that time in developing high quality product, but it would do.

After enrolling at Mesa Community College, he soon became the man to go to for pot. In fact, he spent so much time selling weed, his classes immediately suffered and became only a second thought. Also, there were little lovelies everywhere, and he was constantly tempted. In fact, being the big dealer on campus, he found it was not difficult to dip the wick in wayward cooze. Although he tried to keep it secret from his wife, she knew, and it didn't sit well. But these were new times, and Karen became the earth mother in short order herself.

The metro van they lived in was small, so Lencho struck a deal with the lady who rented to Powder and his wife. She owned another house next door that was badly in need of repairs, and Lencho offered to rehabilitate it for rent.

Then came the acid.

Lysergic Acid is possibly the world's most potent psychoactive substance by molecular weight. The military saw it as a truth serum; the CIA as a weapon; the psychiatric community as instant schizophrenia. The hippies had found it, and the nation was becoming obsessed with it. LSD was now transforming the world in subtle and spectacular ways. "I'm gonna try acid," he announced to Karen. "Can't believe I haven't already."

"No!" Karen wailed in terror. "You'll go crazy. You'll think you can fly!"

"That's the idea, isn't it?" he replied.

"Then I'm going to take it with you," she declared, and they did.

Neither of them jumped out any windows or went mad. The sugar cubes melted on their tongues, and their consciousness moved to another realm of swirls, colors, and giddy euphoria. Nothing made any sense, but everything became clear. Clear for the first time. The clear light.

The two couldn't move for the first two hours, they lay side-by-side in their house all alone, vaguely hearing the cacophony of the Sunday beach crowd outside their windows. If anyone came or went, they didn't notice. After the harlequin shadows of their minds climbed down from the trapeze, they wandered out into the dusk and walked awestruck in the surf. The cool water curled around their toes and feet; they were sinking into wet sand under the sky patterns of paisley. Later that night they made love and experienced an ecstasy that cannot be quantified. Twelve hours later, they were still in each other's arms, smoking a joint with the spaced out calm and a bliss that was stunning. Then a memory. Then, after a badly needed bowl of granola, they slept at last.

That was LSD.

Lencho became a true flower child and certified weed man apprentice. He began taking acid once a week, and then several times a week, which was really not that much in the opinion of the newly reborn.

In an early hint of ugliness, his pot connection, Mitch, was found dead of an alleged heroin overdose. Mitch was not the junky type, and most believed it was some sort of murder. Probably a rip off, which was becoming more and more common.

Before Mitch died, Lencho procured a lot of product and other pot sources, so he was able to supply his growing customer base with little problem. The most valuable of this base, ironically, was the U.S. Navy.

Sailors came down to OB seeking fun and girls. A couple lads stationed nearby became valuable customers. At first, they would buy a dozen ounces and a few tabs of acid to take back to the ship to resell to their mates. It wasn't long before the volume swelled to pounds of marijuana at a time and one hundred dose bags of acid. Lencho's pockets bulged with cash, his hair grew long, and his once skinny frame filled out from good living, fine food, and fine weed.

Despite his relative wealth, the weed man eschewed materialism. To prove the point, he simply abandoned his late model car on the streets and forgot all about it. He preferred to hitch hike instead. He never went back for it because it was a symbol of crass commercialism. Besides, hitching was a way better way to meet new customers and chicks.

Karen's brother had a spread back in Arizona that everyone called Maggie's Farm after the Bob Dylan tune; Lencho would hitch back and forth to it frequently. There he could both sell and buy weed. On one such journey a young guy named John picked him up outside of Phoenix. "Want to smoke a doobie?" John asked.

"Does a bear shit in the woods?"

"This dope is all I got left, man," John told him savoring the bite. "I've been all over the place trying to score, but I just can't find any weight."

"How much weight are you looking for?" the weed man asked.

"I got two thousand dollars in my jeans. How much will that buy?"

"Want to go to San Diego? I can fix you up, my man."

"Groovy," John grinned. He became a very good and regular customer.

After the first seventeen bricks for his two grand, John flew in every couple of weeks for the next year to buy pot and sent it back home. So, when he suddenly vanished, Lencho chalked up his disappearance to the diaspora of the nomads called hippies. There were many new customers that showed up almost daily.

The quality of the product began to improve as well. At first the growers did not give much of a shit on that, but as demand accelerated, better stuff with more punch was demanded by the gringo buyers. Even though weed is synonymous with Mexico, it had never been cultivated in such large amounts, so it took some American experts to show the way. The growers started to cull out most of the male plants to allow the buds to mature to total ripeness. What once had been piles of stems and seeds was now looking like real pot. A community of brokers emerged in the San Diego area, and Lencho knew them all.

He was talking to a customer who came down from Berkeley. "Seems to me," the guy said, "you are sitting right here beside the international border. Instead of buying your weed from smugglers, why don't you become a smuggler? You could get it at a much better price, sell for less, and do way more business." Not a bad idea indeed. He did know a guy down there who might be able to help.

Manuel was a young Mexican he and Karen bought bags of pot from when they went camping down in Guadalupe Canyon, south of Mexicali. He was a good natured fellow, around Lencho's age. When Lencho asked, he said, "Sure, I can fix you up. No problema."

"Let me work on the logistics, and I'll get back to ya," Lencho answered.

Lencho contacted his friend, Danny Pope, who was fresh back from Nam. Danny had been a recon man; his training was in the realm of locating the enemies, tracking them, and reporting back their positions. "Smuggling dope will be a piece of cake compared to those gooks I used to hunt. Let's do it," Danny agreed.

The difference in price for the same weed was a savings of a hundred dollars a block. From $130, the cost plunged to $30. The first smuggling run commenced with Pope gathering his gear, map, compass, binoculars, face paint, water, and food. Lencho rounded up the cash while Manuel procured the product, which he stashed in the desert between Mexicali and Tecate. Danny Pope took his position, spending the next two days watching the comings and goings of the border patrol along the line. He learned the lay of the land, the times when patrols passed, and how many officers there were. On night three, he lugged the twenty kilos across the border himself, and met Lencho at a predetermined spot along Highway 8. They whooped with glee and raced to safety. The load was hidden in the trunk. "Piece of cake," Pope told him. "Can't wait to do it again."

"We will, my friend," Lencho replied. "And soon." After the first time, Manuel arranged for some hired help to do the lugging after Pope gave the "all clear." Profits zoomed.

Around the same time, a Bostonian came upon the scene in OB. His name was Charlie, and he was pretty slick. Well dressed and a head for numbers, Charlie was all business and intended to make a killing in the dope game.

"I'll buy all the weed you can provide, Lencho," he said. "I got a big market back east, and it's only getting bigger." He wasn't kidding.

All Lencho had to do was put in a call to Boston, and Charlie was there in a flash to pick up the product. Then, he started to send his mom and grandma out as well! These two little ladies were so straight looking it was a shame. They dressed nicely and had expensive luggage, lots of luggage packed with reefer. They flew it back to Boston time after time. Profits increased exponentially.

Lencho moved into a bigger house, got his hair cut, and dressed nicer—he had to look straight, considering his line of work. He also expanded his buying. His smuggling wasn't keeping up with the demand, so he had to buy from other brokers. Charlie also went elsewhere for material. As America developed its taste for the mota, it seemed they couldn't get enough. Soon they had a regular syndicate full of sharp dressing young men who all seemed to drive a Porsche.

Charlie kept hundreds of pounds of material ready for shipment. He also considered himself to be a connoisseur. A man who only partook of the very best, be that pot, women, cocaine, or even heroin.

"You ever try H, man?" Charlie asked Lencho one day.

"Hell no!" He exclaimed. "That stuff will kill ya."

"Heroin, in moderation, can be a very sophisticated experience in the realm of pharmacology, my friend."

"Really?" Lencho replied.

"Oh yes, especially with a pinch of cocaine. Heavenly." Cocaine and heroin, the classic goofball.

"No way would I ever do any of that," Lencho told him. The next day he tried some. Heavenly.

During the early seventies, Global Brand #4 heroin flooded America. It was brought from Southeast Asia via organized crime and the U.S. military. The scourge began on the east coast, but made its way to the west coast as well. It was far more potent and dangerous than the usual junk from Mexico—so pure it could be smoked, so potent it could be deadly. Lencho snorted China White blended with Pink Peruvian flake cocaine, and it put him in a narcotized euphoria that lasted hours. He lay on Charlie's floor in dreamland listening to Charlie Byrd bop on the stereo. When he finally came down, he swore that it was such a pleasant experience that it was far too dangerous to ever try again. The next day, he came back and tried some more. Then he stopped. Charlie was the kind of sly devil that might just get a guy hooked on purpose. The ruthless capitalist type.

Business with Charlie was good, and the times were an awful lot of fun. Until one morning Lencho stopped by to see what was up, and he found Charlie and his crew of slick young dudes very freaked out. They were arguing and shouting at each other. Pacing the floor like caged animals.

"Why the agitation?" Lencho finally managed to interject.

Charlie just stared and pointed to the bedroom. "Got any ideas?" He asked blankly.

The weed man looked at the door, and a sudden apprehension came over him. "What's in there?" he asked.

"Johnny's in there," Charlie replied. "He's dead. We don't know what the fuck to do. There's sixty grand in cash in this house and half a ton of weed in the garage, and I got a stiff in the back room. Jesus Christ!"

"I'll see ya later," is all Lencho said.

*****

Charlie and the boys finally calmed down. Their good bud Johnny must have decided he wanted one more sniff of the white powders after the others had retired from their partying the night before. When they got up the next day, they found him face down in a plate of it, his eyes wide, his flesh stiff and cold. Eventually they placed him in an area rug, rolled him up, and hauled him out to an old Ford pickup one of them owned. From there he was taken to the marina and loaded onto a pleasure craft recently purchased. He was ferried out to sea ten or fifteen miles. His gut was slit open so he wouldn't float, and with two hundred pounds of chains and anchors wrapped around him, they sent him to the bottom where he remains today.

Chapter Two

"Good Ol' Boys"
Released 1980
Waylon Jennings

Just'a good ol' boys
Never meanin' no harm.
Beats all you never saw
Been in trouble with the law
Since the day they was born

Makin' their way
The only way they know how
That's just a little bit more
Than the law will allow.

THE MARINE

A young man walked into Lencho's house, plunked his butt onto the overstuffed sofa, and declared to the heavens, "My God, there are so many bitchin, naked girls up in Big Sur. The freaks up there just lay around all day in the sun smoking dope, dropping L, and screwing. It's unbelievable."

That's all Lencho and his brother Bobby needed to hear before they were out the door. Together they hitched up Highway 101 to Monterey, and then veered over to scenic Highway 1 to the cliffs at Big Sur. Rides were never hard to come by in 1970, with the highways full of rock and roll gypsies and flower children of every description. A psychedelic van dropped them off at the entrance to Pheiffer State Park.

Heavily laden with backpacks, they hiked up into the great stone strewn canyon. Just as the oracle had prophesied a day or two before, lovely young girls abounded! It seemed as though at least five hundred maidens were walking around and lying on top of the rocks. The sun shined, redwood trees native to the coast were fragrant, and little birdies flitted about with the colorful butterflies.

A young runaway named Jeff, who appeared to be around fifteen, suddenly said the magic words: "Hello, want to smoke a doobie?"

The boys soon formed a bond and became fast friends. "I got some acid, man. Let's trip."

The three sat on a boulder watching the girls and their bouncing breasts. Every girl had a dozen breasts and giggled manically. Then they smoked another joint, and as the sun began to go down, Bobby announced he was heading back to San Diego.

"But man, you just got here," Jeff told him.

"Naw, man, I've been here for centuries."

"Tell my old lady I'll be home soon. Stay cool, Bro," Lencho called out, and then Bobby was gone.

"Do you want to check out where I'm staying?" Jeff asked. "You can stay, too. It's a commune, and it's really far out!"

They hiked back a couple of miles to the park entrance, and then they stuck their thumbs out. It wasn't ten minutes before a car picked them up, and they smoked another joint. The Nepenthe Restaurant sat seven miles south of the park on the ocean side of the highway. The property occupied about five acres. There were numerous out buildings adjoining its borders and a stately coastal live oak to greet travelers at the entrance.

The restaurant was a world all unto its own. It was very large, and included a sprawling deck overhanging the cliffs with views of the mighty pacific. Angry waves crashed upon the rocks eight hundred feet below. The place was named after the Nepenthaceae Malaysian climbing plant from whence the ancients brewed a potion to dispel sorrow, and induce forgetfulness.

A woman around thirty greeted the boys as they entered. It was clear that, although she was at work, she was high on LSD. "Well, hello, Jeff," Mary Ann said warmly. "Who's your friend?"

She wore a billowing gown of mauve and lace that just reached the floor. It was cut low across her bosom, and blonde ringlets fell to bare shoulders. Mary Ann was a vision of gossamer loveliness, but even high on acid she was clearly on top of things. "We need some help around here," she said slowly. "Do you want a job?"

"What do you want me to do?" Lencho asked.

"Our drink waiter had an emergency and won't be back for a week or two. All you would have to do is deliver drinks to tables. It's easy, and you'll meet some groovy people. The tips are good, too."

He went to work immediately, and was soon delivering white wine to Joan Baez and her party.

The chef, Peter Rabbit, took an immediate liking to the weed man. Peter was a bisexual necromancer in his late thirties. Slender at five foot nine with luxuriant black hair that reached to his shoulder blades, he pranced about the kitchen working his magic on exotic culinary. He also read the Tarot and threw the I Ching. He dressed like a wizard most of the time, except when he was cooking then donned the white jacket and tall chef hat. He seemed to always be in cerebral motion

"I do many things besides cook," Peter Rabbit purred. "I am a seer, a sage, a mystic, and a prophet. I prophesize that you and I will get along famously." Lencho winced uncomfortably, but agreed to take boarding in Peter Rabbit's large cabin on the outskirts of the compound. The motif was baroque with a hot tub. A central mega bed for orgies sat beside a metal fireplace that vented through the roof. Naked people were wreathed and tangled on top of the silk sheets. The smell of incense blended with pot filled the room. It was all quite bizarre, decadent, and homey. Lencho was amazed by the set up, and took the bed in the far corner.

His time at Nepenthe moved quickly, and he enjoyed the job. When he first arrived he had less than fifteen dollars in his jeans, and a week later he had a couple hundred. It wasn't the money he was used to making with weed sales, but for something actually legal, it wasn't bad. He got himself a new set of duds to fit in; a pair of bell bottom velour pants in blazing burgundy, a long sleeved tie dye shirt in lime and crimson, and leather sandals to complete the ensemble.

He met a particularly beautiful young girl named Maureen one night on the dance floor. She insisted on introducing him to an up and coming author who was nursing a scotch and soda with a side of cocaine at the bar.

"Hunter," she exclaimed, "please meet my new friend Lencho. He says he sells pot, and only the best."

Hunter Thompson turned and looked disdainfully through aviation sunglasses. He removed his cigarette and holder from thin lips and sneered, "He'd make a nice rug." Then turned back to his drink.

Lencho didn't know who the father of gonzo journalism was, but didn't care for his attitude. "What a dick," he said to Maureen.

"Oh, that's just how Hunter is. A genius you know."

The libidinous and hedonistic quality of the Nepenthe was a revelation to Lencho, and he enjoyed the place immensely. Cocaine, a fairly new drug on the scene for the upwardly mobile, hip white people, was first introduced to him there, and of course LSD still reigned supreme. Fine quality locally grown marijuana was abundant, and then there was the sex. "Lencho, I want you to meet Jessica," Peter Rabbit said one day in the kitchen. She's eighteen, and so beautiful."

He looked at this angel, and was beginning to believe there were no homely women in Big Sur. She was a petite brunette with a slender waist and firm breasts. And that face. She had beauty to die for. But she was bait, as it turned out.

That night as the weed man began to make his moves on the pliable young wench, his manhood stiff and proud as he rolled around under the silk in the orgy bed with the young Jessica's breasts in hand, he suddenly felt the presence of another. It was the necromancer. He slithered in between them with the subtly of a car crash. His own member erect, and ready to take orders. As he looked hungrily into Lencho's eyes, it was clear that he didn't want Jessica. That was enough for the weed man. There was no boxing the clown that night as he sprang to safety, shunning the embrace of the Rabbit.

"No, Peter. I don't think so," he mumbled.

"But Lencho—my weed man! Why not?"

"You're a nice guy and all. A great cook, but I'm a cowboy for God's sake. How would it look? This isn't my thing! There are limits!!"

"When you discover there are no limits, my love," he purred, "you will discover true consciousness."

As Lencho dashed out of the cabin and into the night, the lovely Jessica fell into Peter Rabbit's embrace, but there was a look of longing and disappointment in Peter's eyes.

The wonderful fantasy of Nepenthe ended that day, as he gathered his back pack, put on his hitching threads, and said his so longs. They all said they loved him, and would remember him. He found himself out on Highway 1 with a thumb out heading south. A VW van stopped within ten minutes, and he climbed in. "Wanna smoke a doobie?" the driver asked.

*****

Lencho, Karen, Bill, Pat, Diana, Pope, and usually about fifteen complete strangers, now resided in a big old house on Muir Street in Ocean Beach. It was essentially a commune where hippies of every stripe, both young and old, stayed for a while and then were gone. Often in the morning, Lencho would get up and stagger into the living room muttering, "What the fuck?" as he viewed all of the bodies crashed on the floor. The doors of Muir Street were never locked.

A load of weed was ordered up for Maggie's Farm, so Lencho left with it in Danny Pope's 1968 Dodge van. Typical of weed men in those days, he would travel the byways of America plying his trade. Often he'd leave with seventy pounds, deliver it to the customer, and then head straight back home without even one single joint to smoke.

Between Phoenix and Gila Bend, he spied a couple of hitch hikers with thumbs out, so he stopped to give them a lift. The two young men climbed aboard; one sat up front and the second laid in the back on top of a mattress. The first kid was about eighteen, and very loquacious. He went by the name of "Free" He promptly broke out his little stash of pot to roll up a joint, which Lencho had just been thinking he really needed. The second was about the same age and said little. His hair was short.

It turned out the boy was a Marine, just back from Nam and heading to Camp Pendleton to be discharged. He declined the joint, which was all right with Lencho and Free since there wasn't much anyway. "I got some beers back there in the cooler, Marine," Lencho said. "Help yourself."

Free told Lencho that he and the Marine had just met on the road, "I guess he seen some shit over there," he added.

"See some shit, Marine?" Lencho inquired, leaning over his shoulder.

The boy nodded and replied, "Did what they wanted, went into the service right out of high school. Two years was all I could take, terrible stuff."

"Yeah," Free said, "this fucking war really sucks. How long has it been going on for?"

"Oh, about eight years, I think," Lencho replied. "Started under Ike with those advisors. Now it's big time! I was in the Navy myself a couple of years ago, and hated it."

"Did what they asked me to do. Man, a lot of killing." The Marine repeated. They drove on in silence.

"Where you going, Free?" Lencho asked between puffs.

"Heading up to San Francisco. Hear there are a lot of naked flower girls there. Also, the draft is after me, man, and there is no fucking way I'm going to go into the Army."

Lencho replied, "I hear ya. You want naked girls, man? Ya gotta go to Big Sur!"

The Marine stirred in the back seat and appeared uncomfortable, even fidgety. Probably fucked up in the head from the war, Lencho thought to himself. Maybe even paranoid. Fucking government and their fucking war. Fuck it.

"Hey, man, let me out at this restaurant. This is as far as I'm going," the Marine said.

"You sure, man?" Lencho said as he pulled over. "Kinda out here in the middle of nowhere, don't ya think? Pendleton is straight ahead!"

"Here is good. I left my parents in Phoenix, and I think I'd better call them. Thanks again for the ride."

"Sure, man," and he let the boy out in the hot afternoon sun. They drove on, and finished the skinny little doobie. A half mile outside of Gila Bend, a Sheriff's car appeared in the rear view mirror. Lencho saw the red light go on, heard the telltale siren, and pulled over. A burly deputy wearing a cowboy hat and boots climbed ponderously out of his Maricopa County Sheriff's car and waddled up to the two hippies.

"Where ya'll going in such a hurry?" he inquired from behind dark sunglasses.

"I don't think I was speeding officer," Lencho replied, hoping the smell of reefer wasn't lingering, but knowing that it was. "We're just going back to California."

"Are ya now?" the fat man replied, "Do I smell mar-i-wana by some chance?"

"Hell no," Lencho huffed. "What are you talking about?"

"Step out of the van, son, and keep your hands where I can see them. You too, buddy," he said to Free.

The boys climbed out knowing that none of this was good. Due to his girth, it wasn't easy for the deputy to make his search, but he gave it his best law enforcer once over, and emerged triumphantly with a tiny roach and two seeds he had plucked from the dirty carpet.

"You boys just stand still," he said with a slight smile. "I got me some probable cause now, and I think I'll get some backup to search your vehicle."

He simultaneously reached for the police radio in his squad car and pulled a .357 magnum from a holster. While pointing it at Lencho and Free, he spoke into the mic. "Sheriff, got us some dope fiends out here on Highway 85. You coming out to toss the van?"

The radio crackled, and then the Sheriff's voice came on to tell the deputy, "Good work, Steve, I'll be right out."

Steve motioned for the pair to climb into the patrol car's back seat. The three of them waited for the Sheriff to show up. It took him around twenty minutes to arrive, and when his car pulled up alongside the other two vehicles, Lencho and Free saw handcuffed Marine sitting in the back seat. He had a distressed look on his face. "What did you arrest that kid for, Officer? He's just a jarhead that I gave a lift to. He's on his way back to Pendleton."

The fat cop smirked, "He ratted you boys out, son. Called us up from the diner back yonder. He said you all was smokin that wacky tobacky, and he thought you were maybe smugglers."

Lencho replied, "You're kidding me."

"Not likely. We arrested him too, for vagrancy."

The two coppers ransacked the old dodge, but found nothing except a few more seeds. The cops took the three men to a little metal and brick jail in downtown Gila Bend. The jail had four small individual cells enclosed with a lot of bars. Each cell featured a smelly toilet and a hard metal rack with a thin piece of foam as a mattress. It was hot as hell with no air conditioning. The place made Lencho long for home; he just sat there looking around thinking of his parents back in Prescott.

His Mom was a sweet woman who always worried about her independent and errant son. The old man was another story entirely. He and Lencho had never really gotten along, even when Lencho was just a child, and the boy never really understood why.

The most praise that he had ever received from his old man was the time a few years earlier when he had cut the hair off some hippie dudes who had the misfortune of wandering into town. Now he was the one with the long hair, and he was sitting in a shitty little jail, in a shitty little desert town.

"Hey," He bellowed, "I want to make a phone call. I know my rights."

He kept that up for about fifteen minutes until the fat deputy who arrested them came in. "Shut the fuck up, boy. I hear ya! One phone call out in the lobby. You probably wanna make bail? Ha, why these here charges are so serious, you're lucky if you get ten years."

He wasn't worried about getting ten years for less than a gram of pot. He just all of a sudden wanted to touch base with his parents. His mom answered on the third ring; he could hear her heart break the second he said, "Mom, I'm in jail. Ah, Mom, it ain't nothing, just a roach?"

"Bugs?" she asked, "they arrested you for bugs?"

"Not that kind, Mom," he replied. "I'm okay. How's Dad?"

"I don't even want to tell him, Lencho. He'll just about die. Hold on." She put the phone down and was gone for a few minutes. When she picked it up again she said, "Your dad said to tell you we'll be down tomorrow, or maybe the next day. He told me to tell you that, and then to hang up. Goodbye, son, I love you."

All three men got their own cells. Lencho and Free's cells were side-by-side, but the Marine's was around the corner from them. He could be heard and bitched at, but not seen. Lencho and Free bitched at him the entire weekend they were forced to stay in that miserable little place.

"Well, jarhead, nice going," Free taunted. "This is your reward for snitching us out. I hope you're pleased with yourself!"

"Yeah, man," Lencho agreed. "I help you out with a ride in the middle of the desert, and this is the thanks I get! What the fuck is the matter with you?" Silence, for the most part, just silence. As the hours dragged on, Lencho and Free told each other hippie war stories about all of the girls they had fucked and the best dope they had smoked. Plus, all of the usual guy crap that guys that age talked about. The Marine would moan now and then from behind his wall.

Jail food was as bad as one would expect it to be. It fit the surroundings, but in jail, meal times were still looked forward to. It was brought in by a little Mexican trustee who handed the trays through a square opening in the bars. The Marine either ate in silence, or not at all. The two hippies needled him unmercifully. It might have seemed cruel, but the little shit had brought this misery down on all of them, and for what purpose? What makes a man a rat?

On Sunday, the Marine finally spoke, his words coming between gasps and sobs. "I did what they wanted for God's sake. I killed people for them. I was taught to be good and quiet, and do what I was told. You bastards broke the law with that dope. I seen lots of guys I knew over there smoke that shit. Heroin, too! Not for me, man. I seen what happens, makes them nuts. Zombies, and they don't give a shit anymore! But I do! I give a shit man."

Unsettled by the Marine's anguish, Lencho replied in a kinder tone. "Hey, Marine, I hear you! I bet you seen some bad stuff, didn't you? Fucked up your head, I think. Can't be good to see stuff like that. Take it easy, man. We ain't really mad at you. This ain't no big deal, we'll live."

"No, no, you don't get it. I've done bad stuff! I can't forget what I've seen, what I've done."

Lencho replied, "Well, shit man, it's over, and you're home now. You're getting out of the military. Go home, get a job. Raise a family. Have kids, you know, go on with your life. It'll be okay."

"You sure, Lencho? You sure I'll be okay?" He asked.

"Sure, Marine, we both forgive you. No worries. Take it easy, and stop crying."

"I don't think God may forgive me. I hope that he does. I just don't know for sure."

It was ten o'clock when the lights went out. At 6:00 a.m. the next morning, the deputy who was supposed to make the rounds still hadn't made his check on the three prisoners. The Mexican trustee bringing breakfast found the Marine hanging in his cell. The Marine had taken off his boot laces, tied them together and made a noose. He then placed the noose around his neck and tied the laces to a horizontal flat strap through the bars above his head where he lay on his rack. Then he just rolled right on off and hung himself.

The Mexican turned pale, dropped the tray, and ran screaming into the other room yelling for help. The deputy who was on duty that night came flying into the cell area and exclaimed, "Holy Shit!" as he grappled with his keys to open the door. Lencho and Free sat up dazed as the guard cut the long boot lace from off the bar with his pocket knife. "Boy, Boy!" he screamed, slapping the Marine sharply across the face, with no response.

"Hey," Lencho called out. "What's wrong?"

The deputy screamed, "This motherfucker killed himself. Oh my god!"

Lencho then yelled to the deputy, "Give him CPR. Give him some CPR! Is he breathing at all? Let me try, I had CPR training in the Navy."

The guard was almost as stunned as the trustee. He flat didn't know what to do. If he had been in on his rounds earlier, this might not have happened. There would be hell to pay now! He quickly opened the door to Lencho's cell, and Lencho bolted around the corner to the body. The shoe lace was so tight around the Marine's neck that it dug deeply into the flesh.

"Give me your knife!" Lencho demanded. "Got to get this off!"

The guard obediently handed over his blade, and Lencho forced his fingers into the folded flesh, grasping the string. The Marine's eyes were open and bulging, and his lips had turned blue. Lencho got the tip of the blade underneath and cut it. The body lay on the floor with the head dangling. That's how people hang themselves in a prison cell. Not from the ceiling, but from small heights, and this boy had done a fine job of it. Lencho pulled him by the feet so he lay flat, then he raised his head so that his scarred throat jutted out and the head was tilted back so that Lencho could administer mouth to mouth. A finger to the carotid artery showed a pulse. It was slight, but steady. The Marine was still alive. The paramedics arrived at the same moment, and they quickly took charge by putting him on a gurney while continuing the CPR Lencho had started. In another moment, it was over. The Marine's body was rushed to the hospital, and Lencho was returned to his cell to tell an incredulous Free what had just happened.

"The poor fucked up kid went to war because they said he had to, because he was afraid to disobey them. He even refused to smoke a joint with us. He went squealing to the cops, and, for his reward, they arrest him. Then he kills himself."

Two hours later, a State Trooper came to inform Lencho and Free that they would be moved out of the jail that afternoon. In the meantime, Lencho was led into the visiting room where it was partitioned off by two big, scratched plexiglass walls. His old man, lean and sinewy, with a Camel cigarette dangling from his lips, sat on a straight backed chair. His sad little mom stood meekly behind him. All five feet six inches of him just radiated disgust. Lencho sat down and waited for the first word. The older generation of that time were nothing, if not conformists. Unquestioning robots: hard work and the law! That's what they believed and that's what they preached. That is what was demanded in 1970.

The young people were taking a new direction and the whole deal—this so called counter culture—just made them sick.

"Don't try and tell me otherwise! You are a filthy, disgusting bum! You are not my son! This place is a cage and you belong here. God damn you, boy!" Lencho's father spat. He then got up and left the room with Lencho's mom following obediently behind him. She glanced back at her boy with a tear trailing down her cheek. The guy drives over two hundred fucking miles to insult me, Lencho thought. To tell me that he hates me and is sorry that I was ever born.

A couple of detectives were waiting to interview Lencho down in Phoenix. They were not interested in the skinny joint or the four pot seeds the Sheriffs had found in his van. They wanted to know about the Marine, and if the jailor had missed his rounds.

"Of course the jailor missed the clock," Lencho told them. "If he had done his job, the Marine might still be okay. I got him to breathing with CPR, so he must've hanged himself only a little while before, don't ya think?"

"We think you better just show up for court kid," one of them said. "It's no big deal, you'll get probation, and then just forget that you ever got busted in Gila Bend."

The Marine was on a ventilator for a week before he died. Lencho and Free were cut loose on O.R., and they climbed into the Dodge van and split for California. Free went off to San Francisco to hunt for naked girls. Lencho showed up in court a couple of weeks later on the matter in Phoenix. The judge sentenced him to six months of probation, and the clerk gave him half a dozen coupons to mail in; one for each of the next six months. On the way out of the building, Lencho tossed them into a trash can before he jumped into the van and left town. He had one hundred pounds of weed in there with him. It came with the territory after all. He was a weed man and his customers were waiting.

Chapter Three

"It's The World Gone Crazy (Cotillion)"
Released 1979
Waylon Jennings

It's the world's gone crazy cotillion
The ladies are dancin' alone
Side men all want to be front men
And the front men all want to go home

Villains have turned into heroes
Heroes have turned into heels
The dealers all want to be lovers
And the lovers all want to make deals

SPAWN OF SATAN

"Amigo," Manuel reported, "there is no weed. No weed anywhere."

"How is that possible?" Lencho cried with alarm.

"Oh, it is possible. It is August now and all last year's product is gone. The harvest will start in mid-September, so no weed until then. Sorry."

The news was stunning. What would he do? What would he tell his customers? Would he lose market share?

"I have some contacts in Mexicali that move the perico. Want to try some of that?"

"What's perico?"

"Cocaine. They say it will be all the rage."

"Oh," Lencho replied. "I like cocaine. Tried it a few times. Kinda a short high, leaves ya jittery. But it's nice. Sure, okay. If you can line some up, we'll give it a go."

"Give the blow a go," Manuel laughed.

Manuel set it up with his friends in Mexicalli. With a fifteen thousand dollar deposit, they were fronted two kilograms of Peruvian Cocaine hydrochloride at $25,000 a key. They took it back to Lencho's house, and along with Danny Pope, decided to try a little taste. In just three weeks flat, they whiffed one entire Kilo, 2.2 pounds, up their collective noses. Everyone was in a daze and had a constant nosebleed, but they kept on sniffing. Lencho found that he had to take hot showers to clear his sinuses so that he could snort even more. They barely ate or slept.

Manuel had a room downstairs in the basement. He would start hitting the coke at six a.m., shoveling it into his head using a butter knife off of a dinner plate. They all became paranoid. Never venturing outside, they continually peered out of the blinds from the front windows watching for the cops. Their world was filled with fear. At last, Lencho realized that this stuff was an evil substance. He came to his senses and called a halt to the orgy of self-destruction.

They were all mental and physical wrecks by that time; and, of course, there was still the little matter of money that Lencho owed to the Mexicalli boys for the product that they had fronted. A small amount of profit was made selling to friends over the past month, but he still owed thirty-five large, so he went to see his old friend, Joe Corrola, who took the rest off his hands at a considerable discount because he knew Lencho was in a tight spot.

Between what Lencho got from Joe and borrowed money, he was able to come up with the $35,000 to pay off those vatos in Mexicalli.

"What are the lessons I learned from this terrible experience?" the weed man asked himself. First, never become your own best customer; that is a real hazard when dealing in truly addictive substances. Second, cocaine use costs too much money! Thousands down the drain. These observations led to the most important lesson of all: only a fool thinks he has a handle on drugs like cocaine or heroin. "Why would anyone think they are immune to addiction when they have seen it happen without fail to all others?" he pondered. "If you are going to sell dynamite, do not play with fire. Case closed. But, man, that stuff does have a lure." He decided it was best to stick with weed, and never, ever sell anything else ever again. Marijuana is holy, the sacred herb.

Powder had this old truck. A Holsum Bread truck that had delivered bread down many streets in days gone by. They painted the truck orange sunshine, hung tapestries inside of it, and rebuilt the engine. They now had their very own Hippie Wagon.

They climbed aboard and headed down to Mexicalli to pay off the coke debt. Wearing a wig and straight clothing, Lencho walked across the border and went to see them.

"Ah, Amigo. We were wondering what had happened to you?" Ortiz said.

"Sorry, it took a little longer than I thought," Lencho lied.

"How did it go with the coke? Good shit, no?" Ortiz asked.

Lencho replied, "I think I'll stick to weed from now on. I don't think there is any future with this stuff for me."

"Sure," Ortiz said with a sly grin. "But just wait. This is the wave of the future."

"I'll take another ounce for myself though!" He stuck it under his wig and bopped back across the border. "Arizona, here I come," he thought.

Danny Pope, the recon man, was gone now. Never to be seen again. Probably the coke binge, Lencho figured. He'd had enough and gone back to Georgia.

Now it was just Powder and Lencho. They needed to recover fast and make some serious money. When a hippie says that he is broke, it's only relative. In truth, there were several pounds of weed floating around; not the very best stuff, but it would do in a pinch. So Lencho proceeded to dig the pot stash up from his backyard, and soon they were back in Prescott. He had left Karen behind once again, but that was part of the deal, the old lady was excess baggage.

Lencho's little brother, David, bagged up the pot and sold lids around town. In a short time, he had accumulated sixteen hundred bucks.

"We're gonna make a pilgrimage to San Fran," Lencho told his youngest brother. "Do you want to come with us?"

"You know I do," David replied, "but I can't. Mom is real uptight these days, and pop would kill me. He says you are the spawn of Satan. Maybe after I graduate next month they'll let me go."

"Shit, boy," Lencho spat, "you're almost a man. You gonna let mom and dad order you around your whole life? You're getting pretty good on that guitar.

25

What if I buy you a new Gibson? You can sing folk tunes in Golden Gate Park, and all the young cooze will go ape shit." They all laughed.

"You buy that guitar and watch for me on the edge of town tomorrow. How's that?"

The next day Lencho bought a beautiful Gibson down at Prescott Music Center. At six p.m. sharp he pulled up to David in the bright orange Holsum Bread truck, and they were off into the night heading to the counter culture mecca: San Francisco and the Height-Ashbury.

"I left mom a note," David said. "I told her I would be home in a week and she shouldn't worry. I'm with my big brother."

"Yeah, the spawn of Satan," Powder laughed. Back in Prescott mom read the note with sorrow and anguish, and burst into tears.

The boy played his new Gibson all the way to the city. They tooted on the ounce of perico Lencho had scored from Mexicalli, but kept it to a dull roar. There would never be a repeat of the great white powder madness. The weather was warm, and the night was mild. Eight hours later they were approaching the bay area; it became cooler once they got to the California coast.

A road trip to San Francisco was de riguer for all flower children. It was the early 70's, and even though the glow had dimmed for the earlier hippy veterans, it still shone brightly for millions of America's youth. The place to go was the Height.

It wasn't only in the city where the drug culture thrived, but also in the east bay of Oakland and Berkeley, and across the Golden Gate Bridge into Marin, and beyond. There were many small cartels running the marijuana trade and distributing LSD. These were wealthy elites of the hip culture. They laundered their ill-gotten gains through stores along Telegraph Ave, the Height-Ashbury, and all over San Francisco itself. Up and down and all over, the early years of the revolution had brought astonishing changes. The Bay Area was a wild and crazy place tolerant of those who were different, on the run, or sinful. It was the west coast melting pot.

The music was as important to the culture as the dope. In San Francisco, Bill Graham, Chet Helms and a host of lesser lights put on shows at the Avalon Ballroom, Winterland, and the Fillmore. The Airplane, Grateful Dead, and Quicksilver Messenger Service with Janis regularly played for free at the Golden Gate Park. The Diggers fed the crowds while the Free Clinic patched them up, giving them shots for the clap and downers for LSD overdoses. It was degenerating badly in many regards, but still there was an excitement and sense of adventure unparalleled in the century so far.

The police seldom busted the freaks for smoking pot or being under the influence. Clouds of pot smoke hung over the Golden Gate Park during the free weekend concerts. The Hell's Angels and the Mafia introduced methamphetamines and heroin into the Height, and its ugly influence spread like a cancer. There was even an annual Crystal Queen festival where a lovely young nymphet was chosen to be the year's reigning deity; when she died a year later from the needle, another one was chosen. People would overdose in the park while the acid heads looked the other way. But with all this, it was still a magical place.

The boys arrived that Sunday morning and parked the bread truck a few blocks from the park on Divisadero. Fingers of fog lingered from the morning and clung to the spires of the Golden Gate. The Height was asshole to elbow in freaks. Word was that the Joy of Cooking and Country Joe and the Fish would be performing from Berkeley, and Blue Cheer might show up as well. Commander Cody and His Lost Planet Airmen couldn't make it because the Commander had been dosed badly with PCP in a bottle of wine someone had handed him, but the Flamin Groovies would take their place. It looked like a fun day to arrive in the Land of Oz.

Planting their butts down on the grass, young David did his own take on 'Morning Dew," and, just like his big brother had said, six pretty young women were soon swaying to the rhythm in front of him. "Walk me in the morning dew my honey," he sang. Lencho and Powder fired up a bowl of Pakistani hash, and all was well with the world.

A girl chased a frisbee and it landed on Lencho's head, but he was gracious. "Sorry," Angel said, "did I hurt you?"

"Not a problem. Want a hit?" A new friend was made, and Angel joined their troop.

She was short and round with bouncing breast sans bra beneath a sheer blouse. Her blue eyes were so merry she reminded them all of Christmas. She was a very giving girl, as it turned out, and an hour later they all were tossing the friz and laughing uproariously. Walking down Height Street, Lencho treated them to organic soy burgers laden with lentils, watercress, and sprouts. They washed down their meal with lemonade. Once they finished feasting, they returned to their spot on the grass and promptly fell asleep. They had not realized how tired they were from the long drive from Prescott.

When they woke up, Lencho saw that Angel had snuggled up in the arms of the budding rock artist. "I see you have a new friend, David," he grinned.

"Oh yeah. I guess so. I think maybe she's everybody's friend."

"I just got some of this orange sunshine," Angel told them, producing six soft barrel tablets from her jeans. "It's from the Brotherhood of Eternal Love. I hitch down to the desert and see them all the time. They used to be in the Canyon in Laguna until the pigs made them leave. They're so groovy, and Leary stays with them now."

"I never tried sunshine before," Powder said.

"It's really strong, but man is it spiritual. Are you experienced?" They laughed nervously at the Hendrix reference, and then each dropped a pill, letting it melt on their tongues.

The Brother Hood were indeed a unique outfit. They eschewed the intellectualization of Tim Leary and crowd, yet embraced and sheltered him from the incessant attacks of the law he endured. They were rough spun lads that had grown rich from smuggling Afghani hash and oils, and now employed their own chemists to manufacture fifty million doses of what they called sunshine. One of the chemists was rumored to have worked for the CIA, but it was also rumored the CIA had safe houses in the Height where they spied on the hippies and researched the LSD genie that was now out of their bottle.

The Sunshine hit them like a freight train. It was not possible to go anywhere because they couldn't get up to go. The stuff was not smooth, either, because it often was fortified with amphetamine or even strychnine for visual effects. But once the bad gut feelings passed, and the trails of unreality moderated a little, the four of them ventured on shaky legs off into the depths of the park laughing, awestruck by anything and everything. They were not alone. The park was awash with others on inner journeys that day. Both Powder and young David had to fight back panic for a while, but Lencho was convinced he was safe since he was really on the moon and what could hurt him way up there? Only Angel was calm throughout. She led them down the pathways to the botanical gardens, the art museums, and finally to the sea at the far end. They stood there and watched the pacific blow with frothy white caps from the mighty winds and of course the winds told them all wonderful stories. Then they trudged the three miles back to where they had begun, and by then it had been five hours and the trip was mellowing out nicely.

Acid like that demanded a long walk to shake off the jitters and the boogeyman of the mind. Finally it was time to go. To where, who knew? But they somehow managed to find their way back to the Orange Holsum van, and when Angel saw its brilliant color she burst into hysterical laughter. "Oh, too perfect," she cried. "I love it. What's left?"

"Where to?" Powder giggled as he powered up the Orange beast.

"Are you sure you can drive?" David asked.

"No," he replied. They all thought that was hilarious.

"In that case, let's go to Mt. Tam," Angel suggested. Mount Tamalpais it was. They got as far as The Presidio, but the patterns and colors proved to be too great an obstacle. Just before they reached the bridge, Powder pulled off and went through a gate plainly marked: U.S. Government Property, Keep Out.

"I think we're safe," he sighed with relief. As one of the Army's most beautiful bases, The Presidio encompassed hundreds of tree filled acres right in the midst of San Francisco. It was a venerable post that housed high ranking officers in classic old stucco mansions, many dating back to World War I. It was largely rural, and this part of it seemed the ideal place to spend the night. "Wow, this is great," Lencho said pulling out his pipe and hash. "I think we should just kick back here until the morning when we're all a little straighter and leave then."

"Good idea," they all agreed. In their mutual approbation, no one noticed the MPs pull up in the jeep beside them.

"Hey," the driver yelled. "You, in the van. Roll down your windows."

Clouds of smoke belched forth as Powder slowly lowered his side. "Can I help you Officer?" He asked sheepishly.

"U.S. Army, Sir. Not the police. I'm enlisted and work for my check, thank you." This military joke was lost on the lot of them. Angel got it together quickly.

"Do you want us to leave, Sir?" she smiled.

The two men in uniform smiled back at the little hippie chick. Clearly they were used to this phenomenon in their duty station. "Are you in any condition to move out?" the driver asked.

The four of them looked at each other idiotically and, in unison, replied, "No."

"We'll lock the gate behind us. If you don't go wondering around, you can stay the night. The gate will be open at 6:00 a.m. tomorrow morning. Have a good day." They left.

"Wow," Lencho said, "you don't see that every day."

"No shit," David agreed.

"Far out," Powder exclaimed with relief.

"Let's fuck," Angel declared pulling off her blouse.

When they woke up the next day, it was Monday. They all were hungry and grubby and the gate was open. They left.

"Listen, Angel," Lencho said, "we're gonna head down to Big Sur. We sure enjoyed your company and the orange sunshine. You are one kind of girl, for sure. Do you want to hang with us?"

"Thanks, man," she replied, "but I gotta get back. My old man will be wondering what happened to me."

After they all dined at a Denny's on Van Ness, they dropped off the little hippie girl with the big, laughing eyes at the corner of Height and Ashbury. They waved goodbye, and she blew them a kiss and disappeared into the throngs.

Driving south on Highway 1, they reached Pheiffer State Park in three hours. They parked back at the end where the road circles and comes to the gorge. That's where the multitudes were camped by the river. They pitched their tent and knew they were home. Young and old came and went, sampling their hashish and eating the food they had bought at a grocery in Castroville. Here, again, there was ample young pulchritude, and David and Powder were like famished foxes in the hen house.

"History will look back on these times," Powder the anthropologist intoned sagely, "and record: At no other time were there so many free and easy females available to the pleasure of men." Lencho was a married man, and now and then he remembered that fact, so he was more circumspect this time.

"I think I'll hitch back to San Diego and pick up some more dope," he announced the next morning. "Hold down the fort, I'll be back in a flash."

As he gazed at all the girls, he pondered the state of marriage in the land and the times that they were experiencing. Things were different, things were changing, he was sure of it. He had been pushed to marry, and though he believed he did love Karen, he resented being tied down to convention. The hippie life was free of constraints. There was something unnatural in the old way of thinking, instead of the other way around. But Karen was forever faithful, and even though she agreed to melt their wedding rings to turn them into an elegant coke spoon, she clearly didn't buy into the mentality her husband had. Oh well, he thought, this is a new world. He brought her back with him, and suddenly Karen came face-to-face with this new reality.

When they reached the camp a week later, seventeen-year-old David was lolling around in the tent with five girls; two of which could have been his mother. Powder was out running around naked, high on acid. And, there was a line of hungry freaks waiting for lunch. She went to work and cooked for the lot of them. The hardworking earth mother seemed resigned to her fate. The feminist movement was about to explode, but hadn't yet.

That night they passed around huge joints of good Mexican pot, and everyone was mellow, listening to David strum his Gibson. Then the cops came bounding out from the shadows. "Hands up," they yelled. "Down on the ground. Don't try and ditch the dope."

The cops had received a tip from Lencho's mother—who was frantically looking for her runaway son, David—that the boys were somewhere near Pheiffer State Park. Lencho's mom wheedled the boy's location out of David's girlfriend, who learned of his whereabouts when he called with the news of his travels (minus, of course, his adventures with all of the girls). It served David right for messing around.

The cops sent an undercover type disguised as a hippie chick into the camp to see what was going on, and she reported back that Lencho had gone south to bring back "a really big load of the good stuff." The really big load consisted of a quarter ounce of hash. After the cops found it in the orange truck, the whole bunch, almost thirty kids, were hauled off to jail in 3 paddy wagons. They were taken to Salinas, boys in two vans, girls in the other. The cops missed the twenty lids that were hidden in the bean bag chair and the LSD one of the kids had rolled up in his cuffs.

"Hey," Lencho said, "before they think to cuff us, want to drop?" Sure they all thought, it's only jail. By the time the cops pulled them out, they were all loose and goosey and giggling madly.

"My god," one cop exclaimed. "What is this world coming to?"

"We should've cuffed them," another replied. "Better do it now before they start bouncing off the walls." But it was too late, they were already bouncing.

So now they were in the can, in Salinas, high on LSD, and up shit creek again without a paddle.

Karen's dad bailed her out, but left her wayward husband there. Karen's dad wired $500 to a local bondsman, and she was free to go. She left with the "Pill People." The Pill People had been in jail in Salinas for illegal possession of pharmaceuticals. They were drug store cowboy types that robbed pharmacies and sold legitimately manufactured drugs. They were always either up or down on legal speed and barbiturates.

David was returned to Mom and Dad, and bragged to friends of his great adventure. The cops sent a bunch of little flower girl runaways home as well. Lord knows Lencho's father was not about to help him out of his latest jam, so he was left in the jail alone.

After nine days in the slammer, Lencho made a deal with the prosecutor to plead guilty and take the entire rap. They granted him release on his own recognizance. He was then able to catch up with his wife and the Pill People at their pad located just outside of town. They were ugly mutts and just too nutty for the weed man. They never slept and were always arguing and fighting. The couple ended up staying there for a few days, sleeping out in the van.

In the middle of one night, an ambulance and police car showed up to haul away someone who had overdosed. He was as dead as a door nail, and Lencho made a quick decision that it was time to move on. This was no place for any self-respecting weed dealer and his wife.

*****

Lencho headed north with Karen and Powder to Mendocino County to a place called Navarro River. They drove up to sign post 297, where some hitchhikers said there was going to be a big hippie wedding in the woods.

After setting up camp, they met a guy whose camp was right next to them. He had in his possession what he called African Mescaline. It looked like dirt and God's own body at the same time. This amazing stuff showed Lencho the death of his ego. He snorted it daily for over a month and came to understand the true meaning of the universe, or at least that is what it seemed like.

Mescaline is a chemical extract found in peyote and the San Pablo cactus. It tastes like shit, and can make the user nauseous, but after all that, it produces sensations of exquisite and sometimes religious rapture. The plains and desert Indians of the U.S. use it widely; for them it is legal. As far as "African Mescaline" was concerned, it is entirely possible that any number of psychedelic substances were to be found in the substance. "Whatever," Lencho thought, "it really was truly great stuff!"

They took it on the Fourth of July when the vaunted wedding was scheduled to occur. It would show them the way!

A Shaman from San Francisco had arrived in the Grotto where all of the tribe had gathered to perform the ceremony. The groom was a slender, bearded man of thirty-two, and his bride was around nineteen. Suddenly word swept throughout the camp that the Oakland chapter of the Hell's Angels were also coming to the party. Coming to ruin the wedding, to rain on the parade, to kick ass and take names. The Angels always sucked in that way. That was clear to most everyone after the fiasco that had occurred at the Altamont raceway in 1969 where they had been hired to "Keep Order" at the notorious 'free' Rolling Stones concert.

These thugs on bikes were on their way, and they had guns. General mayhem and panic ensued, and as the roar of Harley Davidson's boomed on the horizon, freaks fled in all directions. Pandemonium reigned, and even little Karen was not up to the carnage that would surely come from those butt ugly gangsters wearing tattered jeans and chains.

High as the clouds on African Mescaline, Powder looked at Lencho and proclaimed, "We ain't leaving," and they didn't.

Even though the Angels shot and killed a dog that didn't like the cacophony, the lads stood their ground. There were at least 50 with long greasy hair and beards. They wore shades that covered eyes of wrath. The colors of the Death Skull grinned malevolently, and the leader was the ugliest Angel of them all. They carried guns in their belts and holsters. The mean assed 1% had arrived to bring chaos and horror, as only Hells Angels could.

The two lone stragglers stilled themselves and sat back to back in the fire pit, which was now surrounded by the great, roaring machines.

"Be strong Lencho," Powder whispered. "The time comes when ya got nowhere left to run."

"Fuck," Lencho moaned.

The leader climbed off of his hog and sauntered over to the pitiful pair with his hand resting on a 9mm pistol. He was a huge man with many scars and tattoos. His breath stank, and he smelled like kerosene. He stood there with the others looking on, as if waiting for the order to eat the two alive.

"How are you sir?" Powder whispered to the face that was inches from his own.

"I'm fine," replied the outlaw. "Where is everyone?"

"They left. They were afraid." Powder answered.

"Why's that?" he asked.

"Your reputation preceded you," they both answered.

His contours softened and even the scar seemed to smile. Then he gave Powder a kiss on the cheek. Saying nothing more, he walked back to his bike and climbed on. The roar of the engines again rang out, and in two's and three's they turned and rode away behind their leader. They were soon gone, leaving Lencho and Powder, still high on African Mescaline, sitting there in their dust.

After retrieving his wife, Lencho and Powder stayed a few more days in the idyllic woods. The African dope was now all gone, so Powder made a stunning proclamation, "I'm leaving, man. And I want you to have my truck."

"Leaving? What the fuck for?" Lencho exclaimed.

"I got a vision, man, and it's time for me to split. I am going to go to Afghanistan, Nepal, and wherever else my feet take me. It's just time, man."

"But Powder, what are you going to do for bread?" Lencho asked.

He just shrugged and said, "I'll be fine."

"But it takes money to travel to Afghanistan."

Powder laughed and said, "If you have the faith, my brother, the bread will come."

"But your truck, it's your baby, it's so beautiful."

Powder smiled again and said, "Quite right, and that's why I want you and Karen to have her. You'll give her a good home. I know you will!"

Then he just left. Later, Lencho found out Powder wasn't so broke after all. It turned out that he had broken into his lawyer's pad and robbed him of fifteen thousand dollars. Fifteen large was a lot of money in 1971, and he had the dough on him for months. He was only waiting for the spirit world to give him a sign that it was time to split. After the Hells Angels incident, he knew it was, and he left.

What makes a spiritual, dope headed genius steal money from someone who was supposedly a friend? This question was one that Lencho asked himself quite often, but was never able to answer. Life is full of mystery after all. Perhaps it was just the algebra of need, as Burroughs might have put it, or maybe just a sudden impulse. Lencho took the truck, and he and Karen headed south once again to Arizona. They brought a mad man named Sal with them. Sal was a piano playing, re-incarnated grizzly bear who would howl at the moon and claw off the bark on the trees. He got a check each month from the Government, and was a very deep guy. He helped pay the bills for a while, even though Lencho had a thousand dollars in his jeans.

The motor blew up in Kingman, so they stayed there for four days while a mechanic put in a new one. Then they drove down to Prescott to visit both

33

friends and family. They returned once again to OB where the grizzly bear disappeared into the sand.

*****

The friends came and went, but two new friends on the scene, Malcom and Doc, would end up becoming lifelong pals and associates of Lencho's.

Malcom was a Bakersfield cowboy, and Doc was the slick dresser, drinker, partier, and unbelievably lucky son of a bitch who made millions in the years to come. To this day, the police would love to nail him, but have been unable to do so, as he is only known by his legend.

Malcom was the same age as Lencho. The two men got into a discussion one sunny day as Lencho passed Malcom's little cottage. Beer was the subject. Lencho preferred Coors, Malcom's favorite was Heineken. He told Lencho that it was a way better buzz, and after sucking down some of the brew, Lencho had to admit that Malcom was indeed correct and he gave up Coors forever.

Malcom was also a weed man and one of those intrepid souls of that era who traveled the world in search of adventure and fine bud. Thailand was his favorite place, and he became known as the Thai Stick Guy. This label would eventually lead to both his flight and exile in the future.

Traveling by train in the Chao Phraya Region, he was turned on to a family that was in the "Stick" business. Thailand is a lovely and mysterious land, but also a poor one. Many families make their living by gingerly tying the fine Thai marijuana onto thin strips of bamboo.

Tons of the stuff was stored in warehouses in Bangkok ready to be shipped on a moment's notice.

Over time, Malcom sent large quantities of sticks back to the States. His methods of transport varied between the very elaborate to the very simple and straight forward approaches. Boxes within boxes or plain old letters. One way or another, Malcom got the job done.

He traveled back himself quite often to either establish new markets for the product or fine tune his logistics. Once he even freaked out Lencho's mother when he sent a couple of pounds to Lencho's little brother, Bobbby, in Las Vegas. The package had been detected by U.S. customs, and they were going to make a controlled delivery to nab whoever showed up to receive it. But Bobby had moved, and when they asked his landlord what his previous address was, they ended up staking out his Mom's house in Prescott.

Lencho's Mom went outside to get the mail a few weeks later and noticed that the mailman was nervous and anxious. Taking the package with all of the funny postage stamps into her house, she examined it and set it on the counter. A half hour later, David wandered in and all of the Feds staking out the place went, "Holy Shit, it's a Hippie!"

So they swooped in on the poor woman, scaring her to death. The Feds ended up having the wrong house, wrong address, no valid warrant, and the incorrect party to boot. The case was immediately dropped.

The household was in chaos, and Lencho's father blamed Lencho for the whole mess.

The one thing the Feds were able to accomplish in their blunder was to get a lead on Malcom, the international drug smuggler. Upon his return, Malcom found the cops gunning for him. Typical San Diego Narcs, long on gall and short on brains. They decided to place a couple of bricks of low quality weed inside the trash cans that were located outside of his house, and then knock on his front door. Upon answering Malcom was asked, "Is this your trash out here?"

"Yes," he replied, and they proceeded to arrest him for drug sales.

The Feds went inside and found some correspondence from Thailand and a legal handgun. And that's all she wrote. The prosecutor happily informed the smuggler that he was looking at doing some years in the joint. Malcom promptly took off, stopping by the graveyard where he found his new identity on the tombstone of Robert Nathanial Sandlan.

From that day forward, he was known to his comrades as "Nat the Rat."

In the next nine years, he traveled far and wide, and then settled in Costa Rica where he is currently a naturalized citizen. The irony of it all is that after all of those years, he decided that he wanted to come back to the U.S.A. and clear everything up.

Upon arriving at LAX, he went straight to customs and turned himself in. The customs officials, after a thorough search, could not find any evidence of a warrant or that he was a wanted man.

"But, I'm a fugitive," he insisted.

"No, you are not," they told him several times. "Get the fuck out of here."

It turns out that the prosecutor had lied when he told Malcom that he would do prison time. Malcom did not find any of this funny, and was, in fact, seriously pissed off. He then renounced his U.S. citizenship and swore his allegiance to Costa Rica.

*****

Lencho and Karen went back to their house on Muir Street, and resumed weed sales to both new and existing customers. Joe and Denise Carrola were expatriates from New Jersey. A pot dealing husband and wife team who asked Lencho if he would be willing to take a day off to help them out. They explained that he would make a thousand dollars, and all he had to do was assist them in unloading a PEMEX truck that they had hidden earlier in Santee.

PEMEX is the Mexican Government's oil company. Nationalized in 1937 by the Government of Presidente Cardenas, the third world cheered as one of their own became the first nation to seize back some of the assets that had been stolen from them by the huge American corporation, Standard Oil.

The PEMEX big brown tanker was chock full of weed. Lencho never did learn how it had ended up in the hills of Santee, deep in a rural area of San Diego County, but there it sat on a dusty road, waiting to be claimed. It contained a small amount of gasoline in its tank as well.

Joe Carrola, who had taken the remaining coke off Lencho's hands a little earlier, was there along with Pepe, Denise's chubby brother. Lencho and Pepe held their breath and wiggled into the truck. Between frantic gasps of air, they tossed blocks of marijuana out onto the ground. It was both hard and dangerous work, but after about two hours, they had it all out and loaded into a couple of pickup trucks.

Tossing a tarp over the load, they headed back to a house out on Point Loma to knock down a few brews and celebrate.

As Pepe, Lencho, and Skipper were munching on some chips, they heard the slamming doors of cop cars in unison.

From the backyard alley to the front door, Narcs were everywhere, guns drawn. Pepe took the opportunity to bolt, and for a big boy, turned out to be pretty damn fast. Over the backyard fence he flew, then through the neighbor's yard and over another fence, with the cops in hot pursuit. Skipper then figured, 'What the fuck, if Pepe can do it, so can I' and Lencho was left standing there alone in the confusion. He quickly hid behind the sofa in the carport. It wasn't even up against the wall, just over in a corner. He hid there for five full hours.

The couch was quite exposed with just a few pieces of furniture near it. The cops were so busy chasing the fleeing pot fiends and meeting the customers that were arriving that they never looked behind the couch. Lencho continued to hold his breath, barely moving. Sweat dripped down his face to his chin, and his heart beat like a drum.

Time passed, and he watched feet come and go as he lay there praying. People came to the door, were greeted warmly by the Narcs, and then hauled off in cuffs once they walked in.

This went on for a long time, and finally the informer who had set up the whole thing showed up in the garage and sat on the couch. He had a little chat with the two Narcs who remained.

The scumbag's name was Billy Devline, and both he and his handlers got a big laugh about how successful things had went with the huge PEMEX bust. Lencho listened to them discuss the haul itself, 558 Kilos worth.

"Here's your cut Billy," one said as he pointed to a pile of bricks.

"Eleven....they're all yours, for a job well done!"

Bill Devline hauled off his swag. The Narcs then discussed things among themselves before their boss showed up.

"What's the count now? Let's see, five-hundred and fifty-eight minus eleven leaves five-forty-seven."

"We can snatch a hundred easy. The boss will swipe some too. Come on, let's get them into the car. We'll pass them out to our snitches, and split ten grand. That's five grand apiece. I love the dope biz, man. Not bad for a day's work," Lencho heard them say.

After the Narcs had loaded up their take and left, they posted a couple of uniforms to guard the house. These two walked around for another hour, and Lencho waited for his moment. When there was a distance between the two of them going in opposite directions, he made his move.

Following on the heels of Pepe a few hours earlier, he jumped the backyard fence and was gone. The coppers never saw him. Never knew that he was even there that day. They never knew that he had witnessed them stealing those one hundred and eleven bricks of PEMEX marijuana.

Joe and Denise Carrola, Pepe, and Skipper were all caught along with a lot of their clients. Only the dirty cops and Lencho got away clean. Most of the weed people in that group just split on down the road and became fugitives.

In those days it was common to just grab a new identity from a graveyard and become someone else.

Another important lesson was learned by Lencho. Narcs were corrupt.

With all of the money that was to be made by those who had the ability to hide behind a badge, it was indeed a long line to get into the business of narcotics.

As the years went by, the money only got bigger in the anti-drug business. Nixon named it a "War on Drugs," and that's what it was. Only this was a war that was never meant to end.

The cops got more money to chase down the weed and dope dealers; the courts got bigger; the prisons grew by leaps and bounds; and the corruption— the corruption grew to where it is today, astronomical!

One night, Lencho attended a gala party at the Carpenters Hall thrown by the Blue Sunrise people in downtown San Diego. It had been a good year for this early cartel. The marijuana smoke was so thick in the air that he was almost too freaked out to venture inside. Cocaine was served along with the shrimp and steak, and the music was provided by Miles Davis. Security was provided by off duty San Diego policemen.

It all seemed surreal, but Lencho was told not to sweat anything at all. No worries, everything was under control. The magic component was called, 'Money.'

Chapter Four

"Don't You Think This Outlaw Bit's Done Got Out Of Hand"
Released 1978
Waylon Jennings

Don't you think this outlaw bit's done got out of hand
What started out to be a joke the law don't understand
Was it singing through my nose that got me busted by the man
Maybe this here outlaw bit's done got out of hand

LUZ

One dark night in late 1971 there was a terrible fire in Ocean Beach. A little white clapboard bungalow a few blocks over from Lencho and Karen's place burned to the ground. A family of Italian immigrants—a husband, his wife, and their two children—lived there. The flames leapt into the sky and the husband ran back inside, frantically trying to rescue his babies while his wife wailed on the sidewalk. The three perished, and the whole community came together to support the grieving widow and mother.

Lencho and the other weed men were greatly saddened by this terrible event, so they took up a collection from among themselves. Lencho, Doc, Joey, Ronnie, Buddy, and others donated a total of ten thousand dollars in cash through the Red Cross. The donations were all anonymous, of course, but the Ocean Beach Marijuana Coalition and their generosity made the San Diego Union newspaper anyway.

Such were the times. The dealers considered themselves businessmen as well as civic citizens, but they had to be surreptitious about both.

Karen entered into the vitamin business, so Lencho bought a Dodge van, which he painted nicely and covered with the vitamin logos. He had hidden compartments inside that could hold up to forty keys.

Lencho got together with Manuel and they transformed a large old boat of a Ford Fairlane into their latest "Potmobile." Using the deft touches of an automotive craftsman who resided in Tijuana, it was remodeled to carry around twenty Kilos in a false gas tank.

Lencho recruited an audacious Mexican traveling salesman named Faustro to haul loads back and forth across the Mexicali crossing. Faustro made the run into the U.S. so often that he became known well enough by the border guards that they seldom even searched him. There were days when he would make four complete runs in a twenty four hour period.

Lencho rented a storage building for a few hundred dollars a month in the nearby city of Brawley to store his product. Faustro would pull in whenever he wanted and quietly drop off his loads. A few days later, an employee would show up with the vitamin truck, load up the required weight, and then deliver it to Lencho. It was a very smooth operation.

Things were continuing to get more organized for the weed man. He had to be organized, because the cops were getting tiresome. He figured that if one of his men got popped, he would be there to bail them out; but, if he were the one to get caught, all would be lost.

Palm Springs was a fun place. Things were really cooking and he was making quite a bit of money. But poor Manuel got spotted by the Federales in Mexico, and they chased him for miles, shooting holes in his truck as he fled. They finally cornered him and beat him mercilessly. They tortured him for good measure as only the Mexican cops know how.

Those bad boys really wanted Lencho, but good ole Manuel never talked. It was not uncommon for the Mexican authorities to kill their captives when they didn't get the information they were seeking, so to be a standup guy like Manuel was very impressive indeed.

Once he was in the hands of Mexico, Lencho was powerless to help his faithful and loyal pal. There was no bail down there, and he dare not set foot on the other side of the border, so Manuel just disappeared, never to be seen again. Maybe they killed him after all.

The stint in Palm Springs lasted all of four months, and with the arrest and disappearance of Manuel, the current effort was over, finished.

*****

Malcom, who was traveling in Asia, sent Lencho a couple of ounces of pure opium. Lencho and Karen began smoking and eating it until they came close to addiction. With a thousand dollars in his pocket and the rest of the opium, he and Karen drove their jeep to the enchanted forest of Navarro, where they had been confronted by the Hells Angels awhile back. This time, however, they weren't greeted by a throng of naked hippies, but instead by the silence imposed by the State of California park rangers and their new regulations. The once crowded campgrounds were still serenely beautiful, but now they were empty. Empty except for one other camper: Lencho's old friend, mystic, theologian, musician, and newly minted embezzler of a lawyer's money, Powder! Powder and his girlfriend were hidden off in the trees. They were skinny, sun tanned, and high from eating the hashish they brought back from their world travels.

It was a time of spiritual discovery and wonderment, heightened by mescaline. They met a shaman by the name of "Three Feathers" (a seemingly ageless Jamaican black man with long and gnarly dread locks) who taught them that God was everywhere; in the water, the grass, and the trees—but particularly in the great five redwood sisters that grew together in a lush and green grotto. The redwood sisters surrounded an indentation in the earth, which was covered with a gentle felt of moss. The oldest redwood tree had been hollowed out by fires, but she lived on anyway in all of her majesty.

The wicked State Park Rangers forbade any camp fires, which made it very difficult to camp. Three Feathers taught Lencho how to create a small fire that did not make smoke. "You use the magic wood," he intoned. "It be everywhere, mon."

Lencho looked, but was unable to find any of the magic wood that Three Feathers had described, and being high on both mescaline and hash, he became frustrated. He was in combat with his own ego. What this ego was to Lencho was anyone's guess, but it seemed to him that all of the spiritual hippies of the time were concerned about it. Then, all of a sudden, the magic wood appeared. It was actually everywhere that Lencho looked. He gathered armloads of the red, shiny-like stuff, and piled it upright in a wigwam pattern in the middle of his redwood room. Then he lit it with his Zippo. It burned brightly and did not create any smoke whatsoever!

For the next week, the rangers never knew that Lencho and Karen were both living high in the trees. During that week, they learned that what the wise old Rasta man said was God's truth. God truly was everywhere and nowhere at the very same time. It wasn't even necessary to believe in a guy with a beard and long white hair hanging out in the clouds; you just felt his presence. Nature is infused with God. God was and is nature. God was in the peyote button and could certainly be found in the LSD. God was also in the standard sacrament of the everyday—ganja, mota, boo, weed, grass, marijuana—whatever one wished to call the "herb," God was there for sure.

Lencho knew that his calling was correct. He was a weed man, and the world needed weed, and thus needed him. He was not in this game for the money, but for a higher purpose. Someday it would be legal, and freely available for one and all to enjoy, but in the meantime, he knew it was his duty to continue to fight the good fight. Battle the cops, the park rangers, and the snitches who made their living in betrayal. Fight the corruption that was becoming ever more apparent in the trade that he had chosen, and one day, he would prevail. The redwoods seemed to speak to him, and they told him that it would be a hard journey, a long road with much tribulation along the way. But one day he would finally know victory.

Three Feathers taught Lencho a 'Life Lesson' during that trip to the Navarro. He learned the difference between 'then' and 'now.' The difference in how sincere the hippies were in seeking meaning was different back then. It seemed true that the party of the old days differed from the party of today. Back then, something profound was expected, because they were innocent and naive, and they expected to see God, which sometimes they did. That was what good dope did for you. It was an innocent time.

Before they parted, Three Feathers told Lencho and Karen, "Wherever you go next, mon, it will be cold. It be where your child is born girl."

So they left for what turned out to be Colorado. That's how it was back then, a lot of magic around, mon.

*****

On July 4, 1972, the Rainbow Family had their first big gathering in Granby,

Colorado. At an elevation of 8,000 feet, Strawberry Lake was the site of the Great White Buffalo, and even better, Jesus himself was guaranteed to be there.

Lencho and a San Diego fugitive by the name of Brad Goy, aka, "Peach Seed," had just spent a couple of weeks in Prescott selling pot and acid. When they finally arrived in the mountains of Colorado, they found fifty thousand stoned flower children along with Buddhists, Hindu/Krishnas, Rastafarians, and Urantium spiritual guides among many others. The whole enchilada was on hand.

After setting up camp, they hit the vegetarian kitchens, which were setup to feed the multitudes. Later in the afternoon, the Ghost Dance began. Lencho, who was himself part Cherokee on his mother's side, began shaking on two feet, and then moved into a tight circle along with all of the other dancers. On and on they went as a hundred tom toms thundered a hypnotic beat. The dancing continued for hours.

Many of the dancers were of course using psychedelic chemicals, which gave them both stamina and supernatural sensations. Lencho was certain that his own feet were not fastened to the ground any longer as he danced with the throng. It was like being in another world altogether. Six hours later it all wound down and ended.

He felt akin to his Native American ancestry, and now it was time to meet Jesus. "I know the White Buffalo is there, man. My bud came down from the peak this morning. He saw it, and it was awesome," said one kid to another as they climbed up the path with thousands of others.

"Dig it," replied another. "I can't wait to see the Christ, man!"

"Yeah, I sure have heard a lot about him. The son of God, man. Bitchin."

Around ten thousand acolytes hiked up the hill to meet the savior. Many wondered if he would feed the masses with two fish and five loaves of bread, like he did in the book of Mark.

"He's God, man," one girl exclaimed. "God can sure do that, piece of cake."

Finally, at the summit, on a large glade with a granite cliff still half covered in snow from the previous winter, they arrived. The cobalt sky contrasted with the white snow. They all saw the noble and almost petroglyph image of the Great White Buffalo etched in the snow on the rocks.

The spaced out crowd was spell bound by the sight, and muttered "oohs" and "aahs." Jesus, however, never showed up that late afternoon, even though they waited until the setting sun.

"Bummer, man," the same young fellow said to his companions as they trudged downward from whence they had come.

"Oh well, I still dug the buffalo, man."

"Yeah, the buffalo was great," they agreed.

"Anyway, man, there is a lesson to be learned from this. What I see is that just because they say Jesus is gonna be somewhere, that don't mean he will be. He's the son of God after all. He can do anything he wants or go anywhere he wants, man."

"He hangs out with the Buddha. It's presumptuous of us to expect him to just be somewhere cause we want to see him."

"I dig it, man, that's heavy. Maybe he'll show up at the next Greatful Dead gig."

*****

Lencho, Karen, and Peach Seed set off for Aspen. Peach Seed became a fugitive after the PEMEX bust, and was anxious to get up to the ski town. He was originally known as Brad Goy when Lencho first met him back in Ocean Beach a year earlier, and was instrumental in setting up the ill-fated PEMEX job. He was a great actor, and at the time the Narcs had nabbed him, he had been all contrition and regret, even holding out the possibility that he might cooperate with them and become a rat.

But they found out that he was not going to do any such thing. At his first opportunity, he left town only stopping off at the graveyard to cop a name off a tombstone, in order to establish a new identity for himself.

Peach Seed knew some weed dealers in Basalt, and they in turn introduced Lencho to Jim and Lea, a married couple. Jim and Lea were employed as caretakers for the McCullough Corporation, which owned vast tracks of forest lands near Hunter Creek. They all became fast friends, so Lencho, Peach Seed, and the recently pregnant Karen moved into the Canyon.

This was fortuitous, as it was exclusive and solitary up there. Lencho set about building a little cabin in the woods out of scrap lumber and cuttings. Since his experiences over the previous years had been quite varied, he had become adept at the building trades, and by the end of September, he had created an enchanting little abode that looked like it belonged in Snow White and the Seven Dwarfs. It was small, but featured a kitchen with a wood burning stove, a tub, and a double bed fabricated from planks and then stuffed with straw. There were two little windows looking out on a gurgling brook that ran past it. It was everything an expectant young hippie mom could want. Just as Lencho finished pounding the last roofing nail into the last shingle, the first snowflakes began to fall from the late September sky. The snow continued to fall until it was eleven feet deep.

Peach Seed built himself an A-frame a few hundred feet down river. They had both gone into town and found jobs as plumbers, so they had some under the counter money. There was pot to smoke, and a little business always being conducted on the side. Things were sweet as the winter settled in. Even though it snowed constantly, Lencho was young and happy. He always showed up for work, even when he had to ski through a blizzard to get there.

But he began to get restless, and was casting about for something to sell, dope wise. He met a couple of guys with a burlap sack full of peyote buttons that they had scored in Taos, New Mexico. Big, fat and juicy: these gnarly critters were truly beautiful specimens and chock full of enlightenment. With the intention of heading back to OB, Lencho asked if he could move them.

Leaving his jeep as collateral, he grabbed a ride with a couple of ladies in a Cadillac heading toward the coast. They dropped him off in Prescott, where he picked up his brother David and bought a vintage Pontiac that they named White Cloud.

They sold the little cacti quickly for twenty bucks a pop. The well-heeled residents of the beach towns ate them straight-up, or blended them into a puree for soups and sundry confections—they wretched right and left as one does with buttons, and then they saw God in everything, wherever they turned.

Before they left, Ralph Finnester showed them some really esoteric and rare mescaline sulphate that he had. This stuff was the essence of peyote minus the terrible taste and stomach ache. It was a bluish crystal and very expensive. Lencho could not resist and bought five bags of the stuff. Buy, trade, and sell was his mantra of commerce.

Karen was more than a little sore that her husband was gone so often. To make her happy, he flew her out from Colorado to join them for the trip home. The three climbed into the White Cloud and headed back to Colorado by way of Las Vegas, and sampled the organic product along the way. Picking up a couple of hitchhikers outside of Needles, the five of them tore through the starry night.

By Las Vegas, Lencho had become a trifle weary of them. He dumped them out on the Strip where they were last seen staring in bewilderment at the blinking neon.

The road to Aspen beckoned, so off they sped like characters out of Fear and Loathing in Las Vegas.

Taking a junction route, they headed out to Utah. Whether that was the fastest route or a twist of fate, a Utah State Trooper zoomed by them in the early morning and suddenly hit his brakes, turned around, and chased after them with lights flashing.

Shades of Gila Bend, Lencho flashed back. High as hell with a car full of drugs, and here comes the man. "Give me a fucking break," he muttered.

The trooper advanced with gun drawn, and ordered them to get out of the White Cloud. Complying glumly, Lencho and David were placed by the side of the road. Karen was allowed to stand alone at the rear of the Pontiac, holding her purse. While the cop searched the boys, she remembered she had one of the bags of mescaline on her. Thinking quickly, she reached into her purse, pulled it out, and subtly placed it behind the bumper by her knee. When the trooper went through the car, he found the rest of the stash and some weed.

"Holy Shit," he exclaimed, holding the bag up to the rising sun. "I bet this is LSD! Man, a lot of LSD, maybe even a Utah record." The cop hauled them off to a little jail in the town of Moab, just up the road. At the station, the official paperwork and warrant declared the mescaline to be LSD, and everyone agreed that it was a historic drug bust of epic proportions.

The brothers were locked up in a small cell together, and Karen was taken to a back room with a cot. The food wasn't half bad, and they treated the little pregnant lady with kindness, not even placing her under arrest. On Monday, a court appointed lawyer showed up to chat and put it bluntly: "You guys have $500 on your books, that's what was found on you, besides the dope. You are going to be fined $500, so you can just sign it over to me or talk to the Judge tomorrow."

"I'll talk to the judge," Lencho replied.

"Fine," the lawyer said.

The next morning, they were escorted to the court house, which was located across the street from the jail, and they both stood before the Honorable Judge Wellbottom who intoned, "Your fine will be $500." It turned out the police in Moab, Utah, never really had a warrant, but they needed the money, so that was that. The intrepid little band was released, and they headed out of town in the White Cloud. The police let Karen keep the hundred dollars that she had in her purse, and as they rolled away, she announced that she had stashed the last bag of dope in the rear bumper. Stopping quickly, Lencho fished around and found it, and they toasted their good fortune by getting toasted on two big lines of the magic powder.

Back in Aspen, the peyote button guys were none too happy about what had transpired with Lencho and their product. But, since they had his jeep, it wasn't a big deal. Lencho and Peach Seed went back to their plumbing jobs, and began to pay off debts. And then, Malcom showed up. Malcom moved up to Aspen where he was doing pretty good selling his sticks. He lived in a rented Victorian house downtown. It truly was a small world, and getting smaller by the day as the FBI began to close in on Peach Seed. They had somehow caught wind that the fugitive was nearby, and the resident agent was hot on his trail.

Lencho and Malcom did several dope runs back to San Diego. Once he took a Greyhound bus and brought back forty keys. Things were getting back to normal financially, and he paid off his peyote button debt.

Karen was getting larger by the day. They lived at 9,500 feet, and the snow was twelve feet deep in some places. They had to use snow shoes to get around, as well as skis. Plus, they lived in a small, home-made shack. It was remote, and could get dicey with Karen's pending delivery of their first child looming.

The day before Christmas Eve, Lencho and Peach Seed took some mescaline and tripped out on the beauty of winter while riding horses in the deep snow. They got back at four in the morning, blissed out by the full moon and the fact that it was almost Christmas. But Karen's water broke, even though she wasn't due for another two months.

"Holy Shit," Lencho mouthed.

Nervously waiting for first light, they loaded her onto the toboggan and made their way toward the hospital two miles away in Aspen. The hospital staff went into a small panic, because they didn't have much practice delivering babies. Broken bones, scrapes, and cuts from injured skiers was more their forte, not dealing with a premature pregnancy.

The local doctor was summoned. He came to the hospital at once, leaving a Christmas party he was hosting at his home. The doc was a little tipsy, but brought along a guest, Dr. Marge Spencer who just happened to be a prominent expert in the field of premature births. She was the author of several books on the subject of "Blue Babies," named for infant breathing difficulties which, as it later turned out, was exactly the problem this little creature was facing. The doctor and his staff huddled around Karen in the delivery room, while the boys waited outside in the lobby. Finally, Lencho decided he needed a smoke. He fished out a fatty of Columbian weed from his jacket pocket, and went outside in the crisp December air to fire it up.

He was feeling no pain when someone yelled that the time had come: "Get in here, you're gonna be a father!"

Putting on a white smock and covering his face with a mask, he hurried into the delivery room, where the rest of the gang was all crowded around the soon to be mom. Suddenly, there the baby was, emerging from the secret garden, all slimy and wailing loudly. His little pecker was sticking out, pissing in all directions. Lencho took one look at him, and then passed out like a beached whale, hitting the floor with a thud.

The staff administered smelling salts, and when Lencho finally came to declared, "Man, I saw the white light. What a visual. And now I have a son. Far out!"

But the little man was a long way from being out of the woods. His breathing was labored, and the doctor began artificial measures at once in order to save his life. Since the small hospital was not equipped for such stuff, Dr. Spencer breathed into his little lungs using a device that resembled a straw with a mouthpiece. Fundamental as this was, it was effective for the time being. An assistant called in an SOS to the Coast Guard in Denver.

Heroically, the Coast Guard responded to the emergency during a severe blizzard. A big red and white Sikorsky chopper was dispatched. The raging snow storm gave them virtually zero visibility, but they arrived within the hour. Major David Brown and his crew were used to danger, and duty called.

"Will he be okay?" Karen asked her husband with worry and fear showing on her tired face.

"Sure, babe. They sent the Coast Guard, and the doctor told me that she would be with him every inch of the way."

"I'm going too, aren't I? He is my baby."

Lencho replied softly, "I don't think you can go, Karen. They told the docs here that the weather was so bad that it would simply be too dangerous. He'll be fine. They got the best equipment on the other side of the mountains; he needs to be on a ventilator."

"But I need to be with him," she cried. "What if he doesn't make it?"

"Don't worry dear," Doctor Spencer consoled her, "I'll take really good care of him. The base just called and said the pilot is in heavy weather, but has good enough visuals to find his way through the passes. He has made this trip before. He is sorry you cannot come."

"I appreciate you so very much, doctor," she sniffled through her tears. "This is a dangerous night, and it's Christmas to boot."

The kind doctor replied softly, "He's your little Christmas present, Karen. God won't let anything happen to him or to us."

The chopper was being punished and buffeted by fierce winds and blinding flurries of snow. The radar was all that guided them for most of the first fifty miles. Climbing through the cloud cover out of the Coast Guard Station in Denver, Major Brown called home.

"Victor gulf; bravo echo. What's the latest on weather in Aspen? Over."

"Pretty nasty, Dave. Winds gusting to eighty, ceiling limited. Watch your ass. Over."

"Roger that. Did you call Aspen hospital with our ETA?"

"Roger that bravo echo. Out."

It was a scary ninety minutes. At 6:10 p.m. that evening the group of doctors and nurses along with Lencho were standing outside in the cold and staring into the bleak sky when they heard the distant thump of rotors. As the sound grew ever louder, they all breathed a collective sigh of relief.

The great machine was suddenly visible, and no more than fifty feet above them as it lumbered down through the clouds landing gently a hundred yards away in the parking lot. The skipper and copilot never got out, while a petty officer jumped down, and rushed over to the group.

"Where's the patient, sir?" he yelled above the noise of the roaring jet engines.

"This way," the doctor yelled back, and they all followed him into the building. Ten minutes later, the newborn and his caregivers were safely bundled into the aircraft, and it immediately lifted off into the stormy heavens.

He would be on a ventilator and in intensive care in Denver for the next five weeks, and all would turn out to be just fine. Dr. Spencer tended to him the entire trip using her own lungs to keep him alive.

The bill for the entire operation, including the rescue was immense. The whole expense was written off and Lencho and Karen were never charged a penny.

"It's our Christmas present to you kids," the doctor would later say. "We'll all remember this one."

The State Highway Patrol brought Dr. Spencer back in a car and then transported Karen to Denver.

Lencho returned to his cabin alone as Christmas dawned on that cold December morning. The snow crunched beneath his snow shoes. When the clouds parted and finally let that beautiful winter sun shine through, he knew what he would name his boy.

"We'll call him Luz," he said out loud. "That means light in Spanish, and he is just that. The clear light. Little Luz!"

*****

The FBI showed up a few weeks later and asked if Peach Seed was hiding there. Karen told them that he was not, but they were welcome to come in and see for themselves. "I have no idea where he is," she continued. "I've been in the hospital."

The Feds then asked, "Where is your husband?"

Karen replied, "He had to go out of town and won't be back for a few days. I just had a baby, and I'm here alone."

She knew that she was not exactly 'alone.' In fact, she had fifty pounds of marijuana hidden above the shower to keep her company—one of Lencho's ingenious stash hiding places.

The agents came in, looked around, and then left. A day later, they cornered Peach Seed at his job. They took him into town, chained and shackled. The FBI, like the Mounties, always get their man. They just can't always keep him.

Taken before Judge Brentwald, who was the magistrate in Grand Junction for this custody hearing, Peach Seed sobbed and sniffled in misery. The Feds were very unkind to him, and pushed and shoved him into the courtroom. They snarled vague and horrible threats under their breath.

"Give us any more trouble, you little shit, and we'll pull your fingernails out."

"You can't do that, this is America!" he protested.

"Try us," they hissed back.

The Judge looked down upon the young man and intoned, "Well son, what do you have to say for yourself?"

"Please, Your Honor, I'm so very sorry. I should have never smoked that marijuana," he moaned. "It clouded my judgment. I'm just a kid. I didn't know what I was doing, and my parents are very worried about me. I've really let them down lately. These handcuffs are hurting my wrists sir. Couldn't you take them off? Please Judge, don't let these guys hurt me anymore."

The Judge paused, and then glowered at the Feds. He looked down at the pathetic Peach Seed, and found himself truly feeling pity for the confused young man.

"Before I go on, Agents, I want those manacles removed from this boy's wrists, post haste. This is not the inquisition, and I will not allow any suspects to be treated like animals here in my court room. Am I making myself clear?"

"But Judge, we…"

"NOW!" The judge thundered.

An agent cowered, and produced a key to unlock the restraints. Peach Seed seized his opportunity, and as soon as they were off, bolted from the courtroom like a stallion, knocking one of the agents down, and nearly running over the shocked bailiff.

He was twenty-three years old, and in pretty good shape, but he was still dressed in an orange jail jumpsuit and light tennis shoes. To top it off, it was twenty degrees outside.

"That mother fucker!" The FBI agent screamed.

"Get him!" Yelled the judge. But Peach Seed was gone.

Once in the streets, he hid behind a post office in an alley. Then he darted madly up into a fir tree, where he froze in the snowy branches, watching cop cars cruise the area looking for him. One car drove directly underneath as he shivered in the cold. After it passed, with teeth chattering, he dropped to the frozen ground, jumped over a fence, and dashed across the yard of someone who luckily wasn't home.

He kept zigging and zagging across the neighborhoods until he made his way to the outskirts of the small city. There, he managed to take refuge in a big old barn on a ranch. He curled up in the hay between two horses that didn't seem to give a damn whether he joined them or not. As the day passed, he actually started to think that he might not get caught. The next day, of course, was another story altogether.

Cold, weary, and hungry, he slept there with the beasts fitfully. In the morning, he looked out towards the horizon and realized that he was no more than a hundred yards from Grand Junction High School. He spotted several big, yellow school buses parked by the football field. A number of students were milling around, and he figured he didn't have much to lose, so he put on his best poor me face and sauntered out of the barn. He climbed over a wood fence and headed for the kids. "Hey," he said, looking like the escaped convict that he was, "What's happening?"

There were five of them, all jocks who had beat Grand Junction in a hotly contested football game the previous evening. Winning on the visitor's field made them feel pretty good. "Whoa," one of them exclaimed. "You're the dude who busted out of jail!"

"Well, actually, it was the courthouse," Peach Seed corrected. "Man, the FBI had me on a weed bust for just a little bit of pot. They came, arrested me, beat me up, and dragged me into court. I admit it, I was scared of them, and I just took off. Please guys, help me."

They did. Hustling him into a gym, two of the boys posted themselves as lookouts while the other three dug out some clothes and a razor from the bus. They also found some hair coloring that one of their girlfriends donated to the cause. A half hour later, Peach Seed looked like a new man. They ditched the jailhouse jumpers into a trash can, and led him onto their bus. He ate peanut butter sandwiches and drank Coca Cola as he regaled the kids with stories of smuggling pot in a PEMEX truck and living the life of a fugitive and outlaw.

The bus started up and the only person on board who did not know that they had a stowaway was the driver, who proceeded to drive them all back to Utah.

"Is your real name Peach Seed?" an adoring cheerleader sighed as they rumbled towards the state line.

"Well, not really," he replied tongue in cheek. "When you are in the line of work that I am, you might have many names."

"So you work for the CIA too?"

"Sure," he lied. "Them and the Army Rangers, Navy Seals, and the OBMC."

"Who is that?" she asked starstruck.

"The Ocean Beach Marijuana Coalition!" They all howled with laughter.

In Green River, Utah, Peach Seed got a hold of Lencho, who immediately wired his friend five hundred dollars. And that's how the FBI lost their man.

*****

Lencho and Karen stayed up at the canyon for another five months. They had retrieved little Luz from the hospital, and then decided that they were homesick for San Diego. Once back in Ocean Beach, they found a house to rent on Sumac Street, and resumed business with pals Doc, Joey, Buddy and Ronnie.

People from all of the places Lencho had been were now showing up to do business, and business was good.

The house that he rented was perfect for brokering, because it had a large garage, which was always full of product. He bought a Rambler station wagon for Karen. He made friends with the neighbors, and they all loved him as the new young neighborhood husband with a wife and cute little baby.

Ronnie bought a Ford pickup with a camper attached to it. The camper had concealed panels that could hold six hundred pounds of product. He was a very busy boy over the past two years, and was doing some serious business moving that much weed every ten days.

Lencho would buy pot from Ronnie for his own customers, and was clearing a thousand dollars a day, two or three times a week. Not huge money for the drug trade, but better than chump change. By the late summer of 1973, there were people coming and going from all over the country. Besides his regular customers, there were small deals of ten to thirty pounds at a time.

There was also the storage business, and when a guy showed up one day to ask Lencho if he could use his garage for a few hours to transact a deal, Lencho readily agreed. The deal would net him thirty pounds, but he did not know these new people very well, so he had Karen leave for the afternoon. At a little after twelve noon, the load showed up in front of God and everybody in a big U-Haul rental truck. The transporters quickly pulled into the garage and unloaded thirteen hundred pounds of weed and then left.

That was a lot of pot all at once, even for Lencho. While he was standing there talking and examining the product with the buyer, car doors slammed in unison, and a helicopter could be heard overhead. Oh, Jeez, not again. As Lencho made a beeline out the door, he found a gun stuck in his right ear.

"On the ground, scumbag!" the Narc snarled. As the beefy thug with a badge shoved a boot into Lencho's back, Karen showed up. Since she was not a party to this latest difficulty, the cops didn't arrest her. The nice little neighbor lady, however, stared in horror at the spectacle of a police raid in her quiet neighborhood.

One of the region's most well-known and corrupt Narcs, John Mysner, led Lencho into the house and sat him down on the couch. The snitch who had set up the whole deal and posed as the buyer had a grin on his face from ear to ear, because they both now recognized Lencho as the man "behind the couch," a year and a half earlier.

"Well, I wonder how many bricks this pig is going to steal this time?" Lencho thought to himself.

Mysner left and the snitch looked at the handcuffed weed man and said, "They know that you're not really in on this thing, man. You were just letting those guys use your garage for the transfer. Here is the deal that they want to offer you: Come to work for us. You'll earn big money, and you'll have our protection as well. I just made $3,500. You're good and you know everybody. Mysner wanted me to ask you. How about it man?"

"Fuck you," Lencho replied. The rat just got up shaking his head and left the room.

The swarm of Narcs hustled him off to jail where he met up with about 10 others who were involved in this rather large conspiracy. One of them had some LSD in his boot, and hadn't been searched yet. "Anyone want to drop acid with me?" he asked.

"Why the hell not?" Lencho replied with a smile.

Chapter Five

"How Much is it Worth to Live in L.A."
Released 1988
Waylon Jennings

How much is it worth to live in L.A.?
That land of silk and money where the pretty people play
When they itemize insanity, how much will you pay?
How much is it worth to live in L.A.?

I WANNABE A DUCK

Lencho was taken to the San Diego County jail with the ten other 'conspirators' involved in the thirteen hundred pound pot bust. The load lost two hundred pounds after the Narcs got done conducting their 'inventory of the evidence', but regardless, they still valued the bust at three hundred and fifty thousand dollars, a large amount for that time.

Lencho's close associate, Joey—who, with his smallish features, red whiskers, and pugnaciousness, reminded everyone of Yosemite Sam—decided to piss off the blacks in jail, and ended up getting raped. It's easy to laugh at the old prison joke, "Make sure you don't drop the soap in the shower," until you drop the soap.

"Hey, white boy, that's my coffee cup you're using," a brother said to him one day.

"Fuck you, Nigger," Joey answered.

Waiting for their moment, the five blacks posted two very large fellows outside of the shower area as lookouts, and then took turns fucking the shit out of the little white man.

Very nasty business indeed, designed to demean and punish the victim and strip him of his manhood. It works too. The only thing the jail did to make amends was to expedite Joey's bond so that he was able to get out within a week, before he decided to sue them. Joey then fronted Lencho the five grand that he needed to bond out thirty days later.

*****

Malcom and Peach Seed were both on the run now so Lencho decided to move up to Chico, where Peach Seed claimed that the worlds most beautiful young women resided. These girls attended the State university, and the place was truly crawling with them.

The weed man rented a really cool pad in town and began selling his wares. The boys had it made in those days, with women coming and going by the car load. Karen was tired of her cheating husband who she rarely saw, so she decided to get herself a boyfriend out of sheer loneliness.

Lencho fell in love with a freckle faced knock out named Dottie, who was twenty-three years old and taught junior high school. She was petite, with auburn hair, and a fun loving nature. Her sister, Carol, became Malcom's girlfriend and ended up staying with him for the next twenty-five years.

"You want to go to Tahoe?" Lencho asked Dottie one weekend. "You said you wanted to be a croupier in a casino, and I know people at the Sahara that I can introduce you to." Dottie really impressed everyone in management with her stunning entrance. She wore a short, low cut dress that show cased her legs and her dazzling smile.

Lencho made a cardinal mistake introducing her to Karen, thinking that it would help him ease out of his unhappy marriage. The plan backfired when the two women became friends. Dottie felt bad about coming between Karen and her husband, and decided that she would not be a party to their break up.

"I really like you Lencho, and appreciate all of the things we have done together. It was a lot of fun this past year getting to know you, but Karen is still very much in love with you and I can see the heartbreak in her eyes whenever she talks about you. I think it's for the best that we just say goodbye."

"Goodbye?!" This was not a word the lothario was used to hearing and he was crushed.

The blow to his ego was harsh, but Lencho lived. It was important to stay focused on the pending sentencing for the pot bust of a year and a half earlier. The Judge in the case was in a quandary, because most of the ten young men were from wealthy and prominent families who retained expensive attorneys. Lencho had to fork over sixty five hundred himself, but he hoped in this particular case money would talk. And this time, it seemed to work.

"I'm not going to sentence you at this time," the Judge told them. "There is a new pilot program out of Chino State Prison called the "Z" program, which I am going to send you all into. This program is an in-depth psychological dissection of your collective minds. It is the goal of the state medical professionals up there to try and discover what really makes you counter culture types tick. When I get the reports back, I will then decide the most appropriate sentences. The program takes sixty days to complete, and the good news is that Chino State Prison is a model of both civility and decorum. It is not a dangerous place, so your parents may rest assured that you will be safe. I suggest you all go there with the proper attitude and cooperate fully with the authorities. Try and save yourselves from the degradation of marijuana use, and the inevitable plunge into heroin addiction that is certain to follow. See you all in two months, and good luck!"

Chino State was an abomination and a cesspool of bedlam and depravity, none of which anyone was ready for at the time. If San Diego City Jail was bad, it was heaven on earth compared to Chino State Prison, a central holding facility for California's vast prison population. The worst of the worst were housed there.

They were commingled with ordinary miscreants for about two weeks while the system sorted them out before sending them to their final destinations. Many of the prisoners ended up going to the low end like camps, while others ended up in San Quintin. Gangs were all well represented: Bikers, Aryans, Mexican Mafia, La Familia Nuestra, Black Gangster Disciples, and Angry

Panthers were there in abundance.

Lencho could not believe that he had been thrown into this hell hole. He discovered that nothing was done to correct the situation because the guards were greatly outnumbered by the unruly cons, and in most cases were just as terrified as the more timid inmates. One skinny white boy was thrown to his death over a railing on the second tier by thugs covered in tattoos. These men were killers, and were going to spend the rest of their lives in prison, so what did they care about the rules?

They routinely raped the small and defenseless, which occurred almost daily during the two weeks Lencho was in his holding cell, lying on his bunk wondering what made grown men do such hideous things to one another. Were they all just a bunch of muscled up faggots? Or was this just an act of power over the weak? How could five or six men even attain erections to have forced and brutal sex with one scared little man? Many of these same guys had wives, girlfriends, and children on the outside.

Lencho shuddered when one slug blocked a doorway and leered at him with hungry eyes. The huge man hissed, "Whenever I get out of the joint, boy, it takes me a long time to get a hard on without the smell of shit. Shit on my dick or blood on my knife." And then he blew Lencho a kiss.

Word finally came that Lencho was to be transferred from the big rectangular building that served as the receiving unit to the 'white elephant.' It was the difference between night and day! Originally built to house females, the white elephant was situated in the middle of the property, and featured a swimming pool, walking track, and playing field in the center. Everything was painted white. A guard tower stood in the middle of the compound, and was surrounded by a razor ribbon topped chain link fence. The razor ribbon actually made Lencho feel safe from the deviants next door.

Visitation was open, so Karen came frequently during his stay there. She brought him weed to smoke and food to eat. Once she even brought in a vegetarian sandwich stuffed with bean sprouts and mushrooms. The mushrooms were of the psychedelic variety.

He gobbled it down. After the visit he started tripping on the colors swirling around him as he lay out by the pool. The prison assigned him Lifeguard duty, since he had CPR and rescue training in the Navy. He sat up high in the lifeguard chair watching the less violent types frolicking, still mindful of his recent ordeal only a stone's throw away.

He refused to order anyone to stop running or getting too cozy in the shallow end. He wasn't a cop. He even smoked Thai joints during afterhours right beneath the guard in his tower.

Beans, an old junkie, told him nothing but heroin would do for his head until he smoked some of the weed man's Asian reefer.

"Man," Beans sighed, "This shit is bad!"

Lencho had once again done his duty, and was all the more convinced that weed was indeed a cure all.

"Ya know Beans, this stuff should really be used as medicine. One day these politicians will come to their senses and legalize it—at least for drug addiction, if nothing else."

"Nah man, it'll never happen," Beans replied.

They had a good laugh, and then headed over to see the psychologists.

The "Z" program was a massive compilation of all the psych tests ever devised for the study of criminal behavior. Test upon test dictated by tape recordings required Lencho to answer rapid fire questions very quickly: "Yes or No. Did you ever get molested as a child?" An hour later, the tape would ask the same questions in a slightly reworded format.

There were also inkblot tests. A technician would show him one ink drawing after another, asking him what the blurry messes reminded him of: "What does this one look like, Lencho?" Dr. Breams would ask.

"That looks like a cloud," he'd reply.

"And this one?"

"It looks just like the crack between my wife's legs."

"Um, how about this one?"

Lencho smiled and said, "That's little Luz, making his grand entrance into the world, doc!"

In the end, they would all come to the same conclusion: "You ain't no criminal, boy. Now get out of here."

Lencho again stood before the Judge, armed with all of the reports. Looking down on Lencho, the Judge said, "According to the results of the program, you are not a threat to the public or the community. Despite the results, I would say that the trafficking in cannabis is a very serious crime. I have decided to follow the recommendations of the medical staff, and sentence you to serve six months of labor at the Camp Marina Forestry Farm for nonviolent offenders. You have already served two months, and you are allowed two months off for good behavior, so that means you will only need to serve another two months. Court is dismissed!"

For thirteen hundred pounds of marijuana, Lencho ended up getting a six months sentence and almost raped. But he finished his time at the camp with a smile, and a song in his heart. After being victorious over the forces of evil at Chino, and now being finished with his service to the State, Lencho found himself on probation for a couple more years. He paid his lawyer an additional thirty five hundred bucks to appeal his probation, but in the end he was persuaded to withdraw the appeal, since in the opinion of his counsel, it was unnecessary. His attorney, Charlie Cory, promptly refunded his money, which is something you very rarely see lawyers do.

Lencho now had about five grand in his jeans, and was again ready for travel and new adventures. His older brother Joe also became a convert to the New World Order that was sweeping the young. Joe decided to take a vacation from his job back in Illinois, where he worked for the city and traveled with his brother to San Francisco, smoking reefer all the way.

Shortly after Joe went back to Illinois to collect his wife and kids, quit his job, and head out to Yuba County, where they camped for about a year, communing and becoming one with nature.

Joe set up house in a cabin that was seldom used by an old prospector. Eventually, he called the owner and arranged to purchase it and filed some mining claims of his own, which he still holds today.

It was to these bucolic woods that Lencho, Karen, and baby Luz journeyed. Stopping at the Coleman factory in Sacramento, Lencho bought a huge teepee. He was skilled in construction, and his improvised lodgings out in Aspen had been functional. But the teepee was a true and epic creation. It had a height of thirty-feet, and the floor space inside was thirty-six by thirty-six feet. A stout beam across the center supported the loft that he built above it. He even installed a kitchen and shower serviced by a water pump, which brought water from a flume constructed eons earlier by ethnic Chinese workers. The walls were canvas and they painted faux petroglyphs on them. At the top point, flew a flag with a peace symbol. Little Luz had his own bedroom in the back.

He was now ready to start making some money after his last ordeal with the law. Working together with his friends, he soon became very busy indeed, and the teepee was the least of it.

Lencho had three main partners in those days, all of them he had met in Ocean Beach. Perhaps OB was some sort of tantric melting point for weed dealers. First Doc, then Malcom, and then Joey, (who had finally recovered from his jail degradation). Joey was as frantic as ever, bouncing off the walls, snorting coke, and puffing on endless reefers.

Doc was in a category all by himself. He was a legend in the drug world, especially in the last century, and his luck was also legendary. He was called 'Doc' because, while hunting in the mountains of Colorado, he accidently cut a gash in his leg while sharpening a tent peg with his bowie knife. Bleeding almost to death, he performed a field operation like "Rambo," using a long and dull tent needle to stitch up his own wound. Doc was younger than Lencho, and stood six-feet, two-inches, weighing in at around two hundred and seventy-five pounds. He usually carried a gun, which made him the only member of the group that packed any heat. He almost always brought along a quart of whiskey and a pinch of cocaine for good measure. Nobody messed with Doc. He was a man that could handle himself, and he proved it on more than one occasion.

He became a millionaire over the years from sheer force of will, and by an intelligence most of his peers failed to give him credit for. However, he did bring in the Mafia.

Sitting in a bar one afternoon up on Melrose in Los Angeles, he was indulging in idle chit chat with a guy named John Smart. Smart was forty-one years old, slender, and tan. He wore stylish clothes and aviator sunglasses. He was a long time pilot for the Chicago 'outfit', and was in deep shit with his bosses over gambling debts. A light bulb suddenly went off in Doc's head as they sat there talking. "So what kind of flying do you actually do for those gangsters?" Doc asked.

"All kinds," he replied. "I mostly ferry good looking broads around the country for them. You know, hookers. The cream of the crop. These girls are really stunning, and are exclusively for their big time clients' enjoyment. Then there are other times I fly out with hot property like jewels or cash that may have just got stolen—which I fly to the Caymans, for example."

Booze made John's lips loose, and he continued to spill his guts to Doc. "Ever fly dope?" Doc asked him.

"Naw, man, I never have but the boss was saying to me recently that he wanted to get into the drug business."

"What if I offered you and your bosses a really good opportunity to earn very big money?" Doc said.

John answered with, "Hey, that just might get my tit out of the ringer. If you got the connections, I could hook you all up, and they might even cancel my debt to them. What kind of weight are we talking about?"

"Tons," Doc said with a grin.

These organized crime guys were Italian, the original OG's that became what was usually called the American Mafia. They sent their man, Jackie Fabreeze; or, as the boys called him behind his back, Mugsy.

Mugsy was a dapper little man of indeterminate age, small in stature, astute, ruthless and ambitious. He prided himself on his criminal heritage, and was very loyal to the outfit. He would not hesitate to have you killed if you fucked up, but he could also be counted on to stand by you if you were a good earner. Doc was an earner.

Doc met Mugsy out in the San Fernando Valley, and they struck a deal to do some business, which included a brand new airplane and a fifty-fifty split. Doc and the boys would get the weed up from Mexico and sell it; the outfit would provide the cash, a pilot, and storage facilities. They would also use their various influences in high places—the outfit even had a customs agent in L.A. on the payroll according to Mugsy.

Lencho, Doc, Joey and Malcom formed "The Partnership." Each member had their own area of expertise. All profits were to be split equally.

Doc and Malcom went back to Thailand together to expand Malcom's connections and arrange for mega shipments of Thai Stick. The reasoning was simple: the best Mexican pot sold for three hundred and fifty dollars per pound, while Thai went for two grand. This was indeed a no brainer.

Things in Asia were now in the works, but Doc, being the go-getter that he was, set up the first weed deal for The Partnership down in Oaxaca, Mexico, using a guy named CR. CR smuggled his dope out of the steep mountains, buying it from the Indians and hauling it back in various boats, cars, and trailers.

They purchased five hundred pounds of product from CR, which was loaded into a borrowed Cessna. The pilot was a seasoned one, but also had a penchant for alcohol and often over indulged. During a refuel at an airstrip deep in Mexico, the pilot over ran the runway, nearly killing them both in the process. The plane's nose and prop plunged downward, sticking it deep in the mud. Doc climbed out cursing and rubbing his temple where he had bashed it on the dash.

"You dumb motherfucker. If we live through this, I may kill you!"

"Sorry, Boss. The sun got in my eyes," the drunk pilot responded.

"I'm taking this rifle and going up on that knoll over there. I want you to get down to the town and get some Mexicans to come back and load our product into a truck. You tell them that I'll pay them very well for their efforts. I also want you to make it clear that I'm a beaner-killing secret-fucking-agent for the CIA, and I'll put a bullet into the first son of a bitch that approaches my airplane with the thought of stealing any of my cargo. Do you understand?"

"Yes, sir."

Three hours later he returned with six young men and a battered old truck. They loaded up the dope, and then hauled it back to a little ranch house, where one of them lived with his mama and sisters. Doc found a phone and arranged for another plane to come to pick up them and their cargo. They got the weed back to the U.S. safely, and Lencho sold all of it. The outfit was suitably impressed.

The airplane that Mugsy promised for the Thailand job finally arrived. It was a hot little 210 turbo prop that cost a cool seventy grand. The Italian and his body guards flew it into Durango, Mexico where Lencho's brother Bobby had been setting up a refueling operation and carving out a crude airstrip in the middle of the desert for the last few weeks. The mob boss claimed that he was a mining engineer and his goons were hydrologists. Now the boys were in bed with the devil, big time.

Lencho spent his time bouncing between the teepee—where he was just another hippie living with his wife and little boy—and several expensive suites at the Sunset Marquee Hotel. He'd fly down to Guadalajara, where he would meet with CR. He was a busy boy. And, to top it all off, Karen was pregnant again with their second child.

Several loads came in on the fast little mob plane. The weed was stored in a big meat locker Mugsy owned as part of the outfits interests in the grocery business. It was large and cold and also good for hanging dead bodies on hooks until a better resting place could be found for those unfortunates who had absconded on mob debts.

The Partnership went on a buying spree of Cadillacs. Not new ones, but good reliable used ones with big trunks.

"Let me see the ones with the biggest trunks," Joey told the salesman on the car lot at Dilday Cadillac in Bellflower. He began to sound like the wise guys that he had been hanging around with, and that made Lencho a little nervous. Four Caddies were now in their fleet, so they were able to haul four hundred pound loads around the state, selling the product to the many customers that they had amassed over time.

One of Lencho's biggest clients were some pious Sufi Muslims up in Mill Valley. Living in a palatial house at the foot of Mt. Tamalpias, Ahoon, Raheem, Louiso, and Princess Isis were all Americanized whirling dervishes. They wore bright, loose fitting pantaloons, billowing shirts, and scarfs. They loved dancing and singing, as well as historically indulging in less than legitimate trades and sundry criminal enterprises. Often persecuted, but always lively and spiritual, these Sufi sold weed in their modern day incarnation, and sold a lot of it to boot.

Lencho made several trips to their holy pad. Their leader, Raheem, a young psychologist of about thirty years, said they were ready for the final weight on this particular purchase. Then the Mafia showed up.

Two beefy slugs with no necks and bulges clearly visible beneath their blue blazers arrived in a Caddy with four hundred pounds of fine Oaxacan weed. Lencho had been waiting for them, but when Raheem noticed that they were packing heat, he freaked out.

"There is no place for guns in this house," he screeched. "We can do no more business with you brother Lencho."

The two goons were puzzled by the outburst, and one of them wanted to just shoot everyone and be done with it. Lencho urged patience from all. He said, "But Raheem, they just got the guns on them, what's the big deal? Just take delivery of your pot, and we will all leave."

"No, no, that is not the Sufi way. A weapon is an insult to our faith—we are men of peace."

"Let me kill the son-a-bitch," mumbled one of the thugs.

"Cool off boys," Lencho yelled. "You guys go and find a room at a motel in Sausalito. After I speak with these folks, I'll catch up with you in a couple of hours."

The muscle pulled out of the driveway. For the next three hours, Lencho implored the Sufi to be reasonable. "You have sullied this holy place," was all that Raheem would say when he said anything at all.

Finally, Lencho pointed out two things: "Raheem, don't take the Mafia lightly. It ain't a good idea to throw a monkey wrench into the works. Plus, your man there, Ahoon, is your bodyguard. Even though he does not carry a gun, with his extensive martial arts training, he is a lethal weapon by himself, so it's really the same thing, isn't it?"

Pondering these words, and seeing their wisdom, Raheem finally relented. "I suppose that you are right. Tell those thugs to come back with the product, but they are to leave their weapons behind. Unload the weed in the garage, and I will get your money."

Lencho and The Partnership were also involved in the music business. Living at the Sunset Marquee gave them access to many of the popular bands of the time. Poco, Crosby, Stills, Nash and Young, and the Byrds were just a few that recorded at the nearby Record Plant studios. But The Partnership was careful not to reveal that to Mugsy, who they knew from experience would want to muscle in on the action as well.

On one memorable night at the studio, Lencho took the redoubtable Rusty Kershaw over to record a track on the Neil Young album, "On the Beach." Rusty was the talented brother of recording artist Doug Kershaw, but was basically a madman who had to be kept on a short leash. The Partnership put him up in his own suite, where he never set foot outside the door during the day, and even refused to let the maid come in and clean. Beer bottles, ashtrays full of cigarette butts, and miscellaneous garbage piled up behind the curtains in his room. The man would go completely berserk if he did not have a constant flow of whiskey, pot, and coke to self-medicate. Despite these traits, and a well-known history of mental instability, Rusty could actually be a fun guy, and man could that cat play those stringed instruments!

Impatient and awaiting his turn in front of the mic, Rusty was pacing and howling at the moon. Young was taking way too long as far as he was concerned. Then he simply vanished from an adjoining room, and in the darkness could not be found. Suddenly, Lencho spotted a figure down on all fours in the recording booth with Neil. He was slowly coming at the artist like a hungry wolf. Once he got within range, he opened his great bearded jaws and clamped down on Neil's left calf with a fury. He shook back and forth with slobber flying everywhere. Young let out a mighty howl.

Putting the leash back on, Lencho rushed the crazy musician back to the Marquee, where he found the manager arguing with Doc about the current bill.

"I must have the money, sir. Thirty five hundred dollars for the past three weeks."

Doc replied, "Oh please, Pierre, you can't really be concerned that we won't pay you? I mean how long we been shacking up in this dump now, six months?"

"Yes, sir, you have, but still it is my responsibility to take care of these financial matters for the hotel, and I'm afraid that if this bill is not paid right now, I will be forced to evict your entire party!"

"Why you little French cocksucker!" Doc thundered. "Come outside here on the balcony for a minute, so we can discuss this in private."

Once out on the balcony, Doc reached for his zipper and put his beer bottle on a table. "You know that our guys are in the music biz, Pierre?" He began.

"Yes, of course."

"You also are aware that many of the bands and musical acts that stay here at your hotel frequently end up trashing the place by tossing T.V.'s into the pool or punching holes in the walls. Shit like that, right?"

"Yes," the manager answered.

Pulling out his dong from his jeans, Doc began pissing into the courtyard and onto the trees in pots below. "Well, we never do shit like that, do we?" Doc intoned.

Pierre watched in horror as splashes came close to some late night swimmers sitting at a table beneath them. "So if I tell you that we are gonna pay you, we are gonna pay you! Goddamn boy, have some manners for Christ's sake." He then zipped up and went back inside.

Lencho caught up with a trembling Pierre an hour later with a wad of hundred dollar bills, and brought their bill current. "Do you know what Mr. Doc did, Lencho?" Pierre stammered as he counted the money. "He toss a T.V. into the pool?" Lencho answered.

"No."

"Then it couldn't have been all that bad. After all, we are all gentlemen, right?"

Hollywood was fun, but Lencho had to get back to the main task at hand; the importation of the most excellent Thai sticks. He made a reservation on the next flight to Guatemala City for himself and his long-suffering wife and two little children. He was all business now, no more monkeying around. He planned to stay for a while and line up infrastructure.

Things were in place in Mexico. Lencho believed that they could get their dope aboard the daily Pan Am flights from Bangkok to Guatemala City. And, the Partnership had a great airplane and an excellent pilot, so it would be easy to move the dope up to Los Angeles once it was smuggled into Mexico.

Lencho just needed a few more of the right people, and in 1977 anything was possible for the determined weed man. He parked Karen and the kids at the Hotel Majestica, and took a drive in a rented car down Avenida Secena, which ran straight out from the airport into the city proper. He passed the shops and stalls owned by languid Indians, and breathed the smoggy air that belched out of the exhaust pipes of old American cars. He looked with interest at the high rise buildings currently under construction. As he came closer to the center of town, Lencho noticed the soldiers armed with submachine guns milling about in twos and threes and posted on every corner. This was CIA country after all, and Cuba and Castro were not far away.

Lencho had no problem with any of it. In his mind, if the military and the government were preoccupied with the commies, they were more likely to ignore enterprising pot smugglers such as himself. This was just a theory, of course. "Man," he thought, "I could sure use a joint right now."

At that very moment, a young lad with a Kango on his head passed by Lencho. He was slouched down in the seat of an old Ford convertible listening to loud salsa music and puffing on a reefer. Lencho gestured the international sign language for 'pass the doobie over here,' and the young man smiled and waved back to Lencho in a gesture that said, follow me.

"Are you an American?" he asked as they both climbed out of their cars in front of a hair salon.

"You betcha," Lencho said with a grin. "I just flew in with my wife and kids. They call me Lencho."

"Have a toke, amigo. I am Earnesto. Come inside. My wife works here, and I came to bring her lunch."

Lencho followed Earnesto inside and met Celia, a nice young woman who was a whiz with the scissors.

Taking the opportunity to get to know his new friends better and his hair cut, Lencho sat down in the chair. "What do you do for a living, Lencho?" Celia asked.

"My dad is a businessman from Phoenix," Lencho lied. "He's a builder, and I'm down here scouting opportunities for my family. I was really wanting to smoke some weed when I passed your husband, and he most kindly accommodated me."

"Oh, Earnesto," she chided. "How many times do I have to tell you not to smoke the mota in public? You'll get arrested one of these days!"

"You have that problem down here too?" Lencho asked.

"Sí, la policia will arrest," Earnesto replied, "But they just want your money. If you pay them, they go away."

While they were talking, a flashy young man wearing expensive designer jeans and a sport jacket walked into the salon.

"Mi Amigos, how are you?" He said to them all.

"Meet our new friend, Lencho," Earnesto said. "Lencho, this is the renowned Ricardo Secena?"

"It's a pleasure," Lencho said extending a hand beneath the barber's bib.

"Where have I heard that name before? Oh yeah, of course. The boulevard outside is called Secena."

"Yes," Celia answered, "Ricardo's father is Jose Secena, the film promoter. The boulevard is named after him, and I believe that his latest work, Zebriski Point, is also quite popular in the U.S."

"I saw that movie!" Lencho exclaimed. "It's great to meet you."

Lencho was sure God had sent him just the right people to meet. Ricardo Secena was a hip young member of the up and coming Guatemalan society. He was handsome and wealthy, loved to party, and was not involved with dope dealers. In fact, Lencho was able to convince them all that he was indeed the son of a very wealthy gringo out of Arizona who was trying to direct his wayward son toward a more productive life by sending him abroad to 'find himself.'

The two young men soon became fast friends, and shared the fast life in that exotic city. Leaving Karen on her own, he hit the numerous discos and clubs that thrived there. He went on camping trips in the local mountains to buy psychedelic mushrooms from the Indian kids who sold them from baskets near the grassy hills that interspersed the lush jungles. Eating the mushrooms, they would lapse into a cosmic swoon that carried them to faraway places of the mind. Lencho saw rainbows, exploding suns, and children frolicking in the high trees of the forests.

Guatemala was a magic place with young and beautiful women. Lencho was ashamed of himself when he thought of the women that made themselves readily available to the rich gringos who purchased life's carnal pleasures. Ricardo's mother was from the United States, so he was half gringo himself. But Lencho didn't forget he had come to establish routes and set up the infrastructure needed for their project.

As a test, Lencho had several boxes of electronics sent from Thailand to Guatemala, and it all worked perfectly. Customs paid no attention to any of the packages. He felt safe now to send The Partnership's 'electronics' on the Pan Am flights from Bangkok. But the Mafia had other ideas.

"Those fucking hippies got balls, but they also got their heads up their asses," Mugsy groused. "We give them seventy-five large for the plane, and I ain't seen it used that fucking much. How many loads they bring in so far?"

"They brung in five boss," Roland answered.

"The warehouse is holding a thousand pounds of inventory, but it could be holding ten times that much if they were not so busy fucking around with this bullshit idea in Thailand. Thailand is a fuck of a long way from here, while Mexico is just over the hill. That's what I want to see happening: Mexico!"

"Well, boss, that Thai pot is really valuable shit. It costs fifty dollars a pound to buy over there, and we can get two grand a pound for it here. If you sell it by the stick, it's twenty bucks. They got a load of one hundred and eight pounds that's ready to go, right now. That's a couple of million!"

"Sure, all well and good, but that kid Lencho is a crazy son-a-bitch. He wants to bring it up from where? Guatemala, right? Fuck, he wants to bring it into Mexico from Guatemala, and then fly it to California. That's a hell of a long way around."

"It's a smart plan, boss. Look, they fly it right across from Tijuana, over San Diego, and into all of that traffic, right at the busiest time of the afternoon. Our pilot says he can look right into the downtown office buildings, and then just disappear from the radar. Seems to me that they got it pretty well figured out."

"Fuck you too, Roland," Mugsy shouted. "I don't like it. We could be making some real money on this if we just use Rick at LAX customs. Do it! Tell those dip shits to send the Thai now, and send it to Building 25 at LAX. Rick will take care of all of the details. Piece of cake."

*****

"Lencho, can you hear me?" Lencho's brother Joe shouted into the mouthpiece from Yuba County. "Your parole officer called our neighbor, Jack. You know, the one who said that you could get important phone messages from? Yeah, anyway, he's coming out to Space Acres to check on you and see how you are progressing. He says that he will be here the day after tomorrow, so get your sorry ass back now!"

Lencho climbed aboard the next flight to LAX and headed home. It was time to play the role of the humble hippie living in the mountains again. Lencho was put on probation in 1975, and he and Mr. Reed, his parole officer, had a cordial conversation at the time. "What's your address Lencho?" he asked. "I'll need to call on you one of these days."

"I don't have an actual address," Lencho replied. "I get my mail in town, but I'll be happy to draw you a map."

Following the map, Mr. Reed parked his car in a turn off from the main road that led to the camp. He pulled his pudgy, five foot, seven inch body off the front seat and began to trek. He was a forty-year-old pale white guy who had been a bureaucrat all of his adult life. He never questioned anything: he married young, had no experience with a woman other than that of his beloved wife, and had two fat, little sons, ages six and eleven. He huffed up the trail, breathing in the clean pine mountain air and swatting the occasional fly from his ear.

Mr. Reed marveled at the beauty of the area he so seldom saw, and he wondered about the freedom and ingenuity of the young people he now supervised for various drug offenses. Then he ran smack into a nude Linda Swiggleson. She wasn't just naked, she was Lady Godiva naked! A very handsome woman of twenty-one, with long blonde hair and full breasts, she was a sight to behold. Mr. Reed's jaw dropped, and he turned beet red. He covered his eyes with his fingers in stunned embarrassment, "Oh my, I beg your pardon."

"About what?" Linda giggled. "You must be Lencho's P.O. I've been watching for you. He said he thought you might be coming up to see us from Oroville. Follow me. We live just around that bend, by the flume." He followed her obediently, starring at her ass as they walked. He didn't often run into naked and beautiful ladies. In fact, if it were not for the occasional Playboy magazine, he would probably have forgotten what one looked like all together.

Lencho met him at the door of the teepee, also naked. Seeing the look on the man's face, it dawned on him. "Oh man, I forgot to tell you that we are nudists. I see you met Linda."

They sat outside by the flume for a couple of hours until Mr. Reed was very satisfied that everything appeared to be law abiding. Lencho told him that he had a few part time gigs in town, and that he was making an honest, but humble living. That was not quite the truth, of course. At least ten thousand dollars in cash was stashed in the teepee, plus twenty-five pounds of weed was hidden in the forest close by. They all lived a healthy and self-sufficient lifestyle, which easily met the standards of the State. Then a duck came down the flume, pecking at water bugs and kneading its feathers as it floated by the men watching it. Nonchalantly, the creature swam past, and was gone, disappearing around the corner.

With a faraway gaze in his eyes, the probation officer turned to Lencho and announced that he had always wanted to be a duck. "A Duck?" Lencho asked.

"Yes," said the little man.

"Well, maybe someday," Lencho replied awkwardly.

"So, you gave up all of that pot stuff?" he asked Lencho.

"Oh yeah, no more of the devil weed. We're into Jesus instead."

"That's just fantastic," Mr Reed said as he took one last look at Linda Swiggleson, who sat grooming her tresses, breasts swaying to and fro. "And by the way, you have completed state probation. I'll mail you your certificate."

A little while later, Lencho said to Joe, "Well, that went pretty good I think."

*****

Flight 517 from Bangkok, Thailand, to LAX arrived at seven fifteen p.m. on August ninth with one hundred and eight pounds of high grade Thai pot wrapped in five large boxes marked "Sacred Icons." Buddy and Roy were waiting for it at customs. They were expecting smooth sailing since the customs agent in charge had been paid off by the Mafia. Fifteen Feds were also waiting, four from customs, four from DEA, seven from the FBI. Poor Buddy and Roy never knew what hit them. Taken to the downtown Federal Building, they cooled their heels in a tank buried in the bowels of the building for five hours before being escorted in chains for interrogation.

"How long have you been working for the Mob?" an unsmiling Fed asked bluntly.

"Mob? We don't work for no Mob."

"What do you know about these?" A second agent placed twenty black and white glossy photos of dead guys on the table in front of their unbelieving eyes. The photos were of mangled and mutilated corpses that had been fished out of the ocean or buried in shallow graves.

"The Fabreeze family has been working out of Los Angeles since 1964. They are a satellite of Chicago, and are now in the drug business. We know that you are in it with them. You store your dope in Long Beach. Most of the dead guys in those photos were also stored in the same place. You two are looking at 100 years in prison, or even the gas chamber. It would be a very wise decision if you decided to cooperate with us now."

"We want to call our lawyer," Roy croaked.

Chapter Six

"What'll You Do When I'm Gone"
Released 1985
Waylon Jennings

As right as we were we are wrong
Nothings going to change what we've done
The only thing that keeps me from going, babe
Is wondering what you'll do when I'm gone

CURSED

Everybody ran. Not since the days of Jack Dragna, Frank Bompensiero, and Jimmy Fratrianno vs. Mickey Cohen did the newspapers have such a field day. "FBI Investigates Twenty Mob Murders," shouted the L.A. Times.

Joey the Clown, back in Chicago, was not amused. "Make that little weasel Franzee disappear," were his orders.

The Partnership had also vanished, and Lencho split for Prescott. "What a mess," he moaned to his brother David.

"Working for those guineas was a huge mistake. I tried to tell that dumb fuck, Joey, but he just wouldn't listen. He thought those thugs were the ultimate. It turns out that he was right, at least to some extent. It ended up being the ultimate in madness."

Lencho said he had had it. He was getting sick and tired of the crazy life of the weed man. He needed a break from all of it. He was sweating bullets, afraid that the Feds would be coming after him soon. It was time to find out whether the mob was really into Omerta, the code of silence. Or was that also a load of horseshit?

*****

"Remember," he asked Bobby, "a couple of months ago, when I had to meet Doc and that pilot out in Apple Valley? They were bringing in five hundred pounds from Oaxaca; Joey talked me into digging a hole near the airstrip just in case we needed to bury the weed in a hurry or something. Bury it for God's sake! He sniffs so much coke that now he's beginning to lose it. I mean, the crazy fuck is starting to act like he's a made man himself.

"I'm out there for two full days with Brucie and Meyer, two guys who look like linebackers and work for Mugsy. I gotta live with them at a Motel 8, and the phone is ringing off the hook, every hour, on the fucking hour. They are being ordered to go out and collect some money, or bash someone's head in, or maybe even kill somebody. I mean, that's their job, right? It's what they are paid to do! The dirty work, ya know what I mean Bobby?

"And each time they come back to the room, they bust my chops. They start laughing like hyenas about a guy that they just finished beating the shit out of who ended up swallowing his teeth. So there I am in the middle of the desert, digging this hole and thinking to myself that I could be actually digging my own grave here! I look up and these two killers are grinning at me. Now I start wondering if they are going to steal the load and leave me six feet under in a grave I dug for myself. That's what they were planning all along, I think. Once we got the whole operation organized, and up and running smoothly, the mob would just step in and steal it all from us. They'd probably hang our asses on the meat hooks at their plant in Long Beach."

"Was it worth it in the end?" Bobby asked. "I mean, did you guys make a lot of money with them mobsters?"

Lencho answered, "Naw man! The more I think about it, the more I realize that we really didn't make much. When you add up all of the work that we did, all of the risks that we had to take, and then having to pay our overhead and all of the bills. Plus Joey's cocaine and booze habits. Then, after all of that, we split what was left fifty-fifty. It was pretty lean. I am sure now that I would have made out a whole lot better financially with very little hassle or risk had I just remained independent."

Lencho sighed and said with a fiery determination, "If I do stay in this racket, I swear to you here and now that I will never, I do mean never, do business with the mob again."

David added, "Ever since the first time we smoked pot together, brother, there have been many changes in our world. Nixon declared war on all of us a couple of years ago. He called it his 'War on Drugs.' I don't understand it. I mean what's that all about?"

"I'm beginning to feel like some kind of warrior for sure," Lencho answered. "I mean, I'm really frazzled. Most of my closest friends are now fugitives. I'm afraid that I will be the next target and it all started out so beautifully. Pot and acid were like our sacraments, man. The life we embraced was a cause, even a religion of sorts. I never saw myself or any of us as criminals, and I still don't. I sell weed, and it's fucking harmless for Christ's sakes! It's safer than beer, and it's good for the soul. The damned government gets more and more gnarly all of the time. It's obviously the money. These narcs are not fooling anyone.

"They make a bust, steal half of what they confiscate, and sell it themselves. They are the real drug dealers, but the straight people out there don't see it for some reason. They believe that the guy with the badge should be the one to trust. The truth is the exact opposite, though. It's the people with the badges you can never really trust, because that badge is their license to steal."

"Oh, by the way, bro," David interrupted, "Little George called and said he would be stopping by later tonight. I think he has some hash that he wants moved."

Lencho thought to himself, Little George. Another partner from San Diego whose life had been ruined by a mob; the Mexican Mafia this time.

Not long ago, Little George had been wealthy. His home was full of artwork and tapestries, all of which had been acquired through dealing drugs. But too much of his own product ended going up his nose. He also lost several large loads to the cops and rip off artists who found him to be an easy mark in his drugged up state of mind. The mob didn't care about any of the reasons he lost their shipments; they demanded that he pay them all the money that he owed. When he couldn't, they got rough.

A hippie dealer might get mad at you if you fucked up, but he wouldn't kill you because of it. Not so with the organized crime boys who loved violence and inflicting pain, and also had a penchant for murder. In order to stay alive and payoff his debts to this mob, Little George had to hand over all of his property and assets. He was still hustling, but now he was a mere ghost of his former self.

"Okay," Lencho said, "Maybe we can sell some hash around town, and then I'll lay low, cause I'm fucking exhausted!"

Lencho had met Little George after the thirteen hundred pound bust, right after he'd gotten out of jail. They ended up traveling the 'loop' together, San Diego to Prescott, then to Las Vegas and up to Space Acres. Next they drove down to the Bay Area, and from there made their way back to San Diego.

Lencho sold only weed, while George peddled mini bennies and some cocaine. They even sold sandals for a while during their loop travels. The sandals actually became a popular item, so they founded a new business called, The Tri State Sandal Company. They filled their trunk with the newest thing in footwear fashion. The sandals featured thick rubber soles with bright colored nylon straps. They were made in Japan, and sold like hotcakes. This new business gave them an aura of respectability that George's mom urged them to foster. She was a wise woman who said a good business person should not only conduct good business, but do it in an ethical fashion. She also cautioned, "Never fool around with your friends' wives or girlfriends." She also quipped, "Don't ever blame anyone except yourselves if a deal goes bad, or if you get ripped off."

Lencho was inclined to follow her advice. They made a lot of money together back then, but he wondered if those days were now over.

Although both ethics and trust was generally in decline, Lencho was a stand-up guy, and would go to the mat for his pals. Not long before the trip to Guatemala, he had locked horns with the Feds up in Butte County. He chuckled as he recalled the event. It was fun to sometimes give the good old FBI a hard time.

*****

A guy named Larry Anderson had this totally outrageous pad in the hills, not far from Lencho and Karen's teepee. He had been a pretty big coke dealer, but was about to go on the lam in order to avoid prison. He and Lencho had crossed paths at some point, and he offered to rent Lencho his amazing house for a mere three hundred and fifty bucks a month.

Larry said to Lencho, "I trust you! Just send the rent money to this P.O. Box every month. I gotta split right now before it's too late."

The house was a stunning, two-story A-frame. It was a work of art featuring arched ceilings, stained glass windows, a custom built-in swimming pool, and a view that looked towards the heavens and beautiful Butte Creek canyon. The amenities were endless.

Only three fifty a month? My god, what a steal! Lencho promptly relocated from the teepee to his new diggs.

And it was just in time, because Karen gave birth to a little girl on January 20, 1976. In preparation for the birth, Lencho tutored himself with some books and with the help of nearby Doc Hoffman, a telephone, and a curious little Luz, he delivered her himself. This time he didn't pass out. They named her Callie.

Malcom stayed with them also, and he had two hundred pounds of weed just sitting in their garage awaiting transport. Lencho was exhilarated but as he strolled down the road, he spotted a dust cloud from the wake of a black sedan coming his way in a hurry. Two men in cheap suits barked, "Where does Malcom live? It's near here isn't it?"

Stunned, a quick thinking Lencho answered, "Just down the road at that house on the right. About a quarter mile. I think you might find him there."

Off they roared, while the weed man sprinted back to sound the alarm. In an astonishing twenty minutes, all of the pot was loaded into Brother Joe's pickup, and both it and Malcom were gone like the wind.

Lencho stood out on the driveway, waiting for the Feds to show up again, and when they did, they were not happy.

"You little fuck!" one of them spit. "We know that he's here. Get outta the way!"

They almost knocked the door off its hinges, and then ran like wild, hysterical animals through each room. They, of course, turned up absolutely nothing.

Pointing a threatening finger, the bigger of the two snarled, "Boy, you are gonna be dead meat when we are done with you! Let's see: harboring a fugitive, lying to a Federal Agent, dealing dope, and conspiracy. We're going back to the U.S. Attorney to get an indictment on you that will send you away for the rest of your life!"

"Hey!" he shouted as they left. "Who's gonna fix my door?"

That day, they moved out, chartered an airplane, and flew straight back to Prescott.

*****

As David handed him another beer, Lencho went on, "Even if The partnership did end in disaster, at least Malcom and Doc are safe for now. And

I'm down here. Joey, that little bastard, still thinks he's in the Mafia. The piece of shit actually threatened to hurt my kids."

"Get outta here!" Bobby replied incredulously.

"Yeah, he tried to say I couldn't leave! He called it 'our thing', just like the wise guys do. Then he says to me, 'If you quit, something bad might happen to Luz and Callie.' I grabbed him by his scrawny neck; I just glared at him and told him to fuck himself. I ain't never going to see that asshole again."

"The hell with him, bro," Bobby intoned. He put a hand on his brother's shoulder and said, "You're home now with your family. Come on down to the Palace Saloon with us. David is playing there five nights a week now."

Whiskey Row, ten honky-tonks lined up one after another, is located in downtown Prescott. David had come a long way since Lencho bought him the shiny Gibson guitar a few years earlier. David's band, The Stumbling Buffalo, were rocking the joint that night.

Girls and beer were plentiful, and little George showed up just long enough to dump thirty pounds of Lebanese Blonde Hashish on Lencho.

"Just send me the money when you can," George told him.

David's gig at the Palace was perfect. It provided customers for the hash, besides the beer and women.

The bicentennial celebration rolled around, and Lencho approached the City Council about lending him a portable stage for a concert that he was planning to put on in anticipation of the Fourth of July celebration. Seventy thousand people showed up at the event. Lencho was completely bowled over by the sheer number of folks who turned out for the impromptu musical event. The Stumbling Buffalo headlined with all of the other local bands opening for them. The whole thing was just perfect. There were not many fights, and the sweet aroma of weed and hash permeated the air. The local economy prospered, and a good time was had by all.

Man, Lencho thought, if we can get a crowd like this on such short notice, imagine what we could do with some advanced planning. I gotta get a hold of Richie.

Waylon Jennings thought the idea was terrific, and Lencho formed Diamond K Productions to promote next year's gig. He also set about seeking official permission to hold the event and secure the ideal location. He went to see Bill Fain, who was one of the biggest land owners in the Prescott Valley.

"Sure Lencho," Bill told him, "I like the idea! Let's go for a drive and check out some potential sites." Fain provided Lencho with a great location in a little valley on the outskirts of town with room enough for ample parking. He lined up a team of lawyers to work out all of the legalities. After witnessing the huge amount of money spent during the Bicentennial, The City Council blessed the concert. Waylon even promised Lencho that he'd help to line up some big names to perform. He was pretty sure that he could get Willie Nelson and Hank Williams Jr. to come as well as others.

"Far out, man," Lencho told Richie on the phone. "Hell, we've got plenty of time. I'll see you in Vegas pretty soon when I come out there with Diamond K Productions. I have decided to shuck the weed business and go straight. You always told me to get a hit and run with it man."

Later, back in Prescott, Lencho helped David cut a record at Timberline Productions, which was owned by drummer Roger Pearsall. Pearsall had a long background in the music business, having played with Buck Owens, Tony Bennett, Sinatra and many other big names in the industry. He knew many people in Hollywood from his days working on the Carol Burnett Show. Pearsall urged Lencho to stay the course. "None of this comes easy, so don't get distracted," he warned.

They cut a tune that David wrote called, "Moab County Jail."

When it was completed, the two took the tapes to Nashville and pitched it around town. They found that people had an interest in David's music, but because he was unwilling to go on tour, the efforts failed. Little Brother David was as happy as a clam in mud just performing back in Prescott. A big clam in a small pond.

Lencho came back, and found a wonderful log cabin up on Groom Creek. He moved Karen and his children immediately. They had always been happiest when they lived in the woods. But a sea of change was about to take place.

Wandering into the Bird Cage Saloon down on the row, Lencho noticed a seventeen-year-old girl named Tamara sipping a coke at a table with a couple of bikers. Although clearly underage, no girl that cute would be asked to leave. Lencho was thunderstruck.

The bikers were acquaintances, so they didn't take offense when he invited himself to sit down at their table. He began a conversation that basically went: "What's a doll baby like you doing with a couple mugs like these guys?"

Five foot five and slender with silver blonde hair, she looked like Bardot with sharp features, pouty lips, bouncing breasts beneath a sheer blouse. Lust strikes again, and the weed man was in love. "How about you go for a little ride with me," he cooed.

"Why not?" she responded.

When he found out her age, and compared it to his own 32 years, he backed off with the ardor. Not today, he decided, but he asked her to keep in touch. Especially after her next birthday. She gave him a lingering kiss when he drove her back to town, and told him she would. She lived in California, and was visiting her cousin out on the edge of town. She loved pot, she loved to run around naked, and she loved life. She said she liked Lencho. Then she was gone.

Six months later she was back. She called the bar asking for him, so the bar forwarded the call. When the weed man finally hooked up, she was crying and saying her old man had hit her, and that she was a prisoner in her own home. "Where was this home?" Lencho wanted to know. It was in Long Beach. She asked if he could come post haste and rescue her. And oh, by the way, "I turned 18 in March," she told him.

"Outta site!" he replied.

"I gotta go to California on business," he told Karen. "An emergency."

"But you promised to fix the dryer," she protested. "How can I do the kid's clothes if the machines don't work?"

"Take them to the laundromat. This is very important," and he was out the door. Karen stared after her wayward husband. He wasn't fooling her, she thought bitterly.

The apartment Tamara shared with Bart was typical north Long Beach rococo. He found the place on Seventh Street, and banged on the door. When a grungy kid of 21 with no shirt on answered, he pushed his way in. "Where's the girl?" Lencho demanded.

"Who the fuck are you?" Bart cried.

"The guy that's here to take Tamara away from you buddy. Sit down on that couch before I knock you down." The kid sat and the lithe little girl gathered up some jeans, blouses, and skimpy underpants, and they left. Bart sat sullenly with arms folded.

"Fuck you," were Tamara's last words to him, and they drove out of town headed to Sausalito.

He bought her a new wardrobe. Spent $2,500 bucks on that. They ate and drank in the best restaurants up and down the California coast. They toured Hearst Castle and the wine country of Mendocino. They lounged in a nice hotel in Sausalito, and screwed themselves silly. He watched her tight little butt and legs as she tidied up their room, and she did it naked. Always naked. She was the bloom of pulchritude and youth meeting the old man of the sea. This was dangerous, but too intoxicating to resist. He was the weed man angler, and she was a sleek, vigorous, and joyfully abandoned shark. It never occurred to him that he might be the one that ended up eaten.

"I love you, baby," he told her, "but I'm married with two kids. I can't live with you, but I can't live without you either. I'm gonna set you up in San Diego with a friend. He'll take good care of you, and you'll be safe. I'll pay the bills and come see you every chance I can." This seemed ok by her, so he left her with good ole Ronnie, who (he was pretty sure) would be a gentleman to his new woman. She would clean Ronnie's house, do the dishes, and lay around on the beach and smoke dope. She did all that was required, and always in the nude, which was tough on good ole Ronnie, but he endured honorably.

Now back in Prescott, Lencho returned to his Diamond K Productions, and began to book local acts around the area. He also continued selling all of the weed and hash that he was able to get his hands on.

Every couple of weeks he would drive to San Diego to see Tamara, while Karen wilted and slowly died inside.

The year went by quickly, and summertime was looming. All hell broke loose once again. Just one month from the big event, Lencho got a call from a lawyer who represented the Fains. His name was Keith Quale, and he asked Lencho to come to his office. Quale was a no nonsense, conservative, mover and shaker in the Prescott area, and Lencho could tell by the storm clouds on the man's face that morning that this was definitely not going to be a positive meeting.

"I'll be blunt," he began. "There is no way in high heavens you or anybody else is going to stage some big ass show out there on the Fain ranch. Not a chance in Hell, son."

Lencho sat frozen in the chair, as the lawyer paced back and forth in front of him fulminating. "When Bill Sr. told me about this crazy idea of yours, I about shit. You got no insurance, no medical backup for emergencies, you still have not gotten the proper permits, and to top it all off, you are a goddamn, well-known DOPE DEALER! I personally have a considerable investment tied up in that ranch, and there is no way, let me repeat, NO WAY AT ALL, that I will ever allow you to run this type of risk. Nor, I may add, will I allow the Fains to, either. If you don't drop this right now, I will personally see to it that you go to jail."

That was that. A weed man tries to go straight, and look what happens. So dejected, and still in shock over the lawyer's outburst and threats, he left Quale's office. It was the first, but certainly not the last time something like this would happen with Lencho's Diamond K Productions.

CR had called and wanted Lencho's assistance in a venture involving a fishing boat, so a couple of days later, he headed out west to hook up with him. His new girlfriend was at least some consolation. The whole year with Diamond K was not in vain, as it had opened up new opportunities for the weed man. Lencho met Willie Nelson, for instance.

He also discovered that the music business would forever be in his heart. So the next thing he did was call Waylon Jennings to tell him the sad news. Waylon said to Lencho, "That's a damn shame man, but don't let it kill your spirit. I still love the idea, and we'll keep thinking of ways to pull it off."

"'Appreciate your support" Lencho sighed.

CR bought himself a twenty eight foot Sea Ray with twin one hundred and fifty horse Mercury outboards. It was a beautiful boat. They hauled it over to a boat yard in Newport Beach, and proceeded to tear out the factory flooring, refit the struts, and make it hollow above the keel so that it could accommodate half a ton of product.

"What I'm gonna do, man," CR said, "is go down to Oaxaca and load her up from my Indians, and then replace the floor and fiberglass. There will be no way they can get to my weed. Once back in the U.S., I'll remove the floor and unload. It's brilliant, if I do say so myself. Not only that, but we'll make a mountain of money."

"How do we get the weed across the border?" Lencho asked.

CR replied, "I got me a skipper who's a pro, and he'll bring in the load from out at sea, just like he'd been fishing for the day. The Coast Guard, or whoever starts snooping around, will think he launched from the U.S."

"I like it," Lencho agreed.

CR owned a home on Lake Travis near Austin, so that is where the operation began. He and Lencho drove across the border at Laredo while pulling the boat with a big, white Suburban SUV.

They were all decked out with fishing poles and all the gear one could ever need, plus a German shepherd named Jake. Traveling down through Monterey, Mexico, they cut over to Tampico. They skirted the beaches, fishing. They stayed at hotels and partied. Then, taking Highway 130 west at Posa Rica, they began to work their way toward Mexico City.

It appeared to anyone that they were on vacation. They even used credit cards to pay their way, because that's what legit people used on vacations, not cash. CR was also a tennis buff; he was actually more of a tennis fanatic, and played the part to the hilt by wearing cute little tennis shorts, knit shirts, and a ball cap. He always had his racket handy, and was on the lookout for the local tennis pro wherever they happened to stop.

Those who met them along the way truly believed that they were just a couple of wealthy young guys looking for big fish, beautiful women, and a good time. This was true, but more importantly, every load was worth three hundred fifty thousand dollars in profits.

When they arrived in Mexico City, Lencho was amazed at how large and crowded the metropolis was. CR took him on a tour as they drove through the city around midnight. The history and architecture was astounding, and Lencho found himself fascinated by it all.

In the wealthy bedroom community of Cuernavaca, CR leased a hacienda that became their headquarters.

CR had been in the weed business for six years now, and he had specialized in pot from Mexico. He was fluent in Spanish, and also dressed the part whenever he was not masquerading as a tennis buff. He wore huaraches, loose fitting cotton shirts, and baggy pants. He was a short, trim man, and well connected with the indigenous peoples who grew the best Mexican weed in the high elevations of the Sierra Madre Del Sur.

The Indians who lived there had mastered the techniques of growing sensimilla, which had no seeds. Their product was truly a delight to behold, but not so easy to get to.

CR's hacienda was decorated with ornate rugs, paintings, and statuary, which covered the walls and floors. A swimming pool looked out on rolling hills of green. The guy had it going on.

Once they arrived in Cuernavaca, he mysteriously got in touch with the growers who in contrast lived very simply. They left for Oaxaca City. Lencho stayed for a night or two in a hotel while CR rode in a taxi to the farthest reaches of the town and beyond. At a juncture known only to him, he ordered the driver to stop, paid him, and jumped out, disappearing into the thick brush. CR was then met by the Indians who took him high into the mountains where he purchased the product from them.

He returned the next day, and the day after that. He and Lencho drove the SUV with the boat attached to a pre-designated spot near the area where he had jumped out of the cab. The Indians then delivered to them a half ton of their excellent weed, which they hauled down the mountain on the backs of mules. Removing the floor boards of the boat with screwdrivers, they loaded her up from stem to stern. The boat was re-fiber glassed, and they were ready to begin their journey home. The whole rig looked normal; the marijuana and its pungent aroma were both invisibly concealed. A drug dog may have been able to detect it, but in 1978, those types of dogs were a rarity.

Going east to Selena Cruz, they cut over to Matias Romero, and towards the gulf again, just south of Vera Cruz. In Vera Cruz, they hooked up with skipper John Everton and his mate Ronnie. They would do the last of the heavy lifting, and take her back into the U.S. They all drove up to the little fishing village of La Pesca about two hours north of Tampico. Everton backed the boat down a launch ramp and then set out to sea.

The U.S. was just sixty miles due north from there. The boat trailer, which cost nearly three thousand dollars, was dumped in the ocean. This had to be done, because they could not very well drive back across the border with an empty boat trailer. They chocked it up as yet another cost of doing business. They repeated this many times. The vessel sailed sixty miles out to sea, N.E. of Mexico, and then crossed the boundary into the United States, where they returned in a north westerly direction.

The Coast Guard boarded them several times, but they never failed the inspections. Like CR had predicted, the plan was brilliant.

The caper continued on for nine successful runs, but on the tenth trip, fate threw them a curve ball.

"Damn it, those guys should be home by now," moaned CR. "They left Friday and should have been back here yesterday."

Lencho and CR were both worried. The boat had one hundred and seventy-five gallons of fuel on board, enough provisions for three days, excellent navigation gear, and an experienced skipper and mate, but still there was no sign or word from them. The radio that they had on board was the best that money could buy, but the range could be limited by any number of factors. It couldn't have been bad weather because it was both calm and hot on that particular Fourth of July weekend. Dramatic stuff seemed to happen a lot on the Fourth, Lencho mused.

"Do we call the Coast Guard?" CR asked himself, "I think maybe we should."

For the second time in his life, Lencho bet on the Coast Guard, but hoped that they would come to the rescue without busting them all in the process.

A huge crowd was celebrating the holiday on Padre Island. Barbecues were grilling, beer was swilling, and the boys mingled with the throngs. They were as apprehensive as the people around them were relaxed. Then the call came in that the craft had been spotted seventy miles to the east, and seemed to be adrift. There were two men on board and they were waiving their hands and arms frantically. They appeared to be in good condition physically, and a cutter was being dispatched to tow the craft in. When the incapacitated vessel reached the pier the crowd burst into applause as the Coast Guard towed them in.

Lencho and CR greeted both men warmly with beers and hugs. "What the fuck happened out there for God sakes?" CR hissed with a grin.

"Must have happened when we slid her back into the water in Mexico," Everton explained. "We had a problem with the electrical wires, they shorted out on us Friday as we headed for the line. We've been dead in the water since then, and man am I sunburned!"

The local newspaper carried the story on the front page, and the half ton in the hidden compartment thankfully was not mentioned.

They departed for Austin, and upon their arrival the next morning, broke open the cargo and distributed it to the buyers who had been waiting. To celebrate, they partied at the local joints and enjoyed the music scene Austin is famous for. In a bar, Lencho met a girl with huge breasts wearing a t-shirt that read, "If God didn't want men to eat pussy, he wouldn't have made it look like a taco." Gotta love those Texas women!

*****

Louiso was one of Lencho's Sufi friends. He was now transplanted from Mount Tam to the Hollywood Hills. He introduced the weed man to a dark figure on the scene named Richard Soldoff. Soldoff dealt weed and had a considerable clientele among the elite, but his current claim to fame was the emerging niche cocaine activity of freebasing. Richard Pryor had recently set himself ablaze, too much publicity using a blowtorch and ether. Soldoff struck

Lencho as a mad scientist type; he claimed to have a laboratory on his estate complete with a concrete ceiling that would fall at the touch of a button onto the evidence and anyone present without his permission, crushing everything into a lifeless ooze. The house was all concrete and glass with motion sensors and cameras everywhere. Inside were banks of monitors that he scanned constantly. Also, a fortune in gold bars, silver, and diamonds were said to be secreted away. It all gave Lencho the creeps, especially after he had tried some of this new coke concoction, and it nearly blew his heart out of his chest. "How are you my boy?" Soldoff greeted him merrily on the phone. "Your money? Why of course I have it. Come up to the place tomorrow at noon. I'll see you then."

Lencho put Karen and the children up at the Hollywood Hilton Hotel for the next couple of days, and drove out to the huge house in a rented Cadillac. There were two other cars parked in the driveway upon his arrival. He rang the doorbell, and a stranger answered the front door. "Is Richard around?" he asked.

"Oh, sure man, he went to the store. He told me that you were gonna stop by. Come on in!"

Knowing how secretive and security conscious that Soldoff normally was, Lencho smelled a rat. He just said, "Oh, no thanks. Just tell him that Lencho stopped by and to give me a call when he gets home."

"No, wait a minute, that's silly. Just come in and wait. I know he wants to see you, and he'll be back in about five minutes."

Lencho repeated, "Just tell him to call me. Thanks." He turned around and started walking towards his car when he heard the guy say, "Freeze, Asshole, you ain't going nowhere." Two other cops were inside. On the kitchen table sat a pile of gold, cash, jewelry, cocaine, and some lab equipment.

"What is this?" Lencho protested. "I ain't done a thing. Why are you rousting me like this? Where is Richard?"

"He's in the hospital getting the remains of his spleen removed, pal. Last night he apparently went out to confront an intruder and it appears as though he was shot in the back by someone standing in the shadows. They don't expect him to live. Want to tell us what you know about it?"

"I don't know squat about it, man! I'm just a friend of his, nothing more."

"Maybe you like this new freebase shit? Really makes you dope fiends go loopy, don't it?"

"I wouldn't know. I'm gonna leave now. You got nothing on me!"

"Take this little cocksucker down to the glass house, and feed him to the niggers," a cop barked

The downtown holding tank was full of blacks, and it was called the 'Glass House' for some unknown reason. The cops brought him in to sweat him, and that's where he stayed for three days.

83

"I smell a fucking cracker," one big black fellow hissed as they led him in. Lencho was scared shitless for the millionth time, with scenes of what happened to Joey in San Diego flashing through his mind.

"Hold on now," an older black man said, leaning against a wall by his bunk. Out of eighty men, Lencho was the only one who was white. He was saved by Gregory Shields, a pimp, dope dealer without whom he would soon have been a very dead hippie weed man.

"Look around you my Niggas" He told them. "The pigs put this white boy in here so that we could do their bidding. They want us to fuck him up. When you brothers going to learn? Don't let the pigs manipulate you into doing their dirty work. Leave the boy alone."

He was arrested on a Friday, and it was Monday before the district attorney ordered his release. They had nothing on him.

He went back and picked up his wife and children. He was out thirty-five thousand dollars that he knew he would never see again. Richard Soldoff had survived his ordeal, but had to wear a colostomy bag and hobble around on crutches during his stay at Solidad State Prison, where he died a year later.

Once again, Lencho had a yearning to go legit. He was tired of the cops and the never ending hassles. The problem, of course, was that his standard of living had really escalated over the last decade, so he ended up just staying put. The lifestyle was both exhilarating and hedonistic. The hippie age had begun on a spiritual note, but experimentation was also a very big part of it as well. Sex was a drug in itself. For the daring young men in the dope trade, there were always going to be beautiful women that just loved bad boys. What's a weed man to do?

Lencho was a very bad boy indeed. He was an outlaw, now and forever. Not a criminal, mind you, but instead a weed dealer who sold a mild escape for some, and medicine for others. Weed was life, not death. Millions used it daily with no ill effects, addiction, or withdrawals.

Still, the cops continued to bust one and all. They'd steal some of it and sell it themselves. The movies, books, and television were jam packed with cops and robbers. The dope dealers were always portrayed as the bad guys and the cops the good ones. Those involved in the trade knew that it was a joke, but the brainwashed masses bought into it lock, stock, and barrel. So, the war on drugs advanced ever further. It had already been going on for over seventy years when Lencho and Bobby made plans to make yet another run to the mountains of Oaxaca. The challenge for Lencho was that he had to deal with both Karen and the children, while at the same time balancing his act for the sake of the lovely Tamara. He kept her stashed away in several different places while he played the family man on the road. Ronnie enjoyed her naked presence in his home, but got pretty exasperated by her horrible driving skills. She was a beautiful young woman but simply could not drive. She ended up wrecking his big, shiny 1976

Caddy convertible when he let her drive him to the store.

Once, while she was with Lencho, she even smashed into a lady as she blew through a red light in Hollywood one afternoon. That car was a rental, and Avis picked up the tab, because Lencho slid over into the driver's seat and made a deal with the other party right there on the spot. He took Tamara back to Prescott where he and David were staying at the St. Michaels Hotel on Whiskey Row, selling weed. One morning, he got up and headed out to get some coffee at the café down the block, only to find Karen standing on the sidewalk.

"I thought I'd see if you were ever going to come home," she exclaimed. The kids keep asking for their daddy. What do I tell them?"

"Oh, sure babe, tell the kids daddy will be home tomorrow. I have been kinda busy," Lencho lied.

At that very moment, Tamara came walking out of the building, and right up to her lover. The look on Karen's face spoke a million words. She stood there with a knowing expression, and a tear of regret ran down her cheek. "I'm not even going to get angry with you, at least not yet. I have had enough of this, Lencho. I have stood by your side for years, good times and bad. I have always been there for you. You lie to me, cheat on me, and then tell me that it won't happen again. Then it's off into yet another woman's arms. I know you will never stop. It's over Lencho. I am leaving you."

Karen ended that day what had been a very tumultuous, ten year hippie marriage. Tamara stared at a stunned Lencho as he watched a piece of his history just drive away, and then said with oblivious understatement, "I thought I'd come with you to get some coffee."

"I need a drink," Lencho whispered. Later, when he finally went to visit the cabin in Groom Creek, he discovered the place was barren. All of the furniture, appliances, his clothes, the kitchen stuff, was gone. Karen had taken everything except a small mirror with a Heineken logo that was still hanging on the wall above the fireplace.

*****

A new trip to Oaxaca would take three months to fully prepare for. The money had to be generated through sales from the last one. New boat trailers, updated communications gear, and navigation equipment all had to be purchased and installed. The Suburban had to be made ready. There was much to do before an operation of that magnitude could be launched successfully. And, there was the heavy partying that went along with it. It took a lot of nerve to go into a foreign country and commit a major crime. The cops were savages. To fall into their hands could mean torture, or even death. Most pot smokers take it for granted that the product they just purchased from their local dealer would always be available. They never really gave any thought to the tremendous danger that a weed man risked in order to provide those types of services to his weed smoking customers.

Lencho had a friend named Greg Mueller, who was their African connection for a short period of time. He would sometimes travel deep into the interior to the high elevations to obtain the fabled 'Black Marijuana.'

This weed was perhaps the most potent strain ever grown. It was as dark as the natives who knew the secret to its cultivation. The countries of Africa were forever convulsed in tribal warfare and political chaos in the 1970's. The CIA was everywhere, along with the Soviet, British, Israeli, and French Secret Services. It was a very dangerous place to be, and Mueller found out just how dangerous it was when a detachment of heavily armed soldiers pulled him and his driver over at the foot of Mt. Kenya one day. Dragging the terrified young guide from their jeep, they made him kneel. Mueller watched in horror as they fired three bursts from their M16's into the kid's brain.

"You will never come back here again," the major leading the squad told him, "if you come back, you will die, just like this cockroach."

Greg never returned to that place, so the lads lost their only connection, and were never able to purchase the Magic Black Marijuana again.

On this expedition to Mexico, it seemed that nothing could go right. Lencho and Bobby made two previous attempts at getting started, but each time something went wrong and they were forced to return empty handed. Once, it was severe weather, another it was a blown engine outside of Tampico. But finally on their third effort, they were on their way. CR was tired of the run. It was his plan all along to groom Lencho into taking over all of the heavy lifting. He would usually catch up with them along the route somewhere and arrange the purchase of the loads with the Indians, but he was no longer willing to make the long drives like he used to do.

Lencho and Bobby had done it alone twice before, and now on the third, it should have been a snap. The boys had changed their look to travel more comfortably down there. Lencho favored the Miami Vice motif, wearing Hawaiian shirts and pleated slacks, while his brother sported western wear, boots and cowboy hats. Both wore dark sunglasses. The boat had been updated with all the newest bells and whistles.

Fishing poles and equipment lashed the gunwale, and the dog was now gone.

Heading deep into the interior, they stopped at their usual ports of call to eat and mess around with the ladies, but without the suave CR, the trips were just not the same. The Suburban lost a rear axle near Antigua when they hit a rut, and the big SUV went into a ditch. The axle separated from the truck and flew down the hill into a little village. It rolled right through fences and backyards, scaring chickens and barely missing some children who were playing in the muddy streets. It was terrifying, and they were thankful that no harm came to either the chickens or the children. It did, however, leave them in a predicament.

The common folk of Mexico are a kind and forgiving bunch; in no time, a crowd had gathered around the stricken vehicle tethered to the big boat. They rubbed their collective chins, and walked around accessing the damage. "You gotta a big problem meester," one young fellow commented sagely.

"It seems that we do," Lencho agreed. "Is there a mechanic here by any chance?"

"Oh, sí, señor. Javier is a very good mechanic. He live over there. I get him for you." Javier was indeed a very good mechanic and a resourceful one at that.

"You will need a new bearing, amigo," he told Lencho. "We don't have one here, but over in Arriaga, they have it, I think. We will just weld the whole thing onto the axle, which we will retrieve from Marta Gomez's pig pen, and you should be fine."

"I won't have all four brakes though, will I?" Lencho asked.

"No, señor, but three will be okay for you." They paid Javier, said thanks to all, and made their way to the Mocambo hotel in Vera Cruz where CR was waiting for them.

"You boys having fun?" he asked, while pulling on a Dos Equis.

"Tons," Lencho sighed. "Where are all the women?"

Partying was a good way to let off the steam that was building. Losing an axle was just one of the many hazards they had to deal with. Soon the boys learned how to make many of their own repairs on the fly, just like the Mexicans did. At a disco, they proceeded to get totally shit faced. They danced with the abundant putas, and then took five of them home. What was surprising to them was that the hotel actually had some standards and refused to allow them to bring whores back to their rooms. They had to sneak them in the back way. Once in their rooms, out came the cocaine, and then they got down to some serious sexual fun and games.

Bobby complained that his whore was calling him a 'communist.' He was beginning to piss Lencho off, and after an hour of bitching, Lencho had heard enough. "What do you mean she's calling you a commie? You're not a communist, you're a capitalist."

Lencho grabbed CR away from his little group of honey bunnies, made him put down his coke spoon, and go over to Bobby's girl to try to clear up this puzzling political misunderstanding. After a brief conversation in Spanish, a laughing CR said to Lencho and Bobby, "No man, she didn't call you a 'communist.' She said that you were an 'economist.' Which means you are too cheap to give her the money she wants for fucking you!"

The next day, the sobered duo hit the road again for Oaxaca. Good luck, however was still elusive.

When they were finally ready for the rendezvous with the Indians, which they thought had been all prearranged, things again got screwed up. The plan was to drive down the highway near the meeting point below the mountains, and the Indians would pass them and merely wave. No one was to stop for fear of attracting unnecessary attention. They would then follow them to where the dope was waiting for pick up. It was a simple plan that CR had always used. All they would have left to do was to load up the boat, fix the floor, and head back. But that did not happen.

They missed the Indians somehow and got lost, angry, and then confused. They finally pulled over and fell asleep in the boat. At two in the morning, the Indians finally found them. Upon some discussion, it was decided by Lencho that instead of waiting until the next day to follow the original plan in the daylight hours, they would go right now and get the weed. The weed was waiting, so they loaded up the boat with a thousand pounds of fresh, high grade mota, fiber glassed the deck, and then headed down the hill for home. But a twenty-eight foot fishing vessel looked seriously out of place in the interior during the day. There was no ocean or lakes nearby, so when they finally pulled up to a Mexican agricultural check point, Lencho made yet another fateful error. Fearing that they stood out like a sore thumb, and that the guard might also smell the still wet fiber glass, he gunned the motor and took off.

They began to relax after two hours passed and nothing happened. Lencho had been driving all night, and he wanted a break, so he asked Bobby to take over while he took a much needed nap.

Upon reaching a fork in the road, Bobby proceeded to turn the wrong way. Two hours later, Lencho woke up and, after looking around at the landscape, knew something did not look right. They were surrounded by heavy jungle, just like the kind you would see near the border with Guatemala. Spying a road sign, he yelled at his brother, "Bobby, you been driving the wrong way for the last two hours at least, you dumb ass!" He made him stop and took over the driving.

He didn't say a word to Bobby for another two hours, and then his brother spoke. "So, I screwed up man. Like you never do. How about the agricultural stop you blew through back there?" Lencho drove on in a huff.

Finally heading in the right direction, but hours late for meeting CR and the skipper, they pulled the heavily laden boat onto a two lane bridge that crossed over a deep gorge.

It was a long stretch, and right in front of them was an old lorry, lumbering along. Lencho, still in a shitty mood decided to floor the SUV and try to overtake the pokey truck. Another large truck was approaching from the other direction, and it became a race with a horrible collision a distinct possibility. Neither driver would back down and it was 'Chicken' time as Lencho pulled into the opposite lane, pedal to the metal. Bobby was praying and sweating bullets. The other guy was not giving an inch either. "Oh Jesus, you're gonna kill us all!" Bobby screamed.

"We'll make it just fine," Lencho calmly replied.

"Oh man, we're going to die!" Bobby wept.

"Get a grip," Lencho cursed, cringing when the oncoming truck did not slow down. Was the driver high, asleep, or fucking crazy? All three vehicles were on the bridge now, and it looked like a mile to the bottom. A collision here would send all of them to a bone crushing death. Maybe even take down the bridge. The Suburban won by a centimeter. Lencho pulled in front of the slow moving lorry seconds before the stubborn big rig screamed past, but he over corrected, and the heavy laden boat fishtailed wildly and went airborne as they reached the far end of the expanse. They hit a dip and the boat shifted violently forward on the trailer; all four tires exploded in unison. Finally slowing, they came to a smoky stop on the side of the road, and Bobby shouted, "Mother of God, I thought we were dead!"

"This trip is cursed," the weed man muttered.

The Mexican people came through again. Scores stopped and offered help. The tires were repaired on the spot, and one truck driver produced a portable pump to give them air again. Six or seven young men heaved the pot filled vessel back in place on the boat trailer and secured it safely. The ingenuity of the people on the primitive roads—a land with no AAA or useful Highway Patrol—was extraordinary, and the two were back on their way within two hours full of heartfelt gratitude. With any luck they would hit Vera Cruz only a few hours late. But the only luck they were going to find was the bad sort. Six miles outside of town, the Suburban began to spit and sputter from a cracked distributor cap. They limped in, and she died in front of the Hotel Mocambo. The manager called a towing service for them, and Lencho and Bobby met Miguel and Poncho, the brothers who owned the towing service, when they pulled up in their shiny new truck.

"Why don't you let us tow your boat to Tampico while we leave the truck here for repairs?" they offered. "That way you can fish. This will take a couple days."

That sounded like a good idea, so as the boys dozed in the lounge chairs in their pot boat, Miguel and Poncho hooked them up and drove the fifty miles towards their destination, where they could finally hand off this miserable run to the next crew.

A river runs at the outskirts of Tampico, and they had to take a ferry across. The big red tow truck hauling the large fishing boat finally arrived on the other side. They were greeted there by the Federal Police, who were sinister looking men in dark suits and sunglasses.

"I am Agent Morales, señor. Is this your vessel?"

Morales spoke perfect English and had most likely been trained in the U.S. He was humorless and all business. "Well, not actually," The weed man explained. "This boat belongs to my uncle. My brother and I were just bringing it to Tampico for him. He is meeting us here for a fishing trip."

"We are looking for a large Suburban towing a fishing vessel, and we will need to inspect your rig, if you don't mind," Morales informed them.

Lencho knew that he could do nothing, and that a protest would be out of the question. Hell, he figured it was time to put that secret compartment to the test anyway. It had passed a Coast Guard inspection, hadn't it?

The Federales looked the boat over stem to stern and found nothing. Miguel and Poncho looked alarmed and were fidgeting uncomfortably. Morales demanded, "Who are you two?"

"We are just towing these gringos sir. It's just our job," Poncho related.

"I see," Morales said. "And why are you towing them? Where is their vehicle?"

"Oh, well, you see, Comandante, they broke down back in Vera Cruz and they needed to meet their uncle. So while their vehicle is getting fixed, we were hired to bring them here."

"Hmm," the agent murmured. "What kind of vehicle did you say they had?"

Miguel, looking at the ground, answered, "A white Suburban."

"Comandante," one of Morales men shouted, "This is not the boat. It's clean and there is nothing on board except fishing gear."

"Maybe," Morales said quietly. "We will call in the Navy for a second opinion, just to be thorough."

While they all waited for the Mexican Navy to arrive, the Federal Officers had a few cervezas in the local cantina. Lencho and Bobby sweated bullets. Miguel and Poncho took a siesta. "Man," Bobby whispered, "if they poke a hole through the floor boards, we are really gonna be fucked."

"Relax, bro," Lencho shot back as calmly as he could. "They won't find a god damned thing. We are almost home free. That fiberglass is dry as concrete now, and just as hard, we'll be fine."

"God, I hope so," Bobby lamented.

A young boatswain finally showed up and was taken aboard. The navy man spent half an hour looking over the starboard and port sides of the boat, inside and out, examining the keel and then declaring, "This vessel could not be smuggling anything."

"What about below our feet?" the agent asked.

"No, comandante. This is what we call a sealed hull. It probably has some ballasts inside, but there is no way to get in there. It's sealed, sir. I have looked it over every way that I know how."

Morales stared at the sky and rubbed his chin. It was clear this was not a man who gave up easily. He paced up and down the length of the boat, twenty-eight feet from stem to stern, very slowly.

Damn that son of a bitch. Give it up asshole, Lencho thought.

Everyone was getting tired of this, including the other Federales. They said nothing, however, as their commander took one final stroll towards the fantail. Then, just as Lencho thought they were clear, his foot touched a soft spot on the deck and he stopped cold in his tracks. He rocked back and forth, and detected a slight groan in the floor.

"Hector," Morales barked, "bring a drill."

The drill pushed through the deck, and when the ten inch auger re-emerged, it had marijuana wrapped neatly around it, smelling sweet and fresh. Morales smiled and declared, "You are all under arrest. Come with us."

*****

Ten miles outside of Tampico is the hamlet of Altamira. Everyone was locked up in tiny cells that were not only claustrophobic, but stank of shit, piss and mold. The next day, they were taken back to the harbor in the back of a pickup truck, where they found a huge pile of marijuana sitting out on the pier. The fishing boat was gone, never to be seen again. Miguel and Poncho were led into an office on the wharf, and in a few hours, both emerged with what appeared to be bruises around their eyes.

Lencho was next. "I have concluded by speaking to these two drivers that you tricked them into bringing you here. We were on the lookout for a large boat being pulled by a white Suburban out of Oaxaca area, but we never found it. You were clever, I must admit, but we, my gringo friends, are also very patient. To try and throw us off, I believe you attempted to lay low and then hired these men to help you. But it is all over now. If you confess, things will be fine. Clearly you are guilty."

"Now just a minute, Agent Morales, that weed is not ours. We know nothing about how it came to even be there. This boat belongs to our uncle, we told you that already."

"Ah yes, your uncle. Is his name CR by chance?" Morales snickered.

Lencho was stunned, and did not know how to answer. "CR?" he stammered, "No, of course not. I told you his name was Uncle Ben. He is in the rice business in Louisiana, and a very rich man. He is the one you want to speak to."

"We have already spoken to Mr. Rosales, the manager at the Mocambo Hotel in Vera Cruz, and he told us the boat owner is a tennis player named CR. He is a young man about your age, and we are currently looking for him. Quit playing your games and telling me lies; simply sign some papers for us, and this will be over with."

At that very moment, Bobby was dragged into the office with fear written over his haggard face. Morales turned to him, repeating the same question and offer. "If you don't sign this confession like the good little gringo dope smugglers we know you both are, we are going to take your brother over to the lagoon and drown him while you watch."

Lencho yelled to his brother, "Don't sign a goddamn thing, Bobby! If we do, we'll never see Arizona again."

"I have no more patience for either of you," Morales snapped, throwing down a sheaf of papers he had been holding in his hands. "Dammit to hell, Vincente, take these two to the truck. I am through with being a nice guy."

The brothers, still handcuffed from behind, were led back to the truck and then shoved into the bed roughly. Vincente drove the three hundred feet to the smelly lagoon that abutted the harbor. Miguel and Poncho sat glumly on a bench and watched the scene unfold. The Comandante walked over and, pointing to the oily water, said, "I will ask you just one more time. Do you sign this confession, or do I drown you right here and now?"

"Lencho," Bobby moaned, "He's gonna do it, man. Let me sign the fucking papers. What would I tell dad?"

"No, Bobby, don't sign anything, he's bluffing. There were at least a hundred people at the ferry yesterday that saw both of us get arrested. How are these assholes going to explain to the press if something does happen to us? Think about it, we're Americans. It would be an international incident. Fuck them, bro!"

A very irate Morales exploded, "That water is twenty feet deep! So you want to die over a pile of mota? Fine with me! Throw him in now, Vincente."

Lencho went flying into the torpid swamp; forgetting to close his mouth, he swallowed a mouthful of the filthy muck. But it was not twenty-feet deep, not even close. Spitting and sputtering, he came up choking for air, while at the same time, trying to get his footing on the slimy bottom. He remained defiant and screamed, "I ain't signing a fucking thing!"

The agents hung their heads in exasperation. "Pull the rat out," Morales ordered. "We will take them both back to the soda room to continue the interrogation. It is time for plan B, as they say in your country."

It was back to the jail, and the Federales were pissed. So mad that they clobbered a drunk in the plaza with their truck as he staggered across the street. He went flying through the air, and then Vincente jumped out and kicked the shit out of him as he lay there. A trickle of blood oozed from the poor man's mouth, and he too was thrown into the back of the truck. They dumped the sod onto the steps of the jail, and then dragged Lencho and Bobby inside to the soda room, as they had called it.

They looked at their stark surroundings. It consisted of a table, four chairs, a lamp, and, in the corners, about twenty soda pop bottles, all half full. Lencho had heard stories about how they shoved the fizz up a victim's nose to loosen lips or get a confession. Torture is a standard procedure used by cops all over the world. In Mexico, they might drown you or shoot bubbles up your snout. In America, they might lock you up in a room full of sodomites.

A smiling Morales came back into the room and said, "Come with me, gentlemen. We now believe that what you have told us is the truth, and only ask that you give us a statement of your version of the events while our stenographer writes it all down. Okay?"

He led them across the hall into the prosecutor's office, where a young woman was sitting by a typewriter. "This is Sylvia," he said genially. "Go ahead and slowly tell her what happened. Start at the beginning, which is when you were in the U.S."

Lencho began by stating they were invited to go fishing with his Uncle Benjamin, a wealthy rice farmer. He had asked his nephews to drive the boat to Tampico by way of Vera Cruz, and have a fun time along the way. He even provided them with a thousand dollars cash for spending money. They took in all of the wonderful historic sites that Mexico was famous for, and were really impressed by the country and its hospitable people. They had then somehow taken a wrong turn and ended up way down by Oaxaca. "Oh, I need to also mention that we did not have a boat at all when we left the U.S. Uncle Ben asked us to pick it up in the town of Tabasco, where his tennis pro buddy CR would meet us."

They did just that and then got lost once again, missing an agricultural check point along the way. Instead of going back, they made an honest mistake of continuing on their journey, trying to find their way.

"We realize now that it was a foolish thing to do," Lencho continued. "We're really very sorry to have missed the check point. I admit that by that time we were kinda rattled, and not thinking as clearly as we should have. We honestly did not think that it would be such a big deal, because we had never been to your beautiful country before now. The next thing we knew was that we suddenly found ourselves getting arrested by the Federal authorities, and then we find out that all of this marijuana was apparently hidden on the boat all along! We knew nothing about it or even how or when it had gotten there. We never use drugs and are not pot smokers. That's our story, and it's all true."

"Is that all you wish to say?" Morales asked courteously. "Is there anything else that you wish to add?"

The brothers looked at one another, and then Bobby said, "No, I think that is it. Except to say that we were treated very fairly by the authorities in this great Country of Mexico, and we thank you for your professionalism and kindness."

"Excellent," Morales said, and asked Sylvia to read it all back to them, which she did verbatim. It was exactly as Lencho had declared, and both signed the paper with a flourish. "Very Good, my young friends. Wait here and I will be back in a moment."

While they waited, an older woman walked into the room and introduced herself as Martha Keeler, a representative of the U.S. embassy. The boys shook her hand eagerly. "I've been trying to find you two for three days now," she began. "It's against international law to hide an accused suspect. America really frowns upon it. Have you two been abused in any way or tortured?"

"A little," Lencho replied. "I think we're okay now, though. We finally got a chance to tell our side of the story."

"You didn't sign anything, did you?" she asked with alarm.

"Hell no, just our statement is all. We signed our truthful statement that we had no knowledge of any marijuana being smuggled or otherwise."

"Wait here," she said, "I'll be back in a moment."

Ten minutes later she returned and she didn't look pleased. "I just read your so called statements. You confessed to towing a large fishing boat down to the Oaxaca area, buying half a ton of marijuana from the Indians, and then smuggling it through Mexico, with the intention of taking it across international borders. Your signatures are very clear and legible. You two will be in prison in this country for a very long time. Nice going." She walked out of the room as Lencho and Bobby sat in shock trying to digest the magnitude of her words.

"I knew this trip was cursed," Lencho sighed to Bobby.

Chapter Seven

"Ain't No God in Mexico"
Released 1973
Waylon Jennings

There ain't no God in Mexico
Ain't no way to understand
How that border crossing feeling
Makes a fool out of a man

ANDONEGUI

It's the third world in Mexico, and even more so if you get arrested. What passes for justice and the law is an abomination. Lencho had been arrested enough times to know. In Mexico, he had been tossed into a lagoon and nearly drowned by Federal Cops determined to coerce a confession, and when that effort had failed, he had been duped into signing a confession that had been written in Spanish and pitched as his own account. Morales was a cunning devil, but Lencho had only himself to blame.

Martha showed up and informed the boys that they had visitors.

"Who the hell are you?" Lencho asked the young man with short hair. "Another Cop? Get the fuck outta here."

"It's me, Lencho. Your brother David. I decided to clean up my act before I came down."

The last time he had seen David, the guy had long hair and a beard.

Lencho honestly did not recognized him. "Dave, is that really you?"

"It's me, brother, and Ronnie is outside. The folks are worried sick. Even dad, if you can believe it."

The four of them had a long talk, and it made them feel a whole lot better about their current state of affairs. David had brought with him five hundred dollars in cash, and Lencho wasted no time in cutting a slot in his trousers where he tucked it away.

"How long will you get?" they asked.

"No one tells us a thing. A lot less if I can get a hold of ten grand. You can buy anything in this country, including an escape."

"Consider it done." David replied. "The next time we come down, I'll bring you the money."

It was a happy couple of hours they spent together, and it was great to see friendly faces. Finally the two left, and the boys were escorted over to Morales office. "I am glad that you enjoyed your visit, because now it is time for you both to go to our jail. I know you will love it. It is very comfortable."

Tampico City Jail was beyond dreadful. It was a huge cavern of steel and concrete with little glass in the whole structure. With a mixture of tropical humidity, general filth blending with the mold everywhere, if you slipped, there was no telling what sort of crud you might land in.

They entered from the busy street. The front was receiving, while in back was a courtyard with cells on three sides.

The great open caves were segregated with homosexuals and nut cases on the right, the general population of miscreants on the left, and the Navy in the middle.

Sailors on leave get into trouble as any Navy man can attest. It is no different in Mexico. The inmates on the right and left yelled and screamed insults at the swabs in the middle, and some threw human excrement at them, along with any rocks and bottles that they had not yet used against one another. Lencho considered it the nastiest and strangest jail he had ever been incarcerated in.

A portion of the five hundred dollars, was used to buy a couple of bed springs and mattresses to lay down upon. The cell was gloomy, and housed fifty other inmates, all Mexicans.

Suddenly, Lencho started to get pelted on the head by cockroaches; some joker was messing with him, tossing the big insects. This continued for over half an hour until Lencho blew his top. The peace and love, pot smoking hippie could get angry if pushed hard enough, and suddenly enough was enough. He leapt from the springs and pounced on the fellow who had been tormenting him. Lencho beat the shit out of him until he cried like a little girl. There was no trouble after that.

Miguel and Poncho had also been sent into the jail. The poor guys never knew what they were getting into when they offered to drive the big boat to Tampico. Now they were both in jail, lost their truck, and could be sentenced for smuggling. But they were both still friendly, even after all of that happened. Lencho felt exceedingly bad for getting them mixed up in all of this shit. What a great difference between the bad people down there and the good ones. On the third day, however, Morales had Miguel and Poncho released.

The two cops that had transported Lencho and Bobby to jail let it be known that, for the right sum, an escape could be arranged. "Nothing to it Amigos," Officer Domingo had told them. "When you are transferred, it will be us who drives you. It is twenty kilometers through the suburbs, and on the way we will have a little engine trouble. While we are messing with the motor, you two vatos will overpower us and then make your escape. For this to happen, it will cost you ten thousand U.S. dollars."

It sounded pretty damn good, so they arranged for David and Ronnie to bring down the money and hand it over to Martha at the Consulate.

Once she received the money, she came by and had a little chat with the boys that gave them pause for concern.

"I have your money, Lencho," Martha said. "And you can try and bribe your way out of here, but mark my words, you will be very sorry if you do."

"How did you know about our plans, Martha?" he asked her.

"It's standard procedure in Mexico. What will happen is that those two jackals you are talking to will betray you. Hell, they already told Morales what's up. He'll keep half of the money, they'll get the rest, and you two will get the beating of your life before they continue your trip to the prison."

The plan was scrapped, and Martha held onto the ten grand for the time being.

David and Ronnie had been hanging around waiting for the word. They arranged for an airplane and devised an escape route, but it was all in vain.

On the seventh day in jail, Agent Morales informed them that they would be transferred. "But don't feel so bad my friends," he said. "You will still have your marijuana. Look for it when you get to your new home. I think you may end up having to buy it all over again, though," he laughed.

In Mexico, you are guilty until proven innocent, and anything is possible. Many inmates are kept incarcerated for years, and then released when the right wheels are greased properly. Sometimes the convening courts even rule that there was some sort of mistake, and you're free to go. There is always hope in a corrupt system.

At the turn of the century, Admiral P.P. Andonegui owned a very large mansion that had been given to him by the government in appreciation for heroic service rendered by his tenure in the Navy. A long driveway reached from the highway to the arched entrance. Massive gates and double thick walls encircled the two acre estate. Beyond the gates was a gorgeous courtyard filled with tropical vegetation and tiled in the colors of the rainbow. That was then. Now, seventy years after his death, the land had been deeded back to the government and converted into the prison that was to become Lencho and Bobby's new home. The Palacio de Andonegui was not as lovely as it was in its heyday, but it appeared to be much more organized and somewhat less filthy than the jail they had just been moved from. Like all prisons in Mexico, it was run by the inmates, so if you had money, it could be reasonably comfortable.

Shaped like an oval, the entire compound was constructed of concrete, rock, and steel. There were two walls: a fifteen feet high outer wall with six gun turrets, and an inner wall that stood ten feet. The guards on duty in the towers were said to be crack shots. You entered the compound from the front gate only. There was no back gate, and over five hundred prisoners were crammed into various buildings within.

In the days in which the Admiral occupied the place, the front buildings by the gate had been where he and his family resided. It was still a pretty impressive structure, with marble colonnade, ornate tile, and statuary. They had lived there long ago in revered splendor. The complex had also housed their servants, horses, and even his wood working industry. The grounds of the surrounding area had been rich in hardwood forest, and at nearby Madera there was a large seaport.

Immediately to the right of the gate, just across from the old living quarters, was a second building that now housed the Mexican Mafia. These were the organized crime groups and members with the most dinero. Behind the mafia was a patio with the prison kitchen to the right and a fully equipped restaurant on the left, which was owned by Paco Espernusa and his wife. A birthday, holiday, or anything else was a reason to celebrate in that establishment. Paco featured excellent Mexican food and Mariachi music. Young ladies danced in colorful folk costumes.

Beyond yet another iron gate, to the left, is where they housed the murderers. In Mexico, there is no death sentence. For all of its harsh treatment of suspects and prisoners, if you were in prison for committing murder, the sentence was sixteen years or less.

The interior patio was about half an acre, with an old barn that had been separated in two. It abutted the wall on the left, and housed some of the federal prisoners. On the right side, however, the ladies dwelled. There were as many as fifty women prisoners of all ages and descriptions living there. Their crimes ranged from theft to murdering wayward husbands. They were a tired and haggard looking lot.

From midway on the patio to the first wall stood two structures side by side. Each were approximately three thousand square feet apiece, and the one on the right side housed the rest of the federal inmates, while on the left were the state inmates.

A number of courtyards interspersed the state compound, and that's where hundreds of the very poor lived, virtually out in the weather. These desperate souls slept on flimsy cots underneath ramshackle roofing held up by poles. They rolled up their bedding each day and pushed it against the wall. They used the area to cook and work in.

Homemade rooms were attached to walls and this is where the 'Middle Class' inmates lived. Toilets and shower facilities were laid out in wash rooms located inside each of the courtyards. They consisted of five commodes that were fastened over a primitive sewer line. Once a person was finished doing their business, they filled a bucket with water from a fifty gallon drum and dumped it in the toilets. The showers were aligned opposite the toilets and were gravity fed from a tank located on the roof. The tank was filled with water by a pump each day, and was cold.

The floors were concrete and the prisoners washed their clothes by hand on long cement tables with drains. They used powdered soap and hung their wash on braided steel cables, which were stretched across open areas. Occasionally, the clothes lines and the electrical lines got crossed and sparks would fly.

The entire place was homemade, jerry-rigged, and slapdash. It was a work in progress, constantly evolving. One day it was being built up; another, torn down. Materials were recycled and reused. Or, if you had the money, you could order practically anything in the way of construction materials from the outside. The same was true of food and other supplies. A woman would show up each day at the entrance to take orders that she would fill for the inmates at the local stores in the city. There were also tiny 'general stores' run by inmates that sold flour, beans, bread, or whatever. Some of these stores were no bigger than a closet. On Thursdays, the whores came to service those who were lonely.

Everyone had a trade. They manufactured toys, jewelry, furniture, ships in bottles, shirts, pants, boxes, culinary items, and rugs. If it could be sold, it was made. The entire prison was like a huge hobby shop. But the two largest enterprises were drug sales and pop bottle cleaners.

The state inmates had the later concessions, and there was always a mountain of empty soda bottles that were scrubbed by hand in hot water and soap, using a long bristle brush. Dozens were employed doing this.

Father Brito held mass on Sunday, and collected many pesos in his bejeweled hands from the impoverished faithful. Little old ladies near starvation would hand over the last of their earthly possessions to the church before they departed their earthly coil. The whores were allowed back in on Sundays, after the church held its services.

The prison kitchen prepared two meals each day, which consisted of gruel, tortillas, and beans. All other food was brought in and cooked on innumerable kerosene and propane stoves. The ice man showed up daily to reload chests.

Palacio de Andonegui was a self-contained city. A microcosm of diversity and industriousness born of need where nothing was given the inmates except years of servitude to the state, which the state made them pay for themselves.

As the paddy wagon pulled up front, the boys were amazed at the bustle from the moment they arrived. Outside was a cacophony of horns and bellowing vendors being disgorged by a stream of taxis.

Lencho and Bobby were filthy beyond description after not being able to bathe for a week at the jail. They stank and were in dire need of clean clothes and a shave.

The first people they dealt with blanched. "We are placing you initially up front," said a secretary with disdain. "Since you are Americans, you are treated with some regard. The rooms are nice for this place."

"No," Lencho announced. "We don't want to be there. Too noisy."

"Too noisy?" Bobby whispered. "What the fuck man? I want to be as comfortable as possible."

"Shhh!" Lencho whispered. "I got a plan, and being up front ain't no good for us. Look around at all the activity. We want some privacy."

"Where then do you want to go?" she grumbled. "Since you are federal prisoners, it will be in the back. It's not as nice, but it's up to you. I certainly don't care one way or the other."

A young man named Carlos was summoned, and he took them into the prison. Carlos was well educated and civilized. He was a Pocho, which meant he lived on the U.S. side of the border, and was doing his time for dealing in marijuana. He directed them through the second gate and into a world of women doing laundry, children running around screaming and playing, and gamblers laughing over card games. There were men busy carving religious icons by hand as well as cleaning, painting, and building. And everywhere there was the lingering smell of marijuana. The boys had vowed they would not smoke weed out of fear of getting into trouble, but it immediately became obvious how absurd that was.

"There are no guards back here," Carlos explained. "The guards keep us in, but they enter our world only when they are ordered to do so. The inmates run this prison. If you have money there is nothing you cannot have. But if you are broke, it is no different than being anywhere without money. It sucks. Look around at the poor. They toil tirelessly to make things that they can sell. Their crafts are sold in town and everywhere. If you want women, it is easy to arrange. Mota? Cerveza? No problem. Just remember one important detail: the Mafia is the real power within these walls. I am now going to introduce you to El Segundo."

"Isn't that a town in L.A. County?" Bobby joked.

"It means 'the second' in command," Carlos replied.

At the federal compound, Carlos presented them to Pablo, a.k.a. 'El Segundo.' Outside of his room, the net makers were weaving fishing nets for the local fishermen and hammocks to sleep in. An interpreter offered them seats and explained in English what Pablo and the mafia expected of them.

You must pay protection to the mafia, so you don't get beat to a pulp by the mafia.

"So we pay you not to hurt us?" Lencho asked.

"Yes, of course," the interpreter replied. "A standard arrangement. We also make sure no one else hurts you. And if you want a room, you pay us. If you want mota, you pay. Liquor, glue, you pay."

"Glue?" they both choked.

"Sadly, many of these hombres use glue. Women also, and liquor. Pay your monthly mordida and things are fine with us and will be fine with you also."

"What if we need a doctor sometime?" Lencho inquired. "It looks like there is TB in here."

"My advice is don't get sick," he laughed. "Keep away from the coughers, because you are right, there is mucho consunción."

But it wasn't as terrible as it sounded, because the fees the Mafia charged were actually pretty affordable. Lencho handed over two hundred dollars, which caught them up on six months protection, and made them quite popular with El Segundo. He rolled up a fat joint, and they smoked the first doobie since they had gotten tossed into the city jail over a week before. Then Pablo said, "Oh, by the way Gringos, you should take a bath because you both really stink! No offense, of course."

101

Once the financial arrangements had been made and the rules explained, everything went well. You could always expect protection from the 'Cops' who worked for the boss. They carried clubs, but were not really cops; they were muscle for the mafia. They were inside enforcers who kept order for those who paid. It became clear why the prison did not need guards.

They rented a little room from a fellow whose wife had gone back to Mexico City to visit her family and wouldn't return for a month. After that, they took showers and even got a shave. Digging fresh clothes out of their suitcases they were allowed to bring with them was a huge joy. Paying the money was no problem because Lencho had the five hundred stashed, and he was expecting his ten grand from the American Consulate. They now enjoyed all the creature comforts provided by the den of thieves they dwelled amongst.

The real bad part of the deal was the sentence. In Mexico, they never bother to tell you how long you will get; they just toss you into the penitentiary after you have been arrested, tortured, and forced to sign a confession. Then later, sometimes a lot later, you find out how long you will have to serve. From what he could gather from talking to the other men, he and Bobby were looking at seven to twelve years. But, he wasn't sure. He was, however, sure of one thing, and that was that they were both going to escape. Their opportunity came the first day they were there. After relaxing for a few hours and getting to know some of their brothers in arms, a young fellow named Pete Martinez from Del Rio Texas came in to meet the two new Americanos. The subject of sentences was discussed, and, as is natural when in prison, they discussed escape.

"You want to escape? I will tell you how to escape my friends, and you must try this at once. Had I known what I am about to tell you to do, I would have tried it as well. Tomorrow you both just walk right out of here."

"Say what?" Bobby choked. "How are we gonna just walk out?"

"Simplicity itself," he replied with a chuckle. "This place is full of visitors. Wives, children, husbands, and girlfriends. They come here in the day, and they stay overnight. At six thirty in the morning, after the shift change, the guards take count. Just before all of that happens, the visitors must be gone. They leave out of the gate by six a.m. You are new here, so they don't know you yet. And so, you just walk out. I am sure that this plan will work!"

"Let me get this straight," Lencho said, his eyes lighting up. "It's that simple? No one will attempt to stop us?"

"I am pretty sure that it can be done," Martinez answered. "After tomorrow, it will be too late because by then they will know you and recognize you. Just wear nice clothes, which I see that you have. Look clean and go with the crowd."

In the morning, the throngs lined up to exit, and a new shift of guards led by a new Comandante relieved the last. During that time, there was enough hustle and bustle to make their move, and the weed brothers were up for it.

Regarding the etiquette of escape, Pete had also explained to them that the outer wall with the guard towers had armed men, and that they were very good with a rifle.

He had seen men shot while trying to flee, or even sometimes just causing a ruckus. The prison paid the guards a stipend for all shootings. No one was sure if this money was for a good aim or because the guards were traumatized by what they had done. It was, nonetheless, foolhardy to even try and make a run for it.

The Mafia guys generally didn't try and escape even though they had all of the resources to do so. If a man who was in the Mafia was given some time to do, he did it. That's just the price of doing business.

Those guys frequently left the prison anyway with paid permission to do so by the director. They might wish to visit a nearby beach with their families, and they were allowed to while under escort by off duty officers. They often spent the weekends away or even at home, if they lived close by. But they always returned to the prison afterwards. It was a matter of honor. Then, of course, there were the rackets that they operated inside the prison. Since they were paid handsomely for just about everything that happened, there was no reason for them (sensible businessmen) to abandon their enterprises. And anyway, almost any offense could be 'forgiven' by a judge, if the money was right. The common or poor inmates were just shit out of luck.

At six a.m. the next morning, the crowd of visitors dispersed. Women holding the hands of their small children, whores, boyfriends, girlfriends, parents, and others began the arduous process of checking out. Lencho and Bobby were right smack in the middle of the jostling crowd trying to act nonchalant. They got out of their building and were then in the large courtyard. So far so good! Word of the daring effort began circulating and quietly their advance towards the gate and freedom was being observed by dozens of fellow inmates who whispered among themselves. "Look at the crazy gringos," they muttered.

They reached the inner gate and waited their turn to pass by the visitors table. Several ladies were stationed there, including the wife of Carlos Caldaroni, whom they had met the day before. It was these women who were doing the checking. "Name please?" A pleasant middle aged lady asked Lencho as he stood like a deer in the headlights before her.

"Umm, Richard Tracy ma'am, and this is my partner Ralph. We're Americans."

"I can see that, Mr. Tracy, but I don't see your name on my list. When did you check in?"

"Oh, about seven last night," he lied.

She searched diligently for a few minutes and then said, "I'm sorry, do you know where you signed in? What page?"

"Uh, no I don't know what page," Lencho said with a crooked grin. "Look ma' am, I'm sure that we are in there someplace. We really have to be going now. Thank you so much." Then they both began to shove their way forward. Comandante Santana was standing just five feet away engaged in an animated conversation with a little old lady that was probably someone's grandmother. He looked very dignified in his neatly pressed uniform and expensive tejana. He just waved the boys through and they suddenly found themselves out on the sidewalk. Taxi cabs beckoned. The two gulped and strode towards freedom.

"Halt," prison guard Juvenile Limon bellowed, his M16 rifle held at the ready. "Where do you think you are going?"

The entire prison was now aware of the escape, and all of the inmates close to the front gate watched in suspense, while passing the word back to their compadres.

"They are almost free."

"The Comandante has let them through."

"Now, they are about to hail a cab."

"Oh no, Juvenile has stopped them and asked to see their pass."

"Where is your pass?" The guard demanded. "I must have your pass before I can allow you to leave."

"Ah, our pass? Of course. Give the man our passes, Ralph?" Lencho said brightly. He thought about making a dash for that taxi at the curb, but he knew he could not leave Bobby behind. Not to mention that he would more than likely be cut down in a hail of gunfire for which Officer Limon would most probably receive a nice stipend for his good aim.

"Comandante, Comandante!" Limon called out. "These men do not have passes, and I think there is something fishy going on here." The jig was up.

With a rifle stuck in his back, Lencho led the way to the visitors table where the Comandante was waiting, and the man was clearly not amused. He called Carlos over to translate and to find out what the hell was going on.

"What the fuck are you two doing?" Carlos asked incredulously. "Let me guess, you were trying to escape? Just like that. You've been here for one day and you already wish to leave us?"

"Well, yeah," Lencho admitted sheepishly. "Guess it's not gonna work, huh?"

"If you had told me of your little plan, I could have had Sandra put your names in the guest book. She could have written Mickey Mouse or Donald Duck and just given you both passes. No way that can happen now. What do you want me to tell the Comandante?"

"Well shit. Tell him that we just didn't know any better cause we're new. Tell him we wanted to go out to the field to play a little fútbol. Tell him we're real sorry."

"I bet they're gonna beat us half to death for this," Bobby moaned. Carlos had a discussion with the Comandante who seemed very upset. He glared at the gringos, and burst forth in a tirade of profanity in Spanish, culminating it all in English. "Take them both back in, Pronto!"

The boys were led to where they had begun their adventure amid hoots, whistles, and applause from the hundreds of men who had been following the effort. They were not beaten, but instead confined to their building for a week. They had become famous in the little fish bowl they now resided in, and all Lencho had to say after all of this was: "The next time I'm gonna dig a fucking tunnel."

"You guys were lucky that the Comandante didn't mess you up," Carlos explained. "It was not so long ago that a couple of hombres kidnaped some visitors. They tied them up and stole their passes to get out. When you escape from prison, somebody must take your place. That's how it works, and obviously no guard wants to switch. That's why you could have easily been killed. But it was a nice try and everybody is talking about it." He went on to explain how escaping was a natural thing. All prisoners have the right to escape; you are almost expected to. Not the mafia guys, of course. They could buy their way out, but the regular guys, they are almost expected to attempt an escape.

Two other things happened then in quick succession. Tamara arrived, and Martha brought in the ten grand that Ronnie had given her. Tamara made life much easier for Lencho, and she stayed for the duration. The money paid for all of the creature comforts, as well as the lumber, tools and whatever they needed for the coming construction.

After the month's rent was up on the two rooms, Lencho set about buying real estate. Another man had a perfect spot, but he also had a wife and two children.

"How much do you want for your area?" Lencho asked him.

"No, señor, I do not wish to sell. I have my family to think about."

"I'll pay you six hundred dollars," Lencho retorted.

"No, no. Gracias, but I cannot sell."

"Seven hundred then" Lencho exclaimed.

"I am tempted señor, but the answer is still no."

"Seven fifty!"

The man's wife was now on the scene and gave her husband a look that clearly said, Take the fool's money! Are you loco?

"I'll pay you eight hundred dollars! That is my final offer."

One more look by the wife, and they had a deal. They moved out on the spot with eight crisp C notes to take with them. Seeing this spirited commerce, the fellow next door offered his property as well. He left with five hundred. Lencho and Bobby then made arrangements with the lady at the gate to buy some lumber.

"Here's my plan," he told his brother. "We'll tear out this old shack. The ceiling is twenty-feet high, and perfect for a loft above my room, which I'll access through the room that we'll build for you right beside it. Then we'll put in an air conditioner, which we'll install in the windows way up there, and it won't be so damned hot. We'll buy a stereo to play loud music, and we'll set it up over in the corner there, where we will start our dig."

"Our dig? Are we gonna be miners, or what?" Bobby asked timidly.

"Nope, we're going to escape. We are digging us a tunnel, bro."

His experience in construction had begun when he performed what could only be described as slave labor for his father as a youngster. And then, he gained even more experience by building several cabins and a giant teepee. His knowledge was considerable, and he was confident in his abilities as he scoped out the lay of the land.

Andonegui Prison sat on a hill that overlooked the ocean. It was reached by a busy highway that came out of Tampico, and the entire place sat on what he figured was a shallow foundation. The earth was sand and silt. Solid enough, but certainly not hard packed like clay. The floors inside were almost all concrete, poured over the years by inmates. Once they punched through it, they would dig X number of feet under the first wall. Then dig a little further until they reached the outer wall. Dig underneath that, and voila! They would pop up and vanish. Let someone else take their place. When the lumber truck pulled up in front, hired men carted the wood back and the fun began. They tore out the flimsy shanty the previous resident had strung up, and in short order a rather significant abode began to take shape. Two rooms, the first 10x10 and the second 8x8. A door opened from Bobby's room out into the main building, but you couldn't get into Lencho's unless you first came in through Bobby's. This guaranteed privacy and distance.

Above his room, Lencho built a loft where he and Tamara slept. He bought a double bed and installed A/C. They cut a vent into the wall for Bobby and it was a wonderful seventy degrees in what once had been a virtual sweat box. They painted, put down rugs, set up a Pioneer stereo and Bose speakers. Lencho decided to kiss off television, because everything was in Spanish, and the reception was very poor. The boys now had the nicest digs in the place.

Bobby set up a small wood shop in a corner of his room, and made a couch. Ronnie was a huge help, traveling back and forth to bring stuff they needed, but could not find in Tampico. He brought the A/C and piles of Playboy magazines.

Two things Lencho wanted to establish was noise and naked girly pics for the walls. They played the records of Molly Hatchet, Blue Cheer, and Led Zeppelin full blast along with the constant whir of the A/C unit. The photos of the playmates would be a great diversion for the occasional visits by the guards. The couch would sit over the hole they were going to dig.

Although Tamara was often a ditz, she was still lovely, soft, and provided companionship to Lencho during his time at the prison. Unfortunately, a nineteen-year-old that looked that good was a sore temptation for the other inmates, and on more than one occasion, Lencho warned them to back off. When the cat calls and whistles got too annoying, he called for the mafia with their big clubs. He had, after all, paid for protection, and he got it. Pretty soon she was only a beautiful fixture in the world they now inhabited.

At the same time that the boys began their long march at Andonegui Prison, President Jimmy Carter initiated a prisoner swap program. He was touched by the plight of Billy Hayes, famous from the movie 'Midnight Express.' The movie was the story of an American who had been arrested in Turkey for possession of hashish, and was sentenced to life in prison, which included various forms of torture. So there was now a movement to trade out the many Americans that were rotting away in foreign prison cesspools on various drug charges. But Lencho had a record at home, and was fearful that even if he could qualify for the swap, he would end up in the soup again once returned to the U.S.

It helped, of course, when the cheerful and happy to be of service Martha from the U.S. Consulate stopped by to deliver their cash. The brothers began their epic task.

Analyzing the layout of his room in the far corner of the federal unit, Lencho decided the best way to begin was to go through the wall. It was made of cinder block and was a couple of feet deep, but easy to penetrate. An entrance was cut by using a quarter horse electric motor with masonry bits, chisels, and a hammer. Soon they had enlarged the opening inside the wall to where they could stand up. Then it was time to dig straight down. The floor was not very thick and easy to punch through. They shoved the chunks of concrete aside and hit soil that was soft, but still substantial enough not to require shoring. From there, it became a matter of expanding the hole, which they did with gusto, and after one month they had created an opening that extended from where they had begun to the outside of Lencho's room. The accumulating dirt was put into buckets and taken out with their laundry where, to the wonderment of many, they did their wash late at night. In reality, they were washing the dirt down the drains under the wash tables in the courtyard. It was slow going, but effective. In just two months, they had expanded the starting point to four feet by five and were now ready to head towards the outside wall.

"It's time for us to go home, Bobby," Lencho told his brother.

The prison was a hell hole, but remarkably clean considering as many as twenty men might be crowded into a corner of one building that was barely large enough for five.

The trash can man was a fine example. It was his job to empty the fifty gallon oil drums that were filled with human waste day in and day out. It was his job, and also his bed. Each night, he would place a plank on top of the trash cans and climb under a frayed blanket to sleep, coughing and spitting up blood from a terminal case of tuberculosis. Others scrubbed down the toilets and showers daily with water, soap, and bleach. The women had their own facilities, which, though humble, were spotless. They had fixed up their quarters with frills and ruffles, as ladies will do. Tamara was able to bathe in relative comfort and free from attack. It was a different story, however, when she ventured out to meet with Lencho and Bobby's judge regarding their sentences. One of her contributions was that she was able to come and go at will. After all, she was just a guest and not a prisoner. Lencho had been told by the American Consul that Judge Ernesto Mejia was the man to see regarding such matters. All important issues were up to him, and that included determining if any mitigating circumstances might exist in their cases.

Months had passed and they had heard nothing regarding their fate. It was decided that maybe it would be helpful to send Tamara to see the judge, accompanied by the girlfriend of an inmate named Cruz who knew where the judge lived in town. Lencho felt uneasy as he checked out the short hemline and the low cut blouse of Tranquila, the woman who was to lead the expedition.

"You sure you want to wear that particular top?" he asked Tamara. "Kinda flimsy, isn't it?"

"Tranquila tells me that the judge is a gentleman. She looks so cute, I thought I'd dress the same."

Judge Mejia lived in a nice section of Tampico. A winding driveway reached a New Orleans style house. Palms and hibiscus fringed the entryway. A maid answered the door and told the girls to wait as she announced their arrival.

"I will see them now," the Judge intoned. "Bring them to my study."

"Sir," Tranquila began, "we appreciate your time. We have come from Andonegui Prison where our men are, and we wish to inquire about their sentences."

The judge pressed his thin mustache with chubby fingers as he gazed at the two attractive young women who stood before him.

"I may be able to help," he replied, "but you have come just as I was about to have lunch. Will you join me?"

Before they could answer, the maid appeared again and he gave rapid fire instructions regarding the meal. All Tamara could understand was one word: "Tequila."

The day wore on and the judge received several friends, all of them lawyers. Little was said about the business they had come to discuss, and Tamara was running out of excuses to refuse the constant entreaties to drink. Tranquila, on the other hand, was far less abashed. Soon it was five in the afternoon and getting dark outside. Being both shy and nervous, she didn't want to press the issue, but they had come for information and by this time Judge Meija and his cronies were getting downright rowdy.

"Your Honor," she finally implored. "What about my man Lencho and his brother Bobby? How long will they be in your prison?"

The judge leered at her as he sank his considerable girth into a chair beside her and breathed boozy breath into her face.

"It all depends, chica, on how nice you are to an old man," he slurred as he leaned into her, placed a paw under her chin, and tried to plant a big wet kiss upon her delicate lips. Tamara screamed, slapped him hard across the face, and bolted for the door. As she ran down the drive, the judge called out, "My darling, come back! Let us talk. I am not so bad."

"Old goat!" she yelled over her shoulder.

"Puta!" he responded as he slammed the door.

Even in a dangerous place like Mexico, there are still saviors. An elderly man and his wife drove by the hysterical girl as she raced into the evening. They drove her back to the prison where she tumbled out and was escorted inside to the ladies stationed at the desk.

"Call for Lencho," Sandra ordered as she fetched the sobbing girl a glass of water.

"What in the hell happened?" Lencho demanded. "I've been worried sick about you."

"The man is a pig," she cried. "He was all over me. Tranquila didn't seem to care, but I finally ran for my life. It was awful, Lencho, and this from a judge!"

"I can't believe it," Lencho bellowed. "This country is out of control. It's bad in the U.S., but this place is fucking insane. I'm gonna kill the piece of shit!"

Lencho went straight back to the offices and asked to use the phone where he called the consulate and demanded an interview. Martha obliged, and then filed a formal complaint against Judge Mejia for very bad behavior towards an almost underage American girl. The shit did hit the fan for the judge. A senior adjunct from the American consulate flew in from Mexico City, along with a senior Mexican Federal Judge, and they kicked ass and took names. They told Judge Mejia that he better never pull a stunt like that again. They then flew back to Mexico City, and that was that. In Mexico, a judge like Mejia is virtually untouchable. He got his seat on the bench as a political favor from the PRI party, and that appointment was for life. After the dust settled, Lencho and Bobby received word on their sentences: eleven years each.

"Man," Bobby moaned. "We can't catch a break in this fucking country. It went from seven to eleven, just like that."

"Martha tells me that he'll take a bribe," Lencho said hopefully.

"Yeah?" Bobby asked. "How much?"

"Fifty grand each," said Lencho as Bobby let out another groan.

Word also reached them that the cops and the judge were arguing about whom would get their boat. The odds favored the judge. Resigning themselves to their fate, the boys went back to work. Bobby was a good worker and built a table. It was unique in that the legs were hollow. They sold several and bought a couple of pounds of nice weed from some Indians on the outside. Tamara brought it back into the prison in a table.

Perez was numero uno and ran their section for the Mafia. It was his copistas who kept order. He lent a sympathetic ear to Lencho when he was feeling sorry for himself over the fiasco with the judge. In broken English, Perez commiserated and passed along some Mafia wisdom.

"That judge, he is a pig," Perez told him. "I know him well. But he will be gone soon enough because the government rotates judges around. The money and bribes are too hard for them to resist. Men like us buy and sell them. They have no honor."

"What are you in here for, Perez?" Lencho asked.

"Me and my men are in here because Pepe was on a job and he got caught by the Federales just like you did. Only Pepe was not so lucky, and they beat him badly. They beat and tortured him for days and he almost died. You see that he still limps? Well, when La Policia beat a man as bad as they beat Pepe, he has no choice but to give them the information they desire. He gave them us."

"So, he was an informer?" Lencho asked.

"No, my friend, not that. We don't blame him for talking, because he had no choice. That's the difference between my country and yours. I been doing this a long time; in the U.S. they seldom torture you, but here in Mexico they almost always do. So, if you talk to La Policia, it is not very surprising. It's when a person does not talk to them, now that is a surprise! So we all ended up here for the next seven years

"Really though, it's not so bad," Perez continued, "We do pretty good for ourselves. I got only one big problem."

"What's that?" The weed man inquired.

"Chuey. That cockroach over in the state section. He owns the bottle cleaning and he thinks that he should be the boss. I am keeping my eye on him, Amigo."

Weeks went by, and then months, and they settled more and more into a routine. Ronnie came down once a month with money and supplies, and they would sit up all night drinking Heinekens, smoking weed, and talking about the future. Lencho decided that it was time that he establish some juice. Influence of the political kind. Everybody kept telling him that's how it worked in Mexico. He called on Martha at the Consulate, once again, and asked her who in town knew all the big shots. Who was the best person to see for help?

"That would be Señor Legerata. He is a wealthy man and owns the Chevy dealership in Tampico, plus a couple of ranches and some fishing boats. You should let me introduce Tamara to his wife. Señora Legerata is a lovely woman with a good heart. If they like you, who knows? Good things might happen."

The ladies of Mexico were often saints, it seemed to Lencho. He was truly amazed at the differences between the women and the men. The men were lying, cheating, skirt chasing scoundrels, while their wives seemed resigned to their fate. After the introduction, the Legeratas were charmed by the beautiful young American girl and Señor Legerata agreed to come and visit Lencho at the prison.

On the very morning of the expected visit, however, a few of the prison guards decided to also pay him a visit! Lencho knew the reason: it was Tamara.

"What is this woman doing here?" Officer Hector Aureliano demanded, as he and four others stormed in unannounced. Bobby stood there seething.

"Sorry, Lencho, they just pushed their way in and I couldn't stop them."

"What do you mean, Aureliano?" Lencho barked back. "You know full well that I pay her way. She has permission to be here with me. Now, get out!"

The five of them pounced on Lencho as one, and then dragged him from the room, bleeding from a split lip.

"See how tough you are after a few days in the bartolina," Aureliano chided.

The bartolina was the 'hole.' Every prison and jail on earth has one. It is isolation.

Historically, the hole was a room with a hole in the floor to defecate in. Andoneguis hole was historically accurate. Lencho found himself confined to a fetid cave too small to lay down in. Cold bars were his only companions and he was stunned by this turn of fortune.

"Why me, Lord?" Lencho implored as Job once had. And then he discovered the little pot bud with a single match in an empty cigarette package. He made a makeshift pipe of the foil, pressed the weed into the bowl and lit up. The pain and sorrow went up in smoke. Although some may deny it, this really was the true blessing of marijuana. The reason so many smoke it and love it. It is the giver of peace and the vanquisher of sorrows and he knew at that moment he would soldier on, that things in his life would only improve.

"I am here to see a gringo by the name of Lencho," Señor Legerata informed director Pascale.

"Señor Legerata. Of course, of course. It is wonderful to see you!" the director fawned. "I will have him brought up at once. Aureliano!" he bellowed.

They all sat in the restaurant in the forward area drinking tea. There was Señor Legerata and three of his men, together with Lencho and Bobby.

"How did you get the bumps on your head, young man?" He asked with clear suspicion.

Lencho looked over at the nervous Aureliano standing a few feet away. "I fell, Sir. Slipped on a banana peel. You know how dirty a place like this can be."

"Yes, I think I do," he answered knowingly. "My wife and I have met your lovely fiancée and have heard your story. Many of us in my country know full well how absurd this so called drug war is. I myself have smoked and enjoyed the mota. Of course, that was in my youth. I do believe, however, that it is harmless. Things are unfortunately the way they are, and only God can change them. As you may know, Judge Mejia is a friend of mine. In fact, I own the house he is renting in town. I won't deny that, at times, the man can act the fool. His appetite for the young ladies is well known. I know also that you reported him and that he was reprimanded. Beyond that, I am afraid there is not much that can be done with your current legal situation. I can, however, do a few things that I believe will be of some assistance to you. I will instruct my friend here, who is the director of the prison, that I expect him to see to it that you and your brother are not to be abused in any way. My wife will stay in close touch with the prison, so no more of this "banana slipping" takes place again. Also, I am going to introduce you to my assistant, Fernando. He is my pilot and takes care of all incidentals that I need tended to. He is a very smart and efficient young man who I believe can be of help to you in the future. Here are three phone numbers. Contact him at once. I will tell him to expect your call."

This last favor turned out to be a great one for Lencho. He and Fernando became good friends and business associates for the next several years. Fernando came on a regular basis to visit and see what he could do to make life easier. He was three years older at thirty-five, born into an august family. His father had been a general in the revolutionary army of Pancho Villa, and owned estates in northern Mexico. Fernando's father had been a strict disciplinarian. When the young Fernando had become rebellious, he suddenly found himself exiled to a military academy in Mexico City. Once he completed his education there, he was sent to the U.S. where he attended and completed High School. Now, he was a sharp, educated, and well-rounded contact in Mexico that Lencho sorely needed. He was, of course also full of machismo and a shameless womanizer.

Among his many trades, Fernando wore the hat of a Falluquero. One who smuggles goods in order to avoid taxation. An omnipresent reality in Mexico where so many consumer goods had a surcharge, they were beyond the reach of most.

Flying airplanes was the preferred technique for the Falluquero. This is why Fernando knew the lay of the land as well as he did. The entire country was familiar to him. He knew where all of the airports and airstrips were, even the ones off the beaten path. He also knew how to obtain fuel in out of the way places, and where to go for repairs. Fernando was an all-purpose airplane man.

In the meantime, the tunneling went on and the end seemed in sight. Taking care to camouflage their efforts, they mixed some paint to match the edges, which were scrupulously sealed with wax after each session. Then pulling the couch over the entry, they prayed they would succeed before they were discovered. Discovery was now a real possibility, because word in the courtyard had it that Aureliano and his goons would be making an inspection at any time. They were rare, but periodic inspections could be expected. It would be the end of the world for sure, if they were caught.

"We can't be more than a couple of feet from the outer wall," Lencho grinned climbing back into the room. He wiped the sweat from his brow and said, "To hell with it. I say we power through. We can be outta here by midnight."

"But what about the dirt? Where will we put it?"

"We'll put it in the loft. Let the guards worry about it once we're gone."

The dirt piled up, but Bobby crossed himself like the Catholics all around and said, "Please, God, don't let that fucking Aureliano inspect this place before we escape!"

An hour later, Lencho reached the wall. "Bobby!" he gasped coming back inside, "We're there! I'm going under now. Cross your fingers."

The dirt was soft and pliable. He figured the footings under the wall would be no deeper than five feet, but at four he stopped dead in his tracks. He had hit rock! Moving to the left, he began again and once more found rock. "Don't tell me this whole place is built on rock!" he cursed to himself. But it was – rock, rock, and more rock. They would need dynamite to crack it, and a jackhammer after that.

"Man," Bobby moaned again. "Can't catch a fucking break!"

To top it all off, now there was dirt everywhere in the room, and word had just come down that an inspection would take place tomorrow.

Realizing that, if found out, no amount of juice Señor Legerata had poured into their lives would be enough to save them from the terrible wrath of the director, the commandante, and the jealous guards. The only solution was to fill in the big hole as fast as they could.

"My God, look at that mountain up on the loft!" Bobby screamed. "All is lost!"

"Get up there, man, and shovel it down. I'll do the back filling," Lencho calmly replied.

They did just that, and, except for a lot of dust and a few small piles in the corners, the brothers managed to refill the entry. They left the tunnel beneath their feet empty, since that dirt had been washed away at the laundry. It was all just in the nick of time. As Lencho was splashing a bucket of water to and fro to hold down the dust, in walked Hector Alejandro and his men. He stood there with hands on his hips and stared down at Lencho, who was holding a scrub brush.

"Doing some housework, I see, Gringo. Where is that little blonde puta of yours? She make you a house husband?" They all had a good laugh at his expense.

"Yeah, I guess so," Lencho replied obsequiously. "What can I do for you, Captain?"

"Chinga tu madre, mira todas estas chichis y cutitas!" Alejandro exclaimed looking at Miss October. "And over here is Meeze April. Ooh, Meeze June also!" With those observations, the inspection immediately shifted from the floors to the walls which were covered in Playboy centerfolds in all of their airbrushed glory.

"You live with this beautiful woman, Lencho!" Alejandro said in amazement. "But you still want more? You are a man with a vast appetite! I want your collection of Playboy magazines, because I think you are too greedy."

"Help yourself, Captain," Lencho replied as he escorted them into Bobby's room. "They are all over here on the table."

A day or two later, they bought a few bags of ready mix concrete from Garcia's hardware store in town and the place looked good as new. The disappointment of the latest near miss was still stinging, however. Eight months had now passed in Andonegui prison.

*****

There was something in the air. Something that was just not right. Perez, El Numero Uno mafia guy in their section, had placed guards at the courtyard gate and closed them at night. This went on for a week, and Lencho asked his neighbor Andrew Cacho what was going on.

"It is Chuey again. He wants to be the big boss. Better be on your guard, Lencho."

"What will happen?" he asked.

"War," was his reply.

A day later, Chuey, a tough as nails hoodlum right out of a Marty Robbins ballad, climbed atop the double building that separated the state prisoners from the federals and made an announcement to all those below. "Listen to me! My men and I are taking over," he bellowed. "Give it up quietly or fight. If you fight, you will die! That is your choice!"

There was a long silence in the courtyard, and then a mafia man yelled out, "Fuck you, puto!"

A minute later, the first pop bottle came flying over the roof. It splattered into a million pieces at the foot of the defiant one, and then came the next. Then another. And another. Within another minute, the men, women, and children who had been sunning themselves ran screaming for their lives, the sky now darkened by the thousands of pop bottles that rained down upon them.

Chuey had long been envious of the wealth in the federal ranks. He sold drugs and ran the soda pop cleaning franchise, but he coveted the money and power of the mafia. Lencho knew him and liked him, but he had sensed this dangerous man had an appetite for power. The war was now on. "Stay inside your rooms," Cacho ordered Lencho and Bobby. "Keep the chica out of sight and you will be okay. Don't come out."

Gunshots rang out and added to the cacophony. Men screamed as they were hit by flying bottles and clubs from the advancing army of state inmates. The Chueyistas stormed the gates, but were repelled by mafia men with pistols. They retreated, regrouped, and then advanced again. This time, they had machetes. The dead and the dying littered the grounds while Lencho slammed shut his doors. "My God, he's outside. Lencho. You gotta save Francisco!" Tamara screamed.

Lencho just stood there for a moment. "Go back out? Are you fucking nuts?!" he yelled.

"I love Francisco," Tamara wept. "He'll be killed. Please, go get him."

Francisco was a handsome parrot with flecks of black in a sea of white around his noble red head. The rest of him was metallic green, and he was cursing in Spanish as the bottles rained down upon his cage.

Hunching his shoulders, Lencho left the room for the courtyard once again. Outside his door, he found Jesus gearing for battle.

"Jesus, where the hell do you think you're going?" Lencho asked the young man.

"They say I must fight," he replied. "Perez says I must fight like the rest."

"Don't be a fool, kid," he told him. "You don't stand a chance. Leave this to the others. It's their war, not ours."

"Perez says I must fight," he replied. Lencho looked at the young man and put a hand on his arm. Then he dashed out to save Francisco.

Bottles came down by the thousands and they darkened the sky like a middle ages battle with archers sending clouds of arrows upon their foes. He knew that the State inmates had plenty of ammo. Tens of thousands of Jarritos, Mierinda, and Victoria soda pop bottles were stacked over in their courtyard. There were teams of throwers lining up to take their turn at heaving the deadly pop missiles. The first row tossed new rounds over the buildings, while the second and third waves re-armed and took the place of the first. Francisco was frantic in his cage as it was battered about in the foray.

"Squack!" the bird cried out. Lencho held his left arm over his head as if warding off the rain. Blood soaked the courtyard as shards of glass crunched beneath his feet. Ten men lay wounded around him as he grabbed the cage from its hook and dashed madly back in the side door to safety.

He glanced one last time to see Toro lose half an arm to a machete blow. Chaos ruled as he turned and fled.

"Here's your goddamn bird," he muttered with relief.

The battle raged for hours and they continued to huddle inside as thudding bottles gave way to sporadic gunfire. Finally, he opened the door a crack. On the floor, sprawled in a pool of blood, was Jesus. He had been shot three times in the gut and his eyes had the faraway look of the dying.

"Oh my god!" Lencho moaned, leaning down over the boy. There was nothing that he could do. Andrew Cacho appeared and also knelt by the dying Jesus.

"I begged him to stay inside," Lencho said sadly.

"Too late for him now," Cacho replied. "He is going to a better place."

"I hope it is better than this," Lencho murmured and went back inside.

Things became quiet after that. A couple of hours later there was a rap on their door. A wild eyed Mexican poked his head inside to announce that the victor was about to make an announcement and wanted everyone out in the courtyard. The three Americans filed out into the glass and blood splattered war zone to hear what Chuey had to say. He stood with a bloody knife in his right hand, high upon his pulpit.

"The battle is over," he announced. "We have won, and I am the new boss. Everything will be as it was. You have nothing to fear. You will still have protection, and you will now make the same payments that you always did, except the payments will come to me instead of those jackals. Those of you who gamble may still gamble. The whores and the drugs are the same, only I am now the boss. To those of you who might disagree, I say this: If you try, you will die! Am I understood?!"

A murmur of assent went up from the crowd. Chuey had won, and he was now in charge, but his victory was short lived. The Mexican army had arrived and was at the gates.

Perez could be seen conversing with men in suits and troops that stood behind them at the front of the prison. Perez was numero uno. The top mafia man. He was only out of power for an hour. Pointing and gesturing towards the battlefield, he made it clear where the insurrectionists could be found. He was equally specific who their leader was.

Soldiers in riot gear and armed with high powered weapons fanned out. Soon the entire compound was locked down and under federal control. Ambulances arrived to carry the dead and wounded from the courtyard. Chuey and fifteen of his top men had nowhere to run. They had not considered the possibility that the government would intervene.

It was off to the bartolina, where they all stayed for two weeks. Perez then issued a decree of his own.

"I want you men to have your way with Señor Chuey and his ladies. You are to show him the love that he deserves for this great disrespect that he has shown us."

For two weeks, Chuey was brutalized. He was taught the terrible lesson of the failed insurgent, and everyone heard about it. They all knew he would never rise up against the mafia again. He was eventually transferred to another prison and died shortly thereafter.

It was just as well, because in a culture of gangster machismo he was no longer a man.

Things quickly settled down. The army occupied Andonegui prison for a month and launched a thorough search and investigation of the events. All weapons, drugs, and booze were confiscated. The wives, children, and girlfriends were expelled. Phones were cut off.

When the Lieutenant in charge got to Lencho and Bobby, he discovered Tamara hiding in the back. "How did you live through this, young lady?" he demanded incredulously. "No matter. The government will not be responsible for your life again.

"You will leave at once."

The director was arrested for incompetence, and all of the guards were fired. The chief of police of Tampico became the acting director, and his cops were made the new guards. When Ronnie came to visit a week later, he showed up at the front gate with a cooler full of Heinekens.

"Who the hell are you? What is in that box?" They asked him.

"Beer, man," he answered. "We're gonna have a party."

He was arrested on the spot and spent ten days in the filthy jail downtown. As soon as it had gotten dark, some tormentor began throwing cockroaches at him.

Chapter Eight

"We Had it All"
Released 1973
Waylon Jennings

I know that we can never live in those times again
So I let my dreams take me back to where we have been
Then I'll stay with you girl as long as I can
Oh, it was so good, oh, it was so good
Oh, it was so good when I was your man.

GOLDWATER

In the world of professional drug smuggling, it is a rarity to find women engaged in the trade. Lencho had never met any until he met Susan Rogue. It was early 1980, and the uprising at Andonegui Prison was still fresh in the minds of all, when a stocky woman of thirty showed up one day to pay Carlos a visit. She was hearty and full of laughter and jokes. Her reason for the visit was to ask for Carlos' help in building an airstrip.

"To get a bulldozer, Susan," Carlos began, "go into town and see my friend Ramon Santos. He is a heavy equipment operator and lives on Calle De Arboles, which is located near the Catholic Church. He will give you a good deal and even load up the dozer and deliver it onsite at the Rancho."

"Is it a good site for an airstrip?" she asked. "I need the location to be out of the way, but not too remote."

Carlos continued, "After you get the dozer, you travel on Hwy 22 for about ten kilometers to a long bridge. The road that you want will be on your left. The Rancho at the end of the long dirt road belongs to my cousin, Jesse Padillo. I have already called him and he is expecting you. His place is perfect, and the cost to you will be very reasonable, because you are a friend."

"How about the load?" she added.

"Two hundred fifty kilograms at seventy-five dollars apiece. It is top of the line stuff from Guerrero. You will not be disappointed."

A week later, she was cutting a strip all by herself on cousin Jesse's property awaiting the arrival of her pilot and plane. She was a seasoned smuggler who had run many loads from all over the country into the U.S. She was both adventurous and fearless. When she was not busy digging up the ground or moving massive boulders out of the way, she hung out at the prison with Carlos and her two new friends, Lencho and Bobby. She and Bobby became an item for a short while until her wandering nature got the best of her and she was suddenly gone like the wind.

Lencho learned a lot from this woman and other air smugglers that he met while in prison. Airplanes were much faster than boats. Using them correctly, however, meant that he had to develop a whole new set of logistics and tactics. Susan showed him that building an airstrip was really not that difficult a task. You first find a suitable location. Next, you move both earth and rocks. And then, you finish it by ploughing away the bumps so that a bush pilot can actually find the damn thing. Once that's completed, you are good to go.

Of all the fellow inmates at Andonegui Prison, few stood out as did Herminio. He was unassuming, but had an inner sense of purpose and power. At forty, he was of medium build, hard as a rock, and athletic. He smoked the mota, but didn't drink, and radiated an aura of ancient wisdom and Indian stoicism. He was serving ten years for running weed down from the Sierra Madre del Sur. He and Lencho talked for hours on end about the trade and prices, and the people that grew it so far up there in the sky.

"You go, my brother, and look at the tall colas glistening in the thin air. You offer them a price, haggle a bit perhaps, and then agree. They harvest your purchase and cure it out as you go on your way to the next village. When you return, it is ready for the descent, packed on mules. You will meet wonderful people that are not corrupted by the greed that has ruined our country. The cost is a fraction of what you would pay in Mexico City. It can be dangerous. There are bandits still, but you will never forget the experience."

"How do I get up there, Herminio?" Lencho asked. "In a helicopter?"

"Helicopter?!" Herminio laughed. "Horses. Can you ride?"

"Does a bear shit in the woods?"

"I'm getting out of here, Lencho," Herminio went on. "I been in this evil place too long and very soon now I will fly away."

"In a helicopter?" Lencho kidded.

When Susan returned to visit a month later, it wasn't Bobby she came to see. It was Herminio whom she had fallen in love with. Herminio who had captured her heart.

"Look, amigo," he told Lencho the day before he left, "you know how to contact me. One way or the other, we will meet again and you will buy the best mota in all of Mexico, and learn what God really is, and where he truly lives." With these cryptic remarks, the two parted company.

That night, around eleven p.m., Herminio went up to the roof of the Federal building. He stood there in the cool breeze blowing in from the ocean. He carefully scanned the horizon and noted the positions of the gun towers, where he guessed most of the guards were dozing. He stood there and stared at the far wall, all fifteen feet of it. He looked down twenty feet below him to the empty courtyard and then removed his shirt and let it fall to his bare feet. Taking a sprinters crouch, he rocked back and forth.

"Be with me, Jesus," he mumbled." He sprang from his perch and flew into the night.

A quarter mile away, Susan sat in an old Ford pickup, waiting at the edge of the vacant fútbol field that Lencho and Bobby had tried to play on so many months earlier. Suddenly, she spotted him in mid-flight. His body emerged from the night; with his head held high and his two legs running in the air, he finally reached the ground thirty feet below. He rolled into a tumble and came up as intact as if he had just walked out the door.

"I was stunned," Susan told them later. "He flew like a stallion with wings!" The lovers had embraced and then vanished in moments. No one even noticed that Herminio was gone until the morning count.

It was a full five months before things began to loosen up again inside the prison. In that time, however, conditions had gotten relatively tough for the boys. Funds were running low and they had to depend on the prison food for sustenance. Diminished capital made it more difficult to pay the monthly protection. If they did not have the protection, things could really get nasty. But resourceful people somehow make the best of situations, and this too was a learning experience for Lencho. He now had Fernando, Carlos, Susan, and Herminio as future allies and assistants.

These people had taught him many things that he knew would open vistas in days to come. As time passed and things began to cool down, the government installed new people to run the prison, and soon a genial fellow named Gustavo Gomez was appointed the director.

Weed returned, as well as the wives, girlfriends, boyfriends, booze, glue, and prostitutes. The whores were once again available on Thursdays and after Mass on Sundays.

"I wanted to speak with you, Señor Lencho," director Gomez began. "Have a seat, please. Lencho, I know you have met La Familia. They have given us a good report on your understanding of our system. There are four components involved – the City, the State, the Federal Government, and, of course, your new made friends."

The director told the weed man that when the day finally came and he was released, if he decided to return to ply his trade he should first seek him out. The director would then be able to clear away any obstacles that Lencho might encounter. He explained there would then be no more unfortunate misunderstandings with the law. It would cost money, of course, but the end result would be smoother transactions for all concerned.

"Thank you, Señor Gomez," Lencho told him. "I agree that your suggestion makes a lot of sense, and I must admit that I do have plans to be back. I now am so much more knowledgeable about your fine country and how things work here. I am sure that we will be able to do business together."

Then Carlos left. His time was up and he, together with his wife and child, walked out of the gate. He would be seeing Lencho again one day in the future, in the U.S.

Lencho began to study aeronautical maps that Susan had provided him. They were tacked up on his walls in place of the Playmate photos the previous guards had absconded with. Many of the inmates at the prison would stop by and go over them with Lencho, pointing out all the spots where airstrips were located.

"You see, my friend," Herminio had said, "here is the Rio Brazo. It is a large river that is chock full of rapids, but we cross it here. We enter the canyon here, and then go up into the mountains of the Sierra Madre. There is a sad story about the airstrip way up here. Two American brothers flew in to pick up loads of weed; they had made the journey many times. They built their airstrip very high up on their last trip. The plane was overloaded; it was an Aero Commander. When they attempted to take off, they were so heavy that the plane plunged in the canyon and crashed into the cliffs. We covered their plane and buried them where they died. No one knows what really happened to them except us. Now, you know as well."

So, there were dangers. Lencho absorbed it all, digested it. He vowed to never use that airstrip.

Now, since the boys were poor, they ate the food the prison provided. The government issued inmate scrip instead of cash. Only Federal prisoners received it. It amounted to about fifty cents per day and everyone automatically handed them over to el numero uno mafia man. In turn, they were able to eat beans, a little meat, noodles in a broth, and piles of tortillas. It wasn't what they had been used to, but it was enough to survive. Everyone had their own bowl and spoon, and the food was ladled out to one and all.

In the past, if they wanted ham and eggs they would simply go to one of the numerous mini cantinas run by the prisoners. Just as everyone had some sort of trade making stuff, many of the men ran their own little eateries out of their rooms. Now, they could not partake in any extras because they were broke.

Lencho also studied Mexican law. Not everyone in Andonegui Prison was a drug dealer or mafioso. In Mexico, you could find yourself in the Penitentiary for all sorts of stuff that one might not even think of as a crime.

There were men who had been in car wrecks or killed someone while driving drunk. Taxi cab drivers, for instance, were very well represented. Then there were the glue sniffers. Many of these wretched souls would get into fights or act crazy and not remember what they had done. They ended up in prison where they continued to buy and sniff glue. And there was Don Lalo, "The Mayor." He really had been the Mayor once of the town of Ciudad Victoria, but had angered an Oligarch by failing to cut him in on some falluca. Now, the man plied his old trade as a lawyer. He had an office up front which included a secretary and a typewriter. It was from this makeshift office that he advised his clients on their respective situations, plotted their legal strategies, and prepared briefs. He did quite well and always wore a suit.

Whenever friends would come to visit, they might dine with them in the nice restaurant up front run by Pepe and his wife, but their guests had to pay.

Lencho continued absorbing and planning. He was learning so much from his new friends that it became clear to him when he finally emerged from this place that he would be very valuable to select individuals back home. He would no longer be in need of someone such as CR, for instance. Granted, CR had his Indian contacts and even spoke the language, but now Lencho was getting pretty good with Spanish, and he too had contacts within the Indian community. And he continued to study the air and airplanes.

The mafias had always beckoned and whispered in his ear that they could get him anything he wanted. Lencho knew that they would follow through with many of their promises, but he simply could not forget his previous experiences with mobsters. He remembered Mugsy and the Italians. He thought about how little George and the Mexican Mafia had threatened him and cleaned him out of everything. For years, he saw the organized crime thugs in action, and he didn't need them. He was always polite and deferential, because it's never wise to piss these characters off but he was a hippy/ independent weed man at heart, and now he had his own contacts to boot. Fuck those guys! Just because marijuana was illegal didn't mean that it would always be so. One day, he believed he would be able to sell it out of a little store like any legal product. The only reason that it was still illegal was because the real crooks, the narcs and politicians, had their own evil purposes. In the meantime, he would continue to play the game but now Lencho was setup to play the game seriously.

* * * * *

Lencho's mom died before he was arrested in Mexico, so she never knew her son had been imprisoned there. He was thankful for that, because she was such a dear lady who had always been on his side no matter what the circumstances. As things continued to get rougher, the brothers decided it was time to reach out to the family in Prescott for help. Fights and threats were becoming common place, and now they were unable to make their regular payments. CR deserted them from the start. He took Lencho's phone calls a few times and then just vanished. The other brothers and close friends had sent money and best wishes, but they were all tapped out. Tamara was forced to go home after the violent uprising, and the boys were becoming fearful for their very survival. And to top it all off, that's when the divorce papers arrived from Karen.

Susie and her husband Arthur began a dialogue with Lencho's father, and it wasn't long before the winds began to shift with the old man. He was still exasperated by the boys' behavior, especially Lencho, but he was eventually persuaded that evil Judge Mejia was a corrupt old shit and was in effect holding his sons hostage. The man assaulted Tamara, stole the big fishing boat, and was now demanding a one hundred thousand dollar bribe to set Lencho and Bobby free. The alternative was another ten years in that rotting hell hole and that was too much for him to swallow. It was time for him to seek out some juice of his own—one of the biggest cats in Prescott, Budge Ruffner.

Budge was a patriarch in the local republican party. He called a very prominent fellow who he thought might step in to help. "Hey Barry," Budge said in his most down home telephone manner. "How ya doing? I appreciate a few moments of your time. Oh, yeah! The parade's gonna go off like it always does on the fourth. You will be here, won't ya? We love having ya. Got a shiny new Cadillac convertible and the prettiest little cowgirls in Prescott to ride with ya. Say, Barry, the reason I called is we got ourselves a little problem with a couple of our boys down in Mexico." He went on to detail the situation Lencho and Bobby were in to Senator Barry Goldwater.

Ever since the presidential campaign of 1964, Budge Ruffner had been a confidant of the conservative senator and believed that, despite his politics, Goldwater might be inclined to use his influence to help a couple of native sons in a pinch. He was also mindful that former President Jimmy Carter had initiated a prisoner swap program a few years earlier.

Within a week, Senator Goldwater made a personal call to Mexican President Jose Lopes Portillo. On the following Friday, director Gomez summoned Lencho into his office. With great excitement, he informed him that he had just gotten off of the phone with El Presidente of Mexico himself! He informed Lencho he and his brother Bobby were to be transferred from Andonegui Prison on Monday, and they would be taken to Juarez to be repatriated to the United States.

"I knew it would happen one day, my friend. I would now like for you to meet two of my associates, señor Flentez and señor Mapulla." Lencho shook hands with the two gentlemen. They were dressed in expensive suits and were obviously some sort of government or law enforcement officers. "Señor Flentez is the Chief of Police here in Tampico, and señor Mapulla is with the Judicial (F.B.I.). I, of course, work for the State of Tamaulipas. You have now met the four corners of a perfect circle," Gomez laughed.

"In this country we are not greedy Lencho. We want you to be successful. If you win, we all win," interjected señor Mapulla.

"Here is my card, Lencho, and I have put my home phone number on the back. I have also spoken with your new friend, Fernando, and I am pleased with your choice of assistance in your endeavors. I have known Fernando's father for many years. The general and I belong to the same golf club, along with Judge Mejia by the way," señor Flentez added.

"Wow, just one big happy family," Lencho quipped.

The director stood and shook Lencho's hand and said, "We can be your best friends or your worst enemy, Lencho. Be sure to call the next time you decide to visit our country."

By now, it was late November and he and Bobby both climbed aboard a small jet to Mexico City. Once they arrived there, they and several other Gringos were rushed to the main jail in the middle of the sprawling metropolis in a six car caravan, lights flashing and horns honking. They felt like the winning team in a Rose Bowl parade as they were swept along towards freedom. Once they had arrived in the downtown facility, they joined a few dozen other Americans. The cell they were placed in was clean and well lit, and all of them were in a pretty good mood as men tend to be whenever a horrendous ordeal is almost over.

Not all of the men were in the dope trade. One good old boy was from Arkansas, and he had been incarcerated for smuggling hacksaw blades and small tools in order to skirt paying taxes. Then there was Gringo Alex, a weed guy from Oxaca who had a big ball of hash shoved up his rectum. When he was able to pass it, it was gonna be party time!

"Gosh darn, fellas," he bellowed, "I swear it's up there. I wrapped it up real good in cellophane back in Gabito, and then I shoved it up my own ass just like that guy over there told me to. Now, the damn thing is stuck and I can't seem to get it out. Any ideas?"

Everybody just looked askance at Alex. "You got it in, pal," one guy told him, "now you can get it out."

"It's your duty, dude," said another. "What kind of Christmas is it gonna be without some hash to smoke?"

"Ok, I'll go sit on the shitter and try harder," Alex moaned.

Finally, after another two hours of constant grunting and cussing, the stuff popped out of his poop shoot.

"Man, I ain't never gonna do that again!" he said as he washed, rinsed, and dried the large ball of hash clean. Once it was sanitized, they all sat around and had a smoke. It was great "shit" and became the cherry on the banana split of their homecoming.

After two more days, the paperwork was completed and fifteen of them boarded another jet, whereupon they winged their way to the border city of Juarez. This is where they would be transferred. By December 2nd, the desert winter had settled in and it was cold. The facility they now found themselves in was not so nice. It was new, but had no heat and they were in misery for weeks. Twelve of the transfers were placed in one large room, and they all thought that they were going to freeze to death. Naturally, the officials at the facility would not lift a finger to alleviate their pain. The boys and their comrades had to wait for a U.S. Federal Judge to come over and explain things to them. God only knew how long that would take.

One bright spot in all of this was the arrival of Tamara and the mafia's assistance once again. A mob guy had a large room all to himself nicely appointed with chairs, tables, lamps, a television, and a king-sized bed. "We were told you were coming and to take care of you. I will make my room available to you and your señorita for a small fee, of course" the goon said. Lencho's family had sent some money, so he rented the room, and he and Tamara cuddled in the chill and did a little catching up on their cusimundo.

This resulted in a new life being presented to the world nine months later. But for the moment, the gang was slowly freezing to death, so they got Tamara to go and find the International Red Cross. As is often the case, the squeaky wheel gets the grease; the Red Cross came to the rescue. They complained to the prison officials, filed protests, and finally prevailed. The officials relented and issued blankets to one and all!

On the morning of Christmas Eve, the Judge showed up so they could be brought before him as they made final preparations for the transfer. Not shackled during their short trip to the municipal building, it occurred to Lencho this was a perfect time to escape. It would be easy. All they had to do was jump out of the car and vanish into the crowd. They could just walk across the border to freedom. He decided not to, however. What if Bobby didn't make it? He could not abandon his brother. He also did not want to disappoint his friends or Senator Goldwater, who had gone to bat for them and made all of this happen. So, they went before the judge who specialized in international legal matters. The judge reviewed their whole case in detail, and it boiled down to this: "You were arrested in Mexico and served some time there. That sentence will continue to run, because that is the way that they do things in their country. It does not matter if you are physically present or not. The time continues until it is up. Now, however, you boys are back in the U.S. where no criminal charges were ever brought against you for all of that marijuana. So, the question you must be asking yourselves is, are we now free to go about our lives as before? Well, the answer is yes and no."

"Yes and no, your honor?" They both asked.

The judge further explained, "The language of the treaty that you are being repatriated under clearly states that there will be a period of probation which will be decided upon in the next few months by a Federal parole board. Most likely, you will be released and placed on probation, but alas, it is not up to me. You are being transferred to the La Tuna Federal Detention Center until that happens. Good luck to you both."

Somehow, it still sounded like the government was getting their pound of flesh on what was in reality a fabricated confession brought about by torture. It was another important civics lesson in the game in which Lencho had chosen to play.

On Christmas Eve of 1980, the boys finally got back to the land of the free. It was a great feeling and since they were down to a hundred and fifty pounds each, they were more than delighted to eat again. Across the border from Juarez is the Texas city of El Paso, and this is where the La Tuna Federal Detention Center is located. It was a large concrete gaol and, like all Federal Prisons, was encased in razor wire fencing. It was also a hell of a lot better to be there than their former abode and, even though they arrived late at night, the guards took them to the food services building and broke out the odds and ends in the refrigerators. T-Bone steaks and milk was served, which was heavenly since they had seen very little of that in the last two years.

Life in La Tuna was typical Federal prison stuff. It was Christmas so there were holiday activities, such as ping pong tournaments, miniature golf, foot races, and bocci ball contests. No angry card games with the last of the food scraps hanging in the balances, or glue sniffing zombies to endure. It was quite civilized, actually. You could even find some tiny pinner joints getting passed around in honor of the baby Jesus' birthday.

However, true of all bureaucracies, the wheels grind very fine and oh so slowly. Just because the boys had never been charged with a Federal crime in the U.S., did not mean they would be released in a day or two. It would be two and a half months before that would happen. Finally they ended up being placed on Federal Probation for a term of five years.

While imprisoned in La Tuna, the boys took classes in Spanish and were given jobs. Lencho was put in plumbing and Bobby in the paint shop mixing colors. There is always a lot of painting in a penitentiary.

Tamara moved in with a Columbian guy and his wife whom Lencho had met briefly. She stayed nearby and was able to visit often. The two were the only brothers in the place, and their release date was March 11, 1981. They made the best of a bad situation for the balance of their stay. An old pal named Greg Wimmer, who lived in New Mexico, was happy to pick up their civilian clothes and meet them in the parking lot on the glorious day they were released. He was leaning on his Oldsmobile when they walked out of the gate, and after a hearty embrace and some high fives, they jumped in and tore out of the parking lot. It wasn't five minutes before Greg broke out a little pipe and some bud, and they fired it up. They then pulled into a gas station and left the funky outfits that La Tuna had donated to them in a trash can. Just like that, they were again two hip Miami Vice type guys ready to take on the world. All oiled up in their cowboy boots, hats, and aviator sunglasses, they headed for the airport to catch a flight to Phoenix, Arizona.

On the plane, they had a couple of drinks, and when they reached Arizona, they were greeted by Ronnie and his girlfriend, as well as Tamara.

They climbed into his immense Suburban and turned on the radio. They lit up another doobie and, man, did it feel good to be home. Lencho was a trifle worried about his new probation officer, but they usually didn't give many urine tests in those days. Now it was time to get busy once again.

Lencho's philosophy: Life is like a shit sandwich, the more bread you got, the less shit you gotta eat.

In Prescott, all of their old friends welcomed them back and the party carried on over the weekend. On Monday, they had to be in the P.O.'s office. On the way up in the elevator, Bobby noticed a lump in Lencho's shirt pocket and reached over to give it a pat.

"That a doobie you got there, bro?" He asked. David Kreen was a pleasant enough guy, but he did not like dope!

"I'm your probation officer, gentlemen, and I want to make things perfectly clear. When you came back into the United States, you de facto admitted to smuggling all of that pot. I don't give a rat's ass that your story was about an uncle or that it wasn't your boat. You did it, and as far as the only uncle that matters is concerned, his name is Sam. Is that clear to you?"

"Yes, Sir!" They recited.

"And, if you screw up, I will violate you. That means right back to the penitentiary to finish where you left off in Mexico. Is that also clear?"

"Yes, Sir."

"I hate dope. That damn marijuana will be the end of America yet. It only leads to heroin addiction and the base nature of human kind. I would rather bust you for robbing a liquor store than to find one lousy joint in your pocket."

"Gulp," they responded.

The siren song of the weed trade is an inexplicable force, and it sang its tune of allure to Lencho as never before. Never mind that he had just spent almost two years in a fetid Mexican prison where he had dodged cock roaches, pop bottles, bullets, and death. Pay no mind to the fact that he had tangled with crooked cops and the mafia. None of that made any difference to the weed man, though for many, this was hard to understand. Lencho was not like other people. He went back to work although now in a new direction. Cultivation.

First, he got a room in a house in town while Bobby wandered off somewhere. This was good as he needed to establish a residence for Mr. Kreen, his probation officer. He went to work doing carpentry jobs and was paid in cash.

All of this wholesome activity made his P.O. a happy man. Once a month, he sent in his paperwork and that was about all there was to it. He just had to be careful. Old pal Ronnie was there as well to provide him a bridge loan of ten thousand dollars, because finances were tight. He didn't have squat, and was forced to start over again from scratch. All of his beloved furniture, collectibles, and sundry items had been swept away by an angry Karen. Everything needed to be reacquired. That was not going to be easy pounding nails for a living. On top of that, Tamara was pregnant.

"Pregnant?" He moaned. "How's that possible?"

"What do you mean how's that possible? Do I have to explain the birds and the bees to a big boy like you?"

"Yeah, but you didn't have to take so seriously what was poked at you in fun."

"Well, I guess I did, and what I want to know is, are you gonna be a good daddy to this baby? Cause if you aren't . . .?" She tapered off quietly and began to sob.

"Aw, come on, babe," he said, holding her close. "I was just kidding. Of course I'll be a good father to our child. I may be wild and even a little crazy at times, but you know that I love children. Especially when they are mine."

They moved out to a cabin in Williamson Valley and furnished the place using the last funds that Ronnie had lent him. A few days later, CR showed up from San Diego.

"Hey jailbird!" he yelled as he bounded out of his Mercedes Benz. "Where you been hiding?"

Even though CR had vanished when Lencho needed him the most, all recriminations fell away like dust, and the two were soon busy downing brewskies and discussing the future.

"Man, I got me some killer seeds. I paid twelve hundred bucks for them. It's an Indica strain from Afghanistan. Where can we raise a crop or two out here in these boonies of yours?"

Lencho knew just the place. Walter Coughran owned eleven hundred acres out in Skull Valley. This was range land with a lot of cotton woods, and was far enough out of town to do the deed with little to no intrusions. Walter wasn't the brightest bulb on the block, but he was good hearted as well as industrious and up for the concept. CR wanted to do his own project, so Lencho hooked him up with some boys down in Walnut Creek who were currently working a mining claim. That grow didn't go well, as the cops got wind of it in its third month, and they had to hurriedly tear out the plants. Growing weed is a perilous endeavor and not for the faint of heart.

The only times that he had ever tried this before was by tossing a few seeds in a pot full of dirt and then sitting it on a window sill or putting it under a one hundred watt light bulb in a closet. A lot of people do that and, of course, it never produces any actual smoke. It takes dedication, hard work, and tender loving care. And luck. It was now early April, and that's the time that seeds go into the ground. He figured he had better get cracking.

Taking their share of the magic seeds to Wickenberg, where Walter knew a guy, they built a small green house to start the plants in and set them out in starter cups. The weather was still cold, but under plastic the plants just took off and grew like crazy. Soon they were over a foot tall with the broad water leaf that characterizes the Indica from other marijuana strains. In the meantime, at the ranch in Skull Valley, they found an ideal spot alongside the river and began to prepare it by laying a thousand feet of water line and digging holes. The soil was very fertile along the dry riverbed and the earth worms were a wiggly testament to the land's fecundity. As good as all of that was, to ensure success the crop would require bat shit.

"Man, I hope the bats don't eat us alive!" Walter complained as they clamored up the cliffs to the caves above the Hassayampa River. "You ever seen them vampire bats bite a man's neck in the movies? It's horrible."

"Walter," Lencho sighed, "these aren't vampire bats, and besides that, they are asleep during the day. We just want some sacks full of their droppings. We're doing them a favor removing their do-do."

The bat guano was blended with the river dirt and all seventy five holes were lined up together with a drip system and an automatic fertilizing device that gave each Afghani baby a dose. Those little puppies grew like corn. They grew so big and so fast you could almost watch. Besides that project, Ronnie began working with CR on his other latest smuggling effort way down in Mexico. As with the boat, this one was inventive as well as colorful, although little by little CR was losing his Midas touch.

Somewhere, he had found Pete 'the paraplegic'. A crippled man in his fifties with a flair for the gospel and steely nerves. He traveled in caravans of Christian fundamentalists that crisscrossed Mexico spreading the good news of the precious blood of Jesus. When the others stopped for a few weeks along the coast, Pete caught up with CR in Oaxaca, Mexico City, or wherever CR had made his latest score. They loaded up the thirty foot Air Stream trailer he pulled with a one ton truck. False floor boards concealed a ton of pot. Then Pete rejoined the caravan going home, and when they all got to the border, he would laboriously climb down from the driver's seat, plop his butt into an electric wheelchair, move ponderously to the rear, and enter his trailer on a lift preaching hell fire and damnation every inch of the way. The whole procedure with Pete and his friends would take most of the day, and he always positioned himself at the end. The guards were invariably so tired of all this that by the time they got to Pete, they made their search quickly just to be done with them. Pete was always polite. He left them with a cheerful 'God bless you,' and then delivered the haul to CR on the other side.

But Pete couldn't get CR to cut him in for a bigger share, so they parted company. Pete knew all of CR's connections by then and figured he would go into business for himself. He bought his own rig and hit the hallelujah trail on his own, which really irked CR.

"Ungrateful cocksucker," CR complained to Lencho.

"Well, maybe you should have paid him more," Lencho replied. "He was taking all the risk."

"That's bullshit," CR fired back. "What could have gone wrong? God was on his side!"

And even though the truck and trailer were his, he never could find a bible thumping paraplegic again. So Lencho told him, "Don't worry about it. I'll hook you up with my pal, Herminio. Use the trailer yourself, and once you get it across the frontier, Ronnie can drive the loads."

But to even get in touch with Herminio was a major effort. Lencho needed to call the nearest town, which was Iguala, and ask the operator to get him a 'Caseta Zero,' which was a secondary transmission to an outpost phone way out in the desert of the Sierra Madre region in El Escondido. From there, someone ran a mile up the hill to find Herminio who lived with his beloved Susan and, now, two children. They arranged the details and CR drove the two thousand plus miles down in his customized rig. The special bells and whistles that had been installed for Pete were removed, and it was basically a normal vehicle again, except that it still could hold half a ton of pot underneath the trailer's flooring.

This caper worked well the first time with CR bringing it to the Mexico-Arizona border area, and then hiring some out of work gringos to carry it across the line out in the toolies. The second time, however, was not so successful. He got the load across, and Ronnie was assigned to do the final drive up to Prescott. He didn't get very far before the United States Border Patrol pulled him over on a dirt road. Ronnie never could drive very well after he had sustained a head injury in an automobile accident a few years earlier. When the cops searched the trailer, they found the weed. They did not believe his lame story that he had just stolen the damn thing. "I ended up stealing a rig full of dope?" he innocently proclaimed. He ended up doing five years in the Federal Penitentiary.

But for Lencho, it was a good and busy time. Loads of weed were arriving from Mexico, his plants were now flowering, and Tamara was getting huge carrying their first child. For legal purposes, he held down a ghost job. His boss would lie for him to Mr. Kreen.

"Just make sure, Lencho," Kreen had told him, "that you get your paperwork in to me on time and make me look good."

"Not a problem," Lencho thought to himself.

In late August, a freak snow storm rolled through. It was very unusual that time of the year, but at four thousand feet in elevation, it could happen. Fortunately, the thermometer didn't drop below 38 degrees, and the sudden change in temperature made the abundantly flowering girls go off the chain.

The plants were an amazing sight to see. They were more akin to seven foot Christmas trees, and if all went well for another month, they would yield many pounds of bliss.

On August 26, 1981, Tamara gave birth to little Fred. Lencho once again officiated at the happy event, assisted this time by a midwife. His second son was an easy delivery.

The Skull Valley crop was deemed ready to harvest on September 24th. The buds were lush and full. The fragrance heavenly. Their thick bracts were so sticky to the touch, it took solvent to remove from the fingers. Lencho and Walt worked carefully over the next three days, clipping the branches as they hung heavy with their bounty. They then spent the next three weeks curing the product in the basement of Lencho's cabin using a dozen electric fans, which supplied a constant breeze through the vegetation and prevented mold.

After that, the buds were manicured, which left only the thick clusters. It was packaged in mason jars and stored in a large freezer. The whole place wreaked of fresh mota, nectar of the gods. Their net yield from the whole effort was seventy-five pounds. It was worth about a hundred grand in 1981 dollars.

In the first week of November, Lencho had just returned from tilling the soil when he heard a knock on his front door. When he opened it, there stood a familiar figure in all his self-assured omnipotence.

"Hey, buddy," Doc said. "Can you tell a guy where he can score a load of Avgas?"

Doc and Malcolm hightailed it to Thailand after the mafia caper blew up. There was blood everywhere over that fiasco, and Doc was not the sort to get splattered if he could help it. From there, he traveled hither and yon, moving weed and cocaine. He finally settled down back in Aspen, Colorado.

"Been working on my Ferrari, chasing broads, and doing a lot of skiing," he informed his old pal. "Been in touch with Charlie Gray, and boy have we got a deal in the works. Whoopee!! I'm damned excited about this one, and you should be excited, too. The reason is simple, buddy. It's worth a cool million dollars to you alone. I know you have influential friends down in Mexico."

Doc had hooked up with another old pal in San Diego named Charlie Gray. Charlie was a man of many interests and talents. Some talents even surpassed Doc's. There was one extra caveat, however, and that was that he had sold his soul to the devil and was now bulletproof. At least until the devil came to collect his debt. Charlie had money from both family, his brother owned a Ferrari dealership in La Jolla, and his innumerable escapades as a hit man and gun for hire the world over.

Once in Africa, some adversaries caught up with him at a steamy hotel in the Congo and put a bullet through his gut. It went in one side and out the other. A Band-Aid later, he was as good as new and ready to kill again. According to him, this invincibility was derived by a belief in Satan. In a voodooish ceremony, he had literally sold his soul for a life of living large, and the devil tossed in being bulletproof on the house. He was in his mid-thirties, tall, lanky, and mean as a snake. He was also a racist from his war years in Africa. He considered blacks the lowest life forms on earth. He took this belief to theatrical extremes, such as when he cultivated large fields of marijuana in the British Colony of Belize. Driving out to inspect the crops being tilled by Negroes, he would stop the car wearing a crisp white linen suit, string tie, and a straw hat.

As a cheroot dangled from his cruel lips, he would scream and generally abuse his poor workers relentlessly. Sometimes, he brought a bullwhip. This then was Charlie Gray: soldier of fortune, pot grower extraordinaire, overseer, taskmaster, and now Doc's new partner.

"I bought a great plane, Lencho," Doc said. "A Queen Air, and she'll carry a ton at a pop. We plan to bring back a really big crop."

"How big?" Lencho asked.

"I'd guess that it will amount to around forty thousand pounds. Twenty tons."

"Holy shit! That's twenty trips all the way from Belize?"

Doc continued, "You stand to make fifty grand a trip. I went to CR and presented the rough outline to him, cause we needed contacts in Mexico. But it appears as though things are beginning to slip away from the boy of late, so that's how I found you. He's a little bit miffed at me right now, but fuck him. It is my understanding you learned many valuable lessons in your little side trip to that Mexican college in Tampico."

"You are correct, my friend. I can arrange the logistics and organize everything connected to Mexico. I even speak the language well enough to get by now. Let me make some calls."

Doc wanted to be ready to roll early in the new year. Flush from weed sales over the past few months, Lencho called Carlos Caldaroni from his Andonegui Prison days, who was now living in New Mexico, and put him, his wife, and little daughter up in a nice hotel in Prescott. Then they sat down to some serious discussions.

"I promised my wife that I would get out of the trade, Lencho," Carlos informed him. "I cannot break my word to her, and so I cannot be a part of this new adventure of yours. I will, however, be more than happy to give you any people I have that can help you."

It is a conundrum of the outlaw life that legitimacy often beckons. This is a source of confusion to those that denigrate all dope dealers as hopeless recidivists, captivated by their life of crime and thus unwilling to ever fully leave it behind them. At the same time that Lencho was preparing and participating in marijuana capers all over the globe, he too was secretly yearning to leave it and pursue the music business instead.

"Carlos gave it up. He gave it all up for his wife and kid. I have a woman and a couple of kids, so why can't I get out? Well, for one thing, I sure as hell ain't gonna shovel shit," was his usual lament.

*****

Just like in 1978, Lencho knew it could be a big success to stage a show on July 4th in Prescott, Arizona. His original mentor, Richie Albright, had urged him to keep his dream alive. Waylon himself told Lencho that he would back him all the way, even promising to bring along Hank Williams, Jr., Willie Nelson, and others, if he could find a way to leap the hurdles that the blue noses of Prescott politics and civic affairs had thrown in his way.

Sponsors both large and small were interested in putting up the funds for promotion of the event, and that included names like Budweiser, Pepsi Cola, Ford Motor Company, and Marlboro. He even had the idea cleared with the Arizona State Police, the County Sheriff, the planning commission, and just about every other governmental department. Wide support existed all over the business community.

The reason was simple. The event would bring in thousands of visitors and fill up the hotels, restaurants, and retail shops. It was going to equate to some "Big Bucks" for the community, and everyone was excited!

"I'm going to be out of the dope business at last!" Lencho exulted to his friends. "I'm going to be a legitimate promoter from now on."

He was so confident that things were moving right along that he took a moment in his busy schedule to run down to Nashville and visit with Richie Albright. He jumped on a plane out of Phoenix and was in a hotel room in nothing flat but when he arrived and called Richie, there was no answer. He kept at it, but could not find the guy. He left message after message. On the second day, Lencho's phone finally rang. When he picked it up, Richie said, "Hey Lencho, this is Richie. I'm in the hospital man. I set myself on fire while I was working on one of my cars. Come down and see me; I need some company."

Richie had always been a car buff, and while doing repairs on an old '55 Ford Fairlane, he poured some gas in the carburetor and it ignited. He was burned pretty good. There he was wrapped like a mummy, sitting in bed with tubes, pumps, bottles, and drips hanging everywhere.

"Damn, Richie!" Lencho said. "You look terrible! Good thing I brought some really great weed down here just for you."

"I sure could use a smoke," he groaned. "Pull your car around back and let's get the hell outta here for a little while."

The record producer and Lencho bopped out the back door leaving all of the medical equipment behind and drove a few miles to an old cemetery. There, among the moss covered headstones dating back to the Civil War, the two got reacquainted while smoking the pot Lencho and Walter had cultivated up in Skull Valley. Richie wore only his hospital gown, and it was a tad cool in the late afternoon, but the company of his old friend and the great weed began to warm him up.

"Well, damn son," Richie lamented. "I'm sure sorry about my accident. Sorry for both of us. I had planned to take you around the scene and introduce you to a bunch of people in the industry. I've been working with many of the greats.

Obviously, I can't now, so this is what you should do. Go and see the new gal I'm working with. Her name is Marsha. Take her out, and she'll teach you a thing or two! I'm right in the middle of a production with Waylon Jennings and Emmy Lou Harris and this shit happens to me! I should be outta the hospital in a couple of days and I'll catch up to you. Here's her phone number."

Marsha Beverly was going to be the next big thing. She was vibrant and funny with wit and verve. Her songs were meaningful and she sang them with conviction. She seemed to know everyone in Nashville. Among them was the Cash family, and they were in need of some mota. "She's been bugging me for weeks to find her some pot," Marsha told the weed man. "Can you help her out?"

"I only brought a couple ounces," he replied. "The next time I come, I plan to bring ten pounds. I got a lot of friends here that depend on me. But for the daughter of the legend. I guess I can spare one ounce. It's super stuff, though, and it costs three hundred bucks. Is she good for it?"

"Oh sure," Marsha assured him. "Give it to me, and I'll give it to her. She'll pay you before you leave."

Lencho really liked Marsha Beverly and they hit it off immediately. She liked to smoke and drink and party. A bit too much, he thought, but that was life in the music business. She introduced him to important people in Nashville, some of whom became customers. A few days later, he prepared to fly out to Las Vegas and catch up with Waylon, who was performing at the Stardust. Marsha would be joining them there as well. Before he left for the airport, he asked her about the money owed by Ms. Cash. "I just got off the phone with her," Marsha replied. "I told her you're leaving and she said she would be right over. She wants to meet you."

"Well, damn! I gotta get out of here. I'll miss my flight. I can wait another hour max."

"Let me call her back." Marsha assured him she was going out the door as they spoke. Cash never arrived, and Lencho's feelings were hurt, not to mention the three hundred dollars she owed him.

The gig at the Stardust was a typical Richie gig. Crazy as hell with the booze flowing, the coke snorting, and the air thick with the aroma of weed. Waylon was great as usuall and clearly felt no pain that night. To add to the moment, a little boy in a natty tux was led on stage to be introduced to the audience. It was Shooter Jenninings, youngest addition to the outlaw music tribe and three year old son of Waylon and his wife Jesse Coulter A bit on the blurry side, Lencho told Richie, Waylon and little Shooter so long and headed back to Prescott. He needed to check on the crop and update the ongoing arrangements for the big Fourth of July bash.

Marsha arrived in Prescott a week later and Lencho booked her a one night gig at Matt's on Whiskey Row, where she was fabulous. The world was Lencho's oyster, at least in Prescott, where he could not even buy himself a drink and according to many in town, Marsha was the next big thing.

After the show, Lencho and Marsha were off to Hollywood to the Happy Sack Recording Studios on Van Nuys Blvd. He had difficulty finding Marsha before they left Prescott, although he hunted both high and low for the girl. She had apparently found herself a good looking cowboy and vanished.

At the studio in Hollywood, Brian Ahern was producing an album. He and Emmy Lou Harris had been married, and although now parted, they still made some great music. Lencho's pockets were filled with pot, coke, and cash. He partied with one and all behind the locked doors of the studio. Emmy Lou, passed on the smokes and white powder, but instead asked Lencho to get her a bag of chips and a small bottle of tequila. Since she was a country music goddess, he happily obliged.

After the party ended in Hollywood, he and Marsha headed back to Scottsdale, Arizona, where she was scheduled to make her world debut at a club called Wranglers. Lencho had only seen her perform once at Matt's, which was by comparison a small venue. Wranglers was big and loud, and the poor girl got serious stage fright before she went on.

 All dressed up in her cowgirl outfit, sequins from head to foot, and cute little cowgirl boots, she began belting down shots of tequila. Everyone knows that you can drink beer and get away with it. You can even drink wine and whiskey, but when Mr. Tequila walks into the room, it's all over. So it was for the talented Marsha. She was falling down drunk and obnoxious by the curtain call, and the manager told Lencho to get her the heck out of there. Richie was so mad that he dropped her. He had spent a lot of money promoting her only to have the common curse of drunkenness bring it all crashing down. Marsha left town with her tail between her legs, and no one ever saw her again.

Later, Lencho heard that another reformed drunk picked her up and asked her the age old question, "Have you heard the good news, sister?" That's how Marsha met Jesus.

Lencho found a spot in Chino Valley that was perfect for the 1982 Fourth of July concert. It was owned by an old guy named Bizjack, and was right in the middle of the Tri-City area of Prescott, Chino, and Prescott Valley. This time, he had gone to all the bureaucrats for permission and to every business owner who stood to profit from the huge crowds expected to attend, and everyone was on board. One of his biggest boosters was the Chief of Police in the town of Chino, Pat Huntsman. Pat was a stocky and vivacious woman who was aware of Lencho's past involvement in the marijuana business. She was impressed that he had reformed. Her idea of law enforcement was based on rehabilitation and new found legitimacy, which was a goal that Lencho was warming up to more and more.

On top of all this, he had commissioned a private consultant to evaluate the potential cash influx to the area that the event would generate. He happily passed on the analysis to the City Council and to any business people he spoke to. The figure for Chino alone could amount to as much as three hundred thousand dollars. The total for the entire vicinity would amount to a whole lot more.

Then the letter writing campaign began. Lencho believed that it had been started by an arch conservative named Tom Perkins and then abetted by the biggest gun dealer in the area along with the Chamber of Commerce. It was ironic that the Chamber was so set against a business venture its members were bound to benefit from financially. The letters poured in to the local newspaper with bitter and hysterical complaints that the crowds would be violent and unmanageable. They would cause vast traffic congestion and litter the entire area with country music putrescence. The cash boom be damned! The Tri-City didn't need a bunch of dope smoking weirdos hanging around and dancing like savages to loud music until all hours of the night.

By March, Lencho's second attempt at legitimacy was dead. The great musical dream was over. It had been crushed by reactionaries. Lencho was extremely angry and depressed as he sat watching Tamara nurse little Fred. "What now?" He thought.

"Lencho," she said, not looking up. "I'm pregnant again."

In stunned amazement, he stood up from his chair and smacked a palm to his forehead. "You're what? You told me that a woman can't get pregnant while she's breast feeding."

"That's what the La Leche League told me, but when I asked Amber the midwife about it the other day she said it's bullshit. Anyway, I think it's gonna be a girl this time."

Lencho just sat back down and stared out the window.

*****

Lencho needed money, so he and Walter set about to start their second crop in Skull Valley. All of the infrastructure was in place now. They pollinated some females the previous years, so with the seed stock they began anew. At the same time, brilliant Walter was talking to an old but larcenous pal named Roy Cooper about stolen cows. Cooper worked on a big ranch not far from Skull Valley, and he persuaded Walter to buy some of the stolen cattle. It would be only a couple, but cattle rustling is still a big deal in the west. Even though they don't hang you anymore, it still can mean jail time. After learning of last year's marijuana crop, Cooper suggested to Walter that he knew a perfect spot on his ranch where the boys could grow an enormous crop that nobody would ever discover.

Walter spoke with Lencho about it, and afterwards they both went to inspect the area in question. They had to agree it was ideal for a big grow. It was remote with lots of water and ground cover to camouflage up to five hundred plants. That could mean a million dollars, give or take. So, the two went for the offer and set about buying the pumps and irrigation equipment they would need, and also began digging lots of holes. A second, secret location in Skull Valley was also started just in case.

Starter plants were begun down in Wickenberg just as before, and they worked long hours to get it accomplished within the time frame of spring planting. Although Lencho still dreamt of one day leaving the dangerous world of weed, he couldn't do it yet. Not after being shot down on his Diamond K plans. He would keep on trying because that was his nature, and pot was what he knew best. When it worked, it was tremendous. Besides, going to work each day as, say, a janitor was pretty dispiriting. Also, the marijuana business was evolving. He knew that growers had begun to migrate to Humboldt County and beyond, growing exceedingly fine domestic product. The climate and conditions in California were ideal with long sunny days in the summer and virtually no nasty weather. Even in the farm states, such as Illinois and Iowa where corn was king, people were beginning to plant large marijuana crops. Domestic pot was going to be a happening thing and would only get bigger. The weed that came from Mexico had often been a mixed bag and was frequently of low quality or damaged in shipping. It could be slapdash. Of course, the growers of Michoacán, Oaxaca, and Guerrero were masters of the trade and did a fantastic job, but it was rigorous to bring their product to market, as Lencho had discovered the hard way. It was apparent to many that the Mexican mafias were organizing themselves into several cohesive cartels, and that they would soon run the entire marijuana industry in Mexico as a true vertical integration similarly as they did with opium and heroin: "From the farm to the arm." So, too, it would be with pot. They would grow it, ship it, and then smuggle it across the border with hordes of illegal aliens as their couriers. They would sell it in all the cities and towns across the US, where their Mexican distributors had established beach heads. One day these new cartels would rule the entire illegal drug world, including of course the greatest prize of all, America itself.

So, these things were on his mind as he and Walter set out to grow two really big crops to make up for some of the damage of 1982. However, as it turned out again, Roy Cooper was a rat. He had sold his soul and worked for the cops. In this case, it was for an agent named Dave Grantham who was with the Cattle Inspection Department of the Arizona Agricultural Center. Roy the rat told Dave Grantham that he had a live one for him. Not only can he arrest Walter for conspiracy to purchase a couple of stolen bovines, but also Walter's partner in crime, a fellow by the name of Lencho, who was growing a gazillion marijuana plants out on his ranch!

For an educated man, Walter could be pretty dim as he sat at a table in a bar with Cooper and Agent Grantham bragging about last year's fine weed crop, while finalizing the sale of the stolen cattle. He even showed the two a nice bud. Now that Grantham had got his man dead to rights on the cows, he decided to wait for the pot to grow.

Lencho and Walter had the spot all prepared, and brought up their seedlings from Wickenberg after the last frost. No sooner had they planted them, Grantham swooped on their project in a helicopter with fifty agents and cops from various agencies he had pulled into his posse. Lencho learned about it that afternoon while he was having a drink with his attorney at the St. Michaels Bar on Whiskey Row. It was the big story on "Live at Five."

Lencho's jaw practically hit the bar rail as he pointed numbly at the television. "What's it all mean?" He asked his lawyer.

"It means the cops are looking for you, buddy. I better get on down the street to the Sheriff's office and see what the hell this is all about. Stay here, I'll be right back."

But Sheriff Curly Moore of Yavapai County had no idea what Attorney Howard Hinson was even talking about.

"Well," he said to the Sheriff, "Lencho and I were just watching the evening news and Maricopa County says that they are looking for him in connection with a big pot bust."

"Maricopa?!" Moore thundered. "Them sons of bitches have done it again! Invaded my territory and never told me a damn thing. Get Lencho over here now. I'm gonna make some calls, but since I have not heard a thing on this, I may just O.R. him on the spot."

That's what the Sheriff did, too. Accepted a self-surrender with his attorney present, and then cut Lencho loose on his own recognizance. That enraged Sheriff Jerry Hill of Maricopa County next door as well as agent Dave Grantham. But this was the second time in Lencho's life he had seen the end of another million dollar enterprise and been arrested in connection with cattle.

He had a long rap sheet for marijuana, and had recently been imprisoned in Mexico. Lencho figured he was screwed. He thought it might be time to stop at the cemetery himself on the way out of town. It looked like there was no other way.

Lencho still had some time before his case would go to trial, so it would not be necessary to split until the fall. In the meantime, he was nervous, depressed, broke, and bummed out in general. To earn some money, he returned to working odd jobs and, since the cops didn't know about the second Skull Valley grow, they continued to tend to it while praying that nothing else would go wrong.

Wishful thinking. Everything seemed to be cursed that year. The first of October, when Lencho went out to harvest his plants, they were gone. Almost all of the crop had been yanked up hours before they arrived. "This is fucking incredible!" he howled. "Why me, lord?"

"Why not you?" the Lord seemed to answer. Walter dropped to his knees and sniffed the ground. Being the tracker and hunter that he was, he followed the footprints and water leaves a mile to where a car had been parked. The car tracks let to the highway five miles further. Later on, they learned it was those shiftless Webb boys one ranch over. The Webbs couldn't haul all the plants pulled, so they left behind ten to twelve. Very white of them, indeed. As most weed growers know, getting your crop ripped off is a terrible, yet common, experience.

At the beginning of May, Lencho went to see his new attorney for a last minute briefing. "We go to trial Tuesday," he told him. "I'll be honest with you, it does not look good. I can't get any more continuances, and they have a ton of evidence. The informant is even going to testify, if you can believe that. I advise you to get your affairs in order."

"How long?" Lencho asked.

"Could be as much as fifteen years."

Lencho went out to see Walt after that to discuss the situation over a beer.

"I think I'm screwed, buddy," Lencho said. "Unless there is a miracle, they are going to send me away for a long, long time. I don't see any reason that you should go with me."

"We're in this together," Walt replied. "They got us both."

"Not necessarily. I want you to go to the prosecutor and tell him that you will cooperate. Tell him that you will testify under oath that it was all my idea."

"Testify against you? To save my own ass? That would make me as bad as that shit head Cooper."

"No, it won't. Just do it, Walt. I got my reasons, and no one will blame you for anything. Drink that beer, and then go see the guy. Get it all in writing, and make sure that they agree not to seize your ranch."

By the end of the day, the D.A. and Walt had reached an agreement and papers had been signed. It was a done deal. The following Monday, Lencho left town. A couple of guys who owed Lencho some money settled up with him by handing over the title to a Honda 650. It was clean and in good condition. As he looked at its gleaming chrome spokes he knew that the gods would show him the way as they always had.

To get off to a fast start, Doc called and said he was sending a new I.D. From now on, Lencho would be known as Eric John McKenzie, born in Baton Rouge, Louisiana, in 1947.

"Go out and get yourself a driver's license in New Mexico and start life again," Doc said. "Go and sin no more."

A roommate was found to rent a house with Tamara and the children. The day before he was due in court to face certain imprisonment, the newly minted Eric J. McKenzie jumped on his shiny motorcycle and sped off into the night. He was now officially a fugitive. With the birth certificate provided by Doc, he obtained a social security card and a driver's license in New Mexico. He visited with Carlos for a week, not in any particular hurry to be anywhere. There was really nowhere to go, and it was a nice change from his usual frenetic pace. After a week of idleness, he rode out to the coast and caught up to CR in San Diego.

Always the schemer and high octane entrepreneur, CR was now working with a maniac freelance pilot and killer for hire.

"Where do you find these guys, CR?" Lencho, a.k.a. Eric, asked.

"The guy's got balls," he replied. "I got tired of putting a ton of money into boats, trucks, and trailers. Now, I got Jack the Wack, and he steals whatever is needed. That's a lot cheaper, man. Really reduces my overhead. The plane I'm using now, for example. He stole it."

"Did you get him from Doc, by any chance?" Lencho asked pointedly.

CR grunted and walked off. Lencho went back to work with his old partners. He was sent deep into Mexico to hook up with Herminio for some weed, and to begin serious recon on airstrips, fuel, and communications for what was to come.

Jack met him deep in the Guerrero Region a few weeks later. Lencho couldn't stand the psycho.

"You ever kill anyone?" Jack asked. "It ain't hard. Just like killing a cat when you were a kid. Ever killed cats? No? Pussy!" The guy was right out of central casting.

Jack's life's work of killing people for hire, stealing airplanes, and smuggling dope had been pretty profitable up to that time. He was out of Montana, and his plane was a large Cessna 310. He flew down to meet Lencho who was staying with Herminio in El Escondido. Herminio and Susan had split up and she vanished into the ether. Herminio was alone now and said that he missed her. "But that is Susan, Lencho. She is a child of the wind. She couldn't stay in one place very long."

From Mexico City, Jack left without filing a flight plan, as was required. He met Lencho at an unregistered airstrip in the silver town of Taxco, high in the Sierra Madre Mountains. They flew down to a dirt strip in Arcelia to meet Herminio, who was waiting for them with a thousand pounds of weed for immediate transport. After taking off, Lencho informed Jack, "We're four hours from Saltillo, where I've got Avgas waiting."

"What's wrong with this door?" Lencho asked as they pulled out four hours later. "It's screwed up and I can't get it to latch."

"Oh yeah. It acts up now and then. Push out and then slam it. Don't fallout," he laughed.

But the door wouldn't close, and there was no way that they could land and fix it. So, on they flew across Mexico and over the border without incident towards White Sands, New Mexico. All the way Lencho had to hold the door closed with his very sore and tired hands that were beginning to cramp. The drag from the open door caused them to lose speed so that by the time they reached the airstrip in the desert where CR was to meet them, they were two hours late and it was as dark as doom. It was pushing 8:00 pm and, although the moon was full, they were totally disoriented and almost out of fuel.

"Where the fuck are you guys?" CR bitched over the blue bird radios they were using. "I've been worried sick."

"Long story," Lencho called back. "We know you're down there someplace, but we can't figure out where. Can you see us now?"

"Can't see shit," he called back.

The Cessna made another general pass around the area where they guessed that they should be in, and then, with the luck of the gods, CR spotted their silhouette as it passed in front of the moon.

"La Luna, man!" he yelled. "I see you. Watch close for my car lights. I'm parked in front of the airstrip."

Jack may have been a killer and a maniac, but he was a pretty good pilot. Once he got his bearings, he set the big plane down with a tremendous bounce. The landing gear hit the ground and she blew back up a hundred feet. Lencho simply could not believe that the plane could hold itself together. Then he brought her back for another bounce, and yet another, until they coasted to a stop.

"If I could've seen where I was going, it would have been much smoother," Jack muttered.

In a flash, trucks came out of the darkness and men unloaded the weed with precision and speed, and then were gone into the night. The famous three minute offload.

CR had a house rented in nearby Roswell, so the product was taken there and stashed. For the next week, buyers came and went. They then tidied up a bit and abandoned the place.

Lencho, a.k.a. Eric J. McKenzie, was a man with no country now. He headed back to Mexico looking for new opportunities.

Chapter Nine

"I'm a Ramblin' Man"
Released 1974
Waylon Jennings

I've played in California
There ain't too much I haven't' seen
No there ain't
Lord, I'm a ramblin' man
Don't fool around with a ramblin' man

SIERRA MADRE DEL SUR

Carlos made arrangements for Lencho to meet Roberto in Reynosa on the Texas-Mexico border, and now he was there to make introductions to the fellow that would be his guide and right hand man for the next two years.

Roberto Azua was a legal pharmaceutical salesman by trade. His route ran between the border and Tampico, Mexico. He would stop at drugstores taking orders for medication and pills of all descriptions as well as off the shelf items. Roberto was married to a plump little woman and had two children. He and his wife also owned a small grocery store.

With Roberto in tow, they drove down the Gulf Coast to Tampico, determined to locate Fernando, who Lencho met through Señor Legedeta at the Andonegui Prison a couple of years earlier. They needed Fernando to help set up the airstrips that would be used to run huge amounts of marijuana into Mexico from Belize. A massive plantation effort was currently under way under the supervision of mercenary task master Charlie Gray.

Over the next few months, Lencho flew back and forth between Mexico and the U.S. on an almost constant basis. He had a family to look after and meetings to conduct with Doc and CR. Doc regularly provided him with the funds he needed for coming ventures. It was imperative that he locate Fernando. They began their search by visiting the Andonegui Prison.

"Are there any Gringos here?" he asked the ladies at the visitation desk. He was informed there were a couple of Americans in the prison, so Lencho went to town and bought the men some presents. He bought things that he would have liked to have had when he first arrived at the prison himself, such as stationary, music tapes, toothpaste, and soap. When he returned, he was allowed to visit the rag tag looking hombres who were also incarcerated for smuggling marijuana. They smoked some weed, drank beer for a few hours, and he filled them in on events and news occurring back home. Lencho asked whether they knew a lady lawyer named Sandra Vite. One of them said, "Yes, I met the woman a week earlier. You can find her in Tampico where she maintains an office."

He looked her up in the phone book and gave her a call. She passed along the word to some of Fernando's compadres that a man named Lencho was looking for him.

They finally met at La Perla Restaurante, a quaint little seafood joint where the wealthier locals congregated. He showed up accompanied by a couple of bodyguards, not quite certain what to expect.

"Lencho, my friend!" Fernando exclaimed. "Of course, it is wonderful to see you."

"Fernando," he replied. "Long time no see. Why the pistoleros?"

He looked sheepish, and then answered, "Oh, them? Well, I was not certain that you were not a cuckold husband who wanted to murder me for fucking his wife."

"Same old Fernando," Lencho laughed.

They discussed old times and the future, and Fernando announced he would be more than happy to enter into Lencho's employ as a guide and advisor on aeronautical matters. "Where do you want to start?" he asked, sipping his fifth cerveza. "I got crop duster strips to large airports we can utilize. Desert strips and grass strips. I have personally used them all and know everyone connected to them."

With Azua and Fernando as part of the team, Lencho was convinced all the infrastructure needed for the big venture was attainable.

"Where I have been landing my falluca is on a ranch owned by Señor Kline. He works for Pemex. He allows me to land there and I, in turn, fix him up with untaxed goods. We can also work a deal for you," Fernando told him.

Driving north in Azua's car, the three men reached a town called Aldama. There they turned east and headed towards the beach. The area was marshy and full of cattle. These bovines stood hip deep in the water, chewing their cud. An hour later, they arrived at Sr. Kline's Rancho. It was a lovely property situated amongst rolling meadows. Several small out buildings surrounded a large, custom built swimming pool. Kline resided in the largest unit, which was decked out in African milieu. He was a big game hunter and the walls were adorned with many trophies. A stuffed lion growled silently in a corner and the floors were covered with hand tied carpets and animal skins. African art festooned the place from one end to the other. Power was provided by a generator on the periphery, and the people of Mexico who bought their petrol from the State monopoly paid for Kline's electricity. On the edges of the property, a three thousand foot grass runway greeted the sky. A river passed through the property, and at the dock there were boats that could take fishermen out to the sea.

"Sweet," Lencho smiled. "Very nice indeed. This will be perfect for the Belize run. Right across the Gulf of Mexico to here. It's a clear shot."

Fernando also took them to other nearby strips with many having excellent repair services available, as well as fuel. Pleased with the start, Lencho gave Fernando five hundred dollars and they shook hands on their new partnership. Then he flew to Dallas to meet Doc.

*****

"Here's fifty grand, buddy. Go and buy us some dope," Doc said.

Lencho fingered the bundles of hundred dollar bills and gazed out the window. "This time I'm gonna do it differently," he replied. "This time I'll go to the source. The Sierra Madres with Herminio."

"You mean up the cliffs on a horse? The mule packs? The bandits and all that?" Doc asked.

"Why not?" the weed man replied. "You only live once, right?" He left that night for Mexico City where his compadres were waiting. Their first stop was the currency exchange, where the dollars were changed to pesos.

"This is a perfect time to be doing this, Lencho," Fernando informed him conspiratorially. "Through my friends at Pemex, I got word a huge caper is about to take place!"

"What kind of caper?" Lencho asked.

"Financial manipulation, my friend. The Peso is at 350 to the dollar. Monday, it is projected to be over 800 Pesos to the dollar. We will wait until then to buy Pesos, not before. We will make a killing!"

"If you say so," Lencho told him. "Let's go and see the sights over the weekend. I have been through this city many times, but have never really toured the place."

"I have something in mind that is better than seeing the sites," Fernando replied. "I want you to meet a very important and valuable person. A lady."

Ceaser and Fernanda Biastryos were in their early thirties and lived in the penthouse suite of a seven story apartment building in the downtown area near the Vatican Embassy. It was also just a stone's throw from the University and the couple were part of the upper social echelons. He was a television producer, director, and choreographer. She was a pilot, among other things, and her father was with the Port Authority and enjoyed a lot of clout. Fernando believed her father could help Lencho with his never ending headaches regarding aircraft paperwork. This had been a problem ever since he had become Eric McKenzie, and when using aircraft in the smuggling trade, it was necessary to have authentic looking paperwork showing that a plane was owned by someone other than yourself.

Fernanda reminded Lencho of Charo, with her bright red hair and lipstick. She was busty and vivacious and spoke excellent English with a British accent, as that is where she had received her formal education. Lencho thought that this was all very cute, even humorous. The two hit it off at once. He felt instinctively that he could trust her. He also recognized that their relationship would be strictly as friends and business partners. He wasted no time in telling her his life story, and about his business interests. When they finally left the home of the Biastryos at one a.m. that morning, Lencho told Fernando how much he enjoyed meeting this woman and how impressed he was with her.

"She truly is a lovely lady," Fernando agreed. "And by the way, her husband is a fag."

*****

On Monday morning, they entered one of the many exchanges that dot Mexico City. On a big board above the counter was posted the current rate of exchange, and sure enough, it now stood at 810 pesos to the dollar. He exchanged the entire wad of dollars into over 30 million pesos, accepting ten thousand peso notes, Mexico's largest denomination. They nervously jumped into a cab and headed directly back to their hotel room. Lencho spent the next two hours sewing currency into his pants and shirts. He doubled up pairs of underwear and padded them with millions. Money was taped to his legs and around his waist. He could barely walk, there was so much. He was a human money bag, but it was the only reasonably safe way he could carry that much cash. The very favorable exchange rate had tripled his capital.

Stiff and sore from his cash burden, he climbed into Azua's Ford. They waved goodbye to Fernando and drove south on 95 towards Iguala. It was time to meet up with Herminio and climb the great mountains of the Sierra Madre Del Sur. Seven hundred miles of rugged peaks, marijuana, soldiers, and banditos. It would be an epic journey, and he would glean invaluable experience learning and becoming an expert at understanding the many complexities of the marijuana trade. It also meant the difference of hundreds of percentage points in savings. A kilogram of weed purchased at 8,000 feet from an Indian grower cost 2,500 pesos. In Mexico City, the same kilo was 35,000 pesos.

Reaching Iguala, he called Herminio using the casita transfer. A few hours later, they finally reached the remote outpost of El Escondido at the base of the Sierra Madre range. They had traversed from marshes through verdant meadows, then to mountains and now desert flat lands that were harsh and inhospitable. It was the real Mexico down there. Right out of a Sergio Leone movie. Hard bitten characters with bad teeth dotted the landscape. He patted the money taped to his body and whistled past the cemetery.

"I'm glad that you are here," Herminio greeted Lencho. "The trip down can be a little perilous at times."

"The roads were rough," admitted Lencho. "But we did alright. I look forward to the mountains. Now, we are going to go after our own treasure of the Sierra Madre."

"I have bought you a horse. He's a very good one. You told me once you were a cowboy. Now we shall see."

A tiny general store doubled as the town center and rodeo grounds. This was cowboy country after all. Lencho walked with Herminio to where the three-year-old stud quarter horse was tied up. He was a handsome devil, saddled up and ready to go. There was a look of bemusement on Herminio's face, and by the size of the crowd, the weed man had an inkling they were looking forward to a show. Maybe this caballo was actually el diablo, and they were expecting him to get flung off onto his head. This called for a conversation. Lencho stroked the big fella's muzzle soothingly, and then he leaned close to a flicking ear to have a chat.

"I'm gonna climb aboard, my friend, and I don't want to be embarrassed. We're gonna be going on a long journey into uncharted territory, and it would be best if we got off to a good start. You treat me good and I'll treat you better. Is that a deal?"

"Amigo," one of the audience called out, "that caballo is just a little rank. Don't hurt yourself!" The crowd laughed heartily.

The horse leaped into a spin the second Lencho mounted. Then he started to jump; he acted like he had never been ridden before. This horse was a sun fishing son of a gun, and the weed man raised his right arm. It was like being back in Prescott when he was a kid.

"Eeeooo!!" he hooted. The boys on the rails hooted back and the dust thickened. Then the quarter horse settled down. It was like he had made his point, showing his spirit and independence. This horse was not for the faint of heart, but Lencho had passed the test. He strode proudly in an arch, and the assembled burst into applause. Lencho pulled off his hat and waved it to one and all with a nod of his head. They would leave the next day.

"This is late September. Is the weed ready for harvest, yet?" Lencho inquired.

"Not quite. The growers judge it by the corn. When the corn is ripe, so is the mota. By the time that we reach them, it will be perfect."

Lencho and Herminio waved goodbye to Azua, and he drove back the way that they had come. His pharmaceutical route was in need of servicing, and they would hook up again for a refuel stop later.

Lencho and Herminio left early the next morning, but they were not alone. Ten men had been hired by Herminio; with their rifles, the men accompanied them as guards for the caravan. If they ran into bandits, they stood a better chance surviving with a small army. Lencho rode his chestnut colored stud, a fine strapping beast. The others walked. They began at the Rio Balsa.

When the river reached the base of a great cliff, it disappeared into a rocky gorge and they began taking switchbacks dug into the sides of the hills that Lencho would never have guessed had been there at all. Fortunately, his trusty and sure footed mount did. After three hours, the desert flats began to fade from the horizon below into a wide expanse of yellow glare. The scrub and cactus turned to greenery, and the men with rifles slung across sturdy shoulders sang corridos about those that had traveled this way before, some of whom had not returned.

Lencho's jailhouse Spanish was good enough to understand words like "mota" and "pistolero."

"What is this song about?" he asked Herminio as they took a turn upward on the trail.

"It's an old favorite," he laughed. "It used to play on the radio all the time. It's about some gringos who go to get the mota, but the bandits get them instead. Very popular!"

At the top, the switchbacks ended and they came into a meadow that crested the two thousand foot cliff they had just ascended. In the distance, waterfalls fell majestically from even more cliffs and the trees became noticeably thicker.

"This is where we will sleep tonight," Herminio announced.

"Where?" Lencho asked, noticing the absence of grass or anything soft.

"Here. On the ground."

The guards were already unfurling blankets and bedding for the evening. It was dusk, and after a spare meal of tortillas, cheese, hard tack, and water, everyone fell fast asleep. Even Lencho, despite the lack of a bed.

At dawn, they were up and gone. Two hours later, the troop reached a set of bluffs attached to a mountain of granite and sandstone. The pines thickened as they climbed ever higher through meadows between the peaks. Brightly plumaged birds flew from the trees gawking and crying as they spied the weed man on his great horse. Abruptly, they arrived at a residence seemingly carved into the rocks. More precisely, it was a stone house nestled between a crevasse, but was so cleverly constructed it seemed to be just a part of nature. A man watched their approach silently.

Inside, his wife cooked tortillas over an open fire in a kitchen area with the smoke leaving an aperture in the thatched roof. Outside, the place was all ups and downs. There were terraced areas, and in those flat places they grew corn and vegetables. Chickens ran in a panic when approached. A couple of lazy hogs soaked in the mud. Two young girls in their early teens, who were built like small tanks, giggled as they fetched water and beans for the meal that their mother was preparing. These were kind and simple people who were not only the first residents of the mountains Lencho met, but were also the 'gate keepers.' Somehow, they could tell who was coming from any direction. Because they were the first inhabitants along the trail leading ever upward, everyone that came by and went past them was duly noted and word was then sent forward. No one residing further up the trail was thus ever surprised by unwelcome or unknown visitors. How they were able to alert one another was one of many mysteries. There was no electricity up there and no telephones. They stayed with the man and his family for one day, and he told Herminio and Lencho where they should go for their mota as well as the best people to see. He also assured the two that they would be expected. It apparently was quite the occasion to have gringos visiting them, and they even insisted that Lencho sleep in their bed. It was an old spring mattress, and though Lencho tried to decline their offer, they would have none of it. The next morning, they ate some breakfast and bid the gatekeepers farewell. As they were leaving, the man took Lencho aside and asked him if he was interested in a wife.

"Actually, Señor, if you would marry one of my fine daughters, I will throw the other in for free. They would be very lonesome without one another, and they are both strong, hard workers. They can carry water all day long. They also can cook and sew, and would give you many sons."

The weed man looked at the squat little girls, with their crooked teeth and giggling smiles, then thanked him profusely for his generous offer and beat a hasty retreat. It was time to visit the one hundred and four year old man.

A half day's journey and two thousand feet later, they reached the home of Diego Spinosa and his seven generations of family that all slept under the same roof. The Spinosa clan had never left the mountains, and they dwelled in a compound among some old oaks, pines, and shrubs. Parrots flitted above them in the branches, and Señor Spinosa's third wife Gloria was cooking up some tasty catamount on an open spit when they arrived. She was seventy years old, and together with his seventy-five year old son, Eduardo, welcomed the men to their abode. Children danced around his feet as Lencho and party trooped in. Six out buildings surrounded the main home of the old man, and more women and children appeared to gaze cautiously at the new arrivals.

"Welcome," Eduardo said with outstretched hands. "We were waiting for you. Are you hungry?"

"What is this meat?" Lencho whispered to Herminio as they sat with the clan cross legged upon mats. "It ain't bad, but it is a little chewy."

"It's kind of a large rat," Herminio said quietly. "Be polite and tell the lady how tasty it is."

Later, as they sat on the porch smoking some excellent, recently harvested pot, Lencho passed the weed to the old man who declined with a little laugh. Eduardo explained that the reason his father declined to smoke mota with them was because he had smoked it for so many decades that he was always high, and thus no longer needed to smoke it anymore. Marijuana cultivation had been, and still was, a family tradition dating back over two hundred years. It had been so long, in fact, that no one in the family could recall when or even how it began.

"I think the cola de burro may have come to us from the gods," he said. "Either that or the Spaniards who invaded our lands long ago. They were explorers and traveled to many lands. As for us, we have always grown it with our corn and beans. In recent years, the Americanos have taken to it, and now there is a big demand."

"When was your father born?" Lencho asked.

"It was in the winter of 1879. He has never left our mountains, and I am his last surviving child. My son is now fifty-six years old, and his oldest son is forty, and so on down the line. Some of us have, of course, left for the great world, but many remain. I believe the youngest Spinosa is two years of age. That would be Tache over there at his mother's breast. We are all children of the Astecah. These mountains were once a part of the Ancient Aztec Empire."

"This is some excellent weed, my friend," Lencho complimented him. "Did you always grow it so well?"

"We just grew it for ourselves until the Americans started to buy it. They wanted the best for their money, and the colas that we grew were not suitable to them after a while. Then, one day, a gringo came up here and lived with us for a few years. He lived in a cave nearby, and while he was there he showed us how the Americanos wanted their colas. They wanted it to have no seeds. Now, our mota is the finest in all of Mexico."

That night, everyone slept in the shack. They slept on tables, four at a time. Just before he drifted off, Lencho took a count from squinted eyes and it looked like forty-two Spinosa were crammed into the shack. Don Diego was snoring loudly as his seventy year old bride nuzzled in his crooked arm. The next morning, they took a half day hike to inspect some of their marijuana crops and make some purchases. One of the guards was sixteen year old Cortez. He was an eager young man who had been urging Herminio to hire him for this journey, but Herminio had been reluctant to do so. He was too young, plus the trip would be a dangerous one. Lencho finally relented, however, and took the boy along as his personal valet, equine groom, and all-purpose joint roller. Cortez ran alongside Lencho's horse, acted as a scout, and rolled cigar sized doobies from a roll of piñata paper he had brought along.

They reached the grow by noon, and Lencho set about inspecting the colas on the towering cannabis plants that reached up into the clouds. Some of the plants were ripe and sticky and ready for the cutter's knife, while those in shadier areas needed another week or so. He gave orders to harvest the bulk of one hundred kilos with special emphasis on leaf removal. The expedition had been led by Moses Spinosa, one of Eduardo's grandsons. At thirty-three, he was a protean man with a look of one who had witnessed the beauty of his world tempered by the uncertainties of the newfound demand for their product. He assured Lencho that the plants would be manicured as per his instructions. He reminisced about his own youth, growing up and living in the Sierra Madre Del Sur.

"We have more money now," he said. "But we also have more bandits and more soldiers, too."

"Does the army destroy your crops?" Lencho inquired.

"A little bit," he replied. "The gatekeeper tells us whenever they are coming.

We know that they will demand their mordida, and we give it to them. Many of those men also come from families in these mountains. They know we must eat, and this is our life they hold in their hands. So, we pay them a little, they cut down a few plants, and usually it happens early in the season so we really don't lose much. The soldiers can now inform the government that they have struck a great blow to the mota growers in this region, and then for the rest of the year, they leave us alone. The banditos are another matter."

"We have not run into any, yet," Lencho said.

"You will, Señor. Be on your guard. El Guano is the one to watch. He has a big scar across his face and he is missing an eye. There are many of his kind in the Sierra Madre, but I believe that he is the worst in this region. No woman is safe either. We pay him to stay away. The army will not go after him either."

Moses said goodbye to the weed man the next morning. He cut down the plants and took them back to his compound for manicuring and drying. When Lencho returned from his buying trip, there would be two burros packed for the descent back down to the lowlands.

Riding and walking up another thousand feet through glades and meadows, they came upon a canyon carved between the peaks that surrounded them. On the left of a sheer cliff, water tumbled and fell into what appeared to be a bottomless pit. An ancient trail, wet and mossy, led past it. It was very dangerous in Herminio's opinion, and he urged Lencho to get off and walk while he led his horse across the path.

"I think that maybe I should even blindfold the horse," he said nervously.

"No, my friend, I'm fine," Lencho said. "I've been riding since I was a little boy. The horse and I will take our chances."

He bent over and whispered into his graceful ear, "Don't look down, boy. I won't if you won't." An eagle flew above him hundreds of feet and another soared below in the canyon. He and his mount were in the middle and off they went very, very slowly.

The path was so close, he brushed his hand along the slick cliff wall to his left and kept his eyes trained on the group of men gathered watching apprehensively on the other side. It seemed to take forever. Then the stud horse stopped and snorted, his head bobbing with what seemed indecision. "Come on, boy," he soothed, "almost there. Just a little further." He began again. He reached the wider path and safety just as a trickle of stones slid off into oblivion. The weed man earned a large dollop of respect that day from his men. Especially young Cortez, who rolled him a big, beautiful spliff and gifted the noble horse with a bowl of corn when they stopped later to rest.

Five miles beyond the abyss, they came upon a near perfect rendition of a Swiss Chalet. Lencho did a double take as they passed by. Mr. and Mrs. Burgos from Austria lived there. It was a stately old home with a peaked roof and heavy thatch. Large stones had been used for the walls, and to the left sat a row of solar panels.

"We cannot stop here," Herminio told him. "This fellow is very eccentric and I don't trust him not to report our presence to the Government. He is a merchant who sells some needed items to the Indians in exchange for gold and silver. He hauled most of the materials up here on mules to build this house in the sky. Very odd."

Yes indeed, thought Lencho.

It had been five days since they set out on this journey, and they had not exactly been eating extravagantly. Lencho was famished, and he knew that the other men were also. Seven hours and another thousand feet later, they arrived at what appeared to be a rock quarry. In the recess of years of mining sat a dozen small buildings. They were the homes of the Barajas clan.

Señor Barajas was not one hundred and four years old, nor was he a young man either. Just how old he was, Lencho could not tell. The usual chickens ran from the feet of the men and the horse. Lencho caught sight of a fat little hog wallowing in some mud.

When Señor Barajas greeted him amiably with a toothless smile, Lencho's first words were, "How much do you want for that pig?"

A price was quickly agreed upon, and in another hour fresh pork was roasting on a fire spit. That night, the whole crowd feasted. Lencho peeled off thousands of freshly minted peso notes as a dozen little children, along with several adults, watched with fascination and glee. It was more money than many had ever seen all at once.

The next day, they spent time in their field, and Lencho purchased two hundred kilos. The clan treated him and his men like royalty, because they were beyond delight to sell their entire crop all at once to Lencho. The crop would be manicured of water leaves and then loaded onto the backs of burros for the return trip. As they were going over the details, Barajas put his hand over his eyes to shade them from the afternoon sun. "Our neighbors are coming," he announced.

"Where?" Lencho asked straining to see.

"Across the meadow and on the cliff. They are riding their mules. It is Alvaro and Maria. They come to meet you."

Lencho had always had good eyesight, but try as he might he could not make out any movement on the distant trail. Sure enough, though, an hour later he spotted two handsome mules trotting purposefully up to where they stood. A young man and a woman, sitting upon the mules' backs, gazed beneficently down upon those who congregated before them. The man climbed down and then helped his woman from the side saddle that she was riding. They were dressed in traditional costumes cut of the finest quality. Their sombreros were embossed with silver conchos, hers with a braided leather strap tucked beneath her chin. They wore ponchos of dazzling colors. His pants were leather and his boots gleamed. A belt of silver around his waist held a pouch and a leather sheath where a stag horn knife handle protruded. Her woven blouse was hand stitched with designs of ancient origin, and a long feminine skirt reached to handmade boots with silver spurs. Their mules were regal beasts, and the bridles and saddles were of exquisite craftsmanship. Lencho was enough of a cowboy to recognize fine workmanship. The man was handsome and his woman beautiful. Since everyone had been sampling the cola de burro rolled up in a huge joint by young Cortez, the sight of these ethereal creatures was stunning.

"I forget my manners," Barajas suddenly chimed. "Señor Lencho, please meet our fine young neighbor and his wife."

Alvaro and Maria were both Aztecs in their twenties. They had been together since childhood and only recently wed. They did not have any children yet, but were planning on several. In the meantime, they were industrious and very well-liked by those who dwelled in the mountain community. It was said the mota that Alvaro grew was the best of all. He had made the trip to meet Lencho and invite him to take a few days to come to his home for a visit. He told Lencho that he had two hundred kilos ready to go right now, cured and trimmed. He could easily provide burros for transport, if the weed man found his product to be satisfactory.

Lencho would be stopping at one more farm, and then he would travel to the young couple's. It all seemed surreal to him as they rode off into the shadows of the waning day. He was so very far from home that it felt as if he had traveled to the end of the earth. He was in the very mountains where the ancient Aztecs claimed life itself had begun. As he watched the two vanish, it seemed to him that they were probably gods. Not people, really. They were too exotic and too beautiful. He thought back to when three feathers had told him that his road in life would be a long one, hard at times, but also fruitful. Moments like this proved the Shaman correct.

"Man," he sighed to Herminio, "too far out for words. This whole place is magic. Sacred even. Hate to sound corny, but . . . man!"

Herminio just smiled and said to his compardre, "I told you once that you will buy the finest mota and see a world like no other."

The Rancho of Alvaro and Maria was at the far end of the ancient trail. It was located at the highest altitude yet, just over six thousand feet. Their home was a modest one. It did have some comforts, however, because the two were prosperous by mountain standards. Their hogs had pens and they had several free ranging cattle. Fields of corn, oats, and thin wheat were worked by paid help. Several meadows were given over to marijuana cultivation, although only a few dozen plants were left in the ground now in early October. Most had been harvested.

Inside, Maria luxuriated with a wood burning stove and even a portable radio that ran off batteries purchased from Mr. Burgos. The building was actually quite spacious, with glass windows offering a view that seemed to stretch into infinity.

"Well, I guess they are human after all," Lencho said to Herminio. "But they are still extraordinary."

Their mota, as had been promised, was of the absolute finest quality. For some reason, here at six thousand feet in elevation, these final four hundred pounds of weed were more potent than all the rest.

He made large X's on the burlap packings that held this portion. After counting out two and a half million pesos, three thousand U.S. dollars, the weed man and his men now turned to go back the way that they had come.

He had purchased four hundred kilos of marijuana, and it was all packed on fourteen burros. Along the way he had hired an additional ten men, all of them armed, and now a caravan laden with enough pot to satisfy thousands made its way down the winding trail to civilization.

They had been on this road for twelve days. Herminio expected that, without any mishaps, they would be down in three more. At every place they stopped to buy mota, they picked up several more burros, until they came to the final place: the clan of the one hundred and four year old man. They waved farewell as they passed the home of the gatekeeper, who called out to Lencho, "Are you sure that you do not need a bride?"

"I'm sure, but thank you anyway," he called back.

Both coming and going, Herminio sent out two or three men to act as scouts. They would leave hours earlier than the rest. Half a day past the gatekeeper, Cortez came running back to meet the caravan. Breathlessly, he reported there were bandits up ahead! "No more than six kilometers," he told them. "There were fifteen of them, I think. The man who was leading them had this great scar on his fat face. It was so big, I could see it from far away."

"Holy shit!" Lencho barked. "That sounds like this guy Guano that I've been warned about."

"I don't know about that," Herminio replied, "but we must move the whole team off of this trail. Up here, this way."

He raced to the lead burro while the entire troop of guards pulled, shoved, and swatted the butts of the pack animals trying to make them move quickly. They had only just managed to hide the whole ensemble behind a thick hedge of pine and scrub when Guano and his rag tag army passed below. Lencho studied these feared men and was almost disappointed in how ill equipped they seemed to be. Most of them were on foot and did not even have shoes. The scarred one rode on one of only three horses. Lencho could only see four or five weapons. Banditry didn't seem to be a very profitable enterprise, he thought. When they had passed, he relayed his observations to Herminio. "That is what makes these men so dangerous. They have nothing. That means, of course, that they also have nothing to lose. Let's hope they don't smell the donkey shit and decide that it is nice and fresh."

On day fifteen, they were back at the Rio Balsas, and it was even more ferocious than when they had started. One at a time, Herminio and the men led the heavily laden beasts across the rapids. It would not do to have any swept away in the current. "Easy. Easy." He called as the little animals slipped on the stones beneath their feet and half swam, half walked to the other side.

Young Cortez pulled on the ropes along with the other men, and Lencho was proud of the way the boy had handled himself on this excursion.

By 3:00 pm, the job was completed. The caravan had only to traverse the five remaining miles to the airstrip. The tiny town of Arcelia lay just two miles beyond, and as Herminio had the men unload the burros and hide the pot underneath a mountain of tumble weeds, Lencho walked in to make a phone call at the relay station. It took three hours before he finally made contact with "Jack the hit man," who had been awaiting instructions in Tampico.

"Man, have you seen any weather reports? Have you scanned the sky over the mountains?"

"No," Lencho replied. "We just got down and I can't see beyond the trees leading up the trail. What's wrong?"

"Monsoon. Towering cumulus situation. Torrential rains and possibly hail at that altitude. I don't dare fly in there until it lets up. Call me again tomorrow."

The next day it was the same, and the day after that. The extra men that Lencho had hired were paid and they went back up the mountain with the string of burros. Lencho, Herminio, and the rest hunkered down praying that no one would begin to wonder what they were doing loitering out at the airstrip. Even though the town itself was small and the area remote, that did not mean it was vacant. There were a lot of people who lived there, and the place was surprisingly busy. The flinty eyed hombres in Lencho's employ were heavily armed and unafraid to shoot anyone who became a menace, and he was sincerely hoping that it wouldn't come to that. Finally, Herminio pointed to a little shack a few hundred yards from where they were encamped. "I have seen an old woman over there and I think that she lives alone. I am going to go and speak with her.

"How are you, grandmother?" Herminio called out in a friendly voice.

She was in her seventies and stooped from a hard life. Skinny, plenty tough, and now alone. Her children had either died or moved away.

"Sure, I see you," she answered. "I am old, but I'm not blind. What do you want from me?"

"How about I pay you to let us stay with you until our plane arrives? I will give you five hundred dollars. I would also need to store our luggage in your old barn over there."

"Luggage?" she chortled. "I bet I know what kind of luggage you have, my boy! For five hundred dollars, you can stay a year if you want."

She treated all of them wonderfully. She cooked for them outside on her fire pit and drank Cerveza with them as well. She did decline to smoke the mota, however. "I might get addicted if I did," she said earnestly.

Every day, Jack told Lencho over the phone that he would be coming out, but the heavy rains refused to let up. Finally on the fifth day, the weather improved and the men lugged the bales to the strip. Suddenly, there he was winging in out of the clouds in his Cessna 310. There were twenty contoured packages with a total weight of eight hundred pounds, and as soon as the plane coasted to a stop, they began to load it aboard. They were not alone in their excitement, because no sooner had Lencho tossed in the last package when he saw the entire population of Arcelia running towards him.

They had all seen the airplane come out of the sky, and when a plane came it was a big deal for them. Almost a hundred people were whooping and hollering with glee. It dawned on Lencho that these fine citizens knew what was up. They had always known and were celebrating with him as he climbed aboard. The Cessna roared to life and began its taxi down the dirt runway directly towards the running crowd.

"Get the fuck out of my way, you idiots!" Jack bellowed.

They scattered as he passed through them, and Lencho pulled a wad of peso notes from his underwear. With a yell and a big grin, he opened the side door just enough to toss out about a thousand dollars to his newfound friends. The prop sent the money flying into the crowd, and he waved at one and all as they scrambled to pick it up. Their euphoria was obvious, and he knew that he had made their day. Then they rose into the sky and headed north in the direction of Saltillo.

Not everyone was so pleased down below. The local police got wind of the whole episode and were mighty miffed that they had not been paid off. The following day, they caught up to Herminio and beat him half to death for the slight. They also took all of his earnings for themselves. The lesson that Lencho learned from all of this was that next time he would catch the plane on the day that it was scheduled, weather be damned.

After the unforgettable trek into the Sierra Madre del Sur, the plane ride home was anticlimactic. That was a rare, but appreciated, event in the weed man's hectic life. They breached the international border in New Mexico with no one the wiser. CR met the plane during the daytime, and his crew unloaded and vanished with precision. Lencho said goodbye to Jack until the next time, and then he slipped back into Prescott as Eric McKenzie to visit Tamara, Fred, and baby Liz.

*****

Halloween was in a few days, and Bobby told him there would be a wild party down at Matt's Saloon where Stumbling' Buffalo would be playing. "Ya gotta come," he told him. "Everyone will be jazzed to see ya."

"Are you kidding me?" he laughed. "I can't be seen, for god's sake, I'm a fugitive. But I got an idea."

Prescott is known for Halloween celebrations. The little kids love it like they do everywhere, but the older hip types are probably more enthusiastic than their kids. The only other town he ever saw with such enthusiasm for Halloween was maybe Berkeley, but those people were just plain crazy anyway. So, he borrowed some wheels and drove down to Phoenix where he rented a tuxedo that was white from head to toe. White pants and tails, ruffled white shirt, white spats and gloves. He passed on a top hat, because he needed a mask. He went to the Movie House Theatrical Emporium on Central to look some over. A Wolfman latex with long snout, flashing fangs, and a foot of snow white hair capped his ensemble. On October 31, he strode into the crowded bar with Little Red Riding Hood, a.k.a. Tamara McKenzie, on his arm. Between the two, they stole the show from the outset.

He joked and danced and drank mixed drinks with a long straw through a slit in the mouth, but never removed his mask no matter how hot it became underneath. The men ogled the always fetching Tamara, but one look at her werewolf escort inspired distance. At midnight, the contest was held and out of hundreds of participants all decked out in their weird finery no one beat shapely Red Riding Hood and her mystery Wolfman. When the winner was decided by crowd acclamation, the couple won hands down. "Take off the mask! Take off the mask!" they yelled. David put the mic to the snarling fangs, and the man inside replied with a hearty laugh, "No can do! No can do!"

"But the prize is five hundred dollars!" David yelled, even though he was in on the joke.

"I donate the prize to drinks all around," he yelled back and let out a boozy "Oowoooooooo!" The crowd roared their approval.

As the last of the revelers filed out around one a.m., a bleary eyed bunch of diehards were hosting their final salutes to the gods of darkness and another great party. Most were Lencho's oldest friends, whom he hadn't seen in a couple of years. "Here's to you, mystery Wolfman," Derick said raising a shot glass. "Thanks, Derick. And here's to you all as well," Lencho replied as he raised the mask to his eyebrows. The look of astonishment and glee could have killed a buffalo. As they laughed and pounded him on the back, he reached over to a passed out Tamara asleep with head on her hands at a table and said, "Come on, babe. Time we got home."

*****

Catching a flight out of Houston, Lencho flew to Mexico City and then on to Guadalajara where he hooked up with Jack once again. Always the industrious thief, Jack had stolen a swanky Arrow motor home, and with his underworld connections obtained an excellent counterfeit title and pink slip. It bore Montana plates that were acquired through the state's motor vehicle department where he had friends. CR had done his magic with an entire false floor. Behind it, he hauled a shiny new Ford pickup that he recently purchased. Lencho drove the truck to the coastal city of Puerto Vallarta and Tamara, together with the children, flew down to join him. Before Tamara left, one of Lencho's confederates at a hospital provided her with fake birth certificates for the kids. When bringing children into Mexico, it was required that the parent show proof of birth. She got their visas, and now the two were Fred and Liz McKenzie.

The sun and ocean at Puerto Vallarta was wonderful. After luxuriating for a few days, they headed south on Hwy 200 to the place where the movie "10" was filmed, called Manzanillo. In the spring of 1984, it was unspoiled and a world away from all the cops and his legal troubles. Lencho and his family took in the sites and became typical American tourists.

Moving on to Playa Azul, they drove inland on dog leg 37, then connected to Hwy 370. The twisty roads through the mountains displayed breathtaking beauty, but soon it was time to get back to business. Carlos flew in from New Mexico, and he met them all in the city of Uruapan. Then they traveled on to the distinctly unsavory town of Apatzingan, where Carlos introduced Lencho to some old mafioso pals from his time at Andonegui Prison, Chava and Serrato.

It is common throughout Mexico for powerful organized crime characters to live out in the boondocks. They exist everywhere, of course, but the country is huge and largely lawless, so these types of men are even less threatened in rural environments. The area that Lencho found himself in had the reputation of being the heroin capital of Mexico. The reason was because of the quality opium plants that were grown in large fields in the cool elevations found there. Numerous labs turned out black tar heroin. Apatzingan was a dusty berg, cluttered, and anything but romantic. It was also a dangerous place.

When the two mafiosos met Lencho, along with his woman and his children, they were appalled. On the one hand, it was a typical Lencho tactic to bring them along as he had done in Guatemala, because the wives invariably loved the women and children. He figured that if the wives loved them, it was a given they would be treated with respect and safety. The family comes first with the Mexican people, and perhaps doubly so with the criminal element. At the same time, the bosses told him that he couldn't stay in Apatzangan for more than another day. They would not be safe from kidnappers and bandits with their shiny vehicles and the pretty white children.

"We will move you all to Patzcuaro, which is much better." And they did.

Typical of mob hoods Lencho met many times in the past, the two men were around his age and flashy dressers that wore lots of gold. They also slept with any woman that would have them. They stole, murdered, counterfeited, and dealt drugs, plus anything else that came their way where they could earn a dishonest Peso. They treated Lencho and his family well.

Soon they were ensconced in their new setting, which although only a hundred miles north, was a world apart. The city of Patzcuaro was a renowned art colony and home to the intelligensia. The locals wore colorful costumes from antiquity and played hypnotic pan flute and guitar. They also excelled in the culinary arts for the wealthy tourists that came there. Nearby archeological ruins added to the mystery and ambience, and Tamara was very happy for the nine months they visited. They explored and had picnics atop the grass covered Aztec pyramids that had once been the site of sacrificial slaughters.

While exploring, the family discovered a fully functional, albeit overgrown, home in the jungle. When Lencho asked the manager at the hotel who might own it, he discovered it was the same guy who owned the hotel. The owner lived in the U.S., so Lencho called the man up and gave him a story about being a retired steel worker who had been injured and was now traveling the world. He asked if he'd be interested in renting his jungle home. It was his for two hundred dollars a month. Lencho paid and they moved in. The home had hot water from propane gas, electricity, and a fully appointed kitchen. Furnished, it was perfect. Tamara and the children lived there while Lencho arranged loads of weed for his state side partners.

The big marijuana grow that Doc was working on with the sinister soldier of fortune, Charlie Gray, was behind schedule, but still in the works. So, the weed man had ample time for other projects.

"Oh yeah," Doc told him on one of his innumerable trips back to California and Arizona, "I was in Belize two weeks ago and there was Charlie in his white suit yelling and screaming at his darkies. Growing acres and acres just outside of town. He's paid off everyone that counts. I never seen so much pot in one place. And those blacks actually sing as they work. Just like the old south, and Charlie is loving it. I'd feel sorry for the buggers, except I know they get paid very well. Charlie just likes to pretend he's Nathan Bedford Forrest and those are his personal darkies. But it's still a ways off before we harvest, so keep bringing up loads while we wait." That's what Lencho did.

"I got some stuff to show you," Chava told him. "We got to go out to a ranch in the country. I know that you will like this, Amigo, so you should bring some money."

His new friend Chava was driving, and the drive to 'the country' turned into a journey down muddy roads deep into the jungle. It was hot and steamy through dense stands of mahogany and vines thick with parrots, hummingbirds, snakes, and all manor of other flora and fauna. Lencho, Chava, and one other desperado passed very potent marijuana joints back and forth. The deep green of the jungle blended with the shadows, and the pot made Lencho a trifle nervous as they bumped along. He realized that he didn't really know these guys all that well, and he had brought along over ten thousand dollars.

Suddenly, he heard the distinct snap of an automatic weapon and sensed the presence of a 9mm pistol by his ear. There was an instant of panic before the blast left his eardrums ringing. He was sure he was a dead man.

"Holy shit," Martin Siguenza howled with delight, "I hit that bad boy. Stop the car!"

"Vato loco!" Chava yelled at the gunsel in the back seat. "What are you shooting at?"

"That green iguana, boss," he replied sheepishly. "Didn't you see it there on that big tree? Those things are delicious."

The men backed the car up the muddy path fifty feet, and at the base of a huge tree lay the beast Martin had felled with one excellent shot. It was six feet long, and the bullet had passed completely through its spiny head. Lencho was surprised he had not lost control of his bladder. They got out and Martin threw the lizard into the trunk. Half an hour later they arrived at the ranch.

The place was a series of small shacks where the people had lived for generations. The ground around them was hard packed and swept clean as concrete. A little woman took the lizard out of the trunk with glee, gutted it, and cleaned it expertly. That night, they dined on barbecued iguana, and it was fantastic. It tasted like chicken.

He stayed there for three days, and then CR showed up with the balance of the funds. The marijuana was from the Guerrero region and of truly fine quality. They paid an extra five thousand dollars for alleged safe passage all the way to the border. The mafia men claimed all the mordida was covered for every region, cop, official, Tom, Dick, and Harry from Uruapan to Nogales. The boys didn't believe that, but they paid anyway as a gesture of goodwill. The load made it back safely in the stolen motor home.

A month later, Jack flew another load in his big Cessna, and that also went well. Afterwards, Lencho never saw Jack again. He had moved to Guadalajara with a new woman. Lencho later heard that he was dead. No one was certain if his death had been natural or by lead poisoning. He was just fifty-one when his life force was extinguished.

Back in San Diego, later that month, Doc caught up to the weed man. "We're ready for the first load, my boy," he told Lencho. "Are you set up for the stop overs?"

"When is the start date?" he asked.

"I'll be ready in one month," Doc replied.

"We'll be ready," Lencho answered.

Lencho, Tamara, Fred, and Liz boarded a plane back to Nogales out of Guadalajara in April of 1984, and they all flew as McKenzie's.

"I've got four hundred thousand pesos, which is equivalent to fifty grand. When you get to the border, declare the pesos to customs. Tell them that you made the money from the sale of property in Mexico from a wealthy couple who paid you to be their American nanny. Take the kids along. Tell them that your kids lived and played with their children. You will be charged a three percent tax and the balance will be yours, free and clear. Once you enter the U.S., we can change it to dollars. This will give you legal money to live on, and we may buy a house up in Chico. How does that sound to you?"

Tamara thought it was a great idea and so did the United States of America. The officials at the entry point were astounded, as a matter of fact, that a gringa would actually declare currency and agree to pay tax on it. Money hardly ever flowed from south to north, let alone being declared. Tamara was now suddenly well heeled.

After visiting in Prescott for a week, they drove to Chico where Lencho's many friends lived and found an excellent house located in a cul-de-sac. It had a huge garage, and both Mike and Phillip came over to check it out.

Mike said, "Man, this garage would be perfect for an indoor grow. We could add some capacity at the breaker box, plug all of the light leaks, and set off four one thousand watt halides. What do you think?"

"I like it," Lencho replied. "Go for it."

And so, even as forty thousand pounds of high grade marijuana, grown by a white task master overseeing his Negroes in Belize, was about to start flooding in, Lencho had a hundred plants of his own starting from scratch in his garage in Chico. He was using the then novel indoor technique that would later sweep the pot growing world. After everything was well under control and underway in Chico, he jumped on another flight back to Tampico where he was met at the airport by Roberto Azua, his right hand man.

"Let's get out to that Kline Ranch and catch up with Fernando," he ordered. "We got a flight coming in within the week."

Roberto Kline was the big game hunter who worked for Pemex, and it was on his airstrip they had prepared for the incoming and outgoing flights from Belize. Fernando had rounded up dozens of fifty gallon drums full of aviation fuel and an electric pump that could refuel at a capacity of eighty gallons a minute. It would take no time at all to get the Queen Air refueled and back into the sky. The airstrip was grass, and alongside it they placed dozens of buckets containing fuel which would act as makeshift lighting. Tall cane grew on the left side of the field. The flights were monitored via radio by Lencho and Roberto, who were stationed inside Kline's trophy laden home.

They came in the dead of the night, and the first two flights arrived and departed without incident and with precision. Fernando never asked the elder Kline if all of this was okay with him, a small detail they decided was best left unmentioned. Señor Kline had a son named Arturo, and a deal was struck with him. The older gentlemen didn't mind the falluca being transported on his property, but he might have been less enthusiastic about drugs.

"My dad is old fashioned," Arturo had explained. "He does not think that the profit potential is worth the risk for drugs. He says that the payoffs to the police is too much for drugs, not to mention the rip off artists that are prevalent everywhere."

The property was seldom visited by Señor Kline, since he had a home in Tampico where he lived with his wife and nearby mistress, so this was a smooth arrangement all in all.

Since Jack was now dead, Doc had found a new pilot. He was a mysterious guy who they all called Bill, because no one knew his real name. He was a cracker jack, cool and calm, and was on his way back from delivering their third load. Lencho watched for him to land for fuel at 2:30 a.m. as the others waited inside by the radio.

"Foxtrot, this is Bill. ETA is ten minutes." That was all he said and all they needed to hear as they ran out to the field to light off the torches along the runway. The big plane's engines suddenly boomed in the night and just as quickly, it was taxiing to a halt six hundred feet down the runway. Bill killed the engines as the boys ran up to meet him, and then out of the tall cane stepped ten pistoleros, all armed to the teeth. Five pickup trucks roared from the darkness and surrounded the plane. Bill stared wide eyed from the cockpit as the rip off artists waved their rifles and pistols directly at him through the glass. The leader of the group stuck a mini Uzi 9mm in the nape of Lencho's neck, and he and Roberto were made to kneel.

"Get out of the plane!" they yelled at Bill. "Get out now or we shoot!"

Lencho could see by the light of the torches that Bill was hesitating. He thought briefly that the pilot might actually try and make a break for it, but knew there was no point. He yelled to the pilot, "Get out! Get the fuck out of the plane!"

"We want the pot, chinga tu madre. Open the plane and give it up or we will kill all of you," the leader threatened.

Lencho never had been a man of guns. As he knelt there expecting this to be the end of the line, he knew why. Better to give them what they wanted and be done with it. More of a chance of getting out alive. If he had drawn down on them, it would have ended in a blood bath. Besides, he thought, there ain't no fucking pot in the plane anyway! The plane was returning to pick up a new load. It's empty, you dumb son of a bitch!

"There's no marijuana in there," he protested. "We're fallucarros. No drugs, just falluca."

Bill climbed out with his arms held high. Three of the gunmen marched him over to the other two, and the leader holding the machine gun made Lencho stand.

"I am not stupid. We know you have mota, and we want it. Come on, we will take a look."

Climbing into the plane with Lencho leading, the bandido was astounded to find the plane was truly empty. It did, however, reek.

"Where is it, god dammit? I can smell it, but I don't see it."

"We're just fallucarros, like I told you," Lencho said. "No drugs. Never were."

"I think I am going to kill you," the bandito sighed.

They got back out and a heated debate erupted between him and his men. The three smugglers stared at the ground praying. Finally, the leader walked back and demanded all of the money they had on them. Lencho had about two thousand dollars, Roberto a few hundred, and the pilot had three thousand. The money was gruffly removed from the men's pockets, and spitting on the ground, the leader told them to climb back into the plane, take off, and don't return.

"But we are out of gas," Bill protested.

"That's not my problem," the bandit snarled. "Go. Now!"

With Roberto crouching between the pilot seats, the three men roared into the night. Looking back at the burning torches, Lencho breathed a sigh of relief and Bill just cursed.

"We got out alive, but I can't say for how long. The gauge reads empty."

"Jesus, what'll we do?" Lencho asked.

"We head for Tampico, I guess." Bill answered. "The airport is close by, but it is closed until dawn. My watch says it's now 4:15 a.m. We can either fly around in circles or go back and land again where we were. I vote for the circles."

Bill was a skilled pilot. He leveled off the plane at fifteen hundred feet and flew at the lowest airspeed possible. "This plane's fuel gauge is off. When it reads empty, it's not entirely. But almost. I hope that we can stay aloft for an hour. Then we can land in Tampico. If not, we'll try and coast down to the dirt road below us. It's the only plan that I can think of."

166

"I wonder who betrayed us?" Azua asked.

"It wasn't Fernando," Lencho replied. "Couldn't have been. They thought that we were loaded when, in fact, the plane was empty. They had everything backwards. Dumb move. I figure it had to be Arturo? Miserable little shit."

"And they only got a few grand," Bill said. "Had they looked under my ass where I'm sitting, they would have found thirty thousand dollars in cash. Emergency bribe money for some worthy police officer or politician."

"Arturo should die for this," Azua hissed.

"No," Lencho corrected him. "We got off easy. No big deal really as long as we don't crash. Guys like him get theirs eventually. We're just gonna move to a new spot and continue like nothing ever happened."

The fuel held up, and when they could see, Bill put the plane down at the Tampico Municipal Airport where they filled up the tanks and called Fernando on the telephone.

"He what?" Fernando yelled. "The bastard! I already paid him a couple of thousand and he does this? We will kill him."

"No, we won't kill him," Lencho answered. "Where can we move to continue this operation? Meet us over here as soon as possible."

Fernando was there within two hours, and they flew the plane to a crop duster strip located twenty minutes away, where Fernando knew the manager. The plane was pulled into a hangar and they set out to the waste lands of Saltillo where Fernando's dad had once owned an estate given to him by Pancho Villa. Since the estate had water where very little existed, the new constitution required that he surrender the property a few years later to the government, but the old man still owned a few acres.

"It only rains out here once every seven years," Fernando pronounced with solemnity as they drove into the desert. Upon looking around, Lencho believed him.

It was an excellent place to land a plane. Out in the middle of nowhere with little vegetation to get in the way, they built an airstrip and used it for the next few months. They parked the plane back at the crop duster strip where they paid Señor Mendosa a monthly fee to keep it in his hangar.

On a trip back to Prescott, Lencho got word on his cattle rustling and pot growing offenses. He was found guilty of one count of stealing a cow, which he had never stolen, and marijuana possession and dangerous drugs. They did not sentence him because he had split. They figured they would do the sentencing when they caught him later. Walter took Lencho's advice and got himself a sweetheart deal, which was a work furlough for just six months. They let him go to work on his ranch every day and herd his legal cows, but he had to spend his nights in the county jail. Also, the government didn't seize his property.

Lencho continued to be a very busy weed man, flying hither and yon constantly. Up to see his family and then down to Texas to speak with clients. Then back to Northern California to see his brother in Chico and back again to Tampico. Next he would travel to Saltillo to meet an incoming flight from Belize, refuel it, and set it off to the U.S. By this time, the group had a second Queen Air twin engine. On the twelfth trip, the guy who was piloting landed at the dusty strip with a big complaint.

"I got too much weight on this aircraft," he said. "Had a tough time getting off the ground in Belize, and I ain't risking my ass again unless we off some poundage."

"How much poundage?" Lencho asked him.

"Four hundred pounds, at least," he answered.

"Man, you are nuts! We never had this problem before. We can't just shit can almost a quarter ton of product."

"We can and we will," he insisted with arms clinched across his chest.

Lencho was briefly furious, but had little choice since he could not fly the plane himself. He warned him that if they off loaded that weight, it was on him. The loss would come out of his pocket, because he would have to destroy the weed. Couldn't just leave it out there for the Federales, after all.

"Fine," the pilot agreed and they pulled it off.

Lencho yelped with joy as the idiot flew off into the sky. He and Azua hauled the well packaged material to the side and then buried it beneath a pile of tumble weeds. Then he hightailed it into town and made a long distance call to an old pilot pal named Al Hanson.

"Al," he said. "Get that hot rod tail dragger of yours gassed up! The god's are smiling."

Al was out of Marysville. He met Lencho in Chico and picked him up. His plane was a small one, but souped up. It had no seats in the back and could easily accommodate two hundred kilograms. Since Doc and Charlie Gray had purchased an industrial wrapping machine for the project, all blocks were vacuum sealed and the product that the pilot had jettisoned was safe from the elements while they winged their way back down to retrieve it.

"The guy wouldn't take them and I made sure that he told Doc what he had done, so it's assumed this stuff is lost. You get half and I get the other. Sweet!"

On the way home, they landed to refuel at the executive terminal in Las Vegas, hoping to be in and out. But this being Vegas, the brass insisted they come in to the terminal, have a few drinks, and gamble while they were getting petrol. A group of scantily clad babes escorted them inside while they hoped no one would question what was underneath the blanket in the back of the little airplane.

✴✴✴✴✴

It was a fine Christmas in 1984. A whole lot more prosperous than only a year earlier. By February of 1985, the Belize caper was over. It had gone swimmingly well. They completed twenty round trip excursions hauling just under twenty tons of marijuana into the U.S. The boys were all counting their profits. Doc had cleared three and a half million dollars; and Charlie, five million. Bill the pilot made a half a million, as did Lencho. It wasn't a million like Doc had implied, but it wasn't half bad either. On one memorable weekend, after they completed three trips, he cleared one hundred and fifty grand.

"I want to settle down, raise the kids, and pursue my music business. I'm going to get out of the pot business, I swear!"

"I'll believe that when you don't leave home anymore," she answered.

Okay, he thought. If that's how she feels, then I'll just continue to do my thing as always.

The landscape was also changing with his associates as well. Doc had split once again, saying he too had decided to get out of the business now that he had stashed away enough cash. He bought a large fishing boat out of Miami and took his friends on excursions into the Gulf. Doc was always a lucky S.O.B., as all who knew him would attest, but his reputation went totally over the top the day he snagged a thirty kilo bale of cocaine floating in the water from a failed aircraft delivery. No one could believe it, except himself.

"I just live right," he told everyone.

At the current rate of fifteen thousand dollars per pound, he netted another nine hundred thousand dollars.

CR's fortunes, however, soured quickly. He took his Belize profits and invested it in cocaine. He dealt with the emerging Arillano Felix gang out of Tijuana. He had always enjoyed the white powder, but when he was up to his elbows in it, the stuff got the best of him. Within a year, he owed his suppliers hundreds of thousands of dollars that he could not pay. The mafia boys had him by the throat and, like Lil' George, his life was hanging by a wire. He begged his parents to save him. His folks were well heeled business types who had always been stricken by the life their son had chosen, so now they gave him an ultimatum. They would pay off all his debts, but he must swear to come home and leave the drug world behind forever. CR had to obey Mom and Dad to save his own skin. In the dope business, there is great competition between friends, and now he was disgraced. He was gone and never seen again.

"Bill," Lencho yelled into the phone from El Escondido, Mexico. "You want to make some bread? I'm down here arranging a little business. Kinda boring now, don't ya think? Can you fly down? Great! I'll meet you in Tampico."

Herminio arranged for a thousand pounds of product in March, so Bill the pilot was on his way in the big Queen Air twin engine. He met Lencho at the Camino Real Hotel and they discussed things over dinner and drinks that evening. Afterward, they reviewed the aeronautical charts that Lencho brought with him, and Bill calculated his heading for the flight out the next morning.

"A bright and lovely day it is," the pilot commented, setting switches and pushing buttons on his pre-flight procedures. "Should be an excellent day to make a few hundred grand."

"The weatherman said to watch for rain in the higher elevations," Lencho reminded.

"Rain is a given, my boy," Bill replied. "Not gonna be a problem."

Two hours later, Lencho peered down from wispy clouds and saw breakers far below on the beach. "Why am I seeing ocean, Bill?" he asked.

"What? What the fuck?" the startled pilot gasped. "We should be approaching mountains. Let me check the headings. We're going 33 degrees S.E. That can't be correct. Holy shit, I left out a three! We're ass backwards. The heading should read 333!"

Having wasted two hours of fuel and quite a lot of daylight, the plane was turned around and headed towards the correct destination, which was Iguala, and then over to the remote environs of Arcelia, where they were to meet up with Herminio. Missed directions are a hazard of air travel. Running out of fuel was too, and this was especially true for smugglers because they couldn't just set down at the nearest airstrip and refuel if they were loaded. The boys had no cargo now, so it wasn't so bad. The distances were vast, but they were equipped with an excellent radio as well as pilot controlled lighting for any suitably equipped airfields that they might come across at night. Then, it started to rain. With the rain came lightning, and the next time Lencho did a radio check, he discovered that they were incommunicado. The thing was fried.

"That last flash grazed us," Bill said. "I felt it in my hair follicles."

"Fucking great!" Lencho thundered.

They had left Tampico at 1 p.m., and by the time they discovered their mistake, it was past 3 p.m. Now, nearing 4 p.m., they were still two hours away from Arcelia, but at least their fuel was good.

"We got five drums out there, so no problem," Lencho said.

Now near Iguala, the last rays of the sun dropped behind the horizon. Added to the cloud cover, the men couldn't see squat.

"I know we're over the place," Bill said. "But man, we can't be piddling around up here. We got to cut bait or fish. The gas won't last a lot longer."

"How long to Mexico City?" Lencho asked him.

"Just over the mountains, but those things are thirteen thousand feet. Remember that the fuel gauge on this plane is touchy. Sometimes it says a couple of gallons over and sometimes it's the other way around. What do you want me to do?"

"Mexico City," Lencho said with finality. "Go for it."

Another one hundred nautical miles and they would be safe. Not far as the crow would fly, but an eternity when the weather was rough. They flew over rugged mountain peaks on vapors with a dead radio. Finally, they crossed the highest point and Lencho beheld the lights of that vast city spread out before them on the other side. Then the left engine died.

Bill feathered down the throttle and tipped the aircraft back and forth. "If there's any fuel on the left side, she should come to life."

Nothing! With a grimace, he tilted to the right, and on the remaining engine they bounced along toward the airport far away in the distance. They could see the green and white flashing light on the tower beacon. "I got to tell you something, my friend," Bill said sounding like a funeral director.

"What's that?" Lencho asked, not wanting to know.

"It's an unwritten rule of air chivalry. You see the city spreading out before us? Little bits of light from streets and houses joining more and more as we get deeper in? Well, if we run out of gas and go down, we got to crash in a dark place. Can't take innocent parties with us."

Up until then, Lencho had held his cool. Not even a little bit pissed over the navigation screw up, and now he was getting a sermon on ethics and the moral high ground as salvation loomed just a few miles distant.

"Listen to me, sky king!" he yelled. "You're the guy who sent us back asswards today. You made us late for our meeting with Herminio, and now you tell me we gotta crash in a dark spot? Fuck you! Get this plane to Mexico City, and that's an order."

Bill just shrugged and tilted the plane a hair more towards the right engine. They did not have a functioning radio, so they couldn't call the tower and tell them that they were coming in. On top of that, they were going in the wrong direction, directly towards a whole line of incoming commercial aircraft that had been cleared to land.

Lencho beheld the spectacle that was unfolding a mere twenty miles ahead as they brought the Queen Air lower and lower. The Mexico City International Airport used one immense runway for landings and departures. To his left, he saw six or more huge planes taxiing towards their turn for departure, while out in the night sky, the lights of a dozen more planes were slowly heading their way. A Pan American Airways jet had just landed and was moving out of danger, but a second Air France was right behind it.

"Holy shit!" he yelped. "Look at that guy coming in. We're gonna smash into him!"

No sooner had he said it than the pilot of the airliner pulled up and banked hard left back into the sky. "I don't think we'll hit him," Bill said as he approached concrete. "And they know that we're here now."

Bill landed the Queen Air and pulled off the runway seconds later. The long line of incoming planes banked away like the first, off towards the horizon to start all over. Fire trucks and official cars of every description surround them as soon as their prop stopped spinning. Men with weapons were yelling at them to disembark. With hands held high, they climbed out. Lencho's legs could not hold him up and he fell to his knees crying, "It was an emergency! No radio, out of fuel and one engine gone!"

The officials were gruff and unsmiling, but unlike a few of the police types he had encountered, they did not force him to lay on the ground. Instead, they placed a large bucket beneath the fuel stop cock on the left engine, and after no fuel came out, they switched to the right one. From that one, they extracted what appeared to be a gallon or two of gas. Other men were combing the interior, and Lencho was mighty glad that they were going to a pick-up instead of coming from one. The only signs of the trade were a set of night vision goggles and an electronic wand for sniffing out hidden tracking bugs, but he had decided to jettison those over the mountains a few miles back. The officials took the plane off the tarmac and escorted them into town, where they stayed at the Holiday Inn with guards at the doors. They were shaken, but still alive. They dropped any animosity over the mess they were in and ordered dinner and drinks from room service. The next day, they would face a board of inquiry over the whole matter, but Lencho didn't care at that moment and fell into a fitful sleep fraught with dreams of airplanes forced to crash in dark zones.

*****

"You gentlemen have been brought here this morning to explain why you landed a small civilian aircraft the wrong direction at Mexico City International Airport without any notification, interrupting flight plans, as well as endangering the public safety," the chairman intoned.

Bill and Lencho sat at a table in a conference room with six civil aeronautical board members facing them and lawyers from all of the major airlines whose flights they had disrupted surrounding them. The chairman informed the two that Mexicana, Pan Am, American Airlines, and a dozen others had suffered egregious financial damages from the disruption. Not only had they scared the shit out of everybody, but they had caused worldwide delays across Mexico, the United States, and Europe. The estimated damages was three and one half million dollars, and they were lucky it wasn't twice that much.

Lencho got to his feet. They were steadier now than the night before when he had literally dropped to his knees on the tarmac. Still, he hadn't brought along his checkbook and didn't have several million even if he had.

"Sir, we are immensely sorry about what happened last night, but in our defense, I must point out that we had no other options. We were out of fuel, our radio was fried from a lightning strike, and we had only one engine operational. Once we got near the airport, we looked for a dark area to put down in, but could not locate any. So, we had to land and take our chances, but in doing so I believe that many lives were saved."

The lawyers mumbled amongst themselves and the officials huddled, but in the end the chairman announced that they agreed. In an emergency, the Americans had acted prudently and in the only manner open to them. They would not be arrested or even fined. But please, go! Go and sin no more.

After they left the conference room, Lencho stopped at the pay phone in the airport lobby and called his new friend, Fernanda. He needed someplace safe to put the Queen Air and she was the person to assist.

"I'll be down in an hour," she said. "A friend owns some hangars, and I'll see to it that your plane is well taken care of. Then you must come over and have dinner with me and my husband, and tell us all about your adventure."

That night, he dined with Fernanda and Caesar in their penthouse overlooking Mexico City.

"My god that was hair raising. When Bill told me we should land that baby in a dark spot, I started to make my peace with the almighty. This is a dangerous business I'm in. I never would have believed just how dangerous it was when I smoked my first joint almost twenty years ago. I don't think it can get any scarier. Can I use your phone, my dear? Gotta call Doc back home."

His legs were still weak as he dialed the number. He held the phone in his hand and went outside to the deck overlooking the metropolis.

"Yo, Doc. Lencho! Oh, I'm fine. Had another scare, though. But it all worked out. Tell you all about it one day. Listen, the reason that I am calling is about the plane. You know how the cops come around checking at airports and stuff? Yeah, they tend to show up looking for someone to rob, and I keep having to move it. Now, we are done after Belize. What do you want me to do with it?"

"Who in the hell is it registered to?" Doc asked.

"It's registered in the name of Eric McKenzie, you dumb ass. You know that."

"Well," Doc said, savoring the moment, "I guess then it's Eric McKenzie's problem, isn't it?"

When Lencho came back inside, he set down the phone and seemed lost in thought.

"How was your friend Doc?" Fernanda asked.

"He must be fine." Lencho replied with a grin. "Because he just gave me an airplane."

Chapter Ten

"I Ain't Living Long Like This"
Released 1979
Waylon Jennings

I look for trouble and I found it son
Straight down the barrel of a lawman's gun
I tried to run but I don't think I can
You make one move and you're a dead man friend
Ain't living long like this
Can't live at all like this, can I baby?

BADGES

Lencho pulled the package of cash from under his jacket and made himself comfortable in the pilot's seat of the Queen Air. The great plane sat in the back of the hangar on the fringe of the Mexico City Airport, and he patted her instrument panel affectionately. "You are all mine, baby!" he said to himself.

As he daydreamed of future travels and the vast fortunes he would earn bringing loads of fragrant marijuana in to the United States, it was with satisfaction that he now hid the fifty thousand dollars under the backing of the foot pedals by his feet. He got up and climbed behind the front seats and pulled the door lock, and then dropped the stairs to the concrete. As he climbed out a man around forty years old approached him from the shadows.

"Where's the office around here?" he asked.

"Are you American?" Lencho replied.

"Sure, California," he answered.

"Me, too," the weed man said.

"This your plane?" the stranger continued.

"Yeah."

"You got no seats."

"I got no passengers," Lencho replied, and they both laughed.

The man thrust out a hand and said, "I'm Jerry."

"Glad to meet you. I'm Lencho."

Jerry ran a hand through stylish hair as his cowboy boots clacked on the floor.

"I'm looking for a good mechanic and was told that this was the place. That's my Aero Commander out on the tarmac."

"The guy to see is Roberto," Lencho told him. "He's supposed to be excellent. I just met him myself. He's around here somewhere. What's your line of work, Jerry?"

"I work for the government. The U.S. government. Department of Defense."

"Really? I don't fly myself," Lencho replied. "I buy and sell aircraft. Just got this one. I plan to flip it. Hey, let's get us a drink? It's nice to shoot the shit with a fellow gringo."

He said his name was Jerry Strickland and that he was a veteran who had found work as a private consultant and contractor for the DOD after his stint in Nam. The two men hit it off, and the booze loosened tongues. Lencho soon was regaling his new friend with stories of country music musicians biting rock stars on the leg in recording studios.

"Man, my girl is coming into Mexico City tomorrow and we're taking a little vacation. Do you have a gal? We could pal around town and see the sites together."

"I got the perfect lady," Lencho said. "Where are you staying?"

"I'm over at the Century in the Zona Rosa."

"That big modern glass and steel thing? I know the place. I'm just down the block at the Florencia. All antiques and history."

"Sure," he said. "I'll be looking for you guys around noon tomorrow. How's that?"

"See you then," Lencho answered.

For the next week, Fernanda led the group on a tour of the city. In her ebullient and vivacious style, she showed them museums, historical sites, old churches, and theaters, and then wound it all up with a tour of the huge open market where the vendors carried every known variety of goods. Jerry's girlfriend, Cricket, was very impressed with Fernanda and the two became buddies. She was called Cricket because of her petite size, and good-hearted nature. Fernanda took her under her wing. The foursome were fast friends by the end of the week. Over drinks, once again in a bar located near the airport, Jerry looked at Lencho and told him a startling story.

"How much do you make with your airplane sales, buddy?" he asked.

"Oh, on a good week, maybe ten grand. Last year was real solid and I brought in about a half a million. Other years? Not so good."

"Let me be honest with you," he continued. "I ain't calling you a liar exactly, but I don't believe that you are in the sales game. I think you do what I do. Dope."

"Dope? No, heck no," Lencho lied.

"Well, I gotta tell ya, Bud, ten grand a week is chump change. I make on average two million dollars a week and have done that for the year and a half I been in this game. Right now, in my digs in California, I got about one hundred seventy five million dollars, almost all of it in gold. Ya can't beat gold for a hedge, love the stuff. But it weighs tons and there it sits in a dozen big steel crates. I keep digging holes with my back hoe! The rest is cash. I got so much fucking money, I don't know what to do with it. I used to take it down to the Bahamas, but it's too risky and the gold is too heavy. Within the U.S., I got immunity, but I take my chances like everybody else if I leave."

"What do you mean immunity?" Lencho asked.

"I mean I operate with the protection of the U.S. government, as long as I operate within the borders. If any of us gets our tits in a bind outside, well, they got this thing called plausible deniability."

"So, what exactly is it that you do, Jerry?" Lencho inquired.

"Haven't you guessed? Guns, man. Guns and dope. Guns south, dope north. Me and a bunch of other guys fly weapons south to Nicaragua. We're independent contractors. The rebels unload me and then reload the plane with cocaine. Tons of the stuff. We fly it back to Edwards Air Force Base where most of it is hauled off by the spooks. I keep about two hundred pounds per trip for my customers. I get paid in cash by the spooks, and my net since the beginning has averaged two million dollars per week."

Lencho sat on the bar stool with his mouth agape. He was embarrassed and hoped that his face didn't belie the stunned condition of his brain. He thought the man's story was total bullshit.

"So, you're telling me that you work for the spooks? That would be the CIA, I assume?"

"Yeah," Jerry nodded.

"And you're helping with the revolution in Nicaragua? Let's see, that would be the Sandinistas, right? The commies that are fighting those Contras. You're saying that the Contras are backed by the CIA?"

"It's common knowledge," he answered. "I thought everyone knew. I was under the assumption that you already knew what my real business was."

"I've never heard a whisper about any of this, Jerry," Lencho said carefully.

"Well, it's true and I've been at it long enough. It's about time to call it quits, because for one thing there's no telling how much longer this will go on. That's always how it works with the Intel boys. They do their thing till they don't. In and out. But I figured that while it lasts, you may be interested in making some real money."

Lencho wished he had a joint. Liquor was okay, but it made him thick and this kind of conversation called for a lighter moment, if that were possible.

"What happens to all of the coke you bring back? You say that the spooks take it off of your plane. Where does it go?"

"The niggers, I guess. Look, it's just a suggestion. Think about it, why don't ya? I got total protection once I get out of Nicaragua. It can be dicey down there, you know. Those boys do have anti-aircraft capabilities that Fidel gives them, but once you're airborne, it's smooth sailing all the way back to Edwards Air Force Base. Piece of cake, really."

Lencho kept this all to himself, but told Jerry that he'd think it over and let him know. That would be in about a month, because now it was time for both of them to get back to work. Jerry doing his "spook" thing and Lencho heading back to Chico to look for his dream home. He had promised Tamara that he was going to settle down, buy a home, and then pursue his music dream. She had once again refused to marry him, so it didn't bother him much when Doc called from Florida to tell him that he wanted to go golfing in the breathtaking resort city of Ziguantanego on the Pacific.

"Get Bill and I'll be down tomorrow. It's on me. I'm up for some fun," Doc said.

The flight out of Mexico City was the only down side of the wild weekend, because Bill took the Queen Air over the same mountains where they had only recently escaped death and then disappeared into dense clouds.

"God, I can't see diddly!" Lencho yelled. "I hope you know what you're doing."

"What a couple of pussies," Bill laughed. "Do you think I would do anything risky?" Doc said nothing, but was white as a ghost.

The golf course was eighteen holes of emerald beauty beside the pounding surf. They stayed at the Camino Real Hotel in the lap of luxury. After drinks and dinner, the boys went bar hopping and had no problem lining up half a dozen ladies of easy virtue.

"Do you girls want to go for a little airplane ride?" Doc asked them.

The next day at one o'clock, the girls climbed into a limo which took them to the airport where Doc and Lencho waited. Bill was at the controls as they flew out over the waves, gulping champagne, snorting coke, and smoking pot. Bill was the designated flyer, but looked over his shoulder as the boys shared the six young women and became inducted into the infamous "Mile High Club."

*****

Paradise, California is about ten miles east of Chico. Lencho's lease was up on the rental house and now it was time to buy. He wanted it to be special, and he had the money, so he caught up with an old friend, now a realtor, named Paul Abrams. Paul drove him all over the area showing him houses that were listed with acreage.

Anywhere that Lencho lived would have to be pot friendly. The Paradise area was called the banana belt, because of its elevation of about twenty-five hundred feet above sea level. It was ideal for growing a lot of things, not too hot and not too cold. Verdant hills stretched in all directions in the spring, but turned brown in the heat of the summer. Perfect climate for apples, oranges, avocados, and pears. And marijuana. The counter culture invaded the area years before to grow near perfect crops of the sacred herb.

"Hold the boat!" Lencho said to Paul. "That house we just passed had a for sale sign. It grabbed me. Back up!"

Ten acres of fruit trees with an older home also surrounded by trees of all description. There was a lock box on the door handle, so they let themselves in.

The house was a stunner with three bedrooms and two baths. The living room was immense with a brick fireplace. It attached to the dining room, which also featured a fire place. The kitchen and all the cabinets were made of hand hammered copper. A patio sat through the backdoor, and on the left stood the guest house. There was a two car garage and a shop. The place had been the pride and joy of a retired naval officer and his wife, but now they were both gone. Lencho was stunned by the care and craftsmanship the old boy had poured into it. A true labor of love, and now for a mere one hundred twenty seven thousand dollars, it was his.

He had to dig up the cash, literally, from the ground, and it was sort of moldy. The whole deal went smoothly. Paul took fifteen thousand to his office and placed it in an escrow account with a story of how the buyer was a music executive out of Nashville. The realtor used a power of attorney from Mr. Eric McKenzie and did all the leg work. The balance was paid some months later in a similar fashion. Lencho moved his family into the new digs. Then he went to work.

For the next three years he would remodel and expand the house, but because he was a fugitive he could not go out to meet the community. It was rural, but even as his children went to school and made new friends and met the neighbors, Lencho never did.

Men worked on the property week in and week out, and it was all paid for in cash. He also stashed a hundred thousand dollars wrapped carefully in a weather proof container inside a big roll of tar paper roofing that sat in a stack in plain sight. He figured it wasn't likely that anyone would steal some roofing material. Down in Mexico City, he had a safety deposit box at the Bancomer, which contained over two hundred thousand dollars in cash for future buys. So, Lencho was feeling pretty secure with his family now ensconced in a nice house, the children fat and healthy, and the lovely Tamara at his side. He asked her to marry him, but she refused. That was the only thing that tarnished the moment.

To assist in the effort, he brought his brothers out from Prescott as well as close pals in the construction trades. They all worked side by side. Then he wired the barn for Michael and Philip, Helltown's ace clone men. These guys were ahead of the times, and Philip was very interested in grapes as well.

"We're gonna set up a clone shop in here and give you a piece of the action once we're up and running," they told him.

"What the fuck is a clone shop?" Lencho asked.

"We are going to establish mother plants. And from the mothers we develop female clones that we'll sell to the growers in the Emerald Triangle. This concept results in totally female plants, because, as you know, the seed of marijuana are both male and female, roughly fifty-fifty. We will install thousand watt halide lights and keep the female plants, the mothers, in the vegetative state constantly. At eighteen hours the plant will never bloom and from her we will take the cuttings and rootone them to become clones after they develop a root ball. Interested?"

"Very," Lencho answered.

So in what seemed rather dull to the untrained eye, these lads made a couple of hundred thousand dollars a year net at ten dollars per clone. They were responsible for the vast majority of the weight that was produced in the

Triangle.

That summer the boys invited Lencho to attend the annual Emerald Triangle Cruise and Dinner on the San Francisco Bay. Four hundred people wined and dined on a large ferry going up and down the bay from the Golden Gate Bridge to Alameda and back past Alcatraz Island. They devoured lobster, shrimp, and fine wines in celebration of another good year of domestic pot growing. The motto that year was 'Buy American.'

On Sunday nights, he would take a plane to Mexico and resume his ever expanding operations south of the border. As the workers pruned and planted trees and made additions to his Paradise home, he formulated plans that he hoped would bring stability to the future. "The day will come when they will nab me," he told Tamara. "I don't kid myself. They always nab a guy, but I hope this property will be self-sustaining by then. I'm going to build some big greenhouses for various legal products. Along with the orchards, this place will make money. Then I'll get some hot shot lawyers and even do the time, if I must. But someday it will be over and I'll be free to pursue legit efforts. You wait, babe, you just wait."

*****

"I need to establish a bank account, Fernanda," he said. "Can you pull some strings and get that done?"

"In Mexico, a foreigner can't usually have a regular bank account. In your case, it wouldn't be wise anyhow. But I know some people at the Bancomer, and they will help me get you a safety deposit box. How is that?"

"Make it a big one."

A big one it was, and Lencho put another one hundred and fifty grand inside of it in the heart of Mexico City. Now, when he had bundles of cash, he wouldn't have to sew it into his underwear.

He also got together with Jerry Strickland for drinks and discussion.

"Give any more thought to my offer?" Jerry asked. "I mentioned you to my control officer back at Edwards. He said he could use another hand."

"I gotta tell ya, buddy, I have always avoided guns. And though I enjoy a sniff of the white stuff now and again, I'm not keen on getting involved in that trade. I was always told it was the future, but I also have known more than a couple of friends that have bit the dust over it."

"I understand what you're saying," he replied. "I never had any use for it either until I got my badge."

"Badge?"

"Exactly. Who are the guys best positioned to sell dope and get away with it? Cops, of course. That's because they wear the badge."

181

"Ummmmm."

"Down here all coppers are corrupt. They hide behind their badge and drown in the mordida. Same everywhere really; certainly back home. We both know there ain't a narc in the biz that ain't dirty. No honest cop goes into the drug game. They line up to get in because it's so profitable. And nobody doubts their honesty, which is a howl. The citizens are so dense, they never get it. This dope thing will go on forever because there is so much money in it. And I got the ultimate badge, my man: The badge of the CIA. That's federal protection of the highest sort. Total immunity."

"Does that make the coke trade any less evil?"

"It's just business, Lencho. Stay in the weed game, if you want, but I'm telling you, you're missing the boat."

"I sure appreciate the offer, Jerry, but I think I'll pass up the boat and keep myself grounded."

A couple of nights later, Lencho dined with Fernanda and her new boyfriend. She had split from her fag husband. The new man in her life, Yeyo, was at their service, obtaining documentation and running errands.

"Do you know what Jerry does for a living?" he asked her. "Has Cricket told you anything?"

"She hasn't said much. What are you talking about?"

He told her about Jerry's profession, and they both shook their heads in bewilderment. "I seriously doubt this could be true," Fernanda concluded. "I like him, and I think the world of his girlfriend. You know how men are. They got to be bigger than life. Caesar was like that. Everyone thought he was so handsome and such a ladies man, but you see how he really was," she laughed and Lencho left the next day for home.

He had an arrangement with a young law student named Dudley to pick him up from San Francisco International in a rented plane. Dudley was a novice pilot, so Lencho paid for the plane to give Dudley flying time. It was a nice arrangement. The lad dropped the weed man off at the small airport in Paradise. It was a ten minute drive from there to his new home. On the way, this time, he searched for the house and the property that Jerry described as his. It wasn't hard to find; Lencho had seen it many times before as he traveled south on Clark Road. Fifteen miles from the airport, it was the ten acre spread on the rise with a three thousand square foot ranch style house with a hangar, which Jerry told him housed his helicopter. Somewhere on that property there was supposedly twelve steel boxes loaded with cash and gold. "Mostly gold," Jerry had said.

Man, Lencho thought, at two hundred fifty bucks an ounce; that would be a pretty pile.

The phone rang and it was Terry from Prescott. "Lencho, how are ya doing? I was thinking of flying down to Mexico and thought about you."

Terry was a little younger than Lencho. He was a pilot for Blue Bird Aeronautical out of Burbank. In a Leer jet he flew business types and Hollywood celebrities all over the place. He and Lencho had been friends since high school. Currently, he and a partner owned a 185 Cessna that could haul a maximum of five hundred pounds. "I make OK money, man, but I been thinking about a onetime smuggling deal to pick up some weed. We got the money together, and I was hoping you would be interested."

Lencho had just flown in to Prescott and was tired. As the two sipped beers, he gazed out the window of Terry's front room towards the mountains.

"I plan on retiring soon, Terry. Got me a nice place in Cal, my family, and high hopes of straightening out my various difficulties. But sure, if you want to make a run, I'm game. I'll line things up, find us a place to do it. You ready to violate the border?"

"Yup. Me and my partner."

"Who's your partner?"

"Jack. Jack Daniels," he replied patting the bottle in his pants pocket.

*****

Ronnie finished his stint in the pen for the botched driving job where he claimed he had stolen a truck full of pot. Lencho put Ronnie up in a hotel in Mexico City so he could keep an eye on Lencho's expanding operation down there. Fernanda hooked Lencho up with a little old man named Guilermo Tover-Mena, who was the mayor of Sayula in the twin cities region of Coatzacoalcos and Acayucan and the local weed man locally.

The area was oil rich from the Pemex rigs out in the Gulf, and a rare example of prosperity in Mexico. A wide river flowed through with a majestic expansion bridge, reminding Lencho of the Golden Gate. Dams held back the water for hydro power, and out towards the lake a rock quarry produced granite for the natural gas pads that dotted the area. A long straight gravel road ran to the quarry, though it was crossed here and there with high voltage power lines. Between dusk and dawn it made a convenient landing strip.

"How much mota do you want to buy, Señor Lencho?" The mayor asked.

"Let's make it two hundred kilos, Mr. Mayor," he answered.

Having concluded the arrangements with the Mayor, Lencho flew back to Mexico City where Ronnie had met up with Terry. Before the sun came up the next day and the first big trucks rumbled down the gravel road to the quarry, Lencho and Terry would have to land, pick up the load, and be gone. Timing was crucial as they headed in. The road sloped uphill and Terry brought his plane to a halt where a mountain of marijuana was waiting beside a low fence, along with fifteen Indians provided by Mayor Tover-Mena to load them up. Once it was loaded, they disappeared like ghosts, and it was time to leave.

"Now give her some gas and spin her around, Terry. This road is tight, so do it fast."

Terry gave her the gas, but wasn't fast enough, and the right gear slipped off and got stuck in a rut, hitting the fence with the tip of the wing.

"Holy shit," Lencho groaned.

With the prop spinning madly, they climbed out of the plane and tried to lift it a couple of inches so they could manually turn it around to face the right direction. It was no use.

Hollering and cursing and whistling in the hope the Indians were still nearby, they strained under the weight.

"The loaders are gone, and if we don't get out of here soon, the first trucks will show up," he yelled.

Suddenly, Salvador, the head loader, reappeared.

"You got a little problem, Señor?" He asked with a toothless grin.

"God bless you!" Lencho yelled over the roar of the engine. "We're stuck. Can you and your boys help us?"

All the loaders emerged from wherever they had been, and with a lot more grunting, groaning, cursing, and yelling, they moved the plane into position. Thanking them profusely, Lencho climbed back inside as Terry gunned the engine for takeoff.

"Now listen," Lencho yelled, "take note of those power lines ahead. It's a mile from here to there, and you must go under them before lifting off. I walked this road and I figure with the weight and all, we'll never make it if you lift off in front. Is that clear?"

"Quite clear," Terry yelled back. "No more fuck ups. I'm ready."

They taxied forward and Lencho leaned back in his seat with a sigh of relief. He fumbled for a joint in his shirt pocket and reached for his zippo as the little plane gained momentum. Two minutes after they began he felt the wheels begin to lift. But the power lines, all one kazillion volts and six spans of them, were dead ahead. The engine screamed as the acceleration increased. He only got three words out of his mouth before he knew they were airborne: "What the fuck?"

For whatever reason, Terry was taking off in front instead of behind as Lencho had clearly instructed. The huge wires loomed ever closer. The plane lifted faithfully, but slowly. He made instantaneous calculations in his head: No weight, yeah we can do it. Nearly a quarter of a ton will slow us down twenty percent—we're doomed!

He didn't even look at the pilot now. The middle strands of the wires were dead ahead, but the plane kept going up. That was good. What was bad was that they had maybe a quarter of a mile or six seconds to climb another fifty feet.

Five, Four, Three, Two . . .

"Oh Jesus, oh God!" Lencho prayed as the little engine strained and nosed upwards. He said goodbye to his children and Tamara as the end neared. The top tier of the tower was dead ahead, and as Lencho closed his eyes, the left wheel bounced off the wire. It fucking bounced off the top wire as they soared into the clouds!

Shaken, but still very much alive, Lencho gasped in incredulous relief, and then turned an enraged glare towards the pilot. His old pal, Terry, who without another word reached down under his seat for his partner, a bottle of Jack Daniels whiskey.

After the near miss, very little was said between the two as they reached the next stop. A chunk of aluminum striping flapped from the right wing as a result of the rut. That flap resulted in excess drag, which caused them to lose time. Upon refueling in Saltillo, there were still six hours of flight time left before crossing over the border into Arizona where they were scheduled to meet Walter at an out of the way strip called Picacho Peak. The place was normally empty, but this time someone was there as they made their approach. The two noticed the dust rising from the vehicle now heading in their direction. Up and off they flew again, but now their petrol was almost gone.

"We gotta land, Lencho," Terry told him flatly. "If we don't get fuel real soon, we'll crash!"

Deja vu all over again, Lencho thought. Again they spied an airstrip east of the interstate in a town called Eloy.

"I know that we need gas, man, but I can't be found if this doesn't go well. They'll give me life in prison, and that is not part of my plans for the future. Let me out as soon as we land."

Terry knew there was no point in arguing, so at the end of the long runway Lencho jumped out and got as comfortable as he could while hiding behind a knoll. He watched Terry pull up to the hangar, get out, and go inside. He pondered the bundles of weed in the plane wrapped in black visqueen. After an hour, and as dusk descended, he had waited long enough. Fearing the worst, he began to hike across barren fields of sage towards the lights of interstate 10. Two hours of stumbling and cussing, he arrived at a little motel on the edge of the freeway and checked himself in. He called a friend back in Prescott and left word where he was if Walt showed up, and then he showered and fell fast asleep. At 3:00 am, there was a loud knocking at the door. Warily he opened it for a peep and saw that it was Walt.

"Let me in, man," he said, "it's cold out here."

"What the hell happened?" Lencho asked in a daze. "Nothing went right with this load. Did the cops nail Terry?"

"Hell no," Walter laughed. "He's fine! All of the weed is also fine. Off loaded in a Mercedes Benz. The only wheels that he could find after he landed at Prescott."

"Prescott?! He landed in Prescott?" Lencho asked amazed.

"The strip that you guys stopped at didn't have any fuel. The fella there was a champ and he had some coffee with Terry, who told him he was hauling flowers. Well, it was true wasn't it? The flowers! So the guy drives Terry to another airport a few miles away and they find a gas truck and bring it back to fuel up his plane. Then he took off. He just landed out by the golf course in Prescott. He called Derick, who owns that diesel Mercedes. It was just packed with the weed, man. Took us an hour to move it. But in the end, all was well and everything is fine. Terry says to say hello."

"This will be the death of me, yet," Lencho swore to himself.

*****

By now, the weed man had become an organization guy and broker. He had others like Terry calling him, so he arranged loads, found hiding places for the aircraft in use, and took care of the tedious tasks like paperwork. The constant juggling was hard work and he had a couple of people assisting him, such as Fernanda and her boyfriend in the Mexico City area. While up near the border, he continued to work with his Mafia pal Chava, who also had paperwork contacts. This brought him to Cuidad-Juarez, one of the world's most violent cities. Located on the U.S. side of the border is El Paso, Texas, or as the Mexican cartels call it, "The Chicago of the Mexican Mafia."

From there, Lencho rented a car from Avis and made contact with Chava and his partner Serrato. He wanted good paperwork for the Queen Air Doc had given to him.

"Yeah, sure Lencho," Chava said cheerfully. "I'm here. Come on over and we'll talk about it."

Juarez was a big, bustling sprawl with a jammed downtown full of shops and bars. Everywhere you looked, there were merchants, hawkers, and little urchins selling chicklets. Taxi cabs belched pollution and honked their horns into the wild cacophony. On the outskirts were crowded neighborhoods, most of them squalid, but a few much more affluent. There was little vegetation with streets pockmarked and rutted.

Chava owned a nicer thirty five hundred square foot cinder block house located in a Cul-de-sac. It sat in the middle of a dozen others like it, and was painted yellow and lime. Lencho steered the compact car gingerly down the short streets and began looking for a spot to park. Finding one, he climbed out with the address in his hand and began to squint into the noon day sun searching. He was jolted by the sudden squawk of a police radio. It had emanated from a dark sedan he had parked beside. Cautiously, the weed man looked around and realized there were several other vehicles identical to the first police car he had noticed. All of them were Crown Victorias in various hues, and all had radios and portable rotating lights sitting on dashboards.

"My god!" He gasped. "This place is being busted."

With welling panic, he slid back behind the wheel and shot out of the cul-de-sac as fast as he could while peering into the rear view mirror looking for any coppers that might decide to pursue his fleeing vehicle. Another hour of waiting in line at the International border, and he was safely back at the Holiday Inn. He immediately picked up the phone in his room and called Chava.

"Chava," he gasped, "there are cops everywhere at your place. Are you being raided?"

Peals of laughter erupted on the other end of the phone. "Raided? Ha ha ha! Did you hear that, muchachos?" He howled to whoever else was present. "That is so funny, Lencho. Get back here. I am just having a little party with my friends. You must meet them! They are all at work on the riot."

Lencho noticed marchers when he first arrived two hours earlier, but he didn't pay them much attention. The leftist movement in Mexico was largely led by students. Angry labor joined in as well, along with disenfranchised peasants seeking land and reform. They were at war with the establishment, and there was discord and violence all across Mexico.

Lencho went back to Chava's home, considerably relieved but still confused. This time, however, he rapped loudly on Chava's door and could hear the sound of men laughing and talking. Ranchero music blasted from a stereo. When his comrade finally opened the door, he was heartily welcomed inside. His jaw dropped at the sight of dozens of men all with gun belts and pistols hanging from holsters. Badges of the Federal and City Police were abundant, and most of the men wore expensive suits and cowboy boots. A mound of cocaine sat on the coffee table in the living room with a burly Federale bent over from the sofa, snorting huge lines through a short straw. He was a fat man, and his awkward position caused his 9mm Beretta pistol to fall to the floor. He looked down at it and burst into laughter. Others joined in as they quaffed cognac from large round glasses. Marijuana smoke hung in the air and women in various stages of undress ran laughing from the bedrooms upstairs.

Chava slapped his gringo friend on the back and said, "Have some perico. Get something to drink and fuck some whores. They are beautiful, no?"

Lencho was a party type of guy, but this madhouse was even too much for him. He had come here twice to conduct business and that is what he wanted to do, get something accomplished, not find himself in the midst of a dozen loaded policemen, many of whom were waving their guns recklessly.

"My god," he said over the noise. "What are these cops doing here?"

"Oh, they are just off duty. The communists are causing trouble and they will be going out to deal with them soon. Anyway, amigo, they are not all cops. Pancho here is my vato from Apatzingán, and so is Chuey over there with the puta. We do a lot of business up here like I told you, and our best allies are these men. Go ahead, goddamnit, don't be a spoil sport. Go and fuck that pretty girl standing over there. You don't want to hurt Chava's feelings, do you?" He kicked at an AK-47 lying by his feet.

These clowns were clearly out of their minds, and that was punctuated by a blast from a drunken cop's handgun as he took some shots at a marble statue of Aphrodite in the corner of Chava's living room.

"Hey, Nieto!" He yelled. "Don't shoot in my home, ok? Have some respect!"

"How long has this party been going on?" Lencho asked.

"What day is this? Tuesday? I guess since Saturday, then."

The door opened and five more detectives from the Juarez police department entered, one with a bloodied head. They said hello to Chava and began mixing themselves drinks.

"This riot has been going on for a week," Chava said. "That's detective Yeste. He's a real head buster, but it looks like someone busted his also."

Lencho had never been in a room like this in his life. The cops and robbers were thick, and they were partying together, side by side. The world of crime is usually separated by a thin line; here, that line vanished altogether. By the next day, Lencho told Chava he had to get some rest. "And what about my paperwork?" he asked. "I got people who are waiting for me."

"I want you to go with Paniagua," Chava told him. "He's that handsome hombre in the nice suit by the fireplace with the puta. You stay with him until things are ready. He'll get a room at the Presidente Hotel in town and will fill you in on some things."

David Paniagua was a thirty-eight year old Mexican equivalent of an FBI agent. He wore a nice suit with hand crafted boots. He was a good looking guy, but had a glint in his eye that Lencho recognized as that of a killer. He checked them both into the fancy hotel without paying. For two more days, they hung out together, and although it wasn't Lencho's idea of a fun time, it was educational. Over drinks and dinner, they had several long conversations in which agent Paniagua told him that the authorities knew all about him and what he did. They knew that he usually went to the Indians for his weed, and that they thought that he was a dumb shit for being a weed man when everyone knew that coke and heroin were much more profitable. "But to each his own," he told him. Since he did have rather good connections, they would not bother him as long as he occasionally paid his way and did them a few favors.

"Such as?" Lencho inquired.

"We have this Aero Commander on an airfield near here. It was confiscated and we don't have anyone right now who can fly it. We want it moved to another airfield some miles away. Can you help us?"

"No problem," Lencho told him.

He reached for the phone and called Bill at his home in Louisiana. Bill flew down to El Paso and Lencho drove him over the border where, in short order, the Aero Commander was moved as requested. This sort of tit for tat was giving the weed man a certain panache in the world in which he lived. Other gringos didn't have that. He had connections with the cops, the mafia, and the Indians in the high elevations; not to mention that he had personally spent a couple of years behind the walls of Andonegui Prison. Such was the world of illegal drugs. It was a world of smoke and mirrors. A world where governments went through elaborate charades that they liked to call their 'war on drugs.' Where a man had to be connected to even play in the dope game, and even then it could be dicey.

Agent Paniagua finally went back to wherever and whatever he did officially, and dropped Lencho back at the front door of the Mafioso Chava. Cops were still coming and going, and that included the Assistant Chief of Police of the city of Juarez.

"Sure, I can do this for you," he told Lencho when they had been introduced. "Chava has explained what you need. It will cost you ten thousand dollars, but from now on, whenever you need such things in this area, it will be done. Stay at my hacienda tonight, and then tomorrow we will go into town and see some officials at the air transportation department. Excuse me for a little bit while I say hello to that lovely Señorita at the top of the stairs."

That night, he stayed on the edge of the city in the chief's ever expanding palace. A new fountain was being installed in the foyer, but for a change it was actually quiet and he was able to get a good night's sleep.

The next morning over coffee the chief explained, "There is big trouble coming, Lencho. The CIA is infiltrating our country under the protection of the DEA. America is doing this all over the world. Countries allow the DEA in to fight the drug war, but what they're really after is a new way to get in so they can gather information and gain more control the world over. It's not about drugs. They could care less about drugs. What they want to do is cause a division in La Familia by supplying guns and money to the different territories causing a separation of power. Many of our people will be killing one another to take control in their area. Soon it will result in a battle among ourselves. An ancient strategy of divide and conquer. We are hoping that this won't happen, but as you know the U.S. will stop at nothing." After breakfast, they went in to the town as promised.

"Hello Chief," a pretty young secretary said to him. "The paperwork that you requested is ready. Let me get Señor Nobriga to affix the appropriate tax stamps."

Just like that, the Queen Air was now legal for the next six months. A day later, he was ready to leave, but a little worried he might miss his flight out of El Paso. When he asked the Chief to call him a taxi, the Chief waved him off.

"I will drive you to the airport myself, Lencho. Don't worry about a thing."

But he was a wanted man, and so he was very worried indeed. Off they went. As they drew near the customs line, the chief pulled his weapon from its holster and placed it beside him along with his identification. Lencho was sweating bullets, but the border agent passed them through without a hitch after recognizing the Chief. Lencho was dropped off at the airport in plenty of time to catch his flight back home to Paradise.

*****

It had been cold in California, so the more moderate climate of Mexico City was welcome upon his return two weeks later. He visited Fernanda for a couple of days and hooked up with Ronnie, who was living in a small hotel. He also saw Jerry for a few hours as he passed through, and then he flew out to Guadalajara to see the brothers Chato and Mario. Chato was a ladies man who squired the pretty girls to the discos at night while Mario was a quiet guy with a wife and children. They were both younger than Lencho, but very ambitious with plans to open a fancy restaurant and bar in the bustling city. He had met them through Fernanda.

Guadalajara itself was a place of sophistication and fun where Europeans liked to vacation. It was also a center of finance and home of a drug lord named Caro Quintero, aka El Cocho Loco (the crazy pig). Among many other enterprises, El Cocho and his partners ran a couple of huge marijuana plantations in the deserts in the north. These were elaborate affairs with acres and acres under cultivation. The men who tended the crops were virtually slaves out there in the middle of nowhere living in barracks. Water was pumped from artesian wells. The colas were high quality and lightly pressed for smuggling. They fetched a premium price.

Quintero had the paid protection of very high government officials, which was obvious as the operation was totally open to both airplane and satellite surveillance. He did not care if anyone knew that those plantations were out there, because he had paid to be invulnerable. Among those on his pad were the state and federal police and the resident agents of the American Drug Enforcement Agency.

The DEA has field offices all over the world. As lore and legend would have it, they are brave men fighting the drug menace and going head to toe with the forces of evil. One of those American Drug Agents was Enrique Camarena, aka Kiki. He was part of a corrupt unit under the pay of El Cocho Loco. Then he dropped the dime on his masters, and Washington put great pressure on the Mexican government via President Ronald Reagan to shut those pot farms down. The loss of these enterprises were devastating to the Guadalajara cartel, and Quintero was beyond angry. He ordered Camarena executed on February 9, 1985, just as Lencho arrived in town.

The tortured and mutilated corpse of Kiki and his assistant caused a sensation worldwide. No one murdered U.S. Agents. It simply was not done. The DEA and the Reagan administration used the opportunity to ratchet up their so-called "War on Drugs," so the American police presence flooded into Guadalajara.

"You must stay inside your hotel room," Chato told Lencho emphatically. "The city is crawling with DEA and the police have been forced to do their jobs. If they think that anyone is in the trade, those individuals will disappear. If you don't want to be tortured, stay low until things cool down."

"Why in the hell did they kill that narc?" Lencho asked.

"Listen, that guy was paid like all of the others to look the other way. They are making him out to be a hero, but he was dirty. I hear that he was tricked to rat out Caro by the Americans so that he would be killed. That gives your president the excuse to send more American forces. Probably the real reason isn't drugs at all, but the communists. We have a lot of unrest in our country, right now."

"So I noticed," Lencho answered.

The pot deal that he was working on with the brothers was put on hold. This bud was of the finest that he had ever seen in Mexico. Big, fat colas like they grew up in Northern California. Gringos were involved with the supervision, and it was from Indica seed instead of the typical sativa. He had planned to bring it back slowly, so it would be un-pressed. Finally, he ducked out of town and headed back home where he hoped to buy another airplane his old pal Al Hansen had found for him.

"She's a beauty," Al said. "Not new, but in good condition. A Cessna 320. Twin engines with a load capacity of one thousand pounds, and best of all, the cost is just forty grand."

After looking the plane over, Lencho bought it. He once again planned to go down to score a quick load Herminio had waiting, staying away from Guadalajara for the time being. He would go ahead, and Al would meet him in the artistic town of Taxco. High in the mountains of Guerrero, Taxco oozed quaintness. Tight little streets surrounded by houses and shops all bordering on sheer cliffs. The airstrip appeared suddenly from the heights and ended in a precipice. A plane landed and then took off again by flying into the chasm of a three thousand foot gorge that plunged toward a road below that was hardly visible. Al landed with a colossal thud.

"I hate to tell you this, Lencho," he said when they met at the hotel, "but that damned strip has a dip right in the middle of it, and I guess I came in too far before I set it down. I hit that dip and it was bad. Now I'm a little worried about the plane structurally."

"Will we be able to carry the load that I have arranged?" Lencho inquired.

"We'll find out when we take off," Al said.

They toured the town that day taking in the art shops and silver smiths that made it famous. While enjoying a fine meal and wine, they had put the plane out of their minds.

It was a shock when the plane shook and shimmied on the way toward the edge of the airstrip. "Man, this don't feel good," Al said over the roar of the engines.

When they launched over the precipice, Al pulled back on the controls, but instead of rising they began to descend.

"Holy shit!" Lencho yelled as he usually did when some new terror of flying confronted him. "We're sinking!"

Al went pale and pushed the throttle full forward giving the plane all the gas he could muster. The engines roared, but down they went. It was as if they were gliding, but ever downward. Lencho looked back over his shoulder from where they had just departed and instead of seeing the airstrip, he could only see a bare cliff.

"Pull her up, Al!" he shouted.

Al's feet frantically pumped the foot pedals controlling the rudder and wing flaps, but nothing happened and their descent increased in velocity. It was a hot morning, and the thought that it was the weather affecting his new yellow bird crossed his mind.

"Get her up now, Al!" he bellowed.

"Trying to, goddamn it! Trying!"

The plane was not hydraulic, so all of the connections were steel cables. The wings were there for lift and stability, not for strength. They appeared very wobbly now as they continued to drop ever faster towards what looked like sure doom two thousand feet below. Al pulled and pulled on the steering, but it was to no avail. Beads of sweat formed on his brow and he cursed and cajoled. "Come on, baby, come to life. Talk to me."

He reached for the throttle and pulled it back a hair and then forward again, but still nothing. Nothing was the name of the game, now. No response at all and the road that was once thin and distant was looming closer and getting wider. Boats and planes are mysterious contraptions. Just as a boat full of holes and a broken bow might not sink, airplanes too can surprise, and suddenly this one did just that. At eight hundred feet, she came back to life.

Not abruptly, but almost imperceptibly, she began to respond to Al's steering commands and they slowly nosed upwards gaining altitude. At five hundred feet, she was level again. They began to climb. Al heaved a huge sigh and brought her up to a thousand feet as they passed through the canyon and then beyond the range and over the desert. The warm thermals helped as the yellow bird climbed some more. They both knew, however, that she could never handle half a ton of product.

"We're kissing the weed off," Lencho concluded. "Head for home. Let's hope that we can at least make it back."

They did make it, and after Al went over the plane thoroughly, he was forced to inform the weed man that it was a lost cause. The structural integrity of both wings was breached and the internal cables and their workings were tweaked beyond repair. It was truly a miracle they had not been killed. The plane was now a death machine. Lencho's air force was back to just the Queen Air that Doc had bequeathed. His forty thousand dollars was lost. Someone offered him eight thousand for the two good engines, and he accepted gladly. He went home to Paradise to work on his farm until October, when he planned to get Bill and use the Queen Air to retrieve the super weed in Guadalajara. Until then, he said "Fuck it" to the pot business.

Chapter Eleven

"Ride Me Down Easy"
Released 1973
Waylon Jennings

Ride me down easy Lord, ride me on down
Leave a word in the dust where I lay
Say I'm easy come easy go
And easy to love when I stay.

DEA

Home is where the heart is, but to an ambitious man it wasn't long before puttering around the estate became tiresome. Memories of close calls faded, and the urge to make progress went to the front burner. He headed over to Prescott with his Portland, Oregon pal Chuck to buy another gas truck. Chuck was a marijuana dealer that specialized in Columbian weed. Tight little buds that were loaded with seeds, Columbian pot was ubiquitously red and gummy from the early seventies until the mid-eighties. He routinely kept twenty-five thousand pounds of the stuff in his basement, and Lencho occasionally went up there with his son Luz to buy some.

Chuck and his partners also sold tropical foliage and hanging baskets that sold quite well to indoor plant enthusiasts. Lencho had plans to grow them himself for Chuck's Oregon market once he completed building his hot houses. But now they went with a gal named Cheryl Mauritz to get a good deal on a gasser. By this time, Lencho was an expert at meeting a load on some desolate strip; he'd have a crew unload the product, refuel the plane, and have everyone gone in ten minutes. The trucks they used were heavy duty pickups with camper shells and equipped with big tanks, an electric pump, and a long hose. A switch on the dashboard would kill the brake lights in case they were chased by the Border Patrol or some deputies. The most important thing was to make sure the trucks were registered in somebody else's names.

"Want another drink?" Lencho asked Cheryl handing her a flute of wine.

Cheryl was a nice girl who came from a good family, but she did like the grape, so before they headed over to Sanderson Ford, Lencho helped her consume at least a bottle and a half of Dego Red.

"Good stuff, man," she hicked. "I insist on quality!"

"Man, I registered the last truck we bought for the flower business," Lencho lied as they drove across town. "It's your turn, Chuck."

"I know it is," Chuck replied. "But I left all my I.D. back in Portland. Totally forgot to bring it with me when I left home."

"Way to go. Now what will we do?" Lencho replied. "We get all the way down here and we can't buy the damned truck. This really sucks!"

"Pipe down, you two," Cheryl giggled. "I have my I.D. Let's put the damn thing in my name."

"Really, Cheryl baby? You're the best! Here's the cash." Lencho handed her a bundle of moldy currency. "Twenty thousand should do it," he said as she stuffed the money in her purse.

After two hours of combing the lots, they found the beauty they were looking for, a three quarter ton four wheel drive. A little dickering with the salesman, and they settled on a price of eighteen thousand in cash. The salesman expected that to mean a check, but Lencho informed him: "Hell no, man! Cash means cash."

Cheryl tossed a wad of bills on his desk. It had, of course, been buried in the ground and smelled pretty bad. It seemed as though no one in the dealership knew how to count, but after about an hour they finally got the deal done and the piles of moldy bills were neatly stacked on several desks. Happily, there were lax reporting rules in those days.

Back in Paradise, Lencho had a visitor from Mexico. Roberto Azua had come with what he was certain was an offer Lencho would not be able to refuse.

"The Ochoa family wants to speak with you about moving some white powder," he told him. "This could mean a lot of money, Lencho."

"'Those guys are with the Medellín Cartel, aren't they?" Lencho asked.

"Yeah, big time. I met them a month ago in Guadalajara. I'm doing some cocaine myself. The real money is there, my friend. It's so much less bulky than weed and very profitable."

"I hate to see you get involved with that stuff, Roberto," Lencho replied. "A little perico is fun every once in a while, but the trade is deadly. What the fuck, man? You don't even use drugs."

"The money is too big, Lencho. It's important to come down to Riverside and meet these guys. They are the real deal Colombians. Gallardo is now in charge of transportation, but the Ochoas produce the perico. They know all about you, and let me remind you that you work in Mexico and don't pay much in taxes. I think it is at least good manners that you go and meet with them for this little talk."

It was true that the weed man stayed pretty much independent. He would pay the tax whenever he had to, but usually he didn't. So to keep the peace he agreed to the meeting. They flew into Burbank Airport on a Saturday, rented a car, and then drove to a huge Mexican-style home in Riverside on Sunday morning. The place featured a circular driveway like his, only it was filled with luxury cars. Cadillacs, Mercedes-Benzes, and Porsches were parked from one end to the other.

A man with enough gold around his neck to drown if he fell into the swimming pool answered the door, and when he saw Roberto, gave him a hug and escorted them all inside.

"I am Paco," he said extending his hand. "Good of you to fly down. How about we first practice our religion since it is Sunday morning. We call it Sangre Diablo." This turned out to be tequila, tomato juice, and red chile. "Oh yes," he said as he reached for a small mirror and a rolled up one hundred dollar bill, "a taste of perico."

Once the cocaine had been snorted and a couple of Bloody Marys downed, they discussed the offer. Paco laid the C note on the mirror, gave a sigh of contentment, and stretched his back with his arms held wide. The head of Jesus dangled from a gold chain hung around his neck, almost disappearing in the black hair that sprouted beneath the silk shirt he wore unbuttoned to his waist. Lencho thought this guy and the other ten men that loafed around the house were such archetypes, he would have laughed at them if it wasn't so inadvisable.

"The family is always on the lookout for talent, Lencho," he said at last. "We have heard many good things about you. You have a good airplane or two, no?"

"Pretty good," Lencho agreed. "Twin engine Queen Air that I have parked in Mexico City."

"Sí, perfecto. How would you like to get out of this mota business and do some real work? Coca, my friend. For every ton that you fly back, we will pay one million U.S. dollars. Fly one a month or one a day. We have plenty of work for the right man."

"You know, Paco, that I have lost a load or two in my day. It was my money that I lost, but you know how it is. Sometimes shit happens. What would happen to me if I had some bad luck and I lost one of the Ochoa's loads?"

Paco smiled and, putting a fatherly arm around Lencho's shoulders, replied, "My friend, you know that would be no good at all. If you are a pro, then that would not happen. Am I right?"

"Well, I wished to pay my respects to Don Felix, the Ochoa family, and to you Paco, but I gotta decline your generous offer. I would be too afraid of some bad luck, if you know what I mean," he replied.

Paco smiled again. "Of course, my friend. But if you change your mind, come back and see us. Like I said before, we have plenty of work and always are in need of good men."

Once in the car and heading back to the airport, Roberto whistled.

"A million dollars a trip? Whew! That's a lot of dinero. If I could fly an airplane, I would do it in a snap."

"It is a lot of money, Roberto, but you can't spend it if you are in prison or dead, can you? You gotta understand that. Weed is good! Coke is not! Get away from that trade while you still can."

"A lot of money," Roberto repeated, and Lencho knew that he had not been listening.

*****

Terry called again, so Lencho made a second trip deep into Mexico to pick up a load. The trip went far more smoothly than their first. He paid for the weed, but when he and Terry reached the pickup area located deep in the Tabasco region, a heavy fog obscured the landing strip and he kissed it off. That was just the breaks of the game. If the buyer didn't pick up the product, it was forfeited. Fifty grand down the drain.

*****

With Doc being pretty much gone, now that he was down in Florida living the life, Lencho reached out to a dazzling couple from Canada named John and Minerva. They were transplanted Washingtonians now residing on their very own island just off Vancouver. Middle aged renaissance types, they were wealthy from investments in precious stones, gold, and real estate. They were also well connected in the drug world; Lencho met them through the restaurant brothers in Guadalajara, Chato and Mario. They invested fifty thousand dollars, and he placed the cash in his strong box at the Bancomer in Mexico City. It was getting time to bring back a load of super pot the brothers were involved with.

The 'big deal,' as it was called, was really a big deal. A first—ultra high grade marijuana that had not been pressed into oblivion. Big fat Indica colas that would transport the smoker into outer space. It wasn't cheap at $300 per kilo, but it was expected to fetch as much as five thousand dollars per pound in San Francisco. Compared to good Mexican bud, which sold at wholesale for just fifty dollars a pound and then flipped for eight hundred, the math was obvious. Everyone involved was excited.

Bill was stationed at the hangar with the Queen Air getting her shipshape for the flight over to Guadalajara, while Lencho called from Fernanda's penthouse. Her apartment building was both comfortable and high security for Mexico City. Cars entered the building in the basement parking. A heavy mesh steel gate operated by Julio, the security guard, ensured no unfriendlies entered. Julio lived in a converted storeroom with his wife and three kids, so he was on duty 24/7. He was a young man lucky to have a job. He stood ram rod straight in his second hand policeman's uniform with its blue stripe down the pant leg. On his hip was an old but well-oiled Smith and Wesson .38, and on his lips wore a constant and obsequious smile. But now at his elbow stood two sinister men from metro narcotics with alligator clips attached to the phone box on the wall and headsets on their ears.

They had been waiting and listening for two days on orders from the United States Drug Enforcement Agency. They were listening to a gringo named Lencho. He was to be kidnaped and spirited back to America where he was a fugitive from justice.

It was the same tactic the feds had used in the Kiki Camarean case. When they ID'd a physician believed to have been involved in the murder of their boy, they kidnaped him and shoved him under the fence where he was taken into U.S. custody. Then the moment came. Officer Reyonso Paz squinted and lifted a finger to his partner.

"My friend," Lencho said to his contact in Guadalajara. "Yes, I just got back. I'll be down to see you as scheduled. We're on time. But say, I need to change my order a little. Some friends added to the kitty and now I need an additional fifty guitars. Yes, that's right, fifty more. They know how beautiful that music is. Ha, ha. Ok? No problema? Excellent. I'm going to Bancomer in the morning then fly out. See you as scheduled. Goodbye."

"We better call Wayne," Paz said removing the headset. "The gringo is about to play us a song."

Bancomer was located on Insurgente Sur, the streets crowded with office workers, secretaries, moguls, businessmen, and the occasional policeman on the corner. Lencho eyed the cop and ignored the throngs as he entered the glass and steel edifice. The bank had just opened and the expansive lobby had only a few customers. An armed guard stood at attention as he walked up the scissor stairs with stainless steel and glass railing to the upper level where the safety deposit boxes were located. Flashing a smile and shifting the shoulder bag that he had brought along, he dug a key from his pants pocket and asked the young woman at the desk in Spanish if he could gain entry to his box. Once signed in, she led him into the vault where he added his key to hers. She unlocked the door to the two-by-two box he had rented.

"I'll need a moment," he said and she left him alone.

Moving quickly, he shoveled two hundred thousand dollars into his satchel, almost all of it in crisp one hundred dollar bills. Adjusting the weight, he left, said thanks, and trotted downstairs. As he headed for the exit, Fernanda rushed in and stopped him with a look of alarm, "There's two very suspicious looking men outside, Lencho, and I think they are cops!"

"Cops? Are you sure?"

"When I let you out of the car, I found a place to park and went over to a flower vendor for a moment, and that's when I saw them. One small man, the other big with no neck! What'll we do?"

"I'll tell you what we'll do," Lencho replied with a mix of annoyance and bravado. "You disappear. I'm going out there. I got a plane to catch."

As Fernanda had said, the two were waiting. "Eric McKenzie?" The first said.

"Maybe," Lencho answered.

"Wayne Boyd, Drug Enforcement Agency." Boyd's name and badge imprinted on Lencho's memory.

Lencho bristled and the hair on the back of his neck stiffened. "Well, Wayne, in case you haven't noticed, we're in fucking Mexico. Why don't you get the fuck back to America and we'll talk some other time."

The big one was behind him now and suddenly he felt the barrel of a gun in his ribs. "Shut up, puke, and come with us. Quietly," he snarled.

A plaza fronted the bank with tiled walkways and lush greenery. A fountain with a black sedan parked beside it splayed water onto lily pads. The crowds went about their business and didn't seem to notice them as they marched Lencho to the vehicle. The big narc opened the back door and shoved Lencho to the floor. He yanked the satchel off his arm and tossed a suede jacket over his head. "Stay down and keep your yap shut," he ordered.

The two DEA agents climbed into the front with Boyd behind the wheel. "Let's see what we got here," Lencho heard him say. And then, "Holy fucking shit!"

The big one reached over and held the pistol to Lencho's head. There was more whispering. The car engine sprang to life and they pulled away from the fountain. Moments later, he felt the vehicle turn right and then slow down as it made its way into a tight alley. They stopped and locked him in. Lencho lifted his head from beneath the jacket and looked out the rear window. He saw the narcs walk up to two other cars, both of them cop looking sedans. Four snappy looking men in their best under cover Hawaiian shirts and white slacks waited. A conversation ensued and he saw Boyd gesture back in his direction. Then he saw two friendly faces another hundred feet beyond all of the police.

It was Fernanda and Bill in the bright red mustang he had bought for her only a week earlier. He could see even from that distance the look of horror on their faces. The narcs returned and the rear door opened. The big man grabbed him roughly by the arm and dragged him over to the Mexicans. The alley way was bustling with activity, but no one paid any attention, or if they did they preferred to go about their business. A sense of unreality began to set in as he looked at the faces of the smiling men. He saw agent Boyd pat his satchel. One of the Mexicans opened the trunk of his car and then ordered, "Get in."

He felt faint and suddenly clammy, and just before the trunk lid closed, one of them yanked off his fine new boots. He had the fleeting thought that they must have wanted to steal them along with all of his money until it occurred to him they probably didn't want him to make a lot of noise kicking around inside the trunk of the car with his feet. Lencho thought of Susie, his sister, for some unfathomable reason and how she would take the news when someone told her that her little brother had vanished. Just like they always said, his life began to flash before his eyes.

The trunk was a tight fit and there was little room as he lay on top of a spare tire. Lencho was glad that the spare did not have a rim until his active imagination deduced maybe the tire was rimless because it was to be used to burn up his soon to be lifeless corpse. A body incinerates more efficiently when tires are used. They drove on. He knew that it was futile to cry out for help, but he did it anyway.

"Hey, anybody! Help me! Let me out of here!"

No one heard. An hour passed as the car traveled onward. He noticed that whenever they came to a stop sign or traffic light, he could just make out the sounds of the city. For the next two hours or more, there were many starts and stops. Then, it became quieter, and he was thinking that these men had reached the edge of town and would soon be out in the country. What then? He wondered if they were taking him to a remote farm where they would shoot him in the head and then feed his corpse to the pigs. Or maybe they would shove his lifeless body into a fifty gallon barrel of lye. Then he puked in the tight confines. The stench and the mess made it almost unbearable. He also had to take a pee after three long and tedious hours; by the fourth he could hold it no longer and did his business. Lencho's legs cramped and the pain caused him to scream out in agony. His shoulder and back muscles were on fire. Delirium was setting in and he thought for a moment that he was with Tamara, Fred, and little Lizzy.

They were all together on vacation down in Puerto Vallarta, and then they were all back in Paradise having a picnic in the orchard among the newly planted cherry trees. He wept, and after what seemed an eternity, the car came to a stop and Lencho heard the men get out. He expected the trunk lid to fly open and find himself staring wild eyed into the barrel of a gun. He wondered if maybe he should beg and plead for his life like they always did in movies. That somehow struck him as humorous, so he began to laugh. Maybe he would even spit in their faces and scream, "Fuck you, you scumbag beaners!" His laugh became deranged by the thoughts racing through his mind, and the trunk remained closed. It is said that there are no atheists in a fox hole.

~ Lencho's final conversation with God ~

*Lencho: I thought I was doing the right thing, God. Standing up for what I
    thought was right. You set me up.*
God: Ha! It's what I do. I set everybody up.
Lencho: So, you don't really care what happens to me.
*God: Of course not. How many people do you think have suffered doing
    what is right?*
Lencho: So you play us?
God: Like a fiddle.
Lencho: You think this is funny.
God: If you only knew.
Lencho: You're cold.
God: I'm also warm.
Lencho: You could get me out of this.
God: What's the trade off?
Lencho: I can't make any promises.

God: Well, at least you've got balls.
Lencho: You already know what I think, so I can't lie. You would see through it.
God: Wow, I'm impressed.
Lencho: If I live I'll continue with what I started.
God: And if you continue there will be more pain.
Lencho: Excuse me while I puke.
God: Feel better now?
Lencho: I pissed my pants.
God: You're not the first.
Lencho: This kind of stuff is routine for you.
God: Happens every day.
Lencho: Thick skin.
God: I don't have skin.
Lencho: Well, I got a lot more to do.
God: I'll think about it.

"Pretty good frijoles," Lencho heard one of the cops say after another hour had passed and they returned. "Yes, I also like the salsa here, it is excellent."

They climbed back in and Lencho yelled out to them, "Hey, I'll give you money! Let me the fuck out of here. Let me live!"

There was laughter from the other side, and then a man said, "Be quiet, gringo, don't make us tape your mouth closed."

The radio came to life, but he could not tell what they were saying. The engine started and the car moved off. Good thing that he had taken a shit before they all left or he'd be dealing with that smelly issue as well. He thought to himself: It must be at least seven by now and I'm supposed to be down in Guadalajara. Hope they don't sell that primo weed to somebody else. His mind was racing and more thoughts and memories flooded in.

What was supposed to have been his breakout move had come to this. No more middle men or investors. All the money was now gonna be his, and this load as well as future loads would make him rich. He would make so much money that he would be able to quit like Doc had done once and for all. Then he would tend to his legal problems and finish up the ranch. The ranch would provide good income for Tamara and the children while he did a couple of years in the Arizona penal system. Lucidity came and went as time dragged on and on. How, he wondered, had the cops gotten on to him? Had Doc been right? Had Doc really been tailed all the way to New York City as he had comically insisted"

A few months back, after they wound up the great Belize venture, celebrations were in order. Bill, Doc, Roberto, and Lencho were camped out in a nice hotel in McCallan, Texas, drinking and snorting coke. Doc was saying to Bill that he had done pretty damn good, and then asked him what his plans were.

"Well," Bill had replied, "I got to tell you that I dig the adventure angle in all of this as much as the money. I mean, what is life without some danger, right? My biggest trouble is that wife of mine. High school sweetheart kind of a deal. I married way too young and she hasn't changed since we were kids."

"I can relate," Lencho said.

"The woman is a nympho for me, man. Always wanting to have sex!"

"Whoa!" Doc laughed. "That don't sound so bad."

"She's a good enough girl, I guess, but the trouble is that it's still the same good girl. She thinks I'm messing around on her. I don't actually. You guys ever see me with too many other women? But one day I may just leave her, because she's driving me nuts."

"Why don't you clue her into your gig?" Lencho asked.

"Not a chance. The only way that you can stay alive in this business is with secrecy. I don't tell her a damn thing."

Then there was the rasping and thumping from next door. Finally, after a big snootful of cocaine, Doc said that he had enough. "I think it's the cops, goddamn it!" he bellowed.

The others just looked at one another and then had burst out in maniacal laughter.

"Come on, Doc," Lencho chortled, "mice maybe. Even rats. But cops? You are just too funny, man."

"I really doubt if it were the cops they would make so much racket. I mean, what kind of cops let their targets know that they're spying on them?" Bill asked as he swigged a beer.

"For your fucking information, it's well known that when the FBI was spying on the communists in the fifties, they had more informants than they had actual commies. The communists were so broke that they couldn't even pay their phone bill, so the FBI paid it for them so that they could continue to tap the fucking phones."

Everyone howled more than before. "Fuck you," Doc cursed. When they checked out the next morning, Doc was certain he was being followed. He had told Lencho later, "It was a skinny little shit and a big fat fucker."

"You use too much of that nose candy, Doc," Lencho had told his friend. "You'd better layoff of the stuff for a while."

"Bullshit! I know what I know," he replied. "I was followed from the hotel to the airport and these two jokers went right into the terminal with me. So, I'm thinking to hell with Florida, I'll throw them a curve and I bought a one-way ticket to Chicago. When I arrived in Shy Town, I jumped into a cab and took a little trip out into those residential neighborhoods and then back to O'Hare."

"Were they still on you?" Lencho had humored him.

"Fucking A! Same guys, too. So, I went to the United counter and bought a one-way ticket to New York City."

"You're kidding me, right?" Lencho exclaimed. "Then what happened?"

"I took a cab from Newark to Queens, and they were right behind me in another cab. So I'm getting desperate, ya know? I run from the cab down into the subway station there on 8th Avenue and jump onto an F train heading to Manhattan."

"They still on your ass?"

"Right behind me. They jumped on the next car."

"Where have I seen this movie before?" Lencho had mused while rubbing his chin. "Oh yeah, now I remember. The French Connection with Gene Hackman."

"Yeah, yeah," Doc said, getting even more animated. "Exactly like the fucking French Connection. I rode the train to the next station and then quickly jumped off. The cops jumped off, too. I jump back on, they jump back on. The thing then begins to move. But I faked the assholes out, cause I kept two fingers stuck in the door between the rubber thingy and then I whipped around, pulled the doors back open, and jumped back out again. They were not able to follow suit."

"Did you waive bye-bye through the window as they got left behind?" Lencho asked with a grin.

"Na, I flipped them the twig. Then I got an E train back to Jersey. Caught the next flight back to Miami."

Lencho laughed and kidded Doc about that one for months, but now as he was having difficulty breathing with his chest smashed against the stinky old tire and was pretty sure he would never set eyes upon his children again, he wasn't so sure.

The car made another stop. He heard the Mexican cops talking to one another as they climbed out. Something about it now being midnight, and they were tired, and it was time for some coffee. Fuck! He had been in the trunk since eleven a.m. Over twelve hours now. Why didn't they just get it over with? He had resigned himself to his fate. He knew it was over. What had started out being a spiritual quest of obtaining the sacred herb for the true believers had come to this. It had never really been about the money. Sure, money was important. It did buy nice things. It impressed the women. Money bought clothes for the kids and greased the wheels, but a man could make money in other ways. It never had to get this bad. No. He had stayed in the game because he believed in marijuana. It gave happiness and made fear and worry disappear. But it had become so popular and lucrative that murder and mayhem now marched alongside it.

Look at these cops. My god, our own fucking cops are thieves and murderers. He figured that most likely the DEA had been following him because he was a fugitive. Somehow, they got a line on him and Agent Boyd, along with his fat slug of a partner, was supposed to pick him up and then hand him over to the Mexicans for deportation. The U.S. was kidnaping fugitives now, because the U.S. Supreme Court had blessed the practice as being 'legal and constitutional' plus it saved on paperwork. But when they saw the cash in his satchel, their game plan must have suddenly changed. It was easy money, for god's sake. Just take it then and have their Mexican lackeys kill him. Tell the brass that he got away. "Sorry, boss," he could imagine them saying. "We went to the bank to grab Lencho and he made a break for it. We lost him in the crowd."

How often did they do this kind of stuff? All the fucking time, he was sure of it. It didn't just originate with the low level agents either. He remembered the word on the Guadalajara streets about Kiki Camarana and his murder by Caro Quentero.

"He was on the take," Chato had said. "But then he had ratted his paymasters out to the high command anyway, so they butchered him. That's how the game works."

The Mexicans returned to the car and he heard the crackle of a police radio. The car moved forward, and then he finally dozed off. The trunk sprung open and the lights of the Palasio flooded in. He squinted over his shoulder at the cops. "Get out," they ordered.

His legs were numb and he couldn't make them respond. Rough hands grabbed him, throwing him to the ground. He sat there for a second and looked around in a daze. Across the street was the seat of government in all of its splendor. The White House of Mexico City surrounded by the annexes of the bureaucracy. He knew at once they were not going to kill him there.

"What time is it?" is all he could say.

"It's two thirty, Señor Lencho, and I have some advice for you. Get out of Mexico and never come back. Clearly, you have enemies in high places, but it appears that you also have a few well connected friends, as well." They got back into their car and drove off.

Lencho clamored to his feet, and in his socks stumbled the opposite direction. Gathering strength from the realization that he would not die after all, he began to run, glancing back every few seconds to ensure his tormentors were not in pursuit. Half a mile down, he ran into the lobby of a modest hotel and staggered up to the startled night clerk. "Can I use your phone?" he gasped. With a look of disgust and apprehension, the clerk agreed and he dialed Fernanda.

"Please come and get me," he implored.

Fernanda arrived in ten minutes. She burst into tears when she beheld her wretched friend. Filthy, disheveled, and smelly, she embraced him anyway.

Along with a torrent of questions and explanations, she drove him to the Zona Rosa's Century Hotel. She brought his suitcase, and they went up to the room she registered via the crowded discotheque in the back. He showered and put on clean clothes as she proceeded to explain all that she knew of the recent events.

"Bill and I followed the cops to the alley after they grabbed you, and when they put you in the trunk, I went to my father at the port authority. He made some calls to the Federal Police. No one knew what would happen to you; if it was too late to save you or not. Only when you called me did we know that you were still alive."

"This game is really getting dangerous, Fernanda. When I find out how they got onto me, I'll fill you in. I need some sleep, right now, and then tomorrow I gotta tell John and Minerva what happened to their fifty thousand."

Lencho did not know the rich couple well and he was fearful that the loss would really piss them off. Fortunately for him, there were witnesses to his abduction, so he knew that they'd believe the story. But still, they were well connected people and heavy hitters. He really didn't need any more trauma. But John sounded relieved that he was still alive when Lencho reached him in Canada, and even agreed to come down with a fake birth certificate so he could get across the border back into the U.S. He flew up to Reynoso, and John flew down. They met up the next day at a local hotel.

When John came into the room, it was not with animosity that he greeted the weed man, but instead it was with warmth. He put his arms around the beaten down Lencho and hugged him.

"Don't give another thought about the money," he said. "The important thing is you're alive."

Lencho was moved to tears. This was the difference between the decent pot people and the mafia types. He crossed back into the U.S. at the border the next morning and the guards there accepted the new birth certificate without protest.

Chapter Twelve

"Rose in Paradise"
Released 1987
Waylon Jennings

Every time he talks about her
You can see fire in his eyes
He'd say, "I would walk through Hell on Sunday,
To keep my Rose in Paradise

TREASURE OF PARADISE

Back in Paradise, it wasn't the same. Like the pall of unease that descends upon the mind after a bad acid trip, the sun was shining but it stayed dark in Lencho's head. Tamara seemed concerned and professed shock at the horrendous ordeal that her companion had been through. She knew that her man could stand up to just about anything, but this experience had shaken him to the core.

Tamara wanted to be there for him, but couldn't really understand what he was feeling. She asked if he wanted to seek counseling for the nightmares that woke him in a cold sweat at night.

"I'm in these airplanes," he recounted to her almost whispering the words. "Night after night, I dream of airplanes. I'm thousands of feet up when the floor of the plane suddenly disappears. I struggle against the strong winds that are rushing in to sweep me out of the plane into the sky. I am trying desperately not to fall out. And lately, I dream of men standing on dark street corners wearing Hawaiian shirts with pistols in their belts. They grin at me and I want to run away, but my legs won't move. It's like I'm paralyzed. I try to strike out with my fists, but it's all happening in slow motion. The men say to me, 'Get in,' and I want to run but I can't."

The marijuana game was now over as far as Lencho was concerned. This he vowed. Nothing could drag him back into the business. He had just lost two hundred thousand dollars, stolen from him by two scumbag narcotics officers. They had attempted to murder him in the process and cover up their crime. If it had not been for that wonderful lady and her family's political connections in Mexico City, he would just be a memory to his children and siblings.

The marijuana trade was getting more violent and ugly. Where would it lead? When would it end? Never, if the cops got their way. It's much too profitable for them. Why can't the general public grasp the truth? Why do they continue to be fooled by the government and the self-serving politicians? The so called trusted officials singing the same old tune every time they come up for election. Get tough on crime. Lock up the dope dealers and dope fiends. Make the streets safe for law abiding citizens.

The more people arrested, the more prisons they build, open, and staff. The newspapers and television and radio carried the same stories every day. Headlines that read, "Record Drug Seizures made by the narcs with dozens of drug dealers rounded up."

But Lencho knew the truth. Those arrests and raids only made room for some new tough guy to move up the chain and take over the spot just vacated. Large arrests and busts meant pay and career advancements. And the narcotics police kept on stealing and taking payoffs from the underworld. He'd had enough.

But as early months of 1986 passed, things began to get a little brighter, or so it seemed anyway. He looked around at his property with the new trees being planted with drip irrigation, installed by his crew foreman Jeff, and sighed. The two green houses were fantastic, and his Mexican day laborers painted the new additions. Lencho hired attorneys to develop a strategy for his defense, and to try and fix the legal mess he was in with the Arizona courts. His children were doing well in school and had many friends. The major kink in his life, unfortunately, was that Tamara was getting moody and complained that she didn't like this or that about the property. She'd moan the house was too big or that she didn't like the way it was furnished or decorated. She would say that it wasn't her house. Lencho hired a maid to help with the housekeeping and meals, but still she seemed restless.

He chalked it all up to the general tension in the air and promised her once again that the weed business was now a thing of the past. Then, on a foggy Thursday evening at around seven thirty, a car pulled into his circular driveway and a lanky man climbed out and walked to the front door. Lencho saw him coming from the picture window in the front room. Now a teenager, Luz answered the doorbell.

"Dad," he called out.

Lencho asked the stranger what he wanted, but instead of an answer, he got the barrel of a .45 caliber pistol shoved into his gut. Luz saw the gun as his father pushed the boy back inside. He appeared to Lencho to be a junkie, or if he wasn't, he sure looked the part. Disheveled and in need of a shower and some mouthwash, the man had the look of utter desperation. They walked to the car where two others waited. Lencho's first thought was that these lowlifes had been sent by John and Minerva. Maybe they were not as forgiving of the fifty large they lost as he thought. Could it be that they now wanted their money back? The second of the thugs was a big blonde brandishing a long barreled .357 magnum. No sooner had Lencho been marched up to him than he clobbered the weed man upside his head with the gun. Lencho's eyes watered from the force of the blow. He started to fall, but the third grabbed him and threw him against the side of the old Chevy. One after another they pummeled him. Fists fattened his lip, knees were shoved into ribs, elbows to the sides of his head. Blood trickled down his cheeks to his neck and clothing. He put up his arms to protect himself and cried out, "I'll get you your fucking money! You don't have to beat me to death! You won't get anything if I'm dead! I got the plane sold, and I'll have thirty five thousand by tomorrow afternoon."

The thugs were now totally confused. They had come to rip him off, pure and simple. Word gets around in the doper crowd, and someone had told them that Lencho must have piles of cash, because he pays his men each and every day for the work on his ranch. But the words "thirty five thousand dollars" got their attention, though the part about the airplane meant absolutely nothing. They stopped with the violence.

"You can call John right now," Lencho gasped. "Tell him what I just told you. All the rest tomorrow. All I got here at the house is this fifteen hundred dollar money order from Western Union."

He reached into his back pocket and pulled out the wire transfer and cash he just received from Ronnie in Prescott. It was payback of some money that his brother owed.

"Take it. It's all I've got!" He implored.

The third thug grabbed the transfer slip, and the one who had originally gone up to the front door administered a final blow to Lencho's rib cage, and he went down. The confusion that he caused by all of his blatherings worked, and the thieves mumbled amongst each other and fingered the paper that Lencho gave them. He leaped up and dashed for his open garage. He slammed the door before the morons could give an effective chase.

"Come on, you mother fuckers!" He yelled desperately. "You ain't the only ones with guns now."

Although Lencho was not a man who kept guns, the mugs outside didn't know that. In truth, the most lethal thing in his garage was a claw hammer. The rip offs scurried to their car and beat a hasty retreat. Squealing tires mingled with the fog in the air. It wasn't only the fifteen hundred that hurt. Lencho had cuts and bruises, and a cracked rib, but he was okay. Calling Al Hanson for back up, Lencho put his qualms about guns aside for the moment and Al brought over a small arsenal.

But darkness settled once again onto his mind and he wondered if it mattered that he had survived recent nightmare events. The holy herb offered succor, as it always did. The vanquisher of sorrows, the one greatest gift of the gods, but still things sucked. How could his luck get any worse, he wondered? Then a ray of sunshine broke through the gloom in the form of a guitar player named Dugan. "Listen, man. I hear you're quitting the biz. A friend with some cash wants to make you an offer. Sell him your contacts and goodwill. He'll pay fifty thousand, half up front. He's an ape, but a good guy all in all. Interested?"

Does an ape shit in the jungle?

"The guy's name is Migilla. Migilla the Gorilla," Dugan informed him.

"Why do you call him that?" Lencho asked.

"He looks like one, that's why. Low forehead and bushy eyebrows."

"Bring him over," Lencho told him.

When Lencho finally met Migilla, he had to admit he did look like an ape. Besides the head, he was fat and walked with more of a shuffle than a normal gait. He wasn't good looking enough to pass as a silver back, but more like an old circus act. He took speed and, like Bill, had a wife he kept in the dark regarding his dealings. He did, however, have the cash on hand as well as a Cessna 206 at his disposal.

"How well do you fly?" Lencho asked him when they met.

"Real fucking good," was his reply.

So the next day, Lencho, Dugan, and Migilla went for a little test flight.

"See that dirt strip on yonder mountain?" Lencho yelled. "Land on it."

After three or four passes, Migilla finally got his sights half way fixed on the target and began his descent. It turned out to be less descent and more free fall, like a bag of apples falling off of a counter onto the floor. He bounced from two thousand feet to three hundred in ten seconds, and just before everyone on board barfed up their breakfasts, Migilla freaked out and aborted. Lencho proceeded to give the man a thorough tongue lashing as he was unable to navigate a fairly routine and easy landing.

"For God's sake man, in Mexico you're going to find airstrips that are really dicey. That one you just failed to land on was a piece of cake. To be a successful air smuggler, you will need to be able to land and take off from all sorts of strip configurations. Bumpy strips, muddy strips, narrow with deep ruts, grassy ones, and even strips that turn out to be not there at all. How about highways with cars on them? You gotta be able to land, not just fly. I think you better rethink this whole deal."

"No, no," he implored. "I can do it. Give me one more chance. Here, take this twenty five grand. Do we got a deal?"

"I'll take your money, bud, but I ain't sure yet whether we have a deal. We'll go to Mexico and you fly. Just you and me. I'll see how you do on the way down to Chihuahua. If things work out okay, we'll continue. Then you can pick up the weed, and I'm out of there from then on."

"Swell," the Gorilla replied. "I won't let you down, man. I'm on top of it."

They made it to Prescott where they spent the night. The next day when they should have been flying over Nogales and into Mexico, he missed Nogales.

"Where the fuck's Nogales?" Lencho yelled. "What's your heading? I don't see the power line or even the highway. I've been over that town a million times, and I don't see it down there."

The Gorilla fumbled in his pocket for what Lencho thought was candy, but he soon discovered it was a lump of oily amphetamine of the lowly crank variety.

"Well," Migilla moaned, "I'm sure that I flew over it. We're on our way anyhow, no sweat!"

They were running low on fuel about the same time they were due in Chihuahua, but Chihuahua was nowhere in sight. Only thing they could see for miles around was open prairies and a farm here and there.

"Did you set in a course? Did you consult your maps? Do you have any idea what the fuck you are doing?" Lencho yelled at the moron.

"Sure, sure I did. At least I think I did," he answered meekly.

Lencho was exasperated and made him drop to five hundred feet where he could better see where they were. He spotted a farm with a man on a tractor, so he ordered the Gorilla to land the goddamn plane.

"Where?" The Gorilla asked plaintively.

"On that dirt road," Lencho roared.

Once the plane had finally landed and he was firmly on the ground, Lencho climbed laboriously out and trudged the half mile to the bewildered farmer sitting on his tractor.

"Nice cabbages, Señor," Lencho said when he finally reached him.

"Gracias," the farmer replied.

"Can you tell me how to get to Chihuahua?"

The farmer pointed towards the mountains and said, "See that peak? It's on the other side."

Lencho said thanks and hiked back. They took off, and following the directions given to him by the farmer, they arrived at their destination an hour later. Lencho sprawled out on a bed in a cheap hotel. He was so pissed off at the Gorilla that not only was he not speaking to him, but he'd be damned if he was going to share a room with the monkey.

They had fueled the airplane up in Chihuahua, but the seven hundred miles to Mexico City burned it all up and then some. Once again, the Gorilla had meandered off course and by the time they reached the outskirts of that huge city both fuel tanks had only vapors remaining in them.

Mexico City International Airport was not the ideal place to land for such a small aircraft, but given the fuel situation as well as the fact that neither was sure where else they could go, Mexico City International it was.

"Mexico tower, this is Cessna November, bravo, zebra, 433. I'm flying the Cessna 206," the Gorilla radioed hesitantly.

"Cessna 206 calling Mexico Tower, say again?" The tower asked.

"Yes, Mexico Tower, this is Cessna 206 and we want to land."

"Cessna 206, what is your location and altitude?" The controller inquired.

"Holy shit. He wants to know our location. Where the fuck are we?"

Lencho was watching the fuel gauge and thinking this was deja vu all over again.

"What do you mean, where are we? He wants to know what direction we're coming from," Lencho yelled.

"Oh yeah. What direction are we coming from?" Migilla asked.

"Goddamn it, man. It's north and according to the altimeter we're at ninety five hundred fucking feet!"

Pushing the button on his hand set, Migilla said, "We think we are north at ninety five hundred fucking feet. Over."

"Cessna 206, squawk 1347 and identify," the tower replied.

Migilla was pale and sweating profusely. It was clear to Lencho that tunnel vision was beginning to set in on this guy, so he just tapped the transponder with his left hand and told his pilot, "Set in 1347 so that they know which blip is us."

"Cessna 206, we have your indent. You are west of the airport, please state your intentions. Over."

"We are kinda low on fuel and request permission to land immediately," the Gorilla told the tower.

"Say again, Cessna 206? Are you declaring an emergency?"

"Is this an emergency?" Migilla whispered.

Lencho just rolled his eyes. "I'd say it's an emergency, you dumb cock sucker! In another five minutes we'll be bone dry and then we're gonna drop like a rock. Wouldn't you say that was serious?"

"I guess so," he agreed nodding. "Mexico Tower, our fuel is dangerously low."

"Okay, Cessna 206, overfly the airport at ten thousand five hundred feet and enter left downwind on runway fifteen, and then immediately report mid field. Over."

Migilla looked like a deer in the headlights as Lencho had to once again take charge and give instructions.

"I think he wants you to climb above the traffic which is currently lining up to land and get in line, so that you can make your approach."

Migilla was now totally in the grips of frustration and disorientation, a common symptom of inexperienced pilots having to deal with large airports and air traffic congestion. His small brain only registered the part of traffic control's message that had to do with landing on runway fifteen. "Mexico Tower," he answered, "we are on final approach for runway fifteen."

"Cessna 206! My instructions to you were to report on the downwind of runway fifteen! Over."

The ape again ignored what was being said to him and answered, "Okay tower, we are on our final approach."

Lencho closed his eyes and cringed. Obviously exasperated, the tower answered, "Never mind, Cessna 206, you are now clear to land on runway fifteen. Please call the tower land line once you have landed safely. Over."

The landing gear of the six seater touched down with empty tanks.

"Whew," Migilla sighed as he taxied off of the runway. "That went well, I thought. I wonder what they want to say to me?"

"They are going to chew your fat ass off, you oaf!" Lencho fumed. "And so am I. This deal is off. You ain't gonna get my people fucked up like you just about did with us. This racket is way out of your league, Migilla. Understand? I'll take over from here. I will get the weed back to Arizona using your plane, but you will not be flying it. I'm also keeping half of the weed as well as the twenty five thousand that you have already paid me for putting up with this horseshit! Let me out of this goddamn airplane and get out of my sight."

What could Migilla do? He knew the jig was up and that Lencho was just telling it like it was. He wasn't ready for the big time, and so with his monkey tail between his legs, he boarded a commercial flight the next day and went back home.

Lencho dropped by Fernanda's to pay his respects. He had not seen her since the DEA abduction. He found that all was well and that she had not been harassed by any other so called law enforcement. He decided that it would not be prudent to stay at her home, but instead opted for a hotel room at the Zona Rosa. From there, he called Bill and explained to him all that had happened.

"I'm on my way," Bill told him. The next day, he arrived in Mexico City where they jumped into the Gorilla's Cessna 206 and flew to the town of Coatzacoalcos to arrange for the load. The harvest season was in progress, but it always seemed to be a little earlier down there. Lencho called over the day before to talk with the same source he had used for the near fatal power line deal.

Mayor Tovar-Mena and the entire little town were now in on the deal. The airstrip to be used this time was the dirt road that ran through the town. It was so narrow that the plane would hit the orange trees that lined it, so the mayor had many of the trees cut down.

"Nice doing business with you, Mr. Mayor," Lencho said shaking hands. "This may be the last time, though, as I intend to retire."

Lencho grimaced thinking of Migilla attempting to take off down that tight ass little road. Bill, however, had no problem. They flew north to rendezvous with Roberto who was waiting to fuel them up at Saltillo.

Eight hundred miles further, it was time to refuel again. Bill circled the farm land where Lencho stashed three twenty gallon drums. It was raining and the area looked awfully wet, but Bill thought he could land in a field of green grass.

"I don't like the looks of it," Lencho argued. "That road has puddles, but I think it's a safer bet."

"Who's the pilot here?" Bill asked as he put the plane down gently on the expanse of green and promptly sunk into thick mud. The Cessna fell forward and the prop sliced into the muck throwing two or three hundred pounds of it all over the plane. They lurched to an abrupt stop.

They were in a bog with seven hundred pounds of reefer behind the seats. It was approaching five p.m. and getting cold. Neither of them had expected to go camping, so all they had on was light clothing. There weren't any blankets and they had no coats. They put the pot outside on the muddy ground and huddled for the next twelve hours in the freezing cold. It was a misery, but when the sun cracked over the hills at five a.m. the next morning, Lencho went out and had a look around. "I see a ranch over on the hillside," he told Bill. "Hold tight while I hike over there. I'll try and get us pulled out."

While Bill repacked the load, Lencho walked two and a half miles to what turned out to be three small buildings, one tractor, and six Mexicans standing around their early morning fire. "Hola," he said in Spanish. "How are you?"

"We're fine," one replied. "Are you the gringo whose plane crashed last night?"

"Yeah, that's me," he said sheepishly. "I didn't actually crash. Just sort of got stuck. Should have landed on the road."

"The road is no good either," the man said. "Been raining a lot."

"I see you fellas have a tractor. Any chance I could pay you to pull me out?"

"How much would you pay?" he asked.

Lencho had three one hundred dollar bills and that's what he offered. Twenty minutes later, he walked with the men and the tractor to where they were stuck.

The Mexicans hooked a chain to the chassis and slowly pulled the muddy bird out. "If you would take my advice, Señor," the lead man said to Lencho, "you will let us pull you over to that hill. There is a gas line road beneath it, and I think it is wide enough for you to take off from there."

An hour later they were gassed up and perched atop a very narrow swath of fairly dry ground. "My fucking god," Bill marveled, "this is going to be tight."

After wiping what mud off that they could, Bill fired the Cessna up and noted the prop was chipped, but not so bad it couldn't fly. "I'm worried about the mud on the wings," he said. "The extra weight will cost us fuel, and I figure it will be close getting home."

The thin road sloped downhill, and they wondered if it was even long enough. "I can't squint through this muddy windshield and watch the gauges at the same time, Lencho, so you gotta watch our ground speed. When the dial hits seventy knots, I'll pull up. Tell me when. And, oh yeah, keep your head down so you don't bounce off the glass if things don't go well."

Grunting and groaning, the plane lurched along the pipeline. When the magic number was reached, Lencho yelled, "Now!," and up they went. Slowly at first, but still up, and then away.

When the plane approached the border between the United States and Mexico, they made a shot for Bisbee and Douglas, because it was a good place to sneak in with a number of airports in the area. Low and under the radar, they went down and up again, which made it look like they were a local flight taking off. If done right, they would have skirted the local mountains and gone west over Tucson and up to Sun City; from there it was a short hop to Prescott.

But this entire trip had gone badly, and it wasn't about to change. Bill made a navigational error. He was across the line, but too low for the mountains he had to climb now. With fuel ebbing, it was getting hairy.

"I can't get this crate over these peaks with all the mud and the load we're carrying. I gotta do some circles and slowly climb. It's gonna be real close."

On the lower end of the mountain range over southeastern Arizona was a ten thousand foot wall. Massive and sheer. After two go rounds, they had enough altitude to make it, but the fuel was low. At the top they headed towards Phoenix and found themselves over the eastern edge near the Black Canyon Freeway. "I don't know why the engine is still running," Bill marveled. "Keep an eye out for somewhere to land. We're almost to Prescott. We may or may not make it."

"How much farther, do you think?" Lencho yelled.

"We're almost there. No more than fifty miles." Then the prop stopped. The roar of the engine was gone, and only the whistle of the wind could be heard.

At ten thousand feet, they began to sink over Black Canyon. Below them stretched a panorama of boulders and canyons. Ahead they coasted over pinion trees and mesquite, and suddenly before their weary eyes arose an airstrip at the crossroads of Cleator, Arizona.

Descending from ten thousand feet to three took Lencho's breath away. Bill was a great pilot, and he finessed the plane like the pro he was. The engine had seized up when the gas was gone, and the prop caused more drag when it couldn't spin. The mud and the load of pot made them a slug of lead. The strip beckoned, and Bill held her in the glide. It looked good. At least possible. A few hundred yards more and they would be down. He could call for the loaders, it still might be okay. Then the plane's landing gear clipped a barbed wire fence at the edge of the field, and the frozen prop dug into the ground. Just before they began to cartwheel out of control, Lencho jammed his feet between his chin and the dash. The load of marijuana lunged forward crashing into the seats and the plane went end over end two or three times. Since they were out of gas there was no danger of fire, but at one hundred fifty miles an hour the impact was wrenching. Lencho went blank. He knew he was dead. Then he was upside down, still strapped into his seat. The weed was on the ceiling and Bill was bleeding like hell from a head wound; he seemed to be unconscious. He was stunned beyond anything he had ever experienced, but he was alive. Reaching for the quick release, he fell on his neck and clambered out into the Arizona landscape. Pot was everywhere. His ribs ached and his head throbbed, but was clearing. A moan from the pilot's seat got his attention and he fell to his knees and scrambled back inside. "Hold on, brother," he said. "We made it. You'll be okay," and popped the belt. Bill slumped to the ground moaning.

Lencho suddenly realized his left foot was broken and hurt like hell.

Must have happened when the load shifted and pushed him tight against the dashboard. He was grateful it hadn't crushed the both of them. How ironic for a couple of pot smugglers to be killed by bales of pot. He stood and put his weight on his good foot and looked around. Not a quarter mile from where they crashed stood a woman on the porch of her small house staring intently in his direction. He shifted his gaze to the splintered wing sitting twenty feet away from the rest of the wreckage and shivered in the autumn chill. He dragged Bill out of the wreckage and made him stand. He was coming around a little, now, mumbling. He knew the woman had called 911.

"Bill, we gotta get outta here. How bad is it? Can you see?"

"Yeah," Bill replied still in a daze. "I think I'm okay. What's all the blood? Jesus!"

"Looks like a cut on the head. How many fingers am I holding up?"

"Two?"

"Good. Probably just a lot of blood from the cut. Look, you go up in those rocks and hide. Don't let 'em catch you. I'm going for help, and tomorrow I'll be back and get you. Understand?"

"Yeah, I guess so," he said sitting back down.

He saw a Highway Patrol car in the distance kicking up a cloud of dust, and then a helicopter arrived on the scene. "We gotta book. Now!" They both headed up a steep incline towards the boulders above them. "Stay nearby," Lencho yelled as they parted company, "I'll be back tomorrow."

The chopper had trained its ten million candle spot light on the ground and buzzed around furiously searching the rocks and underbrush. Lencho hoped Bill had gotten far enough away to avoid them as he dived beneath a large pinion tree and clung to its trunk. The spot raced over him. Only a stone's throw, two cops got out of the patrol car and were talking. One took a leak. They were so close, he could hear everything distinctly. His foot ached and he prayed he wouldn't scream. The chopper came around again, shined the spot over and over in the area he was hiding, but he clung tenaciously to the tree and hid beneath its foliage hoping that neither infrared nor the bright light from the chopper would betray his position. The search went on for hours and a full moon came out. He didn't know how much longer he could last, and was sure if they stayed all night he was a goner. Then at about two a.m. they packed it up and left, probably to resume the search in the morning. As the cop cars drove off, he stood and stretched and took a leak himself. Then, using the moonlight, he hiked upward again and then down into a canyon. When the moon went behind the hills it got terribly dark, and he knocked himself silly when he crashed head-on into a barbed wire fence he didn't see.

Getting up, he hobbled into the ravine where, although very dark, the sand from the river bed was just light enough so that he could follow its path. He thought it would run downhill and then towards the valley below and the highway. Then there was a blessing. His mind flashed on the black shaman Three Feathers of years before. Ravens!

Like a hand from the heavens to guide his path, two squawking ravens appeared and flitted about his head. They startled the hell out of him at first, but as they came back over and over, flying past his nose and ears with their feathery breath, they seemed to be saying, "Follow us, Lencho. Follow us." He was in pain and perhaps approaching delirium, it was so damn cold, but that's what he felt. So he obeyed, and between the sand and the birds that led the way, he finally caught sight of the highway lights leading into town a few miles ahead. As he left the rocks and canyon walls, the ravens vanished into the morning sky.

Just before dawn he saw the lights of Black Canyon City and heard the roar of traffic on the interstate. He had trekked for miles, too many to even guess, and he sat for a moment and contemplated his next move. He had to get out of there, and soon, so off he stumbled toward a guardrail where he watched the cars from behind a thick bush.

Broken foot, covered in mud, full of cactus needles, and bleeding, the weed man was a sight. Thinking of a strategy for getting out of there, he spied an old pickup truck trundling his way. A good ole boy was driving with his dog in the back. He wasn't going fast, and when he got within a hundred feet, Lencho jumped out in front of him waving his arms. The truck stopped. "Sir, please help me. I crashed my truck out in Crown King. I was drinking out there with my sister and her husband. Man, I been walking all night. Can you give me a lift?"

"Jump in, son," the old man said and took him into Black Canyon City where he stopped at a coffee shop. He still had some change in his pocket, so he called his nephew, Hodi, out in Prescott.

"Jeez, Lencho," Hodi said, "it's all over the TV. You're famous. Good thing they didn't catch you. Sure, I'll come down. Be there in an hour."

Lencho ordered breakfast. He had no money, but was so hungry he was nearly faint. The waitress agreed to wait until Hodi showed up for payment. Two Highway Patrol officers drank their coffee at the counter and never even looked up. They had to have been on the lookout, but when it comes to coffee and doughnuts over a suspect, the former wins out every time. They finished and left, and Lencho sat on pins and needles until his nephew showed up and rescued him.

Hodi drove the fatigued fugitive to Prescott and got him a room in the Prescottonian Motel. He realized this might not be the best spot to plunk his weary and wounded ass, but at this point he thought: What the hell. He watched the local news footage of the cops leading Bill to a patrol car with the anchorman intoning, "Found two miles from the site of the plane crash, the

220

suspect apparently staggered from the wreck and up to Cortes road where he broke into a trailer for shelter from the seventeen degree cold night. Early this morning a passerby noticed a broken window and called police. Authorities have not identified the suspect, but say they believe he was the pilot and pegged the amount of marijuana being brought in from Mexico around at least a ton."

"A ton," Lencho sighed. "Give me a fucking break. Oh, poor Bill. Poor me." He holed up in the room for three days and made a lot of phone calls. His sister in Chicago had seen it on CNN.

He had visitors and callers the entire time he was there, and they got him clothes and some money. Clearly the cops didn't have his name. Maybe they didn't even know there were two guys. But the lady on the porch probably saw two men. He wasn't sure. Had Bill kept his mouth shut? Must have, because no one in Prescott had heard any scuttlebutt to the contrary. His foot still hurt, so he let it rest and smoked pot, of course. He had been through hell, but once again he lived and felt great. Great, despite the ordeal and the danger of arrest and all of it.

He went to see his dad. He hadn't seen the old man for some time, and even though Pops was distant, he thought he detected some love. Faint, maybe, but it was there.

He had always been the bad boy, now he was a wanted man for sure. Some said he should turn himself in. Just give it up, cause it was only a matter of time. Others said run. What should he do? He still had his spread in Paradise. Bill might keep quiet, be a standup guy. He was a helluva pilot. A fucking daredevil and an outlaw like him. He loved the guy and had been through so much shit with him. But there was the plane, it was sure to be traced to Migilla. The gorilla was a pussy along with being a dumb shit. He'd talk for sure. So what to do?

"I won't surrender!" Lencho thundered. He had been through so much, and all those people didn't even know about the DEA robbery and car trunk nightmare. A day later, he flew to California and went back to work on his property like nothing happened. When a lawyer called and said he had been sent by Bill's wife, he took it as a good sign. He never met the lady, but she needed help, and no cops had come, so it must mean Bill was keeping quiet.

Lencho dug out twenty thousand dollars and sent it to Bill's wife so she could hire an attorney and fly to Arizona to visit her husband. He had to be there for Bill. He had to do everything in his power to keep Bill from rolling over. A man in his position was under terrible duress from the cops. They would be threatening him with life in prison or worse, for God's sake. Prosecutors are the Torquemada's of society.

They had Bill warehoused at the Towers jail in Phoenix, and his wife got word back that everything was fine and not to worry. Lencho heaved a sigh of relief. Migilla was a different story.

Migilla showed up at Lencho's place and demanded his plane back as well as the weed. "What are you, a total ostrich with his head in the sand? Don't you read the papers or watch television? Bill and I ran out of gas and crashed outside of Prescott. When you are in a deal and things go south like this, that's just tough shit. My heart was in the right place, none of this was done on purpose. That trip was cursed from the start and you know it."

"Yeah," the Gorilla said, "but I got a lawyer and he says he can't find shit on any of this."

Lencho got ahold of his brothers and they sent copies of the local newspapers to him. When Lencho gave them to Migilla, all he said was, "Well, I'll be damned."

Now that Migilla seemed resigned to his fate, Lencho breathed easier still. Maybe he would pull out of this whole plane crash nightmare intact.

*****

Back on the home front, home improvements and the agriculture end of things were going well. Lencho enjoyed spending time with Luz, Callie, Fred, and Liz. Callie was living with her mother, but spending much of her time with her brothers and sister. Luz had his motorcycle gang made up of neighborhood youngsters. They rode motor cross bikes and used one of the outbuildings for the ongoing wrenching to keep it all running. Liz, being Dad's baby girl, was a joy to be with. And Fred loved playing the part of Federico the Magnifico, standing behind his dad on the back of a horse dressed in a cape as they rode around the pasture. With horses and motorcycles and plenty of room to play, life just couldn't get much better.

Of course, the little woman was becoming more dissatisfied. Always sexy and beautiful, she got her way all of her life. Lencho had not always been faithful, of course, but who knew what she had been up to in his absence. He never asked. She had bore him two beautiful kids, and often helped raise the earlier ones by his first wife, so he had done his best to make her as happy as he could with money and creature comforts. Still, her complaints were becoming a chorus. She didn't like the house because it was "too big," so he hired a maid to help with the upkeep. She hated his line of work, so he continually promised it was over. She spent money like it was going out of style, so he gave her a credit card with daily spending limits of two hundred dollars. She spent every cent of it and accumulated a massive closet full of stylish clothes. Once having run around naked as a teen nymph, she now dressed like a wealthy maven.

He rolled a joint and grabbed a Heineken. Plunking his ass down in front of the TV he put on ABC World News Tonight. Peter Jennings informed, "Today, October 5, 1986, the Sandinista government of Nicaragua shot down a small plane loaded with guns and ammunition over rugged terrain near the border with Honduras. President Daniel Ortega accused the Central Intelligence Agency and the presidency of Ronald Reagan of equipping the Contra rebels in an attempt to bring down his government. The Contras are remnants of the Somoza regime, and have been waging a bloody guerilla war since Somoza was assassinated. At a hastily held press conference in Managua, pilot Eugene Hasenfus, his head swathed in bandages, said he worked with two other men, Max Gomes and Ramon Medina, and they all worked for the Central Intelligence Agency."

The joint dropped out of Lencho's mouth as he leaned forward to catch every word. He watched the wounded Hasenfus surrounded by men in uniforms sitting at a table in front of microphones. My fucking God, all those crazy stories Jerry told me were true, he thought. He heard the part about the guns and switched around to the other news channels. The story was everywhere, but it dealt only with the guns. What about the cocaine? No one said anything about that. He reached for the telephone and dialed Fernanda in Mexico City.

"I was going to call and tell you what happened to me on that last run," he said when she answered, "but I just saw on television that the Sandinistas shot down a guy like Jerry. Have you heard?"

"My God, yes," she replied. "It's everywhere. Huge news all over Mexico and Latin America. But you know what is bigger news for us? Jerry got arrested!"

"Arrested? How? Where?"

"I been on the phone with Crickett. She told me that Jerry was flying back from Nicaragua when the other guy got shot down. He didn't know about it, so he lands at the place he always did—"

"He told me it was Edwards Air Force Base," Lencho interrupted.

"Yes, that's right. Edwards. So he lands there like always, but the people he always met there were gone, and instead the base police arrested him and seized a huge load of perico."

"You're kidding me!" Lencho gasped.

"I think it might be in the newspaper. They say some dumb dope smuggler just landed at Edwards for no good reason. His plane full of drugs, and they arrested him. He's at some place called Safford now. Crickett told me."

"Safford is in Arizona," he answered.

"Crickett was able to see him, Lencho," Fernanda went on. "She said he told her that he might be killed if he doesn't get away. They would get all his money and kill him. He told her to tell you to go to his house, get his helicopter, and break him out. He will pay you two million dollars, a million now and a million later when he is free."

This was overload. Lencho sat down before he fell down. "I guess Bill would be up for it, if he could," Lencho said. "He's a bit preoccupied right now, however. Let me call you back later. All this is heavy. I need to think."

Here he was, on the lamb from a plane wreck smuggling dope, his pilot was in federal detention and now a friend had been implicated in a huge spook scandal. He knew there would be much more to come. Wait till the press heard about the other end of all this, the dope. Guns south, dope north. That's what Jerry had told him. He figured Jerry was toast. No way would they let him live to tell his tale in court or anywhere.

He took a drive to clear his head and wound his way toward town and then out towards the airport. As he approached Jerry's spread on Clark Road, he stopped and watched the wind sock blow eastward in the evening breeze. Lights were on in the house, but he didn't knock on the door. He didn't see any cars, but he looked at the big hangar that Jerry said held a helicopter. And what about the gold and cash Jerry said he hid there? One hundred seventy-five million dollars worth. Man! Would the spooks come and look for it? Had Crickett moved it to safety? Were those twelve boxes full of gold buried somewhere out on that acreage? He suspected that would be a deep and very dark secret for a long time.

All the weed man could do was try and remain calm. The Iran-Contra scandal as it was being called broke big time on November 3rd when a Lebanese magazine reported missiles and other weapons had been traded for the release of the hostages seized by Iran. By late November, Oliver North, the Marine Attache that had headed up the effort for William Casey's CIA, was busy shredding documents that his good looking secretary, Fawn Hall, would later disclose at his trial. President Reagan was making mea culpas big time to the nation. The first allegations that cocaine was brought back by the CIA from Nicaragua began to surface, which would later become a huge outrage in the Black communities of America. The CIA was accused of sparking the crack epidemic and funneling profits back into their dark ventures. At least all the profits they didn't want for themselves.

Since it was too much and too scary, Lencho just put it out of his mind as best he could. He went back to his property and to helping Bill with his case. In December, the pilot was bailed out by his mother-in-law, who put up her house as collateral. His bond was only fifty thousand dollars; amazingly reasonable, considering. Lencho would have put up cash, but just didn't have it to spare, so he was delighted to hear Bill was out. Bill called him shortly after and assured him everything was cool. Sure they were pressuring him, but he was a stand-up guy and wouldn't drop any dimes on anyone. Did the cops want to know about all the trips and deals the guys had made over the years? Sure they did, but they wouldn't get anything from Bill the pilot. Lencho was hugely relieved and believed he could trust his old friend.

"That was a hell of a landing," Bill joked over the phone. "If we hadn't hit that goddamn fence, we would've been home free. Rotten luck."

"I'll say. This game is so awful now," Lencho said. "I swore I was out before. Now, there is no doubt at all. Never again. I'll never make another trip or deal in weed. I'm shot."

"I'm thinking about hightailing it to Mexico," Bill said. "I got some money stashed deep. I could go down there and live large. But I would still need to work. I hate to see you quit."

"No, I'm done. But if you still want to fly, I can ask around."

Lencho called Chuck in Portland. Chuck was interested. He and his friends were big into Colombian pot and were thinking of joining the exodus into cocaine. They were well set up in Florida and could use an expert pilot.

"I know of him cause Doc and you vouched for him, but he did get popped. Is he straight? Do you think he can be trusted?" Chuck asked.

"I think he can be," Lencho replied. "Of course, I'm not psychic, but I believe he is a stand-up guy. Him and me and Doc and the whole gang have been to hell and back. He wants to earn some bucks and go to Mexico. Once he's set there, he says he'll still fly. You can't find many pilots better than Bill. He knows Mexico and Latin America like the back of his hand. He could fly into Colombia just as easily." Chuck and his friends hired Bill to fly their Aero Commander.

By the time Christmas passed Lencho was beginning to think he might slide on the airplane crash. Nothing had happened, Bill was out on bail, and his case would take a couple of years. He had a hundred thousand in cash left and one Queen Air twin engine down in Mexico that was worth a hundred grand. If he sold his property he might make a hundred and fifty thousand. Once it was all added up, it was enough to take off as a fugitive to Mexico or maybe Costa Rica to live near Malcom. If he stayed he knew the cops would nab him eventually, but he was ready for that as well. His lawyers were working on his case in Arizona, and the whole thing was so screwball he just might beat it. If he got prison time he would do it and be done with it and live a normal life for a change. Those were his options. He decided to stay and deal with the law. He was optimistic. Then he gave his old buddy Fernando a call down in Tampico to see how he was and received another shock.

"Roberto Azua is dead," Fernando told him. "It was coke dealers, Lencho. I don't know if he owed them money or they were just loco high, but they put a bullet into the back of his head."

"Man," Lencho said with tears in his eyes, "how many times did I warn him about that perico trade."

"Yes," Fernando agreed. "His fat little wife just cries and cries. Now, she has to run the grocery store and raise his daughters without him. He was a good man."

Lencho hung up the phone and sighed at the loss of another dear friend to the war on drugs.

*****

Valentine's Day was coming up in February and Lencho had a big surprise for Tamara. He had purchased by special order a huge one foot wide by twenty feet long red ribbon, which he would tie into a bow for the 1987 Mercury Cougar he was going to give her on February 14th.

She considered herself the long suffering wife. Well, since she had refused to marry him, she was more on the order of long suffering common law wife, but she was definitely not happy with much of anything these days. The house was luxurious, but "too big." The maid he hired was "rude and didn't take orders well." The credit card he gave her was inadequate with "only" a two hundred dollar a day limit. But she was beautiful and turned heads wherever she went, not because she didn't wear clothes, but because now she wore the best. Long suede boots that reached to her knees were set off by expensive wool suits or favorite cashmere sweaters. Now, the weed man was going to wrap the huge ribbon around the bright red sedan with bucket seats and pearl interior as a gift to the mother of his children, because he loved her and because he felt bad for all the craziness. His other serious relationships had been imperiled by his lifestyle. Women may start out coveting the bad boy, but after the cops come a few dozen times, it gets old and they invariably say so then leave. He wanted her to be happy, but not much seemed to work. Worst of all, he couldn't confide in her his fears and sorrows. If he had told her about Roberto, he knew she would have just said, "I told you so." And to share the tale of Jerry and the CIA would elicit panic in her. His was a lonely relationship.

The past few years of being a fugitive weighted heavily. It messed things up with his kids because he was Eric McKenzie and they weren't McKenzies at school. Constantly looking over his shoulder was making him paranoid, and he longed to get things straightened out.

The car dealer had called with bad news. The pearl interior was special order, and it wouldn't be ready by Valentine's Day. They were real sorry. "I'm sorrier," Lencho groused at the guy. "The damn thing is costing me thirty grand cash, and you can't have it ready. Damn!" To vent some tension, he went golfing with his real estate buddy, Paul. A day on the links was always pleasant. On the way back, he suggested that they get the women together and take them to dinner at Mario's.

Tamara looked great in her long boots, short skirt, and sheer silk blouse. He was always proud of her. They climbed into the back seat of Paul's Cadillac. After picking up Paul's girlfriend from work, they were taking a roundabout route on Forster Road when a police car pulled out from a side street. The cop trailed them for two miles until they reached town and the red and blue lights went on. Paul pulled over and the cop got out. Lencho was apprehensive, but he did not expect to get arrested by just one policeman. It would be a task force for sure, State and Federal no doubt.

After examining Paul's driver's license, he leaned into the window and asked Lencho for identification. All he had on him after the plane crash was a fake DDT 214 with his new name typed in. "Do you have anything else, Mr. Nelson?" He asked. When Lencho said he didn't, the cop asked him to step out of the car. A look of fear swept over everyone's faces. Lencho flashed Tamara a look of defeat and despair; he knew the jig was up. "I need to take you in for some questioning," the cop said snapping the cuffs on.

"Do you need to cuff me for some questioning?" Lencho asked.

"Come quietly, please," the cop said and helped him into his cruiser.

The drive was a short one, two blocks. Inside, the three room building was packed with agents, most of whom were Federal.

A young man identified himself as Special Agent Taft, United States Customs. "Lencho, you are under arrest. You are charged with conspiracy to transport, sell, import, and possess illegal drugs. You have the right—" and he read Lencho his Miranda Rights. The weed man knew each count carried a maximum of fifteen years and that federal time was long time. A very long time, indeed. No one wins against the Feds, either. Or at least that's what he always heard. A 98% conviction rate, serving 87%, and they were real proud of it, too.

One after the other, they booked him. Three federal, one county, and one city. They each made photos and took his finger prints. Customs, Drug Enforcement Agency, Federal Bureau of Investigation, County of Butte, City of Paradise. It took hours.

By eight o'clock that evening, the process was finally finished. Two resident agents from U.S. Customs shackled him from head to toe. He was loaded into a government sedan and driven one hundred miles to the state capitol in Sacramento. No one said a word. Lencho wasn't in the mood for chit chat anyway and the young agents didn't seem to give a shit. Once they got to their destination he was booked into the county jail. Like all jails, it sucked.

The cells were eight man units with ten prisoners each. Eight bunk beds for eight men with the extra two prisoners sleeping underneath the bunk beds. There was one open toilet at the end of the cell unit. Nasty and typically California, overcrowded.

He stayed in that hole for four days, and Tamara visited him with the children. Little Callie was puzzled, but Luz knew what was going on with dad. Luz always knew.

Two days later, he had his first court appearance. It was both an arraignment and extradition hearing. His court appointed lawyer told him the obvious:

"Extradition is a given so if you want to get out of this hell hole jail, agree to it." He pled innocent to all charges and agreed to extradition. The feds are harsh with sentences, but their facilities are nicer. They transferred Lencho to a jail in Colusa with an annex that housed federal inmates. The accommodations were princely by comparison to Sacramento. He got a good bunk, there was a TV and telephones, and the food was edible. The federal government owned him now. They paid the sheriff a hundred bucks a day for his room and board. There were seventy men in there; multiplied by one hundred dollars each, Colusa was bringing in seven thousand dollars a day. That's how it is in the system. Lencho spent one week there, and then got his first taste of federal air transport. Welcome to ConAir.

An immense commuter system for transporting prisoners, ConAir (as it is popularly called), consists of L1011s, 727s, and other older model airliners. They fly daily from city to city all across America picking up and dropping off prisoners. Some are heading to new destinations, others to court hearings. It is fast, vast, and fairly efficient for the government. Lencho was loaded onboard a bus and driven down to Oakland where he and one hundred seventy-five other inmates were flown off to Las Vegas. From Vegas he went to Denver and then to a federal prison in El Reno, Oklahoma, where he was parked for another week. At El Reno, he ran into a guy he had met in Mexico.

Daniel had also been a friend of John and Minerva. It's a small world in the drug game. Daniel had been pulled over by the cops in Houston, and since he was also a fugitive, the Feds were glad to welcome him home. Discussing his case and where he would wind up, Lencho said he was going back to Prescott and needed a lawyer. Daniel referred him to Dave Mackey, whom he assured him was first rate. That night Lencho called his little brother, David, and asked him if he had heard of a lawyer in town by the name of Dave Mackey. "Hell yes," Dave replied. "My wife is his secretary. I thought you knew that."

"It's a small world," Lencho said. One more phone call to Mr. Mackey and Lencho had a new attorney.

The ConAir flew him to San Diego and then finally to Phoenix where they parked him at the Towers Jail. The same jail Bill the pilot had just left. The place was clean and well lit. It was a big pod type jail with a central guard in a glass room watching everybody and pushing buttons to open and lock doors. At least it wasn't overcrowded.

Lencho found himself in a double man cell, and was happy that he had it all to himself for the moment. The second bunk was about to fall off the wall, so he helped it along a little by tugging and jumping on it, damaging it enough that no new guy could use it for a while. Privacy was unknown in the penal system, so it was a rare luxury.

The lawyers he had working on his case prior to his arrest dropped him like a hot rock after he was taken in. "We can't work for you any longer because our theory argued that you were the good guy, and now look. You're charged with all this new stuff like an airplane crash full of marijuana. Nothing we can do for ya."

"How about the money I paid you?" Lencho wondered.

"Gone, spent it. Tough titty."

Lawyers can be bottom feeders, Lencho thought. Ka-ching! So there went twenty-five grand. He gave Mackey twenty thousand up front to get started with a promise of fifteen thousand more in the future. The funds he had worked so hard for and risked his ass over and over were evaporating rapidly. All part of the game.

"You are looking at about seventy-five years, basically," Mackey told him. "Let's see. Four charges that net fifteen a piece. Those are all federal. They want to give you fifteen years in Prescott for cultivating and for going on the lamb. A couple of more years for transporting."

"Well," Lencho told him, "I'm coming up on my fortieth birthday. If they give me seventy five years, I'll die in the joint."

"Like the old joke goes, Lencho: You tell the Judge you can't do that many years, and he'll tell you 'just do as many as you can.' Sorry partner."

All this for the sacred herb. God almighty how the government did hate marijuana! The masses adore it, demand it, but the Feds and States tell them 'no way, and if you disobey our orders, then be prepared to die in prison.' Pretty fucking grim, Lencho thought as he began to really stress.

After his initial hearing, he was sent over to the federal holding facility in Phoenix. The comfort level immediately improved as it usually does in lower end federal detention. The food was alright and he could move around. Always a worker, Lencho got on with the laundry crew to stay busy and keep his mind off the sense of doom that was overwhelming him. He became friendly with the floor cop, Larry Stewart, who was a good guy. Stewart might have been a pot smoker himself, Lencho thought, because he made no bones about how absurd the pot laws were. And because his world was falling apart, Stewart took mercy on the weed man and let him call home from the secure phone in his office. Back in Paradise, the little woman was beginning to panic, and of course complained.

"But Lencho," she whined. "I had to give the lawyer all that money. What are me and the kids supposed to do when it runs out?"

"Damn it, Tamara," he said, "it can't be gone already. I know you still got fifty grand in the household account."

"Oh no, not any longer. There's bills to pay, and I don't see how I'm going to hang on with you gone and the future so uncertain." That made him feel lower and worse than he already did. On the positive side, the irrigation system was being installed by his foreman, Jeff, the exotic fruit fagoya was being planted in the field, and the green houses were ready. This all took about four thousand a month, but soon it would be paid for and some money would start coming in. All she had to do was stay calm and keep the ship afloat. "But I'm so scared," she moaned.

"Okay, baby, stop it. Stop the crying, you're killing me. Here's what you do. Go out to the barn and find the rolls of roofing paper stacked on the tarp on the ground. The one that has a little red mark on the end is my rainy day fund. Take it out and unroll it. There's enough money to keep you and our children safe for two years. Plenty to keep things going until the legal stuff starts to bring in some cash."

"Oh, thank you, Lencho!" she exclaimed. "I figured you had some money tucked away. Me and the kids love you! Bye." Two days later he called again, but it was a different woman he was talking to. Ten years they had been through thick and thin. Now, it was a little too thin, apparently.

"I'm so sick of all the shit," Tamara snarled. "Years of this dope business. Feast or famine, and this fucking house! It's so big and far away. I always hated it. And it's my birthday. I'm all alone on my birthday, thanks to you. No presents, no cards. So I just bought myself a nice present."

"A present? What was it?"

"A diamond necklace and matching earrings."

"Diamonds? How much did you spend?"

"Six thousand dollars, Lencho, and if you don't like it, tough shit."

"Baby, please!" He implored, "Get a grip. Don't waste that money, it's all we have. Things will be okay, I promise. Just pay our bills."

"Not 'our' bills, Lencho, your bills. I'm leaving. I hate this house. I'm getting a condo in Paradise. I'm sorry."

"You're sorry?" he muttered. "How can you do this?" but she had already hung up. The next day he called back. "Just put Jeff on the phone," he barked.

"This is Jeff," Jeff said promptly. "How is it going, bro?"

"Jeff," Lencho snarled, "I gotta tell you, I'm smelling a rat here. Tamara seems to have spent my money, and now she's leaving the house, taking the kids, and moving into town. Are you a part of this? Are you fucking my old lady behind my back?"

"No, no," he protested. "I wouldn't do that, Lencho. I got morals, man. We're pards, for God's sake. I'm watching over your interests out here. I'm on your side."

Then Lencho called his brother Bobby for his opinion. "The woman is evil, bro. I'm sorry to tell you. Never trusted her, and I think she's messing around."

Paul the realtor and his associate Ali confirmed it. "I hate to lay this on you in your time of tribulation," Ali told him, "but I can confirm Tamara has been unfaithful. I think she is going to move to Forest Ranch with your irrigation man. Very sorry."

Now he was alone and so depressed; he felt suicidal. He was experiencing the unique abandonment that a prisoner of war or convict feels when he realizes that most of his friends are only fair weather friends and his wife has made him a cuckold. On top of that, the Feds shipped him out of FCI Phoenix back to the Towers Jail for reasons all their own.

Just as the weed man was thinking about slitting his own throat he was watching the adam's apple on somebody else's throat bob up and down. It belonged to The Kid.

The Kid was a youngster who had a girlfriend that came to visit frequently. She would give him a big sloppy kiss before leaving and transfer two balloons full of pot into his mouth, which he would half swallow right down to that adam's apple and not gag or turn blue. It was amazing. Lencho took the boy aside immediately, because he knew talent when he saw it.

"Listen, Kid," he told him, "I'm so down these days that if I don't smoke some good pot it will be over for me. Tell you what. I'll have friends send your girl some really fine bud, and then she can visit and we'll split it up. Hell, we'll get everybody in here high."

Growers back in the Emerald Triangle sent her two ounces of the absolute best. Within a week, Lencho was rolling skinny, mega-potent joints for the Mexicans, the Blacks, and the Bikers. The Kid and Lencho split the rest, and just like that, his mood improved. Some will say otherwise, but the truth is that weed is magical. Soon he was his old self again; he gained ten pounds and was laughing and joking.

For the next month, it was very mellow in the Towers, and Lencho was a popular dude with one and all. He found a seed in his stash and germinated it using tissue paper. Then he set it growing on a high barred window. It got three inches tall and sprouted initial water leaves. It made him nervous, so he dried it between pages of a book, and then sent it to a girl who ran pot for him back in Chicago. "Things are better now," he wrote. "I'm even bringing in a crop!"

One morning, just like always, he and The Kid rolled a pinner and lit it up. It didn't take much to put him on the moon. As he went back to his bunk to relax and ponder his big toe, a guard came to his cell door. The clank of the lock was jarring. "Lencho," the guard bellowed, "roll it up, bud, the marshals want ya."

"Marshals?" Lencho gasped. "What do they want?"

"How should I know? Get a move on, they're waiting downstairs in the garage."

"God, I'm fucking high!" He thought.

Chapter Thirteen

"Pick Up the Tempo"
Released 1974
Waylon Jennings

Some people are saying that time
Will take care of people like me
That I'm living too fast
And they say I can't last much longer
But little they see
That their thoughts of me is my savior
And little they know
The beat otta go a little faster
So pick up the tempo just a little
And take it on home
The singer ain't singing
And the drummer been dragging too long
Time'll take care of itself
So just leave time alone

BANKROBBERS

Since Nixon declared a 'war on drugs,' jails and prisons had become
an equal opportunity employer. The guard who opened the door and led
Lencho down to the garage was Ms. Brown. A black lady of garrulous nature,
today she sported a high bouffant hairdo with glue-on nails the colors of the
rainbow. Long eyelashes and pink lipstick completed the ensemble, which was
particularly incongruous with her military style bloused trousers and Doc
Martens. "Get hot, honey," she ordered. "The marshals will be here anytime."

"Marshals," Lencho muttered. "What do the marshals want with me? I ain't
got any hearings scheduled."

"Honey, like the Lord, the Feds works in mysterious ways."

Down long corridors shined to a high sheen by trusties in yellow jumpers,
she led him. He had not had time to shower and shave, and felt grungy in
his orange jumpsuit. "I'll miss uniform day," he complained. "Tuesdays and
Fridays."

"You'll live," Ms. Brown told him. "In the elevator, please."

The elevator brought them to a dark hallway outside the garage where she
put him in a holding cell to wait for another twenty minutes. Finally the door
clanged open and Ms. Brown took him outside where a young Federal Marshal
waited with a handful of chains and cuffs.

"Face the wall. Lift your right foot. Lift your left foot. Turn around. Raise
your arms. Hold still. Is that too tight?" When he was finished, the weed man
was bound from head to toe, cuffed from the waist and around the ankles. It
was always difficult to hobble to a vehicle for transport, so he was glad it was a
sedan and not a panel wagon with a step and ten other guys to clamber over.

"Where am I going?" he asked again.

"To the court house downtown. Aren't you glad to get some fresh air?"

The drive took twenty minutes. Lencho was always surprised at how fast
Marshals drove. They were quite reckless, actually, buzzing through changing
lights, never stopping if they could help it. They arrived at the courthouse, and
the driver stuck an access card into the key card scanner outside heavy steel
gates. Up they went. They drove inside and parked beside another Crown Vic.

"Out," the Marshal barked. The weed man stumbled and stood at attention as
the chains and cuffs were removed. All this was a mystery, because they didn't
take him inside as usual. Two new agents got out of the second car and the four
of them went over paperwork on a clipboard. When everyone was happy, the
Marshals went inside and the two new guys put cuffs on his wrists up front, but
left them loose.

"Get in," a silver haired man commanded. Lencho wished he hadn't smoked
the joint an hour earlier.

The driver was handsome, his hair slicked back. He was muscular and rugged, but wore casual clothes with the badge of the United States Customs Service, a large silver buckle, and a nine millimeter Glock on his belt. The second said nothing. He just sipped coffee and looked through wire rimmed glasses as the handsome guy backed up and drove into the bright Phoenix morning. Outside he pulled over at the curb and turned back to Lencho.

"I'm Special Agent Tom Williams, Customs, and this is Agent Simmons. The government has something very serious to discuss with you." Lencho watched the toothpick Williams was chewing on bounce with fascination.

"Oh yeah? What would that be?"

"Let's take a drive." He pulled away with a lurch heading into downtown. "What I have to say to you, Lencho, I'll say only once. I want you to give it serious consideration, because there will not be a second chance. First, let's talk about your pal, Bruce. He works with us, now."

"Who's Bruce? I don't know any Bruce that might work for you."

"You know him as Bill, your drug smuggling pilot. His real name is Bruce Brown, veteran pilot for Eastern Airlines, and a hero. He was flying an Eastern Airlines DC-10 with three hundred people onboard out of Dallas/Fort Worth when one of the four engines fell off. The thing lurched to the right and certain doom but he rode her out and saved all onboard. President Reagan hosted him at a White House event and presented him with a commendation. Danger is this guy's name, adventure's his game. Mr. cool and calm. That is until we threatened to send him away for life, and he wisely switched sides. Now, he works for me, and I work for Uncle Sam."

The weed man was stunned. The words hit him like a hammer. "Say what?" he stammered.

"Bruce Brown rolled on you. On all of you. A couple of months ago. He's already wearing a wire. We got his entire statement about the plane crash, him and you traveling to Mexico on innumerable trips to smuggle marijuana. We know about Doc, Ronnie, CR, all of it. He just helped bust your pals up in Portland the other day."

"You're kidding me!"

"Not hardly. You gave your buddy, Chuck, the thumbs up, so Bruce arranged to fly a load of coke for them out of Florida. We got it all on wire. When he climbed into the plane and hit the ignition last Thursday, the conspiracy was complete and we took 'em down. Conspiracy to import cocaine is going to get Chuck a lot of years." Lencho sat in silence now, sick to his stomach and at heart.

"We also got a statement from this guy you call Migilla. It's reasonably hilarious, I might add, and contradicts what Bruce told us about your crash. We believe Bruce."

"What did that fat fuck say?" Lencho finally asked.

"Let me show you," Williams replied as he handed a typed letter over his shoulder to the shocked weed man. Fumbling with cuffed hands, Lencho read silently.

To Whom it May Concern:

My name is Donald Rambert and I own a Cessna 206. I am a charter pilot, and a very good, honest one at that. Mr. McKenzie called me up and asked if he could charter my plane with me flying. I agreed to fly him into Mexico for a holiday down to Mexico City. Mr. McKenzie came and saw me about this offer in Yuba City where I live. He agreed to pay me my fee as well as buy all the gas, food, and lodgings. I thought this would be great. I said 'sure.' So I flew down to Mexico City with Mr. McKenzie where he introduced me to a woman friend of his named Fernanda. Then, while we were having dinner at a nice restaurant, Mr. McKenzie and Fernanda must have slipped poison into my wine while I went to the bathroom, because I became very ill and I thought I was going to die. This poisoning made me froth at the mouth and vomit. I had to leave the country at once. It was a miracle I got home alive. In fact, I went to the hospital in the nick of time. The hospital told me, yes, I had been poisoned. They pumped my stomach and saved my life. I am so grateful. After that, I called Mr. McKenzie and he told me no problem that he would get a friend down there to fly the plane back and return it to me. Then they filled my plane up with marijuana and crashed on the way back. That's all I know. I will testify to these facts.

Truthfully,
Donald Rambert

"Whew!" Lencho muttered between his teeth. Agent Williams glanced over his shoulder smiling.

"Like I said, we believe Bruce Brown's version. He told us this guy Migilla just couldn't fly for beans, and about how you two ran out of gas and hit the fence. The guy has excellent creds. We love him. You crooks shouldn't ever get married is all I can tell ya. This is an observation I have made as a cop. His wife was the one who did you guys in. She was suspicious; thought he was messing around with the ladies, so she went through his things when he wasn't around and found a pile of money under his socks and some notes he had made about places in Mexico she evidently believed were love nests with his girlfriends. It's hilarious. She called up the local cops, and pretty soon the story reached the DEA and Customs. At that point we added him to our 'watch list' cause ol buddy, the feds had been on to your game for some time. When it was discovered that he was your pilot, we tailed him for weeks. We'd see him in disguise like the time he was wearing an afro and a pillow under his shirt; that was really funny. Then you obliged us with that plane crash. But, in the end, that's how we got onto your group. The suspicious woman."

"The guy never even cheated on his old lady, either," Lencho moaned. "I was with him a lot, even fixed him up with dates, but he never screwed 'em. Pitiful. Still he ratted me out, so he is not that great."

"Sure he did, but he was very kind to you. He hated to talk, but hell man, he's looking at life. Can you blame him?"

"I'm looking at life, too," he replied, "and I ain't ratting out anyone. It is what it is. This is war. I'm fighting for freedom as guaranteed in the Declaration of Independence. I'm a soldier, not a criminal."

Williams scoffed, "Yeah, sure, Lencho. But we got God and the flag on our side, so let's knock off the bullshit and get down to business."

"Open your eyes, Mr. Magoo," interjected agent Simmons. "What the government wants may surprise you. Among all the stuff Bruce told us about your operations, including the huge one from Belize, the one that caught our attention was the Mexican bank robbery."

"Bank robbery?" Lencho replied.

"We know about the DEA agents that robbed you and tried to have you murdered. Customs and I in particular are very pissed off about that one. Bruce filled us in and that's why you shouldn't be so sore at him. We just got back from Mexico City where we talked to your lady friend Fernanda. She confirmed the whole thing. We want those scum bag narcs, and if you help us, I think you will be very happy about that 'life sentence' you just mentioned."

From the back seat, Agent Williams looked like a buff, silver haired preacher to Lencho and the indignation in his voice was not contrived.

"You talked to Fernanda, too?" Lencho asked.

"We debriefed her at her apartment and she gave a sworn statement. She was there when they flashed their identification, and she saw them shove you into the trunk. Those boys are gonna go down. They are a national disgrace, an insult to our country. I personally detest such behavior."

"It's pretty common, Agent Williams," Lencho replied. "And yes, I would be delighted to assist you. They meant to murder me. It was a terrifying experience."

"I want to warn you, Lencho, that you must cooperate with us to the fullest. No lies or evasions will be tolerated."

"There are things that I am concerned about, though," Lencho replied. "I need protection. Agents of the United States have vast power. They can reach out and get me before I even testify. They steal so much money and work for the mafia and stuff. Why, shit, they got rooms full of cash. They can buy anyone.

They can certainly get to me in any prison."

"Agreed. You will be protected. Probably put you in witness protection."

"A fine thing when a pot guy needs protection from opposing branches of law enforcement," Lencho thundered.

"Yeah, I guess it is," Williams agreed as he pulled back to the key card scanner and opened the door to the Federal Courthouse garage. "Now we go inside and have a little chat with the prosecutor."

The weed man was still stoned, but elated. He wasn't going to feel bad about talking to some real cops about the DEA. This was just a magical mystery tour, he told himself.

An elevator took the trio to the top floor. They entered a large conference room with a long table and a dozen stern looking men in suits waiting. The FBI, Justice Department, Drug Enforcement, and Customs were all represented. A large man with suspenders holding up expensive trousers glared from the end of the table, and Lencho could almost see his own reflection in the shine of his Florsheims. This was Deputy U.S. Attorney Tom Connelly of the Western District of Arizona. Papers shuffled and throats cleared as Lencho took his place on the hot seat.

"Lencho," Connelly began, "it is my job to take scum bags like you off the streets. The war on drugs, in my opinion, is the most serious challenge to national security since the A bomb. In fact, it is a bomb. One that exploded and continues to explode daily in the streets and the lives of our people. I am not happy at all to have to deal with the likes of you—a ruthless and obviously relentless marijuana smuggler. You peddle drugs to our nation's youth. But today we are here to discuss a matter that is even worse: corruption in the ranks of our own government agents. Because of that, I am forced to deal with you. I just want you to know up front, that's how I feel."

"Pretty heavy attitude over a little pot," Lencho chimed in. "I am sorry, please forgive me, but I am not the criminal you are painting me. Weed is not a curse, it's a blessing. You got it backwards. I think you guys all know it, but just won't admit it. Everybody smokes weed. I bet the president smokes it. In fact, JFK smoked it with Marilyn Monroe in the White House!"

Smiles could not be suppressed at Lencho's outburst, and chuckles ensued. The ice had melted.

"Everyone is allowed his personal opinion, I guess," Connelly finally replied. "So let's get down to business. We have the basic outline. The serious allegations are that two federal agents stole two hundred thousand dollars from you, and then attempted to have you murdered. This has been alleged and verified by others. But you will have to go on the box. Do you know what that means, Sir? The box is a polygraph. You will be polygraphed rigorously by an expert from Justice. I will tell you that DEA disputes the allegations. They say this is all a lie. Customs believes it happened. We will need total corroboration before we proceed, because, if these charges are true, these agents could face life sentences.

"Once we are happy with your testimony," Connelly continued, "I will go to the judge in your original case and ask for a limitation on your possible sentence to ten years. That's quite a better deal than the seventy-five years you are currently facing. I will ask the judge to suspend the sentence and to put you into a halfway house for one year. We will take you up to Prescott to see the judge on your state case, and help you get that resolved. While I will say I am fairly certain it will go this way, I cannot absolutely guarantee it on the Federal end, but I will urge the judge and probation to agree. I believe they will. We will send you out to the cheese factory at the FCI as well."

"The cheese factory?" Lencho asked.

"Yes, that's what we call it. It's safe housing for informers. Rats, as some might call them. Very nice accommodations, as I understand it. Individual rooms with TV, good food. You may qualify for witness protection after all is said and done. Also, you will be required to testify against Mr. Rambert. He is testifying against you, but we believe he is lying. And then there's your wife."

"My wife?" Lencho asked. "You mean Tamara?"

"Yes," the prosecutor replied. "She's testifying against you."

The woman had just run off with the pool boy, stolen his money, abandoned the house, and now she was going to testify against him in open court. What a gal!

"Of course," Connelly went on, "we aren't totally sure if Mr. Rambert will even go to court over this matter. If he is wise, he will take a plea, but one never knows."

"Is he in custody?" Lencho asked.

"No, but he will be. Please don't speak to him, by the way. That might sound like witness intimidation."

"I got to tell ya, Mr. Connelly, I am not bullish on testifying against Rambert, even after what he said about me. I am not keen on testifying against anyone except those narcs who robbed me."

"Noted," Connelly replied. And that concluded the meeting.

Agent Williams led Lencho back to the basement garage where two federal marshals shackled him once again, and then drove him back to the Towers Jail where he got cleaned up and had another smoke. This time it was less nerve wracking.

*****

A few days later, Lencho went back to FCI Phoenix. Mr. Stuart, the counselor, let Lencho use the secure phone. There was no pot there, but the food was good and he spoke to Tamara a few times. This was not an event that lent itself to sanguinity. He had already talked to Paul who informed him his animals were left alone and abandoned. The gate was open and the dogs were running in circles, the chickens were hungry in their pens, as were the rabbits, and it made him heartsick. "How could you do this?" he implored. "All we worked for you've abandoned. Ten years together meant nothing?"

"Well," Tamara huffed, "I warned you enough times. I never liked that place, and I was so lonely because you were always gone. And there was no telling what you were up to since we were never married."

"Whoa!" he corrected. "I begged you to marry me twice and you refused."

"I don't remember that. And if those animals of yours got ignored, I don't know what to tell you except that you shouldn't have gotten arrested. They weren't my responsibility in the first place."

"You're all heart. How's the pool boy?"

"Oh, Jeffrey? He's so sweet. He knows how to treat a woman. We live up in the mountains where it's peaceful and quiet. The kids are happy. They see him as their new dad."

"I don't believe that!" He thundered. "My kids know who their real dad is, and I'll always be their dad. Any of the money left?"

"Not much. A lot of expenses you left behind had to be paid."

"Bullshit. The bills were almost all paid up. I could use some dollars on my commissary account down here."

"I really can't spare it," she replied. "Look, I gotta go. See ya."

"Miserable succubus," he complained to Gary the bank robber. "Stole all my money, ran off with the pool boy, left my chickens, rabbits, and dogs without food and water, and wants my kids to call him daddy. I'd like to kill her."

"That can be arranged," Gary squinted through flinty eyes.

Gary was a long haul trucker who also robbed banks. He stood five foot eight and weighed a lean one fifty. He would walk into a carefully cased financial establishment, pull on his ski mask, yell 'everyone on the floor,' and then leap gracefully over the counter and clean out the teller boxes before anyone could fart. He was in and out in about a minute, and usually made off with ten to twenty thousand a pop. He avoided the vaults, even though that's where the real cash was, because he didn't have a partner. Running solo, he'd race out the door and speed off in the stolen car left parked at the curb. He never used a gun, and had done this over twenty times. On the twenty third time, his luck ran out when he crashed into a meter maid giving him a ticket. "Nobody's luck lasts forever. I learned something valuable that time: Never park in a red zone during a daylight robbery!"

Gary was also an Aryan Nation type of guy, a walking billboard of tattoos. The illustrated white man with skulls, swastikas, clowns, and naked ladies festooning his lean body. He loved The Order and would extol the myths and virtues of the greatest of all white men, Robert Mathews. "Oh, sure, the fucking feds got him. Burned him alive in his bathtub. That's what they always do, ya know, burn ya up if they get pissed enough. They did it to The Order, the SLA, those niggers in Philly, and they'll probably do it to me cause the next time I ain't going peacefully. But Bob Mathews and The Order, now they're some real white men."

"Well, Gary," Lencho said, "you're a cool guy, but how come you're so xenophobic?"

"You can use your twelve dollar words all you want, Lencho. I don't even know what a zeeno-whatever is. I just got no use for Jews and niggers. Mud people, brother. Get with your heritage as a white man. White power!" Gary said as he strut around their two man cell with his right arm raised in salute. Lencho was tempted to ask him what he meant by 'can be arranged.'

"For a thousand bucks, I'll whack the broad and throw in lover boy for good measure. I'm heading to my sister's place up in Reno next month when they cut me loose. It's just a skip and a jump down to your neighborhood, bro. I know some people that can get me a 30.06 with a scope, and I'll put a slug through her left eye and one up his ass. Be my pleasure. What are pals for, after all?"

"Man," Lencho whistled, "I'll ponder the offer. Ten years with that bitch and she does this to me. Come on, it's time for our air conditioning class."

"Hot dog!" Gary yelped. "I got a good joke for all them jigs and beaners in there. Did you hear the one about these two niggers driving down a country road in their old pickup truck? They drive past a farm and see a black pig in a pen, so they pullover in some bushes and sneak back to steal the pig. The farmer sees the whole thing from his kitchen window and calls the sheriff. The sheriff sets up a roadblock down the road a few miles and waits. A while later, those boys are driving down the road and they see the roadblock ahead. They sit the pig up between 'em, putting a coat and hat on him. They pull up to the roadblock and roll down the window. The sheriff asks, 'What's your name, boy?'

'My name is Rufus Jackson,' says the driver.

The sheriff looks across at the passenger and says, 'What's your name, boy?'

'My name is Jermain Jackson, Sir.'

The sheriff looks in the middle and says 'What's your name, boy?'

Jermain elbows the pig and the pig goes 'Oink!'

The sheriff scratches his head and says, 'Okay, get on outta here.'

The boys drive off down the road, and the sheriff turns to his deputy and says, 'Man! That Oink Jackson is the ugliest nigger I ever seen.'"

Laughing uproariously, Gary asked, "Do ya think they'll like it, Lencho?"

*****

In his rage and sorrow, Lencho did something completely uncharacteristic: He sat down and drew the bank robber a map and directions on how to sneak up on his wayward paramour. A week later, Gary left FCI Phoenix. He gave his sister's phone number to Lencho and waited for the order to proceed. Finally, two weeks on, the weed man gave him a call on the counselor's secure line. Lencho had calmed down and decided it wasn't right to kill his ex, no matter how richly she deserved it. What would the kids think?

"Well," Gary said eagerly, "is it a go?"

"I've been thinking it over, Gary," he replied, "and I can't do it."

"Can't do it?" Gary yelled in astonishment. "Listen, you ain't talking to some shit head that couldn't hit a cow on the ass with a banjo, ya know? I'm a crack shot. It would be relatively painless, if that's what's worrying ya."

"No, no, it ain't that. But killing people has never been my style. I guess I'll just have to live with it. Things are what they are, ya know?"

"Well, how about the horse? Can't I shoot the fucking horse?"

Suddenly Lencho realized Gary had done his homework. He had been out to the ranch where Jeff lived, scoped out the scene and was ready to do the deed. He must have, or how else would he know that Jeff owned a horse?

"No, not the horse either! I gotta go, Gary. Best of luck in the bank game," and he hung up.

The first to put Lencho on the box were the Customs people. A serious looking man with wire rimmed glasses hooked up a blood pressure cuff around his left upper arm, finger sensors over three digits on his right hand, and a couple of EKG like probes fastened to his chest. It made him most uncomfortable.

All the wires and hoses ran into a metal box with a couple of arms that swung over a roll of moving graph paper. He had listened in on a conversation with a couple of fellow inmates talking about polygraphs the week before, so he nervously said to the operator, "I hear these things are not always accurate."

"No, that's not true," he replied. "They are nearly perfect in determining the truth. The government relies on them completely. All the agencies use them."

"CIA even?"

"Especially the CIA."

Two hours of 'yes' and 'no,' 'true' or 'false,' questions later, the polygrapher was finished. He left the room to confer with Agent Williams, and a short time later Williams came in. "The tests show you are telling the complete truth. Those scum bag narcs did rob you and attempted to commit murder. We're gonna hang the sons of bitches."

The next to put the cuff on him was the Drug Enforcement Agency.

They were being accused of owning a couple of narcs that were thieves and murderers, so they insisted that they should get a crack at the weed man.

"So, this guy, Likken, an ex-polygraph man for the government, says these gadgets are bullshit," Lencho ventured before they started. "He says the whole deal is about the operator. Whatever the operator says becomes the truth. Anyone nervous might easily fail."

"Nonsense," the DEA snapped. "David Likken left the reservation. He's a turncoat to the profession of polygraphists. Now be quiet and let's begin."

Three hours later the Drug Enforcement man concluded that Lencho was a lying son of a bitch. "He fabricated the whole story," his report read, "and no doubt corroboration by third parties was disingenuous/obfuscation."

Now the dueling agencies called in a neutral third party from the Justice Department. This polygrapher flew from Washington just to break the deadlock. "Did the guy who invented the Wonder Woman comic and her lasso of truth really invent the lie detector test?" Lencho asked him.

Discomforted by the question, the Justice man said nothing. At the end of his examination he concluded that some parts of the story were true and others were not. "The results are inconclusive in regards to peripheral subjects, like associates of the subject, but truthful in regards to allegations towards the DEA," the Justice reported.

"The DEA and probably all narcs are useless as tits on an alligator," Williams huffed chewing on his ubiquitous toothpick. "I live for the day that bunch is dissolved."

"Do you think the Customs would do a better job?" Lencho asked.

"Well, I'll be honest with you. When it comes to narcotics, honesty goes out the window. There's so much money involved that it is probably almost impossible to maintain integrity. So easy to steal. My own partner stole. It made me sick. A lousy eight thousand dollars and it ruined his career. But not me. I have had many opportunities to steal, but never have. I take my job seriously. But as for drugs, I don't know the answer. Drugs are terrible, but because of the temptation, I doubt they can be stopped."

"How about legalizing them? Wouldn't that stop the corruption?"

"Don't be silly. Do you know how many agents that would put out of business?"

"What's next?" Lencho asked.

"Next we see your judge up in Prescott, and then I want to meet your dad."

The weed man was transferred to the Yavapai County jail, which was another hole. Agent Williams came up from Texas every now and then where he headed up the Federal Air Smuggling Unit for the Southwest corridor. Williams was set about meeting the whole family. "I aim to get a handle on your family and background," he told Lencho. "Your dad seems like a fine fellow." Lencho just looked to the heavens.

While sitting in jail for the next five months, Lencho met a youngster only fifteen years old. He was to be tried as an adult for manslaughter. He and a pal were drinking whiskey, and decided to take a car for a joyride. They crashed into a freeway overpass and clobbered an elderly couple in the process. The man died, and now Christopher Balis was looking at a lot of years. Lencho knew the boy's stepdad, so he took the boy under his wing. The jail let him out every day to attend high school, and he brought his books in at night where Lencho helped him do his homework. Lencho also looked out for his protection from some of the less savory inmates.

After his math was finished, he and Lencho shared a joint while the weed man lectured him on the evils of alcohol. "Some people are teetotalers," he would say, "but most folks like to seek relief from life's travails with an intoxicant. By far the lesser of all evils in this category is marijuana. So the lesson is clear, especially in your case: smoke pot, don't drink."

Later, the boy's mom stopped Lencho on the street and thanked him profusely for his sage advice and help with her boy. He had gone on to a life of alcohol abstinence, and as penitence for the horrible tragedy he caused while drunk, became a spokesperson for Students Against Drunk Driving touring the country in support of sobriety and personal responsibility. But during the time Lencho knew him, he was one scared little kid locked up in jail on Halloween. He wanted to be out trick or treating, so Lencho made him stand still while he wrapped him from head to toe in toilet paper with only a slit to see out from. He hunched over when he was finished, and dragging one leg behind while holding his right arm crossed over his chest, became the mummy of Yavapai County Jail. He went from one cell to another looking for candy. The inmates howled and loaded him up with junk from their commissary.

In the meantime, Williams was working on high with the State of Arizona. He pulled strings, and with the backing of the Justice Department and Judge Sult, who was hearing Lencho's case, court convened for sentencing on November 28, 1987.

After the usual platitudes from attorney Mackey about how Lencho had learned the error of his ways and now deserved mercy, Agent Williams spoke to the judge and asked for a moment in his chambers. The judge returned with a fierce look of anger and frustration on his face. "You, sir, are a fucking scum bag!" he boomed at Lencho who was sitting quietly. After some more paper shuffling the judge resumed, "It is with utter disgust that I am forced to defer to our almighty Federal Government in this case. I sentence you to one year in jail and a period of seven years of probation. Also, you are to pay a fine of thirty thousand dollars. Since you have been in jail for one year, I sentence you to time served. Any questions?"

"Only one," Lencho replied smiling. "How do you suppose I could raise the sum of thirty thousand dollars?"

"I know full well what you will do, Lencho. You will be off to Mexico to smuggle a ton of marijuana. So I don't expect the court will ever see that money, but I am fining you anyway."

Mackey leaned over and whispered in Lencho's ear, "That said, you are off the hook on the fine."

Once back in Federal lock-up, Lencho looked forward to the debriefings by Agent Williams. He already had some dress-out clothes sent by Williams in advance. So, he changed and they went out drinking. Agent Williams was a handsome man, and as it turned out, a player. The two holed up at the bar of the executive terminal in the airport, and went over paperwork with gin and tonics. The place was a cop hangout, and these guys were full of bravado and braggadocio.

"Yeah, howdy," some Fed would brag. "Me and Jimmy had that quem up against the wall in the corner last night, and he was taking her from the rear while I held her by the ears."

"Jesus," Lencho muttered in disgust. "You guys are no better than a pack of bikers. Shit, Williams, you're a married man with a baby on the way. What's wrong with you?"

"Lighten up, Lencho," he laughed. "There's a lot of stress in this job."

And running weed is easier? Lencho thought. Especially when the plane crashes!

"I know you think this dope catching stuff is bullshit," Williams confided. "Maybe some of us do stoop too low. But to me, it's a job. I may not really give a rat's ass if you hippies smoke your wacky tobacky. Hell, maybe I have too, but I get paid to go after you. You're the bad guys, and right now we are after the worst of the bad, these dirty DEA agents. I hate corruption in the ranks."

Lencho and Williams would go flying. "Okay, you crook, today we're gonna violate the international border. Show us some Mexican airstrips."

The cool, quiet agent was the pilot. He took them up in various single engine planes that had been confiscated from other crooks. Williams always seemed to turn a little green on these jaunts, Lencho thought.

"Yeah, we gotta do this. Need your input on where you crooks landed, but I am not much of a flyer myself. Shit, even when they take me somewhere for the job on the jet, I don't like it. Maybe if there was a babe flight attendant serving the cocktails, but that ain't gonna happen."

"See down there?" Lencho pointed to an outline of an overgrown airstrip he and Bruce had used on occasion. This one was just on the other side of Nogales. "We always stopped first at places like that on the way down to leave fuel."

"Oh, so how come you ran out on that fateful day?"

"Running out is all part of the fun. Did I tell ya about the time we landed the wrong direction at Mexico City International?"

Flying across the border the way Williams did it was illegal, but he was a Fed and Feds make up the rules as they go along. At least that was what Lencho suspected.

Other times they flew around Arizona. "What are ya so interested in these little spots for?" Lencho asked him. "Shit, there are thousands just like this in Arizona."

"I'm writing a fucking book, you crook. Gotta have that background for intel purposes. Which reminds me, I gotta proposition for ya. We're after a gang out of Tucson that fly big loads. We got a dipshit narc planted with them, but he's DEA and I have zero confidence in those guys. If he does get us a bust, he'll probably steal all the evidence before we can convict. How would you like to make some points and money?"

"How so?" Lencho asked with suspicion.

"Infiltrate for your government. We'll pay you sixty grand up front. You get introduced by our guy and then become trusted. Smoke weed with them, sell their weed, or buy from them. You'll get a percentage of the gross when we finally take them down. You can't lose, what do you say?"

"These are weed guys?" he asked. "I say no. No way, Williams. The only ones I'm willing to drop a dime on are these murdering narcs. I ain't a rat. No cheese factory for me."

"I thought I'd ask," Williams said grinning. "Didn't think you would, but it's my job. You are a crook, after all."

On February 17, 1988, one year to the day after he was arrested in Paradise, the weed man went to court again, this time in front of Federal Judge Rosenblatt. Rosenblatt didn't like him much more than Judge Sult did. "Lencho," the judge intoned gravely, "I personally believe you are hopeless. A lifelong pot head. A man who has dedicated his life to marijuana. I assume you feel it was worth the trouble, but I don't. I have been briefed by the prosecutor, Mr. Connelly, and by Agent Williams of the Customs Service. This whole situation is most disturbing to say the least. Further, I want to tell you I have little hope you will ever change and become an upright citizen. If marijuana was to become legal, then you might be one heck of a salesman, but since it is not, nor likely ever will be, I fear you will end up back in custody: Marijuana, Lencho, will never be legal. Having said that, I sentence you to ten years. You have served one year, and I suspend the sentence. You are to serve six months in a halfway house. Court is adjourned."

The judge was gone as quickly as he appeared, and just like that, the sword hanging over his head vanished. Seventy-five years in prison evaporated. "Thank you, dirty narcs," Lencho muttered under his breath.

*****

The halfway house was on Roosevelt Street in Phoenix. It was essentially an apartment building that had been converted for government use. Five guys per apartment with bunk beds. Go out and get a job, weed man, then pay eighty-five bucks a week to stay there. More business for the war on drugs down the line. He found a job in short order doing landscaping for the city. Most of the work crew was Hispanic, and since he spoke the language he was directing them almost at once. Then it was time for Migilla, who had insisted to the bitter end he had nothing to do with his airplane being involved in a crash filled with pot.

The trial was a short one, and he lost. Even so, Migilla received probation, but his religious wife was devastated that he could have deceived her. It was hard to argue with the evidence and the witnesses. Large blown up photos of the crash with bales of pot all over the ground. Bruce, Fernanda, Tamara, and Lencho all testified. They had to. But it could have been worse.

"You swore you were innocent!" Migilla's wife wailed outside the courtroom. "Jesus may forgive you, but I never will."

Halfway through his six months stay at the halfway house, Lencho received a letter from the probation department. He was summoned to a meeting at FCI Phoenix on May 3rd regarding his accrued obligation to the federal government going back to the Andonegui Prison days.

"What the fuck is this all about?" He asked Williams a few days later.

"Sit down, Lencho," Williams told him. "There's been some developments."

The weed man didn't like the sound of that nor the gloomy look on the Customs agent's mug. "Here's the deal," Williams began, "you are off the hook on the seventy-five years. That's the good part for you. The not so good part is the crooked DEA agents' case is over. Kaput. It's been handled internally."

"Internally? What does internally mean?"

"Don't sweat it, you crook," he replied with a little smile. "It means just what I said. The Justice Department, in their sage wisdom, has dealt with the matter and it's over. You got a sweet deal, and I suppose justice was served. At least, that's what they tell me."

"No, man. Wait a minute here. Those scum bags robbed and tried to murder me. They must have done this before. I can't believe I was the first. What you're telling me is they walked, isn't it? Scott free?"

Lencho could tell the agent was hurting inside. It was obvious. For all Williams' bluff and his bluster, his womanizing and hard drinking ways, Lencho had come to believe he was an honest cop—for an experienced dope dealer and smuggler that was a rare epiphany.

He looked up from his shoes. "We gave it our best shot, buddy," he said. "I was surprised Justice showed any interest in getting these guys to start with, but in the end, somebody—some people way up there—reached out and saved their bacon. That's all I can tell ya. Forget it. You made out, you should be real fucking glad."

"I am glad," Lencho admitted, "except for this." He held out the letter.

"Oh that. The BOP thinks you still owe them some time. That's all I know."

"How's that possible? I thought everything was cleared up now. New beginning time for this old dope dealer."

"Well," Williams replied, "it's like Judge Rosenblatt told you, you'll never be an upstanding citizen. The government has a way of ensuring that quite often. But don't sweat it. We'll be there to testify on your behalf, and even if you lose, it will only be a couple more years at most. Still better than the seventy five year bullet you just dodged."

"Yeah, I guess."

"But say, listen," Williams said turning back from the door once again. "There's one more thing I should tell ya."

"What's that?"

"I think it would be very wise on your part to consider a career change at this juncture. Not just because I'm a fed and would want that, but also because of the DEA. We tweaked the nose of a very dangerous dragon, Lencho. Going after their boys. The way it turned out made us both some serious enemies. Me, they can't do much about, but they're real mad at you. You got serious enemies in high places, now. Just want to give you a heads up."

Lencho sat for an hour in the gathering dusk of his halfway house apartment contemplating the meaning of life, and in the end he decided there wasn't any meaning at all. It was what you made of it. As for honesty in government, what a joke. Like everybody seemed to know, but could do nothing about, there wasn't any. He had seen in his years of pot selling and importation endless cases of cops stealing and profiting from the drug trade. He was a witness to history in his own microcosm to the Iran-Contra debacle where government agents and contractors commit immense crimes against their own people. And now he watched as a couple of federal agents, who apparently became cops so they could murder and steal, walk away from the fate that people such as himself always had to face. Was this the true nature of government? Did he have to feel so cynical? But they had cut him loose from a life sentence, hadn't they? "You should be grateful." Those were Agent Williams' last words to him.

✶✶✶✶✶

"Lencho," the G12 apparatchik sitting at the table addressed him. "I am Mr. Buell, and it is my job to calculate prison time for offenders. This is assistant warden Brendel, and on my left is Miss Smith from federal probation. According to my figures, you owe the Bureau of Prisons some additional time."

"No way!" Lencho howled.

"Oh yes, Lencho. The report prepared by probation is quite clear. You are a lifelong scofflaw. A seller of marijuana. A grower of marijuana, a smuggler of marijuana. Marijuana has been a schedule one drug since 1970. It has been illegal federally since 1937 and illegal in all states before that. It is bad stuff. It always leads to the hard stuff. A gateway drug. And you, Sir, are an incorrigible profiteer at the expense of our gullible youth. Not to mention that when returned from imprisonment in Mexico on the prisoner exchange swap program some time back, you were placed on probation. Then you absconded on a state charge of cultivating marijuana, and at the time you also violated your federal obligation of probation. My calculation, Sir, indicates you owe the BOP thirty-six more months."

"Thirty-six months!" He yelled. "Hold on here. In Mexico, the sentences run until they end. It doesn't matter if I was there or not, it still ran. That's the law and it's as clear as glass. I finished that sentence a couple of years ago and any so called probation violation would be moot. Void. I just helped you guys chase down a couple of murdering scum bag federal narcs and the judges all cut me loose. How can you claim I have to go back to jail?"

"Have you anything to add Agent Williams?" the G12 asked boredly.

"I absolutely vouch for what Lencho just said about governmental assistance, Sir. He was a great help in our investigation."

"So noted," the G12 replied. "Lencho, you are remanded to the custody of the BOP for thirty six-months, as of now. This board is concluded."

Chapter Fourteen

"Heaven or Hell"
Released 1974
Waylon Jennings

Sometimes it's heaven and sometimes it's hell
Sometimes I don't even know
Sometimes I take it as far as I can
Sometimes I don't even go

MR. WONG

Mang Song Wong was working in the plumbing shop when the prison placed Lencho there. He was five foot five, thirty-eight years old, a Buddhist, and a scion to a very wealthy Chinese family who operated worldwide out of Hong Kong. Mr. Wong had been sent to America to work with his father in their chain of restaurants and imported frozen sea food business that stretched from Baltimore to New York City.

"They say I owe income tax," Wong told the weed man who asked why he was incarcerated. "They also say I have too much cash on hand. Look funny not in bank. Ha, ha!"

"How much did they find?" Lencho asked.

"Ten million U.S. dollar. Ha, ha!"

Mr. Wong liked plumbing and all trades construction oriented. He liked Lencho because he was part Cherokee. Mr. Wong studied the English language constantly, with total dedication. "I don't speak good English when I come this country," he explained. "Now I am in jail, I learn better. It is good to not waste time when you have it. So I study a lot."

FCI Phoenix was a medium security federal prison. In those days, the population of inmates was almost all white, with a smattering of blacks called DC Toads (crimes committed in Washington, D.C.) and some bikers who ran guns. The bulk of the charges were white collar with a few smugglers. Since Mr. Wong had been found with all that cash, the government categorized him as organized crime and limited his movement lest he somehow flee. The diminutive little man never gave that a thought, but only worked diligently and planned for the day he would be freed. As with many Asian prisoners, Mr. Wong was the designated scapegoat for family profligacy. The same is true for industrial crimes brought against Asian corporations. He did his time cheerfully and honorably.

Not everybody liked Mr. Wong, however. His small physical stature made him an ideal target for a fat bully called Skippy who taunted and abused him endlessly. He was called Skippy because one sour day he opened a jar of peanut butter to find the oil had separated. Enraged, he called the 1-800 number on the jar to complain, telling the operator on the other end that he was so pissed he was gonna blow the peanut butter factory off the face of the earth. Shortly after, the FBI paid him a visit and he was sentenced to three years for terrorist threatening of a peanut butter factory. His bad temper again got the best of him when, after prodding and poking the little Chinaman, Skippy decided he would choke him to death.

When Wong's lips began to turn blue, Lencho raised a piece of steel pipe above Skippy's head and ordered him to release his grip or he would be forced to beat him to death. From that day forward, Mr. Wong thanked him endlessly for saving his life, and they developed a strong friendship. After Lencho's first celly went home, he lobbied the counselor to have Wong as his cell mate. The counselor approved after making sure neither of them was a homosexual. Lencho also impressed on the counselor that Wong could benefit from more English language tutoring. With his mastery of construction, Lencho was soon making the rounds of the huge complex tending to the unending work orders. Lencho gave directions, and Wong did the work. This was an equitable arrangement because Wong was driven to improve. It was his nature. "I improve on paying taxes next time also," he laughed.

"Where do you come from Wong?" Lencho asked.

"I was born in the city of Fuzhou. It's across the South China Sea from Taiwan. Big industrial city. Make a lot of stuff there."

"Your family are busy capitalists. I admire anybody that's a go getter."

"We very good go getters okay. Big family, have many business. Food, import-export, fur, clothing. Uncle owns hotel in Las Vegas and business around the world. So you Indian, Lencho?"

"Yeah, sure. About twenty percent, I guess."

"Indian very brave. You different. Not regular white guy."

"Thanks, I guess."

At night, Wong sat with his open books studying English, always taking copious notes. Lencho went to the law library himself where he studied Mexican law and U.S. Mexican treaties. He was convinced that those lunkheads at the time board were totally wrong and had given him three extra years by mistake. The prison was full of jail house lawyers, and many were very knowledgeable. It's surprising the volume of talent inside prisons.

"Hell yeah," Mario Paz told him. "When a guy does time in Mexico the sentence runs till it's finished. A curious practice of law in my country. It's machismo man. You can escape, too, and if you don't get killed trying, they don't add more time to the sentence. It's not like here where these bureaucrats get paid to keep track of every second, and every little change in your status. No, you shouldn't have to do more time, I don't think, from what you've told me."

From Mexican born lawyers like Paz, Lencho found the answers he needed in the United States Treaty Law by Reginald Smyth. "The prisoner swap program instituted by President Jimmy Carter was a god send to the hundreds or even thousands of American born citizens that were imprisoned around the world on allegations chiefly of drug smuggling and drug dealing. The drug laws in these countries having often been inspired by and urged upon them by the United States from whom they were dependent for aid and goodwill dictated the harsh consequences. Proof however was often dubious and so the accused was grateful to be transferred back to his own country where conditions were far better, and the specifics of foreign law were still adhered to, which can mean a shorter sentence."

Further examination revealed that the board had erred. A little research on Lencho's behalf would have been nice. And of course he had to do all this alone because the vaunted firm of Mackey law quit on him after they used up the initial fee of twenty thousand after two court appearances. He submitted his first habeas corpus motion to the court to stand on the sentence. Two months later he received word that the court had ruled the issue was up to the Bureau of Prisons.

Lencho filed with the prison and it went to the Time Manager. "Look," he essentially said, "in Mexico I went to jail for seven years. I did two of them and got sent back to the U.S. on a prisoner exchange thanks to Jimmy Carter and Barry Goldwater. I have been out five years, and since in Mexico my sentence kept running, it's over. Ergo, I don't owe you squat, lemme outta here." To which the reply two months later was "Forget-About-It!"

The regionals were next, and the regional authorities also said 'no.'

That left the National Prison Board. After eight months of trying, Lencho received a letter from the Gods:

Dear Sir,
Your reading of the law and the treaties of United States and Mexico have been reviewed by counsel for the Bureau of Prisons, and counsel agrees with your assessment. We are sorry for any inconvenience and order you released back to a halfway house immediately.
Yours Truly,
Uncle Sam

His elation was palpable, and of course the weed man did not hold any grudges. That night he was talking to Wong, and Wong was as happy for him as he was for himself.

"When I get out, Lencho, I go home to China. I hope you come visit me. I introduce you to my family. You are great Indian."

"Thank you, Mr. Wong," he replied. "I would love to do that."

"I will offer a prayer to the pantheon that you have fruitful and safe journey from now on."

"Thank you," Lencho said to the Buddhist. "You are too kind."

"Perhaps what you need," Wong said slyly, "is Chinese wife. I know this last woman cause you lot of grief."

Lencho agreed. "Big time. She's giving me a hard time now over the kids."

"Yes, we love our children. I have two boys and a girl from late wife," Wong said.

"I don't think I need another wife, Mr. Wong. At least, not right now."

"An arrange marriage maybe? Sometimes those are the best. My dear wife and I were married in arrangement. That common in China. My parents met with broker and they sat on bench in park while the broker passed by with my May Lee, and after they found her okay, a meeting was arranged with her parents."

"What was discussed?"

"Finances mainly. And of course, did she have good temper."

"Ah."

"We had good and happy marriage that produced my beloved children. I maybe didn't love her right away, or she me, but we learned. That's the secret to marriage Lencho. Learning."

"How much more time do you have Mr. Wong?"

"Three more years and then your government let me go."

"Here," Lencho said writing, "this is the address of my father. When you get out, write me there."

Before he left FCI Phoenix, Lencho resurrected his old love, Diamond K Productions. He staged two shows for the inmates. The first was a local band, Bodacious, and the second was the Glenn Campbell band minus Glenn. He was either too stoned to show up or touchy about his reputation, but regardless, the inmates loved it.

The three months he had to spend at the halfway house on Roosevelt Street passed quickly, and then he went back to Butte County to his children. It was a time of new beginnings with the weight of the government off his neck. He had to report to the Federal Probation Department, of course, and was assigned to Miss Bentsen for supervised release. She was pleased right away with his progress, because he got a job hanging sheet rock and always passed the urine testing that was administered regularly. But that was somewhat of a sham since a weed man must smoke the weed. To circumvent the requirement, Lencho invented the 'pissalyzer,' a medium Elmer's glue bottle with rotating red cap that he had a youngster fill up for him at five bucks a pop. Before every visit to the government clinic, he would warm the thing over the stove and then tape it to his belly above his privates. The clinician would stand there while he did his business in a little cup, but would generally not insist on spying his schwanska. Lencho would squeeze the bottle, and it made an authentic racket filling the receptacle. Worked every time.

His two little ones by Tamara were mighty glad to see dad at first, but soon their mother mounted an anti-Lencho campaign that knew no boundaries. Abruptly she forbade them from seeing him, which was a source of great pain and anger. Since he was on probation, he feared to rock the boat. But this could not go on, so he visited the school the children attended in the little mountain town of Forest Ranch. He walked into the office and asked to see them. The children were summoned. When Fred, who was in the fifth grade, and little Lizzy, in the third, showed up, they both ran away in terror having been told their daddy was a bad man. They were told never to speak to him. His heart broke right then and there, and he went to see his probation officer.

The probation department had a policy of encouraging recently released felons to have as much contact with their children as possible to help reorient them and mitigate the trauma to the kids. So, they helped in the court battle that followed. The judge declared to a stunned Tamara that she was to stop the mean spiritedness at once, and that Lencho would have joint visitation. "I don't care if he is living beneath a bridge, young woman," he thundered. "He is granted visitation, and you best not interfere with my order."

*****

Lencho's roommate, Tai, who worked for him on his greenhouse spread before the shit hit the fan two years earlier, was setting up computer programs for some construction guy named Chris in Fremont. Chris had a business startup that was called 'One Call Does It All.' The idea was that if a customer needed any given service from carpentry through landscaping, he could make just one call and they would coordinate the service. Lencho moved to Fremont.

Chris gave him an empty room that he had available. With his building skills, Lencho was soon in demand. He met a builder named Michael Jones, who was working through One Call, and found himself in charge of a crew of Mexican laborers. These guys were inclined to go to sleep when Jones left the site, and since Lencho could speak Spanish, he was able to fire them in their own language, which Jones could not. He was becoming very valuable, and his pay rose accordingly.

Now Lencho was assigned to the probation department in Oakland, he was able to see his kids regularly, and life was ever improving. There started to be a few ladies in his life as well, so he had some uncomplicated companionship, and that was the way he wanted it after the trauma of the beautiful but malevolent Tamara.

It wasn't long before the weed man figured out that, along with the One Call thing, Chris was making ends meet with some pot dealing on the side. In fact, he was moving considerable poundage, but he was paying too much in Lencho's opinion. "You cats are paying too much for this product, you know?" he told them. "What if I can match the quality at half the price?"

Ka-ching!

Bud was one of the boys taken down when Doc's memorable Mafia caper went down in flames years earlier over the Thai pot delivery. And it was Bud,

Lencho turned to now. Bud had done his years in the Fed system, and now back
in the game, he had a basement full of product. "Sure Lencho," he said over
the phone, "you come down and get it, and I'll front you fifty fucking pounds."
Lencho sent a couple of boys to Texas in an automobile, put them up for a night
in a hotel, and fifty pounds was loaded into their trunk. Back they came, and
just like that his fortunes and finances improved big time. A month or two later,
he was sitting on twenty thousand dollars and dreaming large again.

Chris told Lencho that he didn't want him doing any more construction. He
would cut Lencho a ghost check for a grand a week for the benefit of his PO, but
his new work was acquiring good marijuana for the large Bay Area market.

One of Lencho's girlfriends posed as his wife when he met a Chinese fellow
who owned a big house that had just been vacated by an up and coming rapper,
MC Hammer. For seventeen hundred a month, he moved in. Five bedrooms,
four baths, swimming pool and jacuzzi. He had to build a stash under the floor
to hide all the money that was once again flowing into his coffers.

His older son, Luz, got kicked out of high school for being a minor
delinquent, so Lencho took him in and made him go back to school in the
Fremont area. Then, little Fred called one night and begged to come live with
dad also. "I can't do that, son. As much as I would love to have you, your mother
will not permit it." The next day Fred ran away. Well, not really too far away, as
it turned out. He ran into the woods for about five or six hours. The crafty little
boy let his mother get sick with worry and call the sheriff, and then he marched
back home to announce he was so miserable living with Tamara and her 'men'
that he would just run off again if he couldn't move in with his dad.

"Lady," the sheriff told Tamara sternly, "we can't be coming out here again
over this. I suggest you let the boy move to where he's happy and outta my hair."
By the weekend, Fred was with his older brother Luz and his father in Fremont.
Lencho registered Fred at the local grammar school, and he continued to do
well.

Brother Ed moved from Prescott, and Brother Bobby and his son Brian flew
up every week to work construction. One day, some Fremont guys approached
the weed man about a bigger deal. Ronnie was out of the pen now, so a buy
was brokered and over fifty thousand dollars was sent down to Hermino at
El Escondido, the doorway to the Sierra Madre. The pot was purchased, and
Ronnie hauled it to the border of Arizona.

But things went sour, and it was necessary to wait for some time before it
could be moved across by hand. The border patrol had increased their efforts,
and it just wasn't safe. The Fremont people got impatient and also suspicious
that something might be afoot. "Listen," Lencho told them, "I got fifteen
thousand of my own money in this deal. I am not lying to you. It isn't safe to try
and move the pot now. It's there, but you gotta have patience."

Lencho's words fell on deaf ears, and they forced the issue by going down there themselves. Yes, they were relieved to view the product just like Lencho had assured them, but 'fuck you very much, we will hire our own mules to run it across at night because we are tired of waiting.' The whole load got popped by the Border Patrol who was lying in wait. No one went to jail, but a lot of money was lost. Dispirited, Lencho had had enough of Northern California. It was too crowded for the now 42 year old Arizonan, and he didn't like the public schools that much anyway. It was back to Prescott once again where it would soon be time for the annual Kite Fly, a Prescott tradition.

"'All the stars from all the bars,' that'll be our slogan this year," the weed man said to Brother David. "I need a break from the hurly burly man, and I hear they aren't gonna do the Kite Fly this year, so I'll do it for them. I'll be out lining up the acts." He went to all the music people in town and got them to commit for the May event. "All we need is some good wind, a charity to take the money, bands to make music, and I got Budweiser, Ford, McDonalds, and two dozen smaller businesses to participate. We'll have us a party. All non-profit and for charitable purposes."

By the second Sunday of May 1990 the word was out, and a couple thousand parents with their kids showed up with kites in hand. The sky was alive with floating colors. Five bands played all day, one after the other. Beer was slugged down, a little reefer was smoked, and a wonderful time was had by all. Lencho savored the fun and excitement of the whole thing and a pang tugged at his musical heart when he thought of previously thwarted 4th of July epochs he had tried to launch. "Fuck 'em," he shrugged. "I'll try that once again—someday."

Of the participants who put up booths, the most interesting to him was the American Hemp Company. He had been discussing the subject of industrial hemp with some friends, but he had never given it much thought. "Oh yeah," Ronnie pointed out, "Washington, the father of our country, grew it on his plantation way back when. So did a bunch of those dead presidents. They made all sorts of stuff out of the stalks like paper and clothes and rope. Yeah, it was everywhere, but then the Feds made it illegal back in the 30's. Something to do with Dow Chemical and trees."

Bolivia, the hemp lady, and her assistant showed up for the event from Phoenix, so Lencho let them set up for free. They were resplendent in their hemp skirts and shirts and hats, and they brought jeans, dresses, shoes, wallets, purses, oils, and creams for the masses. They even brought hemp lollipops for the kiddies that tasted just like green bud marijuana, but didn't get you high. That, of course, is what industrial hemp is all about. It's marijuana's first cousin without the buzz, but a million uses not the least of which is that it takes the place of forests.

"Hemp is an ancient agricultural product," Bolivia explained to one and all. "Just feel the wonderful texture of the fabric, examine this paper. We can legally buy and sell hemp products in America, but just like pot, it's illegal to grow. Banished in 1937 with the Marijuana Stamp Act. It was a ruse to assist Dupont Chemical, Dow Chemical, and William Randolph Hearst, as well as others so that synthetic fibers could take the place of hemp, cotton, and wool, and newsprint could be made of wood pulp instead of hemp like it always had been. Really sucked, man, but that's what happened. If we could reintroduce hemp as legal crops, it could save the forests and clean the air a bunch. But that ain't likely since the big chemical companies have a lot of money and friends in Congress. Now, even the DEA is on our case. Those crooks chase anything that's related to pot, even if it's benign and industrial." Then they smoked some joints of the non-industrial variety.

"I swear I never gave this hemp thing any thought," he said as they sat around a fire in the park that night. "What if someone grew hemp on an Indian Reservation? The Indians might dig it, and their reservation is sovereign. The Feds can't touch them there."

"Well," Bolivia replied, "if we could get the seeds maybe we could convince them to try. It could be a godsend for them economically. Those people are poor as piss."

"Let me give that some thought. I might know how to get some seeds," Lencho planted the thought rather innocently in Bolivia's head. "Industrial hemp is grown in Europe and Canada, right? I know a lot of people."

The American Hemp Company had a good weekend at the Prescott Kite Fly, and Lencho made some more friends. They also sold marijuana, as it would turn out, so he began moving some poundage that he obtained from them in Phoenix.

*****

"Lencho," Dr. Slatkin said, glad handing the old hippy. "Damn glad you're back in town. Say, you don't have some mota, do ya? I always have trouble scoring when you are not around."

"Sure, Doc," he replied with a wink. "Catch up to me down at the Lizard's Lounge any day around four. I'll fix you up."

Not just the well-respected local surgeon, but also police officers L, K, and N got their weed from him as well as B, C, and D from the fire department. Ms. V, who worked for the District Attorney, picked up bags for herself, the judge, and the principal of the Junior High. Not to mention officer T who headed up the DARE program. They and a million other straight arrow citizens who loved the curative powers of marijuana dropped by the Lounge for their weed. They smoked every day just like many Americans, but just like most Americans, they couldn't admit it.

Lencho went to work at Foxworth-Galbraith Lumber Company when he returned to Prescott, and they put his skills to good use in the specialty woodworking shop. He enjoyed the job, but the money wasn't enough to support himself and his boys. The weed business beckoned as always; half of the employees smoked, so he called up a friend down in El Paso to arrange a front of four pounds. That's how it began, small and intimate, and that was the way he intended to keep things. He got involved with civic efforts, such as the Kite Fly, and he held court down at the Lizard Lounge for a few hours every day after work.

"Lencho," Brad said sliding onto a bar stool, "the Kite Fly was just terrific on Sunday. We at YEI can't thank you enough. The donation you made for our disabled was sorely needed."

"You're welcome Brad," Lencho replied. "It was a lot of fun. We'll do it again next year, although I hear the City wants to buy the park."

"Yeah, no doubt. Then they would demand more insurance and all the bullshit that goes with bureaucracy. Well let's hope that doesn't happen."

The next two years went that way, quiet, peaceful, little drama, zero plane crashes, and Lencho was a contented man as his time on probation wound down. There was a small close call, of course, as there always is in the pot business. He had been selling his bags and passing his urine tests with Federal Probation via his pissalyzer glue bottle when he got tired of his current girlfriend, Debby, the Ballbuster who thought she owned him. When she found out he had been seeing other girls, it was a definite case of a woman scorned, and on Friday evening there was pounding at his door.

"Mr. Demarco," he said, shocked to find his probation officer standing there. "What a surprise."

"I bet it is Lencho," Demarco snarled. "A little birdie told me you been cheating on your piss tests. Also that you've been selling weed. I want some piss right now." And he pressed a cup into the weed man's hand.

"But sir, I have a young lady here right now, we are just having dinner."

"I give a rat's ass. Fill the cup—now. And use your own for a change."

The sample tested dirty and the PO sent it to Judge Rosenblatt. A bad test can easily send a man back to prison, but the judge didn't do that. Actually, the weed man never knew why, but the judge let him slide. But two weeks later, while at a dance with his sister and her husband at the local Rodeo Association, the Federal Judge found himself on the same dance floor as Lencho, who was doing a snappy two step with his sister Suzi. Rosenblatt sashayed his legal butt right into Lencho, knocking him for a loop. The judge just smiled at the startled weed man, but Lencho held no grudges. Maybe it was punishment for the bad piss test, but it sure beat going back to the joint.

The following Wednesday Brother David called him at the hardware store to tell him there was a letter at dad's house postmarked Hong Kong. Tearing it open, the letter read: "Hello Lencho, I am home now, and thought I would write my favorite Indian who is not like other white men. Please come and visit." Lencho called the enclosed phone number.

Mr. Wong provided the weed man with airfare, pocket money, and the motivation for a vacation to the mysterious Orient. Lencho flew to Los Angeles and stayed for a few days with music friends while he arranged for his passport. He thought it best not to tell his probation officer, because he was pretty sure he would say no. What the heck, he was almost done with all that anyway, so what would it hurt to travel across the world for ten days?

The flight on China Airways stopped briefly in Taiwan and then proceeded across the South China Sea to Hong Kong. It was 1993, and that fabulous city was still in British hands, but due to be transferred back to Chinese control soon. The tall skyscrapers on the harbor's edge and the confluence of Asian and European influence was an eye opener for Lencho. Mercedes Benz taxi cabs blended with buses and rickshaw for above ground public transportation, while below ground the newly completed tube with its swift trains connected the mainland with Kowloon. The Kowloon ferry ran constantly between the two points, and naval vessels from the United States, Australia, and England lay at anchor in the harbor. Fishing vessels and water taxis jostled for the right of way. Lencho was bowled over by the hustle and bustle.

Wong and his new wife met him at the Kai Tek International airport in a shiny BMW. Wong looked as boyish and exuberant as the last time they met. "Please meet my wife, Li," Wong said. "We go to the Mandarin Oriental hotel where I get you accommodations."

"Great to see you again, old friend," Lencho enthused. "This is quite a place. I had no idea it was so energetic."

"Lots of energy all right," Wong replied. "Some of it is mine. I own two hardware store now. I will show you later. Lots of fun."

"So it didn't take long for you to get busy once you got out, I see."

"Family give me million dollars to start over. I start stores and buy condo on water front, get married again, life good. I very happy you came. Did you bring sander pole?"

"Oh yeah, the device to sand dry wall. I brought you two, in case one got broken."

"Two?" Wong laughed. "You not too smart, Lencho! Same old Indian. I need just one so I can take to my factory and duplicate. Worth a lot of money in China."

"You old counterfeiter!" Lencho laughed. "I should have known. I also brought you this book on the American West and the Cherokee Indian."

"Oh, I love that," he enthused. "You will have a good time here I promise."

Lencho settled into his suite at the plush hotel and marveled at the view from his room overlooking the city. Beyond Kowloon towards the New Territories he could almost see forever. Pulling out one of the ten pre-rolled joints of emerald triangle mota, he savored the thin wisp of smoke as he changed and prepared to meet Mr. Wong who had promised to take the weed man on a launch out to the Aberdeen fleet and floating garden restaurants where they could pick out live lobsters from huge tanks and feast on delicacies caught only hours before. Then they would visit some night spots featuring both jazz and traditional music. The next day, Wong told the weed man his driver would show up at ten sharp to transport him around the entire place for a guided tour.

"I know you smoke that stuff," Wong cautioned him, "but remember you not in Arizona now. This is China. Remember what you told me how they treat you in that prison in Mexico? Well, they nice compared to here. Be careful."

"Are you going to come along?" Lencho asked.

"Too busy in day. My two stores in Kowloon, they need me, but at night we have dinner party."

The driver showed him Victoria Peak with its panoramic view. He rode the length and breadth of the underground tube, its escalators taking the rider three levels beneath the streets. The meticulous electric trains whisked a passenger to his destination in mere minutes.

"You not worried you get lost?" Wong would ask.

"Heck, no. I am lost to start with, so how could I get any more lost? Anyway, your city is really quite small and compact, so I am able to get my bearing as soon as I pop up from any angle. I am having a great time, man."

Lencho toured the University of Hong Kong, where Wong's boys were matriculating. The next night Wong moved Lencho out of the Mandarin Oriental into his own club where Chinese businessmen sat with intense concentration playing Pai-Gow poker with mounds of chips stacked in front of them. The air in the room was blue with cigarette smoke. They laughed and cursed over their high stakes game.

"Is this legal?" Lencho whispered to Wong as they watched.

"In Macau legal, but not in Hong Kong. Promise not to tell anyone!"

"And you worry about my pot!" Lencho told him.

"Pot not so popular as gambling," he answered. They went upstairs to the apartment he would stay in for the next few days.

Mr. Wong's two hardware stores were both in Kowloon and were packed with customers. He stocked typical hardware store stuff except that all of it was manufactured in China. Presumably the drywall sander Lencho brought would soon be added to the inventory. Wong found time to take him to a huge atrium filled with colorful birds and a cable car that went through an amusement park that was sort of a forerunner of the Disneyland soon to plant its flag in China. The gold district was where he took him shopping, although Lencho was not a gold bug as most Chinese seemed to be. "You so cheap, Lencho," he chided. "You should buy gold, good investment."

"Too damn heavy, Wong," he replied. "I prefer jade and carvings. Just some souvenirs for my kids is all I want."

"Listen, my friend," Wong finally said on the ninth day of his visit. "There is something I would like run past you. That's how you Americans say, right? I got proposition you might find interesting."

"Sure, what is it?"

"My wife like you very much. She agree with me you are not average white man. I tell her you more Indian. You noble savage. Li has cousin. Her name is Jing Yi Chen. She is very sweet and intelligent and not married. She also cannot get passport to travel abroad, and she very much want to go to America for more school. She need American husband, for a little while. Is this possible, Lencho? As a friend, would you marry our Jing Yi, but also not touch her?"

"Not touch her? You mean no sex?"

"Yes, that's exactly what I mean. I know you are gentleman and you save my life from that madman Skippy. I now ask you to save Jing Yi's life too, sort of. I am not saying this is for sure as much discussions must take place. But this would be typical Chinese marriage, arranged. And it would be a good thing for you, if you know what I mean."

"I don't need time to think about it, old pal. And I would not expect anything in return. Certainly not money. We are friends, and of course I will do it if you ask me."

"You are good man, Lencho," Wong said smiling. "I let you know in six months. If yes, you come back to China on our dollars."

The weed man was not back to his job at Foxworth-Galbraith a week when Bobby walked in with a message and phone number: 'Call Susan Rogue.'

He hadn't seen Susan since she ran off with Hermino after his leap for freedom twelve years earlier. Now she was back, and she was broke. But as always, Susan was raring to go. After spending several years in a Mexican prison, she had another little kid and a new old man down at the border town of Bisbee. "Hey man," she yelled over the phone, "great to hear your voice. You selling any reefer? Ya are? Great. I can get the kind?' I'll be up in a couple of days to visit. How many pounds shall I bring?"

She brought four pounds, and it was perfect. Really pretty stuff that everybody loved, and at a good price as well. They agreed to work together and to keep it to a dull roar. "I still got a year to go on my probation," he told her, "and I don't need trouble. Under ten pounds and they will never bother us in my town."

And that's how it stayed for exactly six months. Then he came home at lunch from work to roll a joint and found his son, Luz, stacking bales in his bedroom. "Oh, hi, dad," the boy said startled. "Didn't expect to see you so soon."

"Holy fucking shit!" Lencho yelled at the top of his lungs. "What is this? Where did all these come from?"

Luz looked at his feet. "Well, I guess I better tell ya. I made a deal with Susan. She knows you don't wanna go big anymore, but her people wanted to move some weight. She brought up three hundred pounds at a fabulous price. Man, we can make a killing on these. I'm gonna get Cousin Tommy and Cousin Brian to help me move 'em. Don't worry, I have everything under control."

"Under control? You gotta be shitting me! My PO could walk in here any time. They have the power to do that, ya know? And you got my house stacked from floor to ceiling with weed. Get it out you little idiot! Where do you get off with this shit? Where is that woman?"

Susan had run down to the liquor store for celebratory beer, and when she got back, Lencho made it short and sweet. Out of my house now and take all the pot with you, then don't come back.

So they left his house on Montezuma Street and drove the pot across town where she rented a bungalow that could hardly hold it all. That was the last time Lencho saw Luz and the cousins until Susan showed up once again two months later. "We gotta talk, my friend," she told him through gritted teeth.

"About what?" He snapped.

"Luz was doing pretty good with the money," she began. "We began selling the shit all over the area."

"So I have heard," he muttered. "Flooding the market big time. Selling to anybody that has a buck. Bags to pounds, whatever the market will bear. Very smart."

"Thanks," she replied. "So as I was saying, Luz did okay. It's that little shit nephew of yours, Tom. Apparently he has ripped us off. Disappeared with thirty grand. My man, Lalo, is muy pissed. He wants a sit down with you."

"Listen Susan. I told you from the start, I wanted to strictly go small. Then I came home and found you had filled my pad with weed. You didn't even ask me. Now things have gone south, and you're laying this off at my feet. Where do you get off, woman? This ain't my problem, so go tell Lalo what I said."

"Oh, I'll tell him all right, but be advised, he can be pretty intense when he gets mad. And man, he's mad now. Our deal is this: I fly the weed in and he gets the money. The weed comes from some big time hombres, and you don't burn these people. So now little Tommy has done this deed and his life is on the line. I'll be back tomorrow with Lalo." And she left.

"Great," Lencho muttered, flopping into his easy chair with a hand on his brow. "That's the problem with these fucking Mexicans invading our country!

We need to legalize growing."

"Listen man," the lanky Mexican hood hissed as he strode back and forth in front of the weed man, "I don't give a fuck if you had nothing to do with this fuck up or not. I know where everybody lives. I know where your father lives and your brother, and especially where that little faggot Tommy's mom and daddy live. I will kill them all if I don't get that money. Do you understand what I am saying to you? You been in this business a long time, paco, and you know how it goes with connected guys. We ain't fucking hippies with that shrug of their shoulders when a load gets lost. We are serious. I am in town to collect that dinero, and that's all I got to say to you. Get the fucking money. I'll call you later and you better have it."

"Loco sons of bitches," he cursed under his breath after they left. He had to take this man seriously because he knew he was seriously nuts.

Around three in the morning, the phone woke Lencho from a fitful sleep. "Lencho," Lalo hissed. "Look outta your window up the hill. You see the Buena Vista motel? I'm looking at you this minute through your fucking window."

"You got good eyesight," he muttered.

"Real good through a ten power scope hooked to this deer rifle, man. I could take you out now. Get that money or there will be blood." He hung up.

The weed man threw on his jeans and shoes, woke Fred, and was gone in ten minutes. When the sun came up he called Bobby. "We got a serious problem," he told his brother. "I'll be over to fill you in."

After explaining the mess, Bobby only had one suggestion: "We gotta tell Sue and Arthur. It's their boy that stole the money. I am afraid the cops are gonna get involved."

"Man," Lencho muttered, "I know those two will just blame me for this. Somehow it'll be my fault."

The cops were called in. Susie and her husband were now well to do merchants in the community with a feed store and tac and western wear. They felt about dope much the same way as Lencho's father; it was all bad. As Lencho predicted, they blamed him. Some of their crowd included the state police. Agents Kelly Kasun and Dennis MacMillan were called in for high level discussions. Lencho had little choice but to level with these men. He told them he was selling small amounts of marijuana to adults, some of whom were ranking members of the community, and that this nutty broad Susan Rogue had tossed a monkey wrench into the whole thing by bringing in organized crime, and the consequent mayhem that went with them. Tommy had gotten into crystal meth and ripped them off, and now the lid was about to fly off.

"Well, for starters Lencho, it's very well-known that you are the weed man here. And as far as DPS is concerned, if you kept it under ten pounds we don't give a shit. So we're glad you came to us. Better get Bobby's son to return

whatever weight he still has that belongs to them thugs for starters. And don't
go home for a while. We'll put some security on out here and on your dad."

Bobby's son Brian was pretty wigged out and ready to get out of the mess,
so he was happy to load up the hundred pounds of Lalo's weed still on hand
and head down to Phoenix to return it. But the drug business is a crazy thing
indeed, and as he pulled into the alley next to the house of the bad guys, he
found himself in the middle of a bust engineered by the local narcs. What
timing! Off he went to the Towers Jail while the pot he was returning was seized.
This news caused a sensation of swearing and breast beating in Prescott. "What
more could go wrong?" Lencho yelled at God. This was getting ridiculous, so
he had no choice: he picked up the phone and dialed U.S. Customs in Phoenix.
"May I speak to Agent Williams, please? This is Lencho up in Prescott."

"Williams is in Texas," he was told, "but I will give him the message." A
half hour later, Special Agent Tom Williams called. "Well, well, you crook," he
chuckled, "what kind of mess have you gotten yourself into this time?"

"Thanks man for calling back so soon. Let me start from the beginning."
After imparting the basics, Williams gave him the phone number to a DEA
agent in Phoenix. "I know how you feel about these guys, and me too, but this
fellow is pretty good. I will call him and fill him in, and you call him in an hour.
It'll be okay."

Much relieved, he caught up on the past six years. Williams was still chasing
smugglers in airplanes and Lencho told him he was just about off probation
when all this crap started. "And by the way, how is my old pal Bruce Brown?"

"He's good. Flying helicopters. Transporting oil workers out to rigs in the
Gulf. He isn't smuggling anymore. At least I don't think he is."

The DEA picked up the ball on the terrorists at once after Williams
contacted them. When Lencho and Bobby went down to Glendale for his
preliminary hearing, the prosecutor announced to the judge that Brian had
been assisting the United States of America, and that all he was being charged
with was an ounce of marijuana. The hundred pounds was never mentioned
and the boy walked out of the courthouse a free man. Bobby's jaw hit the floor
with astonishment. Lalo and Susan were never heard from again, and later
Brian told Lencho there was still fifteen pounds of weed hidden underneath the
floor back at his stash house. Lencho went over and got it, considering it to be
some small compensation for all the trouble. But there was one last sad bit of
woe to endure.

When he finally caught up with Suzi and Arthur's boy, Tommy, to tell him
of his peril, the kid went crazy behind a week's worth of speed and paranoia. He
came flying out of his bedroom with a .38 revolver in his twitchy fingers and
nearly shot his uncle, slamming it to his forehead. The kid was wild eyed and
sweating bullets, and of course blamed all his troubles on the weed man. Lencho

left with sorrow and disgust.

But the path the gods had chosen was circuitous and again it was leading back to China.

"Lencho," Wong wrote, "I am sending you the plane tickets once again. Please come and see me. We wish to introduce you to Jing Yi, perhaps your future bride."

The Chinese new year of 1994 was the year of the Dog. It was cold and crisp in January when Lencho arrived for his second visit to Hong Kong. He stood with Wong among the crowds along the harbor and watched splendid yachts glide by festooned with lights and bunting. They were owned by the fabulously wealthy, and the owners dined in splendor. They were attended to by liveried servants as rockets fired from junks and fishing boats exploded in the night sky.

Again he checked into the Mandarin and made plans to dine at the floating gardens in Aberdeen where they would pick live lobsters from tanks and have them cooked to personal taste. There they met Uncle Sing Lu.

"I am pleased to meet you, Lencho," he said with a bow. "My sister has told me so much about you."

Uncle Sing was a slight man of fifty with a regal bearing and dressed in a finely tailored suit.

"Nice suit," Lencho complemented. "I plan to get some clothes while I'm here this time."

"Thank you. I recommend ACE tailors where you are staying in the Savile Row of Asia. Would you like some wine?"

Over a dinner of shark fin soup, Peking duck, and birds nest they discussed the emerging world of China and how it had changed.

"My father was with Mao on the long march," Sing Lu told him. "In those days of fighting both Chiang Kai Shek and the Japanese, it was a time of heroics. It made men strong. Many died. I lost two uncles to bullets and starvation. It was the same for my brother-in-law, Mang Son Wong, and his family. But loyalty to the Great Helmsman paid off handsomely for us both. Times have changed since we were allowed to immigrate to the New Territories after the war, and of course, though we dearly loved comrade Mao, we obviously did not heed his dictum to eschew the 'capitalist' road."

Wong nodded in accord and added, "Our combined families have done wonderfully. Other than the small misunderstanding I and father had to deal with in America, we have in the words of your Methodist missionaries been 'very blessed.' My English has improved also, I think."

"It certainly has," Lencho agreed feeling tipsy. "But it was always way better than my Cantonese, Wong." They smiled beneficently at his compliment.

"Well, Lencho, I want to tell you a few things about our proposition and my niece. Her name is Jing Yi and she is a cultured, gentle woman. She is thirty years old and well educated. She is, unfortunately, the last in our family that still lives in China. Her brothers and one sister all wished to emigrate and now live in Sydney, Australia. That is fine, because our business interests are far flung and we have a major office in that country. But the laws of China are strict as regards the last surviving child of any family leaving. Or even traveling. And that is why we would like to see her married to a foreigner. She needs a passport. Simple as that. We are willing to make this worth your while, if we go forward."

"Stop right there, Uncle Sing. Wong here is a dear friend. We went through some tough times together as guests of Uncle Sam, and I am willing to do this for him. I do not want, nor will I accept, money. The travel is more than enough. I am, after all, an adventurer at heart, and I ain't married at the moment, so I am happy to help."

"You are a man of honor, Lencho," Uncle Sing replied toasting him. "We are in your debt."

"When do I meet the young lady?" he asked.

"Tomorrow we will travel to the border town of Shengzeng and you shall meet Jing Yi and her mother. But I must tell you a few more important details. Jing Yi is a wealthy woman. I would guess her worth right now is about twelve million dollars. That is nothing compared to what the future has in store for her, however. I know China will boom beyond imagination in the next two decades. It has come so far now. So you cannot put a claim on her wealth nor have sex with her."

"No sex?" Lencho asked

"Absolutely no sex. This is a marriage in name only. The purpose of it is only so that she may travel freely to someday work in our family businesses. Do I have your word on this?"

The wine was doing its thing. "You have my solemn promise Uncle Sing. No sex."

"I know you are a normal man, Lencho," he continued. "If you wish for women, you only have to ask. It just must not be my niece."

"No sex," he repeated, like taking the oath of a boy scout.

Shengzeng straddles the border between Hong Kong and mainland China. The railroad took them there quickly, and Lencho was installed in the Palatial Hotel. His room overlooked the bustle below and a skyline littered with huge cranes hoisting steel for the next round of tall buildings. A huge square clogged with traffic lay below, and on an adjoining edifice an immense TV like screen flashed images, messages, and commercials. Things clearly had changed since the days of Mao and the Cultural Revolution. And all in a couple of decades. What would the future hold for this ancient country, half authoritarian and now half capitalist frenetic?

The three men rose to greet two ladies as they walked into the lobby. Leading the way was a petite and very well dressed young woman. Behind her, looking downward and walking with a shuffle, was her mother. The clothing of the first bespoke an almost desperate modernity of Vera Wang, Guess, and Pierre Cardin; the latter, a throwback to a more humble and earlier time.

"Uncles," the young woman greeted them in English, "how are you today?" and then, "You must be Lencho."

"Lencho, this is Jing Yi," Wong piped up.

"A pleasure, Jing Yi," he replied shaking her hand. He thought he detected a somewhat disdainful air, but wasn't certain. Altogether, his wife to be was a very professional looking woman. Almost regal, which wasn't surprising considering her lineage. Her mother smiled shyly and said absolutely nothing. They sat together in a circle of high backed chairs and chatted in stilted English.

"That's a very nice camera you have around your neck," Lencho hazarded. "A Nikon?"

"Minolta," she corrected. "I want take picture of us for historical purposes. Tell me about yourself," she went on. "Uncle Wong tell me you are Indian. Very noble savages."

"Oh, Wong and his love of Indians," Lencho laughed. "Well, yes, I am twenty percent Cherokee. But mostly cowboy you might say. Raised in a place called Arizona in the U.S. You might like it there. Maybe someday you can visit. Uncle Sing tells me you work in the local hospital."

"I do volunteer work, and I also work in Uncle's enterprises. I am what you might call human resources manager. We have over twelve hundred people working. Keep me very busy."

The next day the love birds went on a tour of the city alone and visited the Window to the World theme park. Since it was still difficult and expensive for the masses to travel outside China, this place was an invented microcosm of other cultures as seen through Chinese eyes. Europe, America, the rest of Asia was all there in silhouette and plaster. The place was packed.

The day after, Jing Yi's mother accompanied them on the train ride up the mountain to the People's Paradise resort. They soaked in the warm springs and saunas, and enjoyed professional massages while breathing cool breezes entirely free of pollution. It was a time of getting to know one another a little better. When pressed by the weed man to expand on her previous romantic experiences, Jing Yi was blunt. "I have never been touched by any man." He took that as a warning, and remembered Uncle Sing's admonition about such matters.

Altogether, the sightseeing was fun and rewarding. On their third day together, they rose early from their separate rooms, met in the lobby, and after a quick breakfast, headed into Quanzhou to get married. First stop, the American

Embassy.

"My name is Miss Dupree," the lady from the Foreign Service introduced herself. Her southern drawl seemed quaint and out of place and she must have known it because she continued, "Originally from Mississippi and currently residing in Quanzhou, China. How may I help you today?"

Lencho and Jing Yi explained they wished to be married and that she would be leaving China for America. "And why, Lencho," Miss Dupree had to ask, "do you want to marry a Chinese woman?"

"If you knew my last wife, ma'am," he explained, "you would know how sick I am of American females. Gonna try me an Oriental this time." Jing Yi winced.

"And you Miss? I must ask why you wish to marry this man?"

"I'm in love," she lied.

Miss Dupree smiled benevolently and seemed satisfied. It took an hour to fill out the paperwork and they left. Next it was time for the Chinese Officials.

In the grim and quiet room of the People's Hall of Records an equally grim Major Quat Song stared at the couple through wire rimmed spectacles. His People's Army greens were starched and pressed, and his military cap with a blazing red star sat emphatically upon his bald head. The room was concrete and cold. It had no electricity, and was lit with candles from dozens of dishes and ancient lamps. Jing Yi was comfortable in her expensive London Fog while the weed man shivered in his Hawaiian silk that he had purchased in Hong Kong. The place gave him the creeps.

"I will say to you bluntly Lencho, I personally do not approve of foreign intermarriage. Call me old fashioned, but I am a loyal member of an earlier cadre before all this capitalism crept into mother China. I was faithful to the Great Helmsman and his little red book. I still keep a copy close at hand for the inspiration of his words which are timeless. Why do you wish to marry this daughter of my country?"

"Well sir, I guess it's because we have found a oneness. Jing Yi and I are soul mates. I met her through her uncle, Mr. Wong, while I was in your country on a trade mission."

"What's your line of business?" asked Major Quat.

"Business? Oh, hardware business. Drywall sanders is our specialty."

"Go on."

"So I met Jing Yi and was impressed with her serenity and inner calm. Also she likes baseball and we are both Buddhists."

"And you, Miss Chen, why do you wish to marry this American and circumvent our laws—our strict law on travel?"

"I love him," Jing Yi lied.

"Love indeed," the major muttered. "In the People's Army we have a saying: 'If the army wanted a soldier to have a wife they would have issued him one.' I am not pleased to approve your paperwork, but the law is clear. When 'love' is the stated reason for marriage, it must be honored. The fee is sixty thousand yuan. Pay the cashier over there by the candle and come back to sign these papers. You will then be married, and if the state approves her application your new wife will be issued a visa within six months to leave the motherland. I hope you are happy."

"Well, gee, thanks," Lencho replied surprised. "Is that it then? No ceremony or nothing?"

Major Quat Song glowered and didn't reply. The weed man had little doubt he was considered slime. Maybe even sub slime.

"That sure was romantic," he mumbled to Jing Yi as they walked out into the sunlight. "And I gotta ask, do you really love me?" Like the major, Jing Yi didn't reply.

"Let me get a picture of us here at the Hall of Records," she said cornering a passerby. They both smiled for history and then went back to the hotel after a strenuous day.

Uncle Sing Lu greeted the weed man in the lobby as his new bride went to her room. "I gather things went well?" He asked warmly.

"Oh fine," Lencho answered. "I think I'll go upstairs and take a shower and then get some dinner."

"The restaurant here is very good. My driver is waiting to take me to Hong Kong, so I cannot join you. I just want to say thank you again and that we shall meet again soon. I am in America frequently. We have interests in Las Vegas. And one more thing, Lencho, I really appreciate your honoring my niece's virginity. It is a very important thing to the family. So with that in mind, I have arranged a little companionship for you at dinner. Sort of a marriage celebration you might say. They will meet you when you come back down."

When he returned an hour later it was five p.m. He went into the restaurant and got a table at the far corner of the room where three very beautiful Asian ladies were sipping glasses of white wine and laughing among themselves. They were knockouts to say the least, and as he stared in wonder they looked up at him and waved.

Lencho joined them at their table, introducing himself. The ladies were so beautiful that the weed man was almost scared. Well almost. "What will it be, dinner and a movie?" he asked.

"We are very pleased to make your acquaintance, Mr.Lencho. Your new uncle is a very powerful man, and he has instructed us to make sure that your wedding night is to be a night that you will never forget. Please join us for a glass of champagne."

"Cristal. Nothing but the best tonight," one of the ladies said.

Lencho sat with them and was soon telling them about his youth growing up as a young cowboy, roping and riding broncos back in Arizona.

Sue Lynn was a stunning, dark haired beauty. She spoke with a British accent that was mesmerizing. "We have all three traveled the world over, Lencho, and visited great cities, but have never been to Arizona. Your stories have been delightful, and I wish to see this place someday."

The ladies all carried large shoulder bags, and from one of these bags, Ling Ling, a gorgeous, auburn haired goddess, produced a silver flask. She sat the flask in front of Lencho: "Please drink of this tea. You will find it both relaxing and euphoric, and it will give you the strength and stamina of a young bull."

"You are going to need it to get through this night," giggled Mai Ling, a little pixie and obviously the youngest of the three.

Lencho was in love times three as they left the lounge and walked through the darkness of the courtyard. The ladies picked flowers on the way to the room. In the 32nd floor penthouse, his new found friends set about lighting candles and placing flowers at the head and foot of the bed. Soft music played on a small cassette and champagne flowed from silver ice buckets.

"Lie down and be comfortable," Sue Lynn instructed as she placed bottles of oil on the table beside the bed. Lencho was beginning to feel the effects of the tea and could not control the silly smile on his face and laughter in his heart.

"Excuse us while we go into the other room and change our cloths. When we return, we will perform an ancient Chinese dance that will call upon your ancestors to bring you protection and long life." Lencho took off his boots giggling and removed his clothing, putting on a pair of baggy silk pants that they had left for him. He laid back on the bed in amazement. For the next six hours, the dancing and oiling continued and the young bull stood strong as the ladies had predicted.

The next morning, Jing Yi knocked on his door. He answered thoroughly hung over and disheveled. "What time is it?" he mumbled.

"It almost noon, Lencho. What happened to you?

"Oh, I was just celebrating our wedding like your uncle recommended. Might have overdone it a little."

She could see empty wine and champagne bottles on the floor and a pile of takeout boxes from the restaurant all over the table behind him. "We must check out now. I will take care of bill and be back shortly."

He bumbled his way to the shower, and when he staggered back out in his robe, his bride was standing in the middle of the messy front room with a look of dismay on her face. "How come bar bill so big?" she wailed. "Eight hundred U.S. dollar! My God, I can't believe you drink so much."

"Well," he replied sheepishly, "a man doesn't get married every day you know. I didn't get to have a bachelor's party, so I kinda made up for it last night."

As soon as you marry them, they turn into bitches he thought.

"Well, I wish to buy you a wedding gift. It is kind of you to marry me, and I am grateful. Let's go downstairs to the clothes store."

She picked out an expensive silk tie from Fleishman's that he knew he would never wear, but nonetheless thanked her profusely. It would be a memorable trip. As they passed over to the women's aisle, she ran her hand across a long row of furs hanging from the rack. Fox, mink, chinchilla, leopard from Africa, and silver and black fox from Russia. Wraps and coats, they were all there.

"These are from our lines. We have office in Moscow. Even though fur not so chic in some places now, there still a lot of money to be made. These are the reasons I marry you, to be able to travel out of China for future."

The flight back was fourteen hours and he slept most of the way. From LAX he flew to Phoenix where Bobby picked him up and drove him home to Prescott. Everyone was excited and amused that he married a Chinese girl. Everyone except his dad. "He just can't believe you got married over there," Bobby said. "He just says, 'As if the pot weren't bad enough, now he's gone and married a commie chink.'"

Chapter Fifteen

"Amanda"
Released 1974
Waylon Jennings

I've held it all inward, God knows, I've tried,
But it's an awful awakening in a country boy's life,
To look in the mirror in total surprise
At the hair on my shoulders and the age in my eyes

Amanda, light of my life
Fate should have made you a gentleman's wife
Amanda, light of my life
Fate should have made you a gentleman's wife

FLUSH

Fred was in the seventh grade at Mile High Middle School. The weed man wasn't home for a month when the boy got into a knife fight with a Mexican classmate over a girl. Like his dad, Fred liked girls, and this one belonged to the kid with the knife, or so the kid claimed. Felix, the Mexican janitor, told Lencho about it, and Lencho was mightily distressed over this racial dispute. When he tried to tell Fred about the birds and the bees, and the brotherhood of man, his son told him to fuck himself. Like his mother, the boy was headstrong and willful, and totally convinced he was right and could handle any situation. He was thirteen, after all. Remembering the recent tribulations with his older son Luz, Lencho shuddered.

On top of the fight, Fred decided he was ready to be on his own and ran off to live under a bridge with the homeless wino bums that dotted the landscape. After three days of searching the entire city, his father located his new abode and the pile of cardboard he was sleeping on out near the Safeway market. A forty year old derelict who looked like he was going on sixty said, "Fred lives with us, now, man. He is free of societal constraints."

"I'll tell you about constraints, you grubby asshole," Lencho yelled, jabbing the man's grubby chest. "I'm coming back here in a couple of hours for my boy, and you and your scum bag friends better skedaddle. Cause if you don't, me and my friends are gonna chop all of you into a fine puree of homeless goo, and I promise it will be painful." The old hippy was at his wits end and wasn't kidding. The bums must have believed him, too, because when he returned they were all gone and he found his son sleeping on his cardboard bed alone. When Fred found out what his dad had done, he was tremendously indignant.

"Man!" he howled. "How could you be so insensitive to those poor people? Mr. Whitaker is a great man who has been dealt harsh blows by our selfish society and lives free. I want to live free just like him."

The weed man turned to his old pal Malcom for consolation and advice. Malcom had lived in Costa Rica since the U.S. government had told him years earlier he was a wanted man (only to discover that he wasn't). He had held a grudge since. "The U.S. is a toilet, man," Malcom counseled over the phone. "Arizona is unfit to raise a child. You should flush the whole place."

"I wouldn't say it's that bad, Malcom," he replied. "Yeah, it's strange, but a toilet?"

"Messed up place, man," Malcom answered. "We hear all those hoary old homilies. 'Land of the free, home of the brave, innocent until proven guilty'. Give me a fucking break! You should move down here with us and bring Fred with you. Make all the difference."

Malcom, the ex-weed dealer, had hooked up with a guy who was nearly killed by electrocution on a job site and the settlement he received after losing his arms and legs was substantial. He was building an eco-lodge in the jungle, and there was work galore. And it paid fifty whole dollars a week! The place was tropical with warm ocean breezes, a long left surf break that went for miles, and lots of girls. Suddenly, it sounded like a darn good idea and getting Fred out of there and back to nature an even better one. After all, he had lived in teepees and campsites when he was young and it had been great fun.

"Son," he told his boy, "we are moving to the tropics."

*****

"Have a Heineken," were the first words out of Malcom's mouth. "Hope you brought some weed, cause we got everything but."

"Well, I brought a little," he replied. "How come you didn't tell me? How can life go on without mota?"

"Something about the latitude here, even the Columbian seed doesn't do well. I think we're too low. But other than that, this is God's own country."

And indeed it was. With around two hundred inches of rain a year, the jungle that abutted the azure sea was dense and full of birds, bugs, and critters of all exotic description. The indigenous people numbered a few thousand, but Malcom had loved them and protected and traded with them from the day he arrived, and lived next door to the Gulfo Dulce where they all lived. It was a small village of 400. It had a cantina run by a lady named Guadalupi who taught the local kids what schooling they got, and young Fred was soon enrolled.

On the very afternoon they pulled in from the long journey via Phoenix to the rutted airstrip in the jungle, Fred took just one look at the great lagoon fronting breathtaking surf in the warm Pacific and ran madly in. His father was aghast as he wasn't even sure if Fred understood current conditions all that well. Well enough, it seemed, as a dozen dolphins appeared from the deep and frolicked around him forming a mystical circle to protect him from all danger.

"My God," Lencho exclaimed at the sight, "do you think he's all right?"

Malcom stood at his side and smiled. "It's a sign, brother. A clear sign from on high. You don't see that in Arizona."

Big waves originating off the coast of South America brought the wonderful surf, which in turn brought world renowned surfers from everywhere when it was big. For Fred, it was there every day, big or small, and he became quite a surfer in short order. Lencho knew he had made the right decision in leaving the toilet of America before it got flushed. It was a time of bonding, and he became very close to his son that year of 1996.

Five miles from where Lencho and Fred lived in their new bungalow, Malcom owned two thousand acres of forest adjacent to the reservation lands

of the Guimi Indians. When he had fled there in 1977, he had no other way
of survival beyond gathering coconuts off the ground and later learning to
carefully shimmy up the long curve of the trees and hacking them down with
a knife. Years later, he was the defacto mayor of the area and sold real estate.
"They say America is the land of opportunity," he huffed. "Wasn't much
opportunity for this weed dealer. Here a man can be free even if he does have to
start with coconuts."

"First things first," he told Lencho. "We got to start building the main house
out in yonder lagoon. The basic plans are drawn up, but you are an expert
builder and we need your input as well as labor. I think the concrete pilings will
go in first."

The site of the anticipated eco-lodge was miles down the beach and through
dense jungle. It was secluded and protected further by the incoming tide. To
get the supplies needed to begin, Lencho rounded up a sturdy cart and some
sturdier oxen. If he wasn't fast enough, he got stuck on one side of the estuary
or the other and frequently spent the night waiting for the tide to recede. The
area chosen was lush with wildlife, chief among them birds of every species
and description. The place was going to be a bird lover's paradise. Prescott
College was extremely interested in establishing a satellite campus there for
that express purpose, the observation of rare and endangered species of birds.
Lencho was in his element even though the work was back breaking and the
equipment primitive. With the help of the local Indians, he mixed and poured
the concrete for the footings that would support the floor of the one thousand
square foot primary building. When that was completed, it was envisioned that
outer structures of smaller dimensions would encircle it for residential use. But
next came the walls of jungle hardwoods and then a magnificent thatched roof
woven and installed by Indians he hired at a dollar per hour. The damming of
a river inlet would be next. That would create a fresh water lake for fishing and
swimming, but the work was interrupted after that first year with a phone call
from David. "You remember Motorhead Bob and Gearhardt, don't ya? Well, this
is both an emergency and an opportunity, I think. Those two biker lunkheads
grew this big ol' crop out in Chino Valley. Great stuff, but they got into some
dumb ass dispute over how much each one of them should get. Now, Bob's
girlfriend says they are on the brink of murdering each other. They both got
their guns out. Armed to the teeth. Daisy is begging you to arbitrate before it's
too late."

Lencho knew these boys well. Nice enough guys, but very territorial.
Gearhardt in particular could be dangerous. A big hulking biker who got pretty
wild and mean when he snorted too much coke. "If Daisy can buy me a round
trip ticket, I'll be there the day after tomorrow," he said. The tickets arrived at
the airline counter in San Jose International promptly, and the weed man left

his project and son behind for the trip to settle a blood feud. He needed a break from the hard labor, but wasn't too sure about the outcome. These two guys could be nuts.

He was only back for a few days, but Prescott welcomed the weed man. "Saved your booth," Scott the bartender greeted him at the Lizard Lounge.

"You're the best, Scott," he replied. "I got an appointment with Miss Daisy, ol' Bob's girlfriend. She been in, yet?"

"Just walking through the door," Scott answered looking up.

"Hey Daisy, great to see you again. Been a while."

"Oh man, I'm glad you came, Lencho," she almost shouted. "It's high noon around Prescott. Those two are acting so crazy."

"Calm down and fill me in."

Scott brought a couple of Heinekens and the young woman began her story.

"The year before last, Bob and Gearhardt worked together on a medium size grow out near where you and Walter got in trouble a while back. We all did pretty well on that one, no cops or snitches, good weather, and few bugs. Made some dollars. So, they decided to get bigger this past year. I helped and, man, it was a lot of work."

"Agriculture is like that," Lencho philosophized.

"No shit. Well, so we set out three hundred clones. Went clones this year to side step the little boys. All girls. We figured we could get a yield of about five hundred pounds, if all went well. And we came close. We got three hundred. Lost some weight to a flash flood in August, of all things. Never plant in a gully. But we were real fucking happy. The first part went smooth, but then those two idiots started to squabble. First it was over me. I been with Bob for five years, but one time when me and Bob were arguing I got drunk and made it one night with Gearhardt. I told Bob I was sorry, goddamn it. Just one of those things, and it's not like Bob never cheated on me, neither, cause he has. But anyway, Gearhardt grabbed me by the ass later when he was into the toot, and that started it. Then they argued over who did most of the manicuring. Christ, trimming three hundred pounds of weed is a drag. My fingers were sore and stickier than slack in a raccoon's shorts."

"Oh, I know what you mean."

"So, when we were finally done with the whole effort, the two of them agreed to store it with me and Bob cause we got a big old garage out on my dad's spread near the Vargas Ranch."

"I know it," Lencho nodded.

"We debated unloading the whole shebang in bulk, cause we had buyers, but then we decided to sell it off piecemeal. We woulda netted close to half a million. That seemed like a nice round figure."

"It always does," Lencho smiled knowingly.

279

"But for some reason I still don't understand, Gearhardt started saying he was owed more than Bob. That he had done more work. Well, that's shit, Bob told him. 'I done more work than you. I rounded up the clones.' Gearhardt told Bob, 'Fuck you back, it was my pickup truck we used to get all the stuff there.' Next thing you know, they got into a fist fight and that big ol' Gearhardt beat the shit outta my Bob. But Bob still wouldn't back down, and me and him just keep our distance, now, but Gearhardt has let it be known he don't give a shit what happens. If he don't get more than half within the next week, he's coming after Bob with a sawed off shotgun. So, I called you. You've known those boys forever, so I figure only you can save the day. After all, Lencho, you're the man."

"Well, Daisy, I'm flattered. Where's Gearhardt now?"

"He's living with his mom out on Chestnut."

"Big oaf still lives with his mom?"

"He takes care of her and his guns. He got a lot of guns."

"First, I want to talk to Bob. He out at your house?"

Daisy and Lencho finished their Heinekens and went looking for Motorhead Bob. They found him sitting in the dark living room of their little house on Wardlow Street peeking out of the blinds.

"You been doing speed?" Lencho asked when he walked in.

"Hell no! If you had that big asshole mad at you, you'd be paranoid, too."

"You guys been friends since High School. How did it come to this for God's sake?"

"Shit, Lencho, I don't know. I love the guy, really, we're pards. Been in the weed biz for years together, but you know how it goes sometimes. There be fights."

"Apparently. So, how do we resolve this issue?"

"As far as I'm concerned, it's simple. I keep half, he keeps half. I can't see giving him more though. Fair is fair. Go tell him that, okay?"

Out on the east side where Gearhardt lived on Chestnut Drive, Mom let the weed man in with a smile. "Why, Lencho," she beamed, "it's wonderful to see you. Real glad you got out of that airplane crash alive. You were all over the news. My bridge club just thought it was such a story. We laughed and laughed. You kids today! In my time, it was whiskey coming over the border, now it's pot. Not much difference, if you ask me."

"Yes, ma'am. Is Gearhardt around?"

"Out in the garage, Lencho. Would you like a lemonade?"

"Thank you, ma'am, but I'm fine," Lencho smiled.

Just like Motorhead Bob, Gearhardt was sitting in the dark. His garage spotless with woodworking and mechanical tools hung neatly on peg board walls. He sat at a card table in the middle of the room illuminated by a small lamp cleaning an enormous pistol. His long black hair was braided and fell to his waist. Bulging muscles hugged a black t-shirt with the words Harley Davidson across the front. He wore a look of intense concentration.

"Your mom said it was okay if I came in. How you been?"

"Pissed off," Gearhardt replied. "How you been?"

"Fine. I moved down to Costa Rica last year. Took Fred. Now he's learning Spanish and he is a pretty fair surfer. So, what's this shit all about between you and Bob?"

"Motherfucker ripped me off. I'm gonna kill him."

"Don't you think that's going too far? And what makes you think he ripped you off?"

"The boy is pussy whipped. Thinks he's gonna steal my half of the crop and run off to Venezuela or somewhere with that goofy broad of his. No way that's gonna happen, man. I worked too hard on that crop."

"Yeah, no one knows better than me how much work and worry growing weed is. But I just saw him and he says he's got your half right now. Just say where and when, and he will bring it to you."

"Half ain't enough," the big man mumbled. "I did more work than he did. It should be sixty forty."

"My god, Gearhardt. You both did a ton of work. He even had Daisy helping. Surely fifty fifty is fair. You going to blow him away and go to the penitentiary over a dime you'll never collect anyway?"

"It's the principle," Gearhardt replied wiping the long barrel with an oily rag.

"A quarter million dollars, man. You're going to piss all that away and the cops will put you in jail for life, and they'll steal your weed and sell it. You know the drill. They can't wait for you to do something dumb like this. And what about your mom? You can't do this to that sweet old lady. You'll break her heart."

Gearhardt put the pistol down slowly and turned to the weed man. "I hadn't thought about mom," he said. "That would be fucked up."

"Fucking A it would," Lencho agreed. "And you know what they say, 'you can't fuck an A without a triangle dick.'"

Gearhardt sat there in the dark for a minute contemplating that one, and finally a big grin began to form on his mug and a minute later he began to chuckle. Then, the chuckle turned into a laugh, and finally burst forth into a torrent of hilarity.

"Man, Lencho," he snorted between tears of mirth, "you always could make me laugh. Tell the motherfucker to bring me my half on the double. Bring it here. Bygones be bygones."

And that's how the weed man of Prescott settled a blood feud and earned fifteen pounds of sweet bud for his trouble, and it took about an hour.

So, now an ambassador for peace among his many laurels, the weed man also fell into a steady sum to augment his meager earnings in ecological building down in the jungle of Costa Rica. Forty-five thousand dollars to be exact. He mused on how both easy and hard it was to make money in the weed game. These two silly men in their angry dispute over something they couldn't even explain was a prime example. Or carefully calculated plans and efforts, such as growing a crop, only to have the house fall in over a fictitious stolen cow. Clearly, there was no meaning to any of it. All a crap shoot. And it's the times of random chance that love comes knocking.

"Give me a Heineken, Scotty," he told the bartender down at the Lizard Lounge. "I'll take it over at my booth with my brothers." As he sat down with Bobby, David, and Ed that evening to regale them with his peace overture tale, his eyes lit upon a vision of loveliness sitting at a table across the smoky room. She was having a beer with a group of lady friends in their early thirties, and she had that special something. "Who's that girl?" Lencho asked to no one in particular.

Bobby looked over his shoulder and gave a little shudder. "You don't want nothing to do with her, bro."

"What the fuck are you saying?" Lencho exclaimed. "She's heavenly. I know a babe when I see one."

"Way too bossy, I'm telling ya."

"How long has she been around? Anyone dating her?"

"I think she's been coming in for a few months. Moved down here from Portland. She is a tough nut."

"I assume by that, you mean she ain't easy."

"Exactly," Bobby laughed. "And in my book, if a woman doesn't get with the program no later than the second beer she's trouble."

"That's fucked up," Ed howled.

"You're just a horn dog," David chided him. "You even given her a try?"

"Naw," Bobby admitted. "She scares me."

"That's the kind a woman that would rip your heart out and stomp on it. She's beautiful," Lencho said. And he was out of his booth to meet Connica, newly moved from Portland, Oregon.

Usually glib with the ladies, by the time he reached their table he was tongue tied. He just stood there for a moment holding his brew with a vacuous grin. Finally, all five of the girls stopped talking and looked up at once. "Can we help you?" The blonde one asked expectantly.

"Oh, er—I was just wondering if you'd like to dance."

"Well, which one do you wanna dance with?" she asked as they giggled. "There are five of us, or do you want all of us at once?"

"No! No, of course not," he stammered. "I want to dance with this vision of loveliness. Miss Portland." They howled and reality faded away, and his face got red. "I would love to," Connica finally said standing as they headed to the dance floor to Conway Twitty's 'Only Make Believe' on the jukebox.

Lencho got his act back together quickly and put his beer down on an empty table. He was a good dancer being the cowboy that he was and the flush of embarrassment faded. Man, this girl feels nice, he thought with an arm around her slender waist and the scent of her hair and perfume in his nostrils. He was tempted to nip an ear.

"God, you smell good," he whispered.

"So do you. I can't put my finger on it, but it reminds me of the sea."

"I live by the ocean," he told her as they danced. "The jungle and the ocean in Costa Rica."

"Are you a Tarzan type then?" she joked.

"No, no. I'm really a Prescott boy. A cowboy transferred at the moment to Central America. I'm up here only briefly and will be going back soon."

"What do you do in Costa Rica?"

"My son was getting into trouble up here, so at the advice of an old friend we moved south to get away from the festering pustule of America for a while. My friend calls this place a 'toilet.'"

"You have a way with words," she chuckled. "And has it helped your son to be away from this 'toilet'?"

"Immensely," he answered. "But what about you, Connica? What's your story other than this irresistible presence that knocked me over all of a sudden?"

She was five foot four with curly red hair and the face of an angel. She looked at him with big blue eyes and a wry smile of self-confidence. Self-assured. Not cocky.

"I'm my own person, I'll tell you that. Independent, never married. I'm in the architectural landscaping business. I'm working for a firm here in Prescott that's developing the Antelope Hills golf course. It's challenging work and I'm good at it."

He wanted to ask if she was good at other things, but quashed the impulse. This lady was different, he could sense it. As Waylon Jennings came on over the speaker, they left the floor to sip brews and talk some more. Three hours later, Bobby interrupted the two as they gazed into each other's eyes. "Say bro, we're gonna split. Gotta go to work in the morning. Forgot to tell ya, ya got a call from that Chinese person this afternoon. Here's the number."

"Chinese person?" Connica asked.

"Oh yeah," Lencho choked. "Must be my old pal Mr. Wong out in L.A. I met him at a tradeshow. He is in the hardware business."

They made a date to meet again. Connica had to go to see her father in Portland, an executive with Ma Bell, and Lencho floated home that night on a cloud certain this Connica woman was something special. It was a fortuitous event.

After a night of dreaming of Connica, Lencho woke up to make a call to his Chinese wife. She had come to L.A. six months after the wedding, and with her paperwork complete, was granted a visa. When he reached her, she was in tears.

"Jing Yi," he said. "Calm down. What in the world is wrong?"

"Oh, Lencho," she sobbed, "I been in this country since spring. It's 1996 now and we married one year. I so miserable."

"You miss me that much, huh?" he asked.

"Don't be silly," she replied. "I don't miss you at all. I hardly know you. It's just that here in Chinatown I am working so hard and trying to practice my English and learn how to drive, I just overwhelmed. I so homesick for my family and how you say it? Bummered out." The tears streamed so hard he almost got wet over the telephone.

"Well darn, girl," he said, "you should have called me sooner."

"I did call you sooner, but you were in Costa Rica."

"Well, I'm here now. What can I do to help?"

"I want to rent a nice place to live. Very tired of this Chinatown with smog and mean boss. Can you come help me? I must have husband with me when I go look. I must live like an honorable person. A woman of my rank."

"I totally understand. Can you pick me up at LAX? I can be there tomorrow."

There she was at the Southwest Airlines curb in a little Datsun when he got off the plane. She was as prim and proper as he remembered her, dressed in an expensive skirt and blouse with a pill box hat straight out of Jackie Kennedy.

"I like the hat," he told her as he climbed into the car.

"Thank you. Very fashionable now in Shanghai. First we go to DMV."

"You are driving without a license?"

"Not for long," she answered.

The day got off to a great start as he coached her on the driving tests and she passed with flying colors. They had lunch at the Sea Harbor Restaurant and she filled him in on her Uncle and Mr. Wong. She also told him she hated her job and her boss, who was very cruel, and that he had a habit of grabbing her ass now and then and didn't always pay her.

"Why in the heck are you even working, Jing Yi?" he wanted to know. "You're worth millions and are the scion of a powerful industrialist family. You hardly need the job."

"Must work," she corrected him. "All honorable people hold down job. I always work and always will. Now, we go to Newport Beach to look for condominiums."

"Hold the boat," he told her. "For starters, I have no credit. I am a cash and carry kind of guy. Always have been. When they check my references, they'll find out that I don't even exist. Also, I have somewhat of a police record. And

284

why do you wanna live down there in Orange County anyhow? Nothing but right wing, anti-communists that will hate you. I got a better idea altogether."

Her lower lip was quivering, but before the tears began again she asked, "And that is?"

"You come to Prescott. I am back and forth from Costa Rica, and I can easily be contacted. Also, my family lives there, and I guarantee they will look out for you. The city of Prescott is small and clean, unlike Los Angeles, and I think you will enjoy it a whole lot better. You can go to school there for your English and business subjects, and it will be a big improvement."

"Are there Chinese restaurants in Prescott?" she asked after what seemed like protracted contemplation.

"I will need job."

That weekend she arrived with her escorts, Mr. and Mrs. Chin. Lencho introduced her around and Lencho's family loved her, except dad who they avoided because he was a commie hater.

Ed and his wife and daughter really took a liking to her and threw a dinner party in her honor. Lencho's daughter, Liz, was there and Jing Yi charmed them all with her delicacy and elegant manners. An old friend, the chiropractor Dr. Steve Gayle, had an available one bedroom, one bath apartment with kitchen above his office for three hundred dollars a month, and told her to take a look. If she liked it, she could have it at once. No paperwork, nothing, just a handshake. It was right across from the modern Yavapai College and was ideal. Although she was now legally licensed to drive, just about everything she would need was in walking distance. So, her car sat idle at the curb for the most part.

As the weed man was preparing to go back to the jungle of Costa Rica, Jing Yi's life had greatly improved. She was waiting tables at the Golden Dragon Chinese Diner on Willow Creek Road. "You very good husband," she gushed to Lencho as she got her camera out for some pictures. "I need some of your clothes for the closet here. We married and you must live here if anyone ask. I am honorable woman, after all."

With his Chinese wife in good hands and all things now under control, the weed man headed back to the Lounge in search of his mystery woman. She was mysteriously attractive, mysteriously coy, and wondrous to the eye. And damn if he didn't have to leave. There she was again with some friends. She smiled broadly as he approached.

"I was wondering where you were," she said.

"I just got back yesterday," he responded beaming. "I've been handling some things before I head back."

"I was hoping you would accompany me to a charity event," she said. "Before you go. It's for a good cause."

"Wow. A beautiful woman asking me out for a date. You don't see that every

285

day."

"I told you I was self-assured. The event is at the Bartenders Showdown at Murphy's Fine Dining. All the big muckamucks will be there. You know, doctors, lawyers, and Indian chiefs. As well as the state's greatest bartenders all competing to make the best drink with the most dazzle. It'll be fun. How about it?"

"Just say when," he sighed.

He joined her the next night at Murphy's. The place was packed with the elite. Lawyers, cattlemen, tycoons, and lots of decked out dudes and ladies strutting their stuff while a battle raged behind the long mahogany bar between Tucson Slim and Hot Toddy Todd, competing for the most authentic margarita in Arizona.

Connica was waiting at a table sipping a martini. Lencho got there just in time as several hungry sharks were circling her. All of them wore suits. He had on western wear and cowboy boots with an oversized silver buckle that said 'Mota' in brass relief.

"There you are," he smiled and sat down. "I'll have what you're having."

Three martinis later, they were both feeling little pain when a familiar figure walked up to them. "Hey, you old dog," Terry yelled over the cacophony. "Long time no see."

"Well damn," Lencho yelled back standing up and putting out his hand. "Hit any power lines lately?" Terry and a statuesque French girl with a body to die for sat down and the reminiscing began.

"I'd like you to meet my friend, Connica," Lencho said.

Connica shook hands all around and said, "Where do you two know each other from?"

"This guy scared the shit out of me a few years back when we were taking off with some cargo down in Mexico. He almost flew into some wires."

"You're just a cry baby," Terry replied. "What are you doing now?"

"I been living down in Costa Rica with my son doing construction. What are you up to these days?"

"Me and Harry just bought a Gulfstream G4. Well, he bought it, actually, I just fly the thing. I'm living in Paris with Jenette here."

The conversation went on that way for an hour and two more drinks. Connica found out that "Harry" was the actor Harrison Ford, and that Lencho's cargo was marijuana, and that he had been kidnapped by the Feds, chased by bandits in exotic mountains, crashed in airplanes only to walk away, and a whole lot of other crazy stuff. She didn't believe any of it. All she could say when the couple had left was, "I've heard some bullshit in my time, buster, but that takes the cake!" And then she looked into his eyes and purred in a voice that both made his pulse race and his heart sink, "Are we gonna hook up, big boy?"

He put his hand on hers and looked at that lovely face. This lady was something special. All his wild and crazy ways, his womanizing and skirt chasing, seemed like it had been so long ago. All of his bad boy instincts abandoned him. "It breaks my heart that we can't," he said in a subdued voice. "But you're something special. We barely know each other, but I feel it right here," patting the general area of his heart. "If that weren't true, I would grab you right now and well—you know. God I must like you. I can't even be my usual crude self. But the fact is I'm leaving for Costa Rica at 5:00 in the morning, so I'll have to pass."

"Maybe another time then," she said softly with misty eyes.

*****

"Whoa nelly!" Malcom exclaimed looking at the two fat bags of marijuana sitting on his kitchen table. "No more stems and seeds! Some real mota."

"I can't believe with all the bud we smuggled into the U.S. from Belize that good pot can't grow down here. Well, at any rate, I brought some down from Arizona. This is good ol' American grown weed and it's killer, let me tell ya."

Besides the two pounds that he brought, he now had a steady income from the thirteen pounds that he left with some friends in Prescott. They faithfully sent him two or three thousand dollars a month until it was all sold. The weed man was living large relatively speaking in Costa Rica in that fall of 1996.

He went back to work hauling supplies out to the lagoon via ox cart and built a dam that captured the river water. This was a difficult feat of engineering and was extremely labor intensive. The inlet was about a hundred running feet wide and he had his Indian laborers build forms and sink pilings into the mud and rocks. Then he made a pull up gate that worked off a hoist for releasing the water.

"If I'm not here to do it, don't ever forget to pull open the gate if there's a bad storm," he advised the tribal chief. "Because if you don't, it could bust. That would make all our work for naught."

The original building he had worked on the first year was now done with a beautiful thatched roof created by the Indians. It had windows that looked out to the sea with no glass. It was a design of the tropics.

Also, he did a remodel on a large home owned by a wealthy American yacht captain. The captain worked for a billionaire out of the Middle East somewhere. This guy was so rich that he had his yacht put on steamers and carted around the world where the skipper would catch up to it and then set sail. "Money is an odd thing indeed. Either none at all or an absurd embarrassment of riches," Lencho mused.

Son Fred was getting very good with his surfing and Spanish, and now had a cute little girlfriend and lots of pals. He was a hard worker, and his dad was happy to see him develop a work ethic and an appreciation that was lacking back in the States.

Malcom was single, now, having broken off with his gal, Carol, from those long ago days when she was one of the sisters. He walked in one balmy evening with the announcement of a phone call from the cantina.

"Your wife is coming to visit," he said. "She wants to take lots of pictures."

*****

"Man!" Brother Ed exclaimed taking a hit on a joint after he and Bobby had arrived with Jing Yi that afternoon. "That wife of yours is just super. Sweet as honey, she paid for our trip to paradise. Where did you find her?"

"It's a long story," he told them.

"This most messy house I ever see," Jing Yi complained coming out of the kitchen. "I clean after dinner. Now time for roast duck."

Ed and Bobby stayed for two weeks as Jing Yi cooked, cleaned, complained, and took copious photos for historical purposes. She didn't much care for Costa Rica, and really hated Malcom's twin Rottweilers who cornered her when she was least expecting it with hip shaking and droolly doggy smiles. Slobbering and growling, they scared the shit out of the little Chinese woman.

"Save me! Help, help!" she would yell.

"Oh, Jing Yi," Malcom would say, "Thug and Billy are harmless. They'd lick you to death maybe, but they won't bite. Just pat them on their heads."

"I no pat nothing. They ugly like demons. In China, we eat dog not keep for pets. And they stink."

Before she left with Bobby and Ed in tow, she pronounced Costa Rica far too primitive for her liking. "Too hot and no window here. What kind of house has no window?"

"We love you, Jing Yi," everybody told her as they saw her off, and like everywhere else she went in America, she left behind friends. Lencho escorted them to San Jose International Airport and she shook his hand solemnly. "Goodbye, husband," she told him. "I see you back in States next time you there. Be careful of snakes and those dogs."

"Goodbye, Jing Yi. We had a wonderful time."

"You decide to put glass in window, let me know. I get Wong to send glass free."

Another year passed. The work was coming along, the money owed came, many Heinekens were drunk, and a lot of pot was smoked. Now that Lencho had good weed, he was extremely popular with the locals, including two German guys that ran the sport fishing concession for the occasional tourist fishermen from the States. "Dats zur gut veed, Lencho," they would tell him.

But at last it was time to head back again. Fred was getting antsy to see Arizona and the family, he said. And he might strike out to the Islands to ride the North Shore. Lencho remembered the dream girl Connica. When they got back he went straight to the Lizard Lounge to see if she was still single and still there. As fate would have it, she was still both.

"I think you should forget about her," Bobby scolded. "She ain't your type."

"How would you know my type?"

"Whoa, bro. I know your type very well. I am your brother, for God's sake and we been around a lot of broads in our day, and you like the wild and crazy type that put out and then get out. She ain't that way. Why hell, I don't think she took up with anyone since you were last in town."

"Man, Bobby, you make it sound like that's a bad thing. I couldn't be happier.
"

Just before Thanksgiving of 1997, he found her with her girlfriends once again down on Whiskey Row. "I always seem to find you in a bar," he said as he materialized from the street that night. "I'm just drowning my sorrows, big fella. Have been ever since you left last year."

"Do you want to dance?" he asked tenderly. "I think I hear Waylon about to sing a love song."

They made a date to see David play with his band at the Spirit Room in Jerome. Connica drove.

"How's the golf course business coming along?" he asked. "Still at it?"

"Oh sure. Still a ways to go on that one, and then there are things in the future, I guess. What about you? Going back to Costa Rica?"

"Well, yeah, I kinda have to. I'm committed down there. We're in the middle of a big project and it's remote. Beautiful, but remote. I have to haul everything out on an ox cart and I hire the local Indians to help me."

"They aren't head hunters down there, are they?" she asked wild eyed.

"Head hunters! Give me a break. Well, now that you mention it, I guess the indigenous people Columbus ran into way back might have been cannibals. But I don't think they cut off heads."

"So you're saying it's okay to eat people as long as you don't save the heads for some kinda trophy."

"Well, yeah. In my book, if you were to cook someone in a big old pot and it was really delicious, then that would be trophy enough. Pretty soon all the other cannibals would be singing your praises as a wonderful chef, so that would be your reward. You wouldn't need to collect heads. But, anyway, my Indians don't hunt heads, wise ass." And they both broke up and laughed and laughed some more. He sure liked this gal, and because he did, he came to the conclusion as they had drinks in the Spirit Room he better come clean about Jing Yi.

"Listen," he began slowly, "I think you are a very attractive lady and I will admit I really like you."

"Yes," she replied batting long eye lashes.

"And it's because I like you so much that I am telling you this."

"Hold the boat," she said sitting bolt upright. "I knew this was coming. You're too good to be true. You're married! Am I right? Married bigger than heck!"

He took another sip of his drink. "Yes and no."

"What ya mean 'yes and no?' You're either married or you're not. Which is it?"

So began his Wong story and his trips to China.

"My god, you are so full of shit," she sighed. "So how long does this charade go on?"

"We figure three years. It's been two."

Connica pondered this for another long moment before speaking.

"I'm not going to let you get away again," she said emphatically. "If you have any sense, you won't let me get away either, my friend."

"I don't want you to get away, but I do have to go back to Costa Rica. Want to come with me?"

"I'll quit my job tomorrow. I'll go to a travel agent and buy a ticket right afterward."

"Baby, you don't need to buy a damn ticket. I have money and I'll buy the tickets. Instead of going back with my son, I'm going back with a beautiful woman. Are you positive you wanna hookup with a maniac like me? The things you've heard, the stuff I've told you is true. I kinda march to my own drumbeat. Always have and always will."

"Yes," she told him. "I'm sure. Let's get outta here. Have I ever shown you where I live?"

The next day, he went with her to her job where she handed in her resignation to a stunned boss. After that, they made arrangements to store her belongings and he pulled a wad of cash out of his pocket and peeled off a thousand dollars. "This is for you. You need to buy some appropriate clothes for a tropical climate. And by the way, do you mind windows without glass?"

"What?" she asked.

After that, she introduced him to her mom and her grandmom, and some cousins. "I have family all over the Prescott area," she told him. "I don't know why we never met."

"It's so close to the holidays I think we should stay until the season is over," he replied.

Thanksgiving at her house was first, and pretty soon it was Christmas with his family. A whole lot of parties, a lot of booze, and a lot of fun. When love is young, it is truly memorable. They closed out 1997 with toasts and made love and plans for the future. On January 3, 1998, they were winging their way to San Jose, Costa Rica. "You know," he said, "I had this little financial windfall and work can really wait. I think we should do some traveling. How about Panama? It's just around the corner from where I live." With the future promising no limits, they made plans to buy some property themselves in Costa Rica. They would open a bed and breakfast specializing in bird watching, fishing, and all things natural. "Mom has scads of money," Connica said. "Maybe she would invest. How much would it cost?"

"I think a hundred thousand would do it," Lencho replied. Six months later, they flew back to the States where the weed man brokered a deal up in Portland and then spoke to Ms. Lilian, Connica's eccentric Mother. "Ecolodge?" she asked. "Oh, that sounds wonderful. A hundred thousand? Certainly. More, if you need it."

"Wow," Lencho said. "Your mom is great. Such enthusiasm. And say, look at this article in the morning papers. California has passed something called a medical marijuana law. If you are sick, you can smoke weed for medicinal purposes. I've always known it could cure depression and improve appetite. No doubt it could help other ailments as well. Gotta look into this."

They flew Ms. Lillian down to Costa Rica and showed her the raw land Lencho had scouted. They wined and dined the dear lady for two weeks, and she was most demanding. Finally, Lencho got to the point. "Ms. Lillian, ma' am, it's time for the money. We gotta move on this project."

"Money? Project?" she asked blankly. "I don't have any money for any project, young man. You aren't some kind of gold digger, are you? Getting to my money through the affections of my daughter? How dare you!" Ms. Lillian was shipped back to Prescott on the next flight out. Adios, motherfucker!

"I'm so sorry about mom," Connica apologized. "I should have also said that she is prone to eccentricity."

"No shit," Lencho muttered as the airplane lifted off. But the whole effort wasn't a total loss in the entertainment sense, because while they were at the airport Air Force 2 arrived and a contingent of U.S. Marines disembarked, all in civilian clothing, along with the Secret Service and other spook and security types. President Bill Clinton was due in town the next day on board Air Force 1 for a state visit. The circus had arrived.

All eight of the jarheads were staying in the same hotel as Lencho and Connica, and they met down in the bar that evening. Party animal central was in full swing.

"You guys seem to have a lot of fun with this job," Lencho and Connica said at a table piled high with Heineken bottles and Cohiba cigar butts. A corporal replied, "Best fucking job in the Corps. Bill is a party guy himself and we do our job, but still find time for fun in the sun, and pussy too. Oh, sorry, ma'am. No offense."

"None taken," Connica replied.

"You boys want some pot?" Lencho asked.

"Does a bear shit in the woods? Our stuff or yours?" he howled and they all adjourned to Lencho's room for some sweet Arizona bud and a line or six of Peruvian flake. This was the military Lencho remembered from his youth.

"You know," he said to the marine, "I bet Air Force 2 would be an excellent way to smuggle back some stash. You guys certainly go to the right places."

"Done all the time," the marine replied. "Hell, I wouldn't be surprised if Bill didn't smuggle some back himself on Air Force 1. I know he's smuggled quem on there before. There was that time, for instance, in Fiji. Man, that little lady was hot. And then out in Paraguay. You might think the women would be plain on the pampas, but there in South America those women are cowgirls, and ol' Bill is a cowboy. Gonna get his tit in a ringer one of these days. I feel sorry for Hillary."

The next day President Clinton himself showed up, and the weed man wondered if he made a stopover at one of Costa Rica's putarias.

Taking the opportunity to see the local beaches, the happy couple spent the next night at the Hotel Calypso. It was the off season and the accommodations were luxurious and reasonable. So few guests were registered, they were treated as royalty. At the bar that night, the two tied a fairly major one on and Lencho was seized with an inspiration. Pulling the bartender aside he told him, "Do you know, my friend, this little lady only recently won the world of bartending's greatest honor, the National Bartender Competition for the entire United States?"

"No!" the man gasped.

"Oh, but it's true. Her drink was picked in the most original and potent category. The flaming Ko-Nika."

"Get out, Amigo!" he gasped.

"Oh, sí."

"I must see this drink. I will make them for our patrons here!"

"I see you have all the ingredients," Connica chimed in, "except one I must have, but I don't see it."

"My god. No Drambuie? I will send out for some at once!" and he called Pepe the valet and groom to the bar. "Pepe," he barked in Spanish, "run and fetch some Drambuie from Señor Gomez at his spirit shop, pronto!"

It took no more than twenty minutes for Pepe to return, and in the meantime Connica assembled the necessary precursors for the world famous drink of which she was the inventor and the current intoxicant laureate. Rum and absinthe were the two critical components, because they were flammable and a half dozen others for color, zest, and character. And then, finally, a drop or two of Drambuie that Pepe had returned with. Now, the match.

The flame leaped nearly to the ceiling and all four of them had to jump out of its path. Then, it settled down to a gentle blue flicker. "I need ice," Connica intoned with authority and the bartender provided it expeditiously. The ice doused the fire and she proclaimed, "It's ready. The flaming Ko-Nika."

The two love birds giggled maniacally and stumbled out of the bar to their room as the bewildered bartender called out, "But aren't you going to drink the flaming Ko-Nika?"

"I've had too much already," Connica called back. "And anyway, I made it for you, my good man." They never found out if he tried it.

*****

Since the hundred thousand dollars didn't materialize, they dropped the bed and breakfast concept and after eight months decided to return home. On the way back, somewhere over Mexico, Lencho proposed.

"I thought you were already married," she giggled.

"I guess it's time I got divorced then," he replied.

Once back in Prescott, he took her to meet his Chinese wife. True to form, the little woman loved Connica like a sister and heaped praises on her 'husband.'

"I so happy for you," she gushed. "Lencho very good man and make wonderful husband. He never touch me one time the whole three years we married."

"Is everything finished that needs to be done?" Lencho asked. "Do you have your passport and everything you need to travel now?"

"Oh yes," she told him. "I was going to see you about that anyhow. This perfect. I call lawyers in L.A. I want divorce, husband unfaithful!"

A few months later, the divorce was final on the grounds of infidelities, so the happy couple made plans for their own ceremony. When Connica sent Jing Yi an invitation, she told her she wouldn't be able to come. She was on her way to the London office of her family's far flung empire to oversee mineral rights in Africa. No one saw her again.

One morning in November, Lencho put the newspaper down and looked at his bride to be: "This proposition 215 really has my attention," he told her. "California is always ahead of the curve. Somehow, they got this medical marijuana initiative passed. Maybe the voters aren't as dumb as I thought, and for sure there are a lot of legit voters that are sick of the mafias running the pot trade. Hell, that includes me! I have been a part of organized crime for years, and I'm not a criminal. I believe in weed. I've always wanted it to be legal, even though if it were I'd lose my business. I suppose the corporations will grab the pie when it is, but I think that's still better than those sick hoods. Who would've thought the medical angle would usher in a new era? But who cares? This is the direction pot should go."

When he took a load of good quality Mexican weed up to Chico shortly thereafter, all his friends laughed at him. "Man," they said, "where you been? After Prop 215, the local growers kicked it into gear. No one wants that foreign bud up here. Ours is simply way better." And it was. Fresh and unpressed, the big, fat, Emerald Triangle colas came in all varieties and colors of the rainbow, and were so potent and sweet it knocked your socks off. An instant introduction to God, and it made you laugh as well. Heavy stuff and light. Some made you hungry and some gave you energy. The growers were developing super strains and specialized strains. They worked alone or in groups or even with some of the world renowned universities and colleges. Something indeed was happening here, and Lencho knew he had to be a part of it. He went back to Prescott and contacted the American Hemp Company for information on opening up a hemp store, and he began contemplating legalized growing for himself.

As these things were going through his fertile mind, he went back to construction and remodeling. For a while, Connica worked landscape design, and Lencho started on a carpentry job for Prescott musical veteran Roger Pearsall of Timber Line Productions. Roger let them live in his guest house.

Lencho was down at Lizard's every evening, as always, taking care of small customers, but also discussing upcoming ventures. "I'm telling ya, legal pot is the only solution to the crime problems the Mexican gangs pose to our country. I know them. They are animals. A bunch of killer lunatics. It will only get worse. And think about the billions of dollars that they take out of America. Foreign pot is not patriotic. I hate to sell it and will stop first chance I get. If it weren't for our own stupid government and the crooked cops in the dope game, I would be already."

"Good luck on that one, Lencho," Judge Blake said as he paid him for a bag of weed.

Finally, on February 10, 1998, he opened the Southwest Hemp Company right downtown on Whiskey Row. Stocked with all things hemp, from clothing to candies, the gala opening was a smash. "Now that we—you and me—are legitimate, we have to do something you've never done," Connica told him.

"What's that, dear?" he asked, thinking it was something kinky.

"File taxes."

The outlaw was aghast, but heeded her advice. They opened a business account at the local bank and got a tax number. Then they tied the knot.

On May 24, 1999, Doug, the disc jockey and pastor of the Universal Life Church, conducted the ceremony at their store with a hundred friends and family in attendance. A good time was had by all with champagne flowing. They didn't go on a honeymoon, since they had already been on one all the previous year, but instead dived into the hemp business. Christie Bohling, the mother of the hemp movement, advised him.

High Times Editor and Chief, Malcolm MacKinnon, arrived for a photo shoot of some Oaxacan spears of great beauty that the weed man had on hand. The shoot took place at a nearby lake where Luz's pretty girlfriend obligingly posed nude on a boulder. She was eating an apple and it was titled, "Eve in the Garden of Weed."

Business was building and the word was spreading far and wide as the new millennium approached. This was bothering the Drug Enforcement Administration, however, and one day they seized a load of imported hemp products Southwest Hemp was expecting and had already made a large deposit on.

The consignment came from China and was totally legal, so it was assumed the seizure was out of spite. The Feds ruined most of the products by leaving it out in the elements and on dirty floors. The products were eventually delivered after finally clearing customs. But it was not a total loss. "They are getting scared," he told Connica. "If weed gets legalized, those shit heads may be out the window where they belong. They may need to get honest jobs."

Sitting around discussing the loss with Christie and Patrick Lange, Lencho told her, "I wish there was something dramatic we could do to make some points: For one, industrial hemp products are not illegal, and two, growing industrial hemp should be made legal once again, as it was for centuries in this crazy country."

"Remember when I mentioned Indian nations a while back?"she asked. "You know, maybe growing it on their sovereign lands? I meant them growing it as a viable industry. It would give them something useful to do, make jobs, and income. They are so damn poor. Well, let's approach them and see what they say."

"Damn fine idea!" Lencho agreed.

Going out to the Navajo reservation in Northern Arizona, Christie and Patrick pitched the concept to the tribal elders, and they loved it. "We can have a big laugh on the white man, if nothing else," the Chief said.

A plan was developed whereby the tribe would grow the hemp and then turn it into fiberboard useful in all sorts of products from homes to cars. It would employ a hundred Native Americans right off the bat. In a novel twist of reverse smuggling, they placed an order for five hundred pounds of hemp seed to be sent from Hungary. It arrived in Alberta, Canada in the early spring, and was then brought into the U.S. through Montana alongside a load of maple syrup.

The tribe prepared a hundred acres for when the seed stock arrived. But in the year 1999, a little known battle erupted between the red man and the great white father. Getting wind of the impending heresy, the Bureau of Indian Affairs arrived unannounced at the reservation and delivered an ultimatum: cease and desist this mad idea at once or the federal government will cut off all funding to your tribe. Not one red cent for anything. Is that understood, our little brown brothers?

Apparently it was. The beleaguered natives had been under the thumb of their conquerors for so long that they had lost their stomach for intransigence and they capitulated. This little known event may have been the most vehement effort any tribe mounted since Wounded Knee in the seventies.

So, losing two hundred million dollars a year was too great a burden for the moral high ground and self-sufficiency. Anyway, the Indian nations were developing their casinos and cigarette sales. Tobacco killed millions, but it was legal.

This was all dispiriting, but those in the forefront of legalization, and also industrial hemp, did not despair. In the papers, Lencho read of fifteen year old Todd McCormack, a leukemia sufferer who had flown into the U.S. from Amsterdam with three pounds of pot and a medical chit from his doctor saying he needed it for his condition. He was not arrested, nor was his medicine seized.

The weed man still took care of his customers with Mexican products, but more and more it disgusted him. He should be providing domestic pot. Emerald Triangle pot. Pot grown anywhere in the U.S., but not Mexican pot that was supplied by organized crime. Pot was the sacred herb hijacked by our government and the crime groups that controlled the market. They also brought in illegal immigrants, many of whom were part of the drug trade. Now, they had spread all over the U.S. and infiltrated major cities and small towns. They were everywhere. Like the racketeer elements in the immigrant Italian communities a century before, they helped bring hard drugs, pot, and the violence that always goes along with their presence.

One day, as Lencho tended his store, a man walked in who had to be in his seventies. He strolled around for a while looking at clothes and hats and wallets and oils and other things made from industrial hemp. Finally, he approached Lencho when all other customers left.

"My wife is very sick," he said. "The pills and shots they give her just make it worse. She gets so nauseous. It kills me, so I have gone out and found some of this marijuana from time to time. I bake it into brownies, and when I can get some down her, she feels so much better. I just couldn't believe it. But, you know young man, it's hard for me to find marijuana. I actually bought some from my car when I drove through the barrio in a rough part of town in Phoenix, but it scared me to death to do it. I am not the police, I swear. So, I am asking you, can you get me some marijuana for my wife? I would be so grateful.

Lencho looked at him and believed his story. He did not think the old guy was a cop. He believed his wife was very ill and could benefit from medical marijuana. But he couldn't be sure. He didn't know him. He was a stranger. He had been in so much trouble over pot that he dare not take the chance.

"Sir," he told the old man, "I am very sympathetic to your situation, and I agree completely that marijuana is what you need and what you should have. But I cannot help you. It's still illegal, after all."

Chapter Sixteen

"This is Getting Funny
(But There Ain't Nobody Laughing)"
Released 1977
Waylon Jennings

Get's so lonesome here in L.A., my summers turned to autumn
I don't know if you heard it way out there where you stay,
My heart just hit rock bottom
I'm runnin' round in circles, I don't know where I am
Won't you at least give me a call
This is getting' funny, but there ain't nobody laughin' honey

THE ALL CLEAR

"Whataya mean they want to tear up the sidewalks?" the weed man yelled into the telephone. "We only been open a few months. Things are beginning to happen. If it isn't the DEA trashing up our inventory, it's the city and cracks in the pavement. When is this supposed to happen? Not sure? Well, keep me posted." He hung up and stared out the window around the faux marijuana leaf embossed on the glass.

The shop had been open for six months. Connica had thrown herself into its design and motif. Customers came in and handled the merchandise, and sniffed it as well. "This wallet doesn't smell like pot," was a common remark.

"No, industrial hemp isn't marijuana," they would reply. "There is a big difference."

But Lencho was beginning to wonder if he was the store owner type. He knew he didn't have to do it. He had money, and was always moving the industrial hemp's more famous cousin. Business was brisk as usuall down at the Lizard Lounge, and Connica's interest also seemed to be fading. Always fond of the grape more than the herb, she tippled a bit more than Lencho cared for while on duty. Now, the City of Prescott was talking about tearing up the whole Whiskey Row area for a repair job long overdue, and, if they did that, all the merchants would suffer just as Christmas was around the corner.

Since the Compassionate Use Act of 1996 was passed in California, Lencho had thought of little else. This just might be a harbinger of things to come. The back door approach to total legalization and the great dream of the old hippy cadres who had expected this bit of common sense to have arrived for decades but had not.

Was this the first step? Still, he knew that the few brave souls in California who attempted to sell medicinal weed faced arrests from the detested Feds. The perennial States Rights face-off between federal authority and the fifty states had been ongoing since the civil war. In the war, the Union had prevailed, of course. But still, the States often got into it with the federal government over all sorts of things. Recently, the State of Idaho challenged the sovereigns over the Ruby Ridge incident wherein an FBI sniper had killed the wife of Randy Weaver in a standoff. The State's argument was that the Feds had no jurisdiction there, and therefore the killing was murder. They had arrested the sniper.

But in the case of medical marijuana, Lencho believed the wind might have changed direction, and he longed to be part of the effort. Lencho reached for the phone, and dialed a number he had been given for Woody Harrelson in Hawaii.

"Who is this?" a cranky sounding woman demanded on the other end of the line.

"Uh, yes, hello," Lencho replied. "I need to talk to Woody. I got his number from Christie Bohling. You know, the hemp lady."

"Oh yeah," the voice replied. "Hold on a minute, I'll get him."

"Lencho!" Woody Harrelson yelled. "How's it shaking man? Haven't talked to you since the Hempfest in L.A. Say, how about that medical marijuana, man? Ain't that something?" And so it went, the discussion was animated and went on and on. Everybody was high on the subject, and there was a sense of hope and renewal among the more activist inclined.

Lencho talked to the great and mighty, and the common as well. Willy Nelson was always happy to chat about his love of the sacred herb and how it saved him from the degradation and an early tomb from alcohol. Ed Rosenthal discussed soil depletion in the coming millennium. Jack Herer spoke of the potential for resurgence in industrial hemp and the salvation of the planet. Keith Stroup from NORML postulated the day might be finally coming for legality altogether. Malcolm MacKinnon was planning for what would happen to High Times Magazine if it became legal. There were all sorts of thoughts and points of view, and Lencho enjoyed it immensely. He was even amused when two agents of the Drug Enforcement Administration walked into his store one day and bought fifty dollars worth of hemp items.

"What are you going to do with those?" Lencho asked them. "Give them out at your office Christmas party?"

"Not exactly," one replied behind dark glasses. "The boss was wondering if our dope dog could identify industrial hemp in a blind search. This is for a test."

"Let me know how it comes out," he told them, but they never did.

Lencho thought about his upper and middle class customers. The judges, cops, lawyers, and school principals. The teachers and doctors, the mayor and council members. And about that CEO of a major industrial business and his wealthy neighbors down in Scottsdale? These were the pot lovers that dare not let it be known they had given up booze for weed. A mild intoxicant preferred to the deadening liquor that made their heads throb and fogged out their brain for all of the next day in hangover stupor. He understood their situation and shook his head in dismay that it had to be this way. And why was it this way? After forty years of publicity and controversy, almost everybody had tried it and discovered, like everyone always does, that they did not die. Even if a person didn't like weed, it was clear that all the noise was much ado about nothing. Still, on it went, the Great War on Drugs.

The point: marijuana was a soft drug. All the lies spewed out by the DEA and Justice Department were bullshit. Picked up and championed by the state cops and prosecutors, many of whom smoked it themselves.

And there was the most troubling reality of all, the true crime of marijuana trafficking. Lencho, like millions of other thinking men and women, knew marijuana was now firmly entrenched in the American culture, its psyche and its pallet. It was not going away. But it was completely under the control of organized crime. The Mexicans had taken over the entire drug importation end of the trade by now, and the bulk of their ill-gotten income came from pushing marijuana into the United States. They had squeezed out the independent traffickers like himself over the years. Now, they muled the pot in on the backs of illegal immigrants who in turn created beach heads for further drug and criminal pursuits in American cities. They built tunnels. They had submarines and vast fleets of aircraft, and at the border they paid off U.S. border guards to waive their loads through. It was a joke. It was such a joke that it was simply impossible for the U.S. government to claim that it wasn't aware of what was going on. Nor could the U.S. honestly say it was not part of it. The only people who could not see the sham were the gullible citizens like his father. Since pot was not going away, the only solution in dealing with the vast corruption and evil—as well as the lost revenue and exported American dollars—was to legalize the stuff. And maybe the medical angle was the path. Perhaps God, in His mercy, was finally turning his attention towards sanity over this most serious matter.

Lencho thought often of Three Feathers and his prophecy: "It will be a long road." The phone rang and Lencho snapped out of his reveries. It was a big customer that needed the week's product. He had to go down to Tucson and pick up his bi-monthly bale of imported pot. Imported by the Beltrans or the Arellano-Felixes or any of the dozen other sinister and violent cartels running Mexico and colluding with crooked U.S. narcs and border agents.

Here it was, almost the new millennium and the endless war raged on. Fifteen billion dollars a year spent on the 'fight,' and for what? It was a hoax. Out in California, the growers in the Emerald Triangle were selling their product for up to five thousand a pound, and that was also crazy. The common man couldn't afford prices like that, and it insured the Mexicans would maintain their grip on the industry. And now, more and more, the Drug Enforcement Agency meddled and interfered with the legal hemp market. They were obviously afraid, just like Christie had once said. If pot is ever legalized, they and their collaborators, minions, and political sycophants were doomed. Behind legal pot might come a push for the federalization of the drug epidemic. Give it away. Oh God, how that would freak the criminal organizations of the world! Hard drugs were the underpinnings of global anarchy, and if they were given away, it would mean the end to all this madness. How come so few could see that? He sat on the phone talking to the mighty, to the merely interested, to the faithful. The message was clear, and they all agreed something must be done, but their final word was always the same: "I know what you're saying is true and right, but I can't put my head out there. It will get chopped off."

In California, though, there were a few that had the spine to stand up to the iron heel. Pot was being sold here and there in dispensaries that were legal at the State level. But the jackboots might show up, close them down, and send those brave souls off for five years on Federal charges. The days passed, and the war went on.

It became the new millennium, and the computers didn't cause the world to end or stand still, as was predicted. The year 2001 was the same, until that dark day in September when one earthshaking event caught everyone's attention while another transpired in the shadows of the drug trade.

"My god, the sight of those twin towers coming down in all the fire and brimstone was a sight I never want to see again," Lencho was saying to Ronnie on September fifteenth. "The chickens have come home to roost, I truly fear."

"I got people up the ying yang clamoring for weed," Ronnie replied. "I can't find a joint anywhere in Prescott or Phoenix or Tucson for that matter. Hell, there doesn't seem to be any weed anywhere at all."

"Except in Northern California," Lencho said. "I hear it just went up to six thousand a pound. I got some new information. The border is closed. This terrorist stuff has the country in a panic. You can see it on TV, everywhere. The government has closed the ports, the airports, and especially the international borders. Nothing is coming across. I called all the people I know. I'm gonna call old Paz next. He's with Beltrans. He knows everything."

On the weekend, Lencho grabbed a flight from Prescott down to the U.S. side of the border at Nogales. He walked across as he scanned the long lines of returning cars. They were getting a thorough going over by very determined border agents. The lines stretched into what seemed like infinity. He called ahead, and Señor Paz was waiting for him at the La Chiquita Bar in downtown. The old man looked up from his cerveza as the weed man walked in. Tired whores eyed him balefully. "Sit down, Lencho," Paz gestured. "I already know what you are going to ask. The same question everyone is asking."

"Like, where's the weed and when will it come again?" Lencho laughed.

"Sí, sí," the old man said. "Exactly that. Where's the mota?"

"Well," Lencho replied taking a big gulp from a Dos XX, "where is the mota?"

"It's here, my friend. Tons of it sitting in storage. Safe and sound, but since the attack in your country the word is out. Very high up word. No product will pass over until the all clear."

"The all clear?" he repeated. "What exactly does that mean?"

"What does it sound like? All clear means just that. All clear. We will be told when the time is right. In the meantime, you must tell your people to be patient. Some things are out of our hands. Comprende? Only God knows and He is not talking."

"Okay. I guess I get it. Like from the President or someone very high up in the U.S. government."

"I can't say it's your President. In my country, if it were the Presidente that gave the all clear, no one would be surprised. In America, they are more subtle. But, whoever says it, they are very high up. That's all I know, Lencho."

A month later, the border was still closed to all shipments of weed, cocaine, methamphetamine, heroin, and illegals. The weed man's customers were becoming frantic. When? When? When? That was the word on everyone's mouth. Soon, soon, soon was the reply from on high. Then, on November 2nd, Lencho got a phone call.

"My friend," the old man said, "within ten days the flood shall come. We have received the all clear." On November 9, 2001 there was weed, cocaine, heroin, and illegal aliens everywhere. Weed of every stripe and description. Tons of it, and the price was the same as before 9/11. The weed man's customers gave a sigh of relief, because they were back in business, but the greater lesson was not lost on him. This sudden flood of illegal product back into the United States was proof positive: the war on drugs was a sham. The level of corruption from the days of his youth and his first joint until now had reached the very top. Not just in Mexico where it was expected, but also here in the land of the free.

The product arrived just in time for the musicians. From Nashville, Lencho was getting ten calls a week. "Man," they told him, "the big guy is going out on tour and he needs at least five pounds. You know he doesn't drink any more. What's the hold up?"

Well, now there was no more hold up. The all clear had been sounded from on high, and the weed man hoped his customers were happy. But it troubled him to contemplate the deeper meaning; the musicians wrapped themselves in the flag, while at the same time sending their cash south of the border to the pockets of the cartels. It was time to start being patriotic and buy American. Genuine made in the U.S.A. marijuana that he would grow himself.

Those outlaw musicians had depended on him going way back to the seventies. Richie Albright vouched for his weed at a time when hard drinking was sending a lot of the famous musicians to early graves. Lencho watched as they came to rely on weed in order to minimize their alcohol intake. Apparently, not many of them wanted to die too soon. Life was short and they were having too much fun for an early check out. Medical marijuana was already essentially medicine for men like them, Lencho thought. He had better figure a way to become a medical marijuana technician himself. When the City of Prescott finally tore up the sidewalks, he and Connica took it as a sign and began making plans to move to California. California beckoned, and her siren call whispered, "Medical, is the wave of the future and the door to legalization."

When he thought about it, no country on earth had really legalized weed.

304

In some places, like Morocco or India, it was de facto legal, but you still didn't go into a store and buy it over the counter. Even in Amsterdam, it wasn't really legal, although the State looked the other way. What an irony that the country that prosecuted weed the most, the place that imprisoned anyone who smoked it, would be the place to finally make it legitimate. And he wanted to be part of the effort. If it did become legal, it would not be because of the insight and common sense of politicians, but because of a few who had the courage to stand up to the crooks and tyrants who profited for so long from the very illegality they fostered and pretended to fight. It might finally be 'we the people.' Finally.

*****

While Lencho was making some phone calls in early 2002, he dialed up his buddy, Wong, in Hong Kong. Wong's son, Kenny, answered and told Lencho that his dad was now living in the city of Fuzou on the coast across from Taiwan.

"Hey Wong, you old Chinaman, this is Lencho. How ya doing, man?"

"Lencho," Wong cried, "I just thinking about you. Jing Yi tell me all about your new wife."

"Yeah, that's right, I got married—again. This time for real."

"I must meet her. I sure she is lovely lady. You must come to China again! I pay for everything."

Lencho and his new bride left for Shanghai via Manila on a cloudy October morning after spending two days looking over the Philippine capital city. Their plane carried them to Shanghai where Li Wong met them and gave them their wedding gift: a six week package tour of China.

The tailors of Shanghai made the weed man suits and custom shirts of silk and hemp. They shopped for art of every description, piling up a trove of carved ivory, jade, and teak. On one of their sprees to Beijing, a young man asked if they needed a guide. It cost twenty-five dollars a day in his own car. Dai Cha, their guide, was also a history professor at Beijing University and squired the two around the fabled city. They toured the summer palace of the Emperor, Tiananmen Square, and the Forbidden City. They hiked the Great Wall, and Lencho stopped to smoke some joints while there. They flew up the Yangtze River and viewed the immense dam the government was building to block the flow of the great river. They viewed the epic Granite City carved into bluffs so long ago. Soon it would all be submerged, but the government was removing much of it and hauling it to higher ground.

It was a wonderful honeymoon gift, and now laden with a mountain of artwork, clothing, and gifts, they took a flight to the industrial city of Fuzhou where Wong waited for one last conference.

"How you like to run dollar store?" he asked Lencho with his usual ebullience.

"What the fuck are you talking about?" Lencho asked.

"I mean Dollar Store, Lencho. You know, everything for one dollar. Dollar Store."

"Oh, Dollar Store? Sure, I get it. They're all over the place."

"I been thinking of buying a couple. Make you manager. I send big container of merchandise over worth two hundred thousand American dollars and you send back twenty thousand. We make fortune."

"I'll think about it," he replied, clearly not intending to think about it very hard. He and Connica were about fed up with the store they were running at the moment, let alone getting involved with a huge corporate outfit.

The industrial city of Fuzhou rested on the sea surrounded by verdant hills, but it sucked as far as Lencho was concerned, because it was truly industrial. It was grimy and old with factories big and small, and packed tightly one after the other on crowded roads and byways. The place was full of laboring folks transplanted from across China. The wages were low and the hours were long. It reminded the weed man of how England and America must have looked not so long ago. It was truly depressing.

And when Connica walked around in public, throngs of laborers dropped everything to gawk. She felt like the eyes of the world were upon her, and they were indeed. In Fuzhou they had seldom seen foreigners, let alone American women. It gave her the creeps and she was glad they were not there for long.

Wong's buddies and fellow industrialists, all gunho owners of little factories met for dinner and influence peddeling. All of them were hard chargers, and liked to squabble and barter. Fortunately, it was all in Chinese with a smattering of Vietnamese, Laotian, and Cambodian thrown in for good measure.

Wong translated as he introduced Lencho as his big shot 'American buyer' looking at merchandise and taking orders.

"I tell them you want to see their products. Act interested, please."

"I ain't no buyer, Wong. Not this kind, anyway. You know that."

"I think very funny. Plus, I trying to get better deal on my bamboo. These guys Hung Manh Nguyen and his partner Tin Huu Tran tell me Vietnam bamboo is best and only 5,600 Yuan a ton. I tell them Som Vesaisack from Laos can beat their price by thirty percent, and Pang Chan from Cambodia is even less than that. They all think their shitty bamboo is best. To me, all the same. I only want lowest price for my bamboo factory."

The industrialists loaded him up with brochures and price lists and smiled toothy grins while jabbering away in Cantonese. Lencho just said thanks and longed for a joint.

After touring two more factories that made counter tops and modular homes, Wong led the weed man to a meeting with the bureaucracy. At a long conference table in a State building they sat down with nine men and two women, all dressed in business attire, with looks of great seriousness. The discussion was taxes.

Wong was buying into another factory, this one manufacturing appliances, and he was seeking the most favorable tax break he could wrangle from the government. Once again, all in attendance were very friendly and animated toward their American guest. The powerful and affluent U.S. buyer to whom all the men gestured and exuded friendliness while the ladies smiled demurely. It made Lencho most uncomfortable, but he indulged his old pal and played along. He smiled and pretended that he knew what was going on. After two hours of this, and just in time, the meeting was adjourned for dinner. Wong led the way, and Lencho figured he must have gotten what he was after, because he was all smiles and laughter and pats on the back. Wong held the door open for the crowd as they climbed into cars parked at the curb and were driven to the Pleasure Crown Seafood Restaurant at the top of a hill overlooking the harbor.

The proprietor greeted everyone effusively, and Lencho thought everyone in China must smile and bow endlessly. They were seated in the banquet room, and then led to a large room that must have been called 'the sea tank room,' because a series of ever bigger salt water tanks held their dinner.

Each of the officials, as well as Wong and Lencho, picked a lobster and a huge perch or bass or small shark or whatever they desired from one of the tanks. It all was alive and swimming around before their eyes. No question, this seafood was fresh. Waiters with nets plucked the specimens from their tanks and whisked them off to the kitchen. They all returned to their table, and while everyone else sipped tea with their first appetizers of raw squid and sea worms, Lencho quaffed a Heineken. He passed on the worms.

"I make sure restaurant get you Heineken," Wong whispered. "You not ordinary white man, especially in China."

For the next three hours they feasted on platters of boiled lobster and eel. Steamed abalone with oyster sauce was served with hot bowls of shark fin soup and steamed fresh water shrimp, Peking duck and pork, rock fish and roast quail. Desert was birds nest with pure sugar.

"I didn't know if you like puffer fish," Wong whispered again. "Mostly Japanese dish, and very poisonous if not cleaned right, but delicious. Also, could have barbecued sea snake, but I didn't think Indians barbecued."

Lencho blanched. "No, you're right. Indians never barbecue."

Lencho was indeed stuffed and most content after all was said and done. And it appeared that all had been said that needed to be said, as the feast wound down and his hosts departed with many more handshakes and Cheshire cat grins. Lencho looked around at the mess they were leaving behind as the last table of officials left the room. Expecting Wong to dig out his wallet, he was surprised when he did not as they too headed for the car. "Well, who pays for all this, Wong?" he finally asked.

"Owner pay," Wong said curtly. China was a fascinating country. A land of immense and vast complexities. The weed man really couldn't figure them out, but what the heck. He and his new wife had a wonderful time and saw an awful lot, and it hadn't cost him a dime. It was his turn to express effusive thanks, because they would be heading home in the morning. As Wong's driver took him back to his hotel, he told his friend how wonderful the trip had been, and assured him that if there was ever anything he could do, all Wong had to do was call.

"Well, there are couple of things I want to mention," Wong replied. "First, think about Dollar Store offer. You could be rich man. And second, I would very much like to come again to America. Company has many restaurants back East I need to see again, as well as hotel in Vegas. But I can't get in now, am a convict. A felon. Any ideas?"

"Do you mind crossing the border in a cramped tunnel?" Lencho asked. "If you don't, I think it can be arranged."

Mr. Wong gave him a big smile. "Tunnel fine!" he almost shouted.

Chapter Seventeen

"Ladies Love Outlaws"
Released 1972
Waylon Jennings

Ladies love outlaws
Like babies love stray dogs
Ladies touch babies like a banker touches gold
Outlaws touch ladies somewhere deep down in their soul

SAM I AM

"Hey," Brother Joe said into the telephone, "how were things in China?"

"We just got back," Lencho replied. "They were fine. We had a wonderful time. Those Chinamen sure know how to eat. What's up?"

"You know Mr. Corcoran, the old boy that owns the six acres adjacent to mine? Well, he wants to sell them to me. Nobody but me will do, he says. They're primo, man, heavily forested old growth. Beautiful views. Wish I had the twenty grand he's asking, but I don't. How about you? You interested?"

"I just might be," Lencho replied. "Connica and I will be out there in a few days to check it out. Twenty grand sounds like a steal, and we're thinking of getting into the legal weed game. This could be perfect."

They closed up South West Hemp, packed away all the remaining inventory, and drove out to Butte County in Northern California. With old man Corcoran, they walked the hilly property from one end to the other, all six acres. It was perfect, and the price couldn't be beat. The deal was sealed with a handshake. That evening, the couple went to dinner in Paradise and spent the night at a friend's house who was out of town. At four a.m., Lencho got up with chest pains and staggered into the bathroom.

"What's the matter, honey?" Connica asked, awakened by the light. "Oh God!" she gasped. "You look awful."

"I feel awful. Like a chain wrapped around my chest. Must be indigestion."

"I'm calling 9-1-1. You don't look like a case of indigestion."

It took the ambulance an hour to find them. The house was buried deep in Butte Creek Canyon, but when two shapely young blonde paramedics strode in, the gravely ill weed man cheered up at once. "God has sent angels," he mumbled from the bed. Connica was less sanguine, but glad he was on his way to medical attention.

"Has this ever happened before?" the nurse asked holding his hand while they raced into the sunrise.

"Yeah," he replied, "a couple other times. I never mentioned it cause I thought it was just too much hot sauce or something."

"Well," Doctor Mofftt said, entering his hospital room two hours later, "there's good news and bad news. The good news is your coverage is excellent with the insurance company, but the bad news is that you had a great big heart attack, and it isn't the first, either. Looks from the chart like you have had a couple small ones before this."

Connica insisted on two things when they got married: Start paying taxes and get health insurance. When the doc told him the A team would arrive in a few hours for immediate surgery, it was comforting to know he could afford to live, but if he didn't the Feds wouldn't get any more tax money. A win-win.

Twenty-four hours later, he was recuperating quietly from six-way bypass surgery. All his major arteries had collapsed, and he felt weak and beat up. His doctor told him that, for an old hippy who had lived the kind of crazy life he had, his ticker was amazingly strong. It was his cholesterol that had done him in, and if he didn't fix that, the next time would be the last.

"No more bad diet, booze, or cocaine," he was told.

"How about pot'?"

"I'm not so concerned about that," the doc replied. "For an old guy, your lungs are great. Pink and healthy. You might want to eat the stuff from now on, though, because it does cause coughing, and coughing can put a strain on your heart. But otherwise, you should live to a ripe old age."

"My dad is still going," Lencho grumbled. "Mean as a snake, but he's in his late eighties."

"Mr. Corcoran called," Connica told him when he woke from a nap. "He says he's so sorry you got sick."

"Call the old guy back. Tell him the hiking did me in, but I plan on living. We definitely want the property."

Lencho left the hospital and stayed another week recuperating at Callie's place. His oldest daughter owned a motor home they camped out in. He smoked some weed and began to feel better. They drove back to Prescott and negotiated a deal with Connica's mom to buy a motor home she wanted to sell.

"I'm giving this to you for only five thousand," Lillian told him. "It's worth more than that, but I'm feeling generous toward you since you aren't well."

They kept their rented house in Prescott for the time being and moved out west to his niece's property next door to Brother Joe. The Compassionate Marijuana Act, or SB 420, had been voted into law by the more enlightened electorate of California in 2003. This bill superseded the 1996 Medical Marijuana law, and updated its provisions, rules, and regulations. It was due to become law on January 1, 2004, so Lencho studied it from one end to the other. He was in touch with Harbor, Malcom's young son, who had become a virtuoso pot grower since his days back from Costa Rica. Lencho was stunned by the indoor grow operation the young man had developed.

An old pal of Malcom's loaned Harbor the perfect house. Big and secluded, it was now decked out to cannabis horticultural perfection. In one large room, under a thousand watt metal halide lamp, grew an enormous mother plant. She had been developed from primo seed stock created by mad genius weed scientists, and then kept in a constant vegetative state under sixteen hours of lumens. This guaranteed she would never bloom. From her, cuttings were taken, root toned, and placed in starter cups of vermiculite and perlite under banks of low watt grow lamps until they developed root balls. After that, the clones were placed in the vegetation room under fifteen halides, where they prospered into lush specimens five feet tall and almost as wide. From there, they were moved into the bud room where low sodium lamps, with their eerie orange glow, nurtured the emerging buds after the light cycle was reduced to ever shorter "days." When full and sparkling with resin, the buds were harvested, cured, and manicured. They were then packaged and sent off to eager customers far and wide. All this was done in soil, because Harbor disdained the more elaborate and dicey hydroponics so often in vogue. The system was elaborate enough with a huge A/C setup, vents, filters for the aroma, and twenty thousand watts of juice coursing through all those giant lamps. Drip irrigation and timers completed the ensemble, and the whole setup blew Lencho away. "I want one, too!" he enthused.

Lencho's niece, Melissa, let him and Connica stay on her property in the motor home when he was ailing, and now her husband, Darrell, informed the weed man that they wanted him to go ahead with an indoor grow just like Harbor's. Lencho was very jazzed by the concept after seeing how beautiful and bountiful Harbor's was, but insisted he get the go ahead from Melissa's own lips.

"No man," Darrell insisted, "she's out of town a lot lately, but she told me it would be fine. Go ahead and get started."

"Melissa owns the property, Darrell," Lencho replied, "and I gotta know I have her permission. This thing will cost thousands, and I will shit if it gets screwed up."

"I'm telling ya, she said that it's okay. I'm her husband, ain't I? I should know!"

"Where is she these days? I haven't seen her around for ages."

"Uncle Frank out in Boulder isn't well, so she's been tending to him a lot. She's just in and out, but she told me to tell you that it's okay with her. Go for it." Ronnie and Lencho went for it to the tune of forty thousand dollars.

Two months later, they had built a sturdy and attractive barn-like structure all compartmentalized for the different grow rooms. They installed A/C, dozens of halide lamps, and ventilators with all the bells and whistles Harbor had going, plus a few new ones for good measure. The place was lush with vegetating cannabis indica, and then Melissa finally came home long enough to walk over and take a look. She had a cow right there on the spot. "What is all this marijuana doing on my property?" she screamed at the cowering men. "Who told you you could do this?"

"Now Melissa, sweetheart," Lencho soothed. "I could never find you to talk to you directly, but your husband told me a dozen times you said it was all right. With the profits on this legal crop, I'll pay off your mortgage."

"You can stuff the profits up your ass, Lencho!" she screamed. "If you believed that dense motherfucker, you're as dumb as I was when I married him. Now, get it out. It's all illegal, and I want it off my property."

"But Melissa, it's almost legal. In a couple of months it will be on the books. SB 420."

"Fuck your 420! Out!! Now!!!" And there went another forty grand. Ka-ching!

He had hoped to have a crop ready to go when SB 420 went into effect, but instead he let the plants die, and hauled their corpses to the mulch pile on orders from his hysterical niece. Naturally, Darrell denied all, but Lencho was never one to be discouraged for long, and he corralled Ronnie and Brother Joe to begin setting up a large outdoor grow while lining up patients to form a collective under the new law.

He went to a local clinic that was operated by a lady doctor named Fry. Dr. Fry was quite ill herself with breast cancer, and had been persuaded by her lawyer husband to give medical marijuana a try. She had been so impressed with the results in lessening her misery from radiation and chemotherapy that she was keen to assist Lencho in this new arena of the marijuana cycle. She began signing patients up with letters of recommendation. He got an original twelve patients, and set out six plants apiece for them. Dr. Fry then opened one of the first exclusively marijuana medical marijuana clinics in the country under the new law.

Then he went to the health department to check in with them, but they didn't have a clue what to do, so he began sending them data on his progress. The boys had to hustle, but they got their first outdoor crop in the ground by May 15th, and were off and running once again. Leaving Ronnie in charge, he and Connica drove back to Prescott to tend to his old clientele. There in the Lizard's Lounge, Doc Westin walked in to pick up a bag of super high quality Northern California primo killer bud, but he had a serious set to his jaw this time.

"Lencho," the doctor began, "I hear you're moving out to California for good, and me and the other city elders are most distressed."

"Well Doc," he replied, "I gotta follow the arc of history. California is leading the way to legalize the mota. The time is drawing near."

"That's all fine and good, but here in Arizona the powers that be are not quite so enlightened, and some of us who have been loyal customers for years are very concerned we'll have to do business with these crude ruffians of organized crime just over the border. Can't have that, son, so I have devised a plan that will alleviate our concerns as well as provide a steady income stream for yourself."

"Do tell."

"Molly down at the post office will open up a special PO Box in a bogus name for you to send us a pound or two every couple months. If it arrives in the post safely, she'll shunt it over to me and I'll take the responsibility to distribute it to our friends. If there's any heat from the coppers, she'll reject it. You'll get your money without a problem, and we'll pay top dollar. It must be that great medical stuff, though. No more beaner reefer. We want medical only, and since I'm a doctor, I don't feel any qualms about prescribing here in Arizona. How's that sound to ya?'"

It sounded fine, and from that day forward the good Doctor and all the civic elders began receiving their own medical marijuana from the weed man. The money either was sent back to him in the post or he came down occasionally and collected it personally.

Back at Space Acres, the outdoor plants were becoming huge. Following instructions from the legendary Emerald Triangle veterans so long in the gorilla grow mode, they built three foot raised beds using stakes and three foot welded wire fencing lined with stiff industrial paper to hold the tons of forest mulch. This was mixed with high quality potting soil and chicken manure obtained from Ag Mart Garden Center, which despite its corporate sounding name, was founded for the exclusive provisioning of marijuana growers in that region. The store in Chico was run by young men who were experts in pot farming, and had learned the art at their hippy fathers' knees. To play it safe, a customer didn't say he wanted their products and expertise for marijuana cultivation, but that's what they got nonetheless. Harbor provided the clones, and now in the blazing sun of the low mountain summer, the plants were getting gigantic. By August, the early blooms were forming nicely.

Lencho expanded his visits beyond the health department, and he now visited the local DA and Marijuana Task Force of the tri-county area. "You're the first guy in all of Butte and Yuba Counties to come in here and talk to us about this," the top cop told him. "We're more than delighted. You're doing this the right way under the new law," he said as he handed Lencho his business card, which had the name of a guy on the back who specialized in clones. "If you don't already have some, go see this kid. He's an expert, believe me." Lencho knew at that moment things had changed in his world mightily.

After that, Lencho met with the Sheriff to give him his location and number of plants. "You're always welcome to visit, but to please call ahead," Lencho told him. "If we were to have any trouble, such as rip offs or the like, can we count on law enforcement to assist?"

"Lencho," the Sheriff replied, "we consider legal pot grows to be like banks where robbery is concerned. We know from experience how things are in that regard, so if you ever have trouble, call at once and we will respond."

"Excellent."

But as the marijuana became more legal, the laws remained very gray. The Federal attitude was unbending. For their own evil reasons, a powerful few were determined to keep things as they had always been. The weed man now lived with one foot in both realms. Quasi-legal in California, total outlaw in the rest of the country. It was time to go back to Tucson, Arizona and score a twenty pound bale from the Beltrans, so he could service his regular customers. He also needed to discuss things with those cartel boys regarding his promise to Mr. Wong. It was tunnel time.

Maclovio Acosta was a Beltran lieutenant in charge of the Tucson region. He was thin, well dressed, and wore a lot of gold. He was a killer when he had to be, and his face always gave Lencho a chill.

"Mac," the weed man smiled pulling up a chair in the Mezon Del Cobre on 1st Ave, "how the heck are ya?"

"Like always, Lencho," Mac replied, "busy. I got a lot of problems these days with the Zetas, and those asshole Los Numeros in Juarez are always getting out of line. They don't got no respect for their betters, like in the old days. This violence in Mexico is building. Very bad for business."

"I been reading about it in the papers," Lencho replied. "Seems to be escalating every year. What's behind it?"

"Territory," Acosta replied. "Over on the pacific, the Arellano-Felix brothers are just plain crazy. Ever since that Cardinal down in Mexico City got caped, the heat on them has been heavy and they shoot anything that walks on two legs for the fun of it. Too much perico, I think. Now, they are getting fragmented and people want to move in on them. It's only natural. They can't keep their act together, they gotta get out of the show."

"Right," Lencho nodded.

"The same everywhere. This business is a lot of money. Where there is so much money, there is always someone who wants to get a slice. We are the Beltran-Leyva, and we are allied with Guzman. No one messes with the most powerful padrone in this sorry world but I been hearing things are getting frayed with Arturo and Chapa. I don't like that. Guzman is the real presidente of Mexico, you know. We need him, I think. It was never supposed to get this way."

"Why do you say that?" Lencho asked.

"You know yourself. Didn't you do a couple of years over at Andonegui prison? Haven't you always worked with one family or another in Mexico? Los mafiosos?"

"When I had to."

"Well, that was the old days. That all changed around fifteen years ago. Maybe a little more. After your famous DEA and the American military helped the Columbians finally remove the Medellín and Calle cartels down there, two of our most revered fathers, Felix Gallardo from Sinaloa and Pablo Acosta Villarreal from Chihuahua, met with the Ochoa's from Columbia. They made a pact to shift the transportation of the perico from Florida to Mexico, if organization could be achieved among what you call the many mafias. They were joined by Amado Carrillo Fuentes and that great mota hombre Caro Quintero. Together these founders created The Federation."

"So, that was how the mafia came to rule Mexico?" Lencho asked.

"It was no longer the mafia. It was the time of the Mexican cartels from then on."

"I'll be damned. I always wondered how that change took place. But now the cartels are beginning to war against each other. How come?"

"Things went smooth at first. Felix Gallardo handled transportation and territories all over Mexico with the different people while Carrillo, who had vast political and military connections, made sure the cocaine got to Mexico from Columbia safely, and stayed that way across Mexico up to the U.S. border. There they did business with your DEA—or CIA posing as the DEA—and most of the product made it across. Always, some was sacrificed to make the game look real. Everyone got rich. Very, very rich. Carrillo became a multi-billionaire. Each election in Mexico, the presidential candidate is bought and paid for by our people, simple as that."

"So, then what happened?"

"What always happens?" Acosta sighed. "Everybody wants to be the boss. Gallardo and Carrillo got busted. It's all part of the game. They expected it, but in Mexico that don't always mean much. They had a big meeting in the prison and territories were established. It was supposed to keep the peace. This guy got the Gulf region. Another got the border with Ciudad Juárez. Over in TJ, it was the Arellano-Felix brothers. The Federation then became the cartels. And after that, they still fought cause there was so much money involved, and then your very own CIA working alongside of the DEA began filtering big money and guns into the separating factors and assisting them at various border crossings encouraging a division in the Federation. It splintered, and now we are seeing la violencia grow. You watch, Lencho. In a couple of years, I bet it will get real out of hand."

"Hey, take a look at these," Lencho brightened, removing some glossy photos from a pocket. He spread four shots of six-by-six foot pot plants that were now growing at Space Acres in front of the grumpy gangster.

"You growing these?" Acosta asked quietly.

"Yeah. Ain't they beautiful? And they're legal, man. That's the great thing. Completely legit to grow medical pot in California."

The look on Acosta's face darkened as his cold eyes drilled into the photos. Suddenly, he threw them down on the table. "This is another thing, Lencho," he hissed. "This legal pot thing you got going on in California does not make us smile. Why the fuck should it? At this rate, the mota business will be in the hands of Proctor and Gamble! We have controlled things for many years. Mota is the backbone of the drug trade. If mota goes legal, what will be next? Perico? Chiva? If I were you, I would not be so eager to get involved with this legal mota business. We may have to look up north and deal with this sort of thing, my friend. You wouldn't want that," he prophesied. And he was right. By 2012 the Mexicans cartels had moved in.

"No," Lencho replied meekly, gathering up his pictures, "I guess I wouldn't. But, anyway, I need a twenty pounder as usual, and there is something else I was wondering about."

"What would that be?"

"I have a dear friend I did time with. He's a Chinaman, lives in Hong Kong. He needs to visit our fair land, but since he's a felon, the government won't let him—legally. Is there a way you could assist in this matter? I will pay, of course."

"Not a problem, if he don't mind bending down a little bit. He can cross in our tunnel."

"Those guys are short, anyway," Lencho chuckled. "The tunnel is what I was thinking, too. How do I arrange that?"

Maclovio Acosta wrote a name and address on a piece of paper and handed it to Lencho. "Take this to this guy down in Nogales. I'll tell him you're coming. He'll fix you up."

Three blocks into downtown Nogales, Mexico, Lencho walked into the San Pablo Hotel and asked for Alphonso. He was directed to the bar and sat down with a swarthy young man dressed in black from top to bottom. "I been expecting you," he said. "Come on, let's go down to the basement."

There were two levels of underground parking in the San Pablo. They walked down the ramps to the lower level. Alphonso was a man of few words. He didn't say a thing until they arrived at the far wall where only a new Dodge Ram was parked. Behind it was an opening in the wall that became a dimly lit room, about 15 feet by 20 feet. The weed man could discern a staircase and railing descending in the back. Suddenly, two men in succession, clearly the laboring type, emerged and walked to the bed of the truck where they each tossed a bail of something over their shoulders and then turned around and vanished into the darkness of the staircase. The bails were identical to the one Lencho bought from the Beltrans on a regular basis, so he could guess what was in them.

The two men stood by the truck in the dim light and Alphonso lit a cigarette. "When you are ready, let me know. Bring the Chinaman to me with five thousand dollars. He goes down those stairs, and a thousand meters later he's in the U.S. Comes up in a trucking company over there."

"Amazing," Lencho mumbled. "Could I take a peek?"

"Make it quick. We got men at work, as you can plainly see."

He entered the room and made his way to the fourteen wooden steps that led down into the depths. A one hundred watt light burned from a fixture at the bottom. Once there, he rubbed his chin in wonder at the beautifully engineered rabbit warren that ran straight ahead for about fifty feet and then made an abrupt right turn off into the distance. Every twenty-five feet another one hundred watt light bulb dispelled the darkness. The walls were five feet high and supported by shoring every ten feet, and the ceiling was heavy fiber board. The path was cement. This was not a temporary design to be used once or twice and then abandoned. This hole had cost some bucks and was a thing of beauty, if you were into tunneling. His curiosity quenched, Lencho turned and climbed back up the stairs and headed to the border crossing. The symbol of the power and might of the United States Federal Government was only three blocks away.

Things were now arranged for when, in the near future, Wong could fly into Mexico City and then up to Nogales where he would have his own private entry point into the United States. Lencho and Connica headed back to Space Acres and his newly purchased adjoining property, where they began the task of moving in. This began with brush and tree clearing. Connica proved to be an adept heavy equipment operator, sitting on the back hoe and front end loader pushing levers. She cleared and leveled a pad where they parked their motor home, which was to be their house for the next four years. Next door on Joe's spread, their seventy two plants were getting to be giants, thriving in their immaculate legal environment. They were standing ten to twelve feet high and just as wide with huge colas blooming from top to bottom. The yield looked to Lencho perhaps four pounds per plant, maybe more.

When down at the grocery store in Brownsville, the weed man met Deputy Maney Haas of the Yuba County Sheriff's Department. "How's it going, Lencho?" he asked amiably. "Any trouble out your way?"

"Hey Haas," he answered. "Good to see ya. No trouble at all, which in my experience is certainly a nice change."

"Seriously, we appreciate your honesty and want to work with you new legal growers. Everyone knows these surrounding counties have been ground zero for pot cultivation for decades. What with the lousy economy, pot is just about the only thing that earns money and very few cops want to rock that boat. So, now it's semi-legal with this medical thing, we're delighted. Can we come over and look your grow over? This request is on the up and up, no surprises. Also, we'll know where to go if you have any trouble with rip offs."

"Sure you can," Lencho answered. "When do you want to drop by?"

"How about tomorrow around noon? How do I find you?"

"Go to the logging turnout. My nephew Hodie will meet you there and lead you over to our place. We're kinda secluded."

Space Acres looked largely as it had twenty five years earlier when Lencho and Karen lived in the teepee there with the kids, and everyone ran around naked. They were all older now and wore clothes, but the mentality had not changed much from the peace and love movement of the counterculture in vogue back then. Hodi pulled in with the Yuba County Sheriff's Chevy Blazer behind him. Lencho was bustling around in the garden wearing only shorts and a ball cap. The late summer sun pushed the temperature to over ninety degrees. Four men got out and Deputy Haas shouted, "Good afternoon! Beautiful day out here."

One man in jeans, tee shirt, and dark glasses remained at the vehicle while Haas introduced Deputy Rollins and U.S. Forest Service Agent Michael Bell. "My god," Haas whistled. "Look at these plants! They're huge."

"They are impressive," Bell agreed. "It's my job to hunt for illegal pot grows on federal property and I have never seen such a tidy and downright pretty setup as this. No debris, camp fires, or illegal aliens. This is like it should be."

"Thank you gentlemen," Lencho resounded with pride. "We try and maintain a tight ship, not to mention we're virtually all organic. I just finished fertilizing with some bad ass stuff mixed up down at AG Mart. Costs three hundred bucks a week, but look at the results."

"I've seen thousands of illegal grows and even though I personally quit believing that bullshit about pot being dangerous years ago, we can't allow those crime groups unfettered access to American range. They also cause a lot of the forest fires every year when a chopper swoops down and they vacate their camps leaving fires burning."

"Well," Lencho told him, "Since we're on that subject, just over that ridge you might find an illegal grow. Bunch of Mexicans, I think, on federal land adjoining ours. My kids can't hike or ride up there for fear of getting shot, so allow me to give the crooks to you."

"I'll make a note of that," Bell replied.

"We are experimenting with fourteen strains out here. Marijuana is always evolving in every sense. Notice the leaf structure and stalk dimensions on the different plants. Over here is our pond warmer. Artesian water from the well is too cold at first, so we warm it up in these ponds before irrigating. Over there is the curing facilities, and in here we'll manicure. Come on inside and I'll show you our clinic list of collective clients who we grow this herb for. I think we cross all our T's and dot all our I's. This is the new world of pot—a sensible world that will ultimately be the end of the drug cartel involvement and the corruption. Speaking of which, who's the sinister looking cat waiting at your car?"

"DEA out of Sacramento," Haas replied. "He called and asked to ride along. Sorry to have to bring him, but we got little choice."

"DEA. I suspect this legal pot world has got their shorts in a bunch."

"I think you're right. They are a pain to us, too. Locals can't say much to the Feds. They're always interfering in our affairs and taking credit wherever they can after we do all the heavy lifting."

"Well, can't be rude. He came all the way from Sacto to meet me, so I guess

I should say hello." Lencho strolled over to the narc leaning on the fender with arms folded. "How are you? My name's Lencho. Who are you?"

They didn't shake hands. "Special Agent Sam. As in Uncle Sam."

"Very clever, Agent Sam. All you DEA types are clever devils, and I've met several. Why are you guys interested in us legal pot growers? Aren't you supposed to be after the bad guys? What you see here is essentially a legitimate pharmaceutical operation."

"Don't try and blow your smoke up my ass, pal. We know exactly what this is all about. It's our job to protect America from scum bag dope pushers who sell this poison to our children, and we're gonna continue to do it."

"Ya know," Lencho replied, starting to boil, "I just spoke with another guy who expressed concern over legal pot as well. He was just as threatening."

"Must be a fine individual," the narc snarled.

"Two peas in a pod, that's for sure. But if you're so protective, how come you don't go after the booze farmers? Go out and hassle the guy who grows potatoes for vodka. Corn's another one, and grapes. Those crops are grown to make dope, the liquid type. Those crops go to the manufacturers who turn it into death and destruction, and then ship it out all over the world. I think those are the guys you should be hassling now. After that, you should be busting the tobacco growers. That shit kills three hundred thousand people every year, and little kids pick up a life-long habit. I bet your kids smoke. Those crops are dangerous, Agent Sam. But marijuana? Show me some statistics on marijuana overdoses. How many people die each year from pot? You know as well as I do, there has never been a pot overdose documented anywhere. No proof of cancer or heart disease. I have had personal experiences with your DEA, bud, and I know what you guys are really all about. Now, get the fuck off my property. Go back to your SAC in Sacramento and tell him what you saw here today. Tell him you saw the future, and by that I mean the dawning of the end for the DEA. And don't come back without a warrant and pair of handcuffs!"

"Ok boys, break it up," Deputy Haas chimed in noticing things were getting heated between the weed man, who had once been nearly murdered by DEA, and Agent Sam, who may or may not have been aware of that tawdry incident.

"Fine," Sam snarled as he climbed back into the Blazer. "You're the big man now, Lencho, but your day will come. We got long memories. You're in our databases and indices. Your ass is gonna literally be grass, just wait and see." The police backed out of Space Acres and left in a cloud of dust. As Lencho watched them leave, he felt both elation and unease. It felt good to finally spout off at the vaunted Drug Enforcement Administration, knowing his words would certainly be repeated back at headquarters, but he also knew that the narc's threat shouldn't be taken lightly. This was, after all, the second time he had been warned to watch his back with the federal narcs.

Chapter Eighteen

"Slow Movin' Outlaw"
Released 1974
Waylon Jennings

The land where I traveled once fashioned with beauty
Now stands with scars on her face
The wide open spaces are closing in quickly
From the weight of the whole human race

And it's not that I blame them for claiming her bounty
I just wish they're takin' it slow
'Cause where has a slow movin'
Once quick draw outlaw got to go?
Where has a slow movin'
Once quick draw outlaw got to go?

HUNDRED DOLLAR BILLS

Nephew Hodi, Brother Joe, Ronnie from the old days, and Harbor all stood around the fire as Lencho went over the 2004 pot crop game plan. They smoked joints as the weed man reminded them that the recent fiasco with the indoor crop at his niece's was calamitously expensive. "Each marijuana plant is like a money tree. One hundred dollar bills will be hanging from every branch. It is critical to be vigilant for thieves and righteous in the rejection of greed."

"Damn straight," Joe concurred. "All me and the wife want for the use of our property is stash. Four pounds will do it for us, bro. You been super generous all these years, and this is the least we can do."

"Can Heather and her kids stay here with us?" Hodi asked.

"Who's Heather?" Lencho asked.

"She's a friend of mine. Got nowhere to live for a few months till her old man gets out of jail. She's cool and can be of help, if we need any."

From mid-May until the end of September the plants thrived, all fifty of them. As harvest neared, Ronnie volunteered to be the night watchman. "Yeah, I'll put a cot right in the middle of those babies and no one will get by me."

"Well, how can you be a night watchman if you're asleep on a cot?" Lencho asked.

"I'll wake up, of course. Plus, I got Gus, my faithful German Shepard. He's ferocious."

Heather's boyfriend, Weyet, was released from jail a few weeks later. Heather told him all about the developing fortune over at Space Acres as he snorted meth at their kitchen table. On October 1, Weyet did a few stout lines, threw a bed sheet over his skinny shoulders, and drove over to Space Acres just as the sun was coming up. He made his way into the middle of things, spread the sheet on the ground, and with a pruning tool he clipped a hundred thousand dollars' worth of fragrant bud, piling them in a heap. Neither Gus the ferocious hound nor Ronnie the watchman woke up for a second. With a satchel full, Weyet got away like some heavy laden thief in the night.

An hour later, Joe came out of his cabin and looked at the desecrated crop in horror. He yelled at Ronnie to wake up, but when Ronnie didn't, he went back inside and grabbed his twelve gauge. Joe fired two rounds right over Ronnie's head, but he still didn't wake. Joe ran to get Lencho.

"Holy shit!" Ronnie finally yelled. "We been robbed! How the hell did he get by me? Gus! Wake up, you worthless old flea bag." Gus just yawned. They followed a trail of water leaf a half a mile to where Weyet parked. They examined a still fresh cigarette butt laying on the ground. It was deja vu all over again. Lencho went to see Deputy Manny Hass of the Yuba Sheriff's Department. "I can identify the dope, Manny," he told him. "I know the scum bag that ripped us off and where he lives. He's cleaning the bud as we speak."

"Sorry, Lencho, there's nothing we can do. There are no bona fide forensics for identifying marijuana. At least, not yet. It's sort of like diamonds. You should have called us while the theft was taking place. How come you didn't have a guard on duty?"

Lencho paid off Ronnie and Gus with some poundage, and sent them packing back to Arizona. He was out around a hundred grand. The legal pot growing business was not off to exactly an auspicious start. But most sadly and dispiriting was Brother Joe, who dropped a bombshell.

"You want what?" Lencho cried.

"A third of what's left, man," Joe replied blithely. "I got bills. And, oh yeah, you gotta pay Hodi out of your cut, not me."

"Well, I think that may be the most bluntly avaricious fuck job I ever got from a relative. What happened to the 'four pounds is all I want, bro, you been so generous to me all these years' business?"

"I never said that, man!" Joe lied. "Hey, you're the big shot dope dealer. You're rolling in the mud. But me and Pam got all sorts of illness, and we have to eat. It's my property, and those plants are my plants. I'm dragging their asses over to my cabin." And he did. Lencho's heart broke a little more each day.

After Lencho paid all the bills, giving everyone their cut of what was left, he ended up with eight pounds out of an original fifty plants. He choked back bitter tears. This was the life of a weed man, a life now going on forty years.

One afternoon, Harbor came over to get his cut and bring a new business proposal. "Life must go on," he began, "and what I'm laying down will make you some bucks. You know my pals Mark Bush and James Roberts?"

"Those southern boys?"

"Yeah, originally from Virginia, transplanted to northern Cal. Well, they're enterprising guys and they're sitting on half a million in cash. They need a load of reefer. They could use some perico, also. How about we all meet down in Tucson and do some biz with the Beltrans?"

The idea immediately made the weed man uneasy. He knew these young guys to be go getters, having met them once or twice. Doing big business, especially with a fearsome Cartel like the Beltrans, would be dicey. Anything went wrong and it was lights out with those people. "I'll think about it," Lencho finally replied. "But no cocaine. Not a chance. The coke trade is out of bounds with me. I have lost too many friends to it already."

"Okay," Harbor nodded. "I agree about that. Weed is sacred, coke is death. We'll talk about it some more. We can meet you down there at your convenience. Do those Mexicans usually have weight available?"

"Does a bear shit in the woods?" Lencho answered. "They got weight and they got tunnels."

From the winter of 2004 into early spring, Lencho and Connica worked on their property. They built a greenhouse for young plants and clones, and started working on his latest concept: a bamboo garden and hills terraced with a front end loader. He was also revisiting the practical concepts of industrial hemp, an idea whose time had come and gone, but would surely come again. Now and then, he went to Tucson and scored a commercial bale from the Beltrans.

Eventually, they began work again at Space Acres. They raised beds for the coming crop. Pounding stakes into the hard, piney ground, and then walling in the medium with stiff construction paper, they created spacious beds for what would be a seventy-two plant crop. Three feet tall and layered with mulch, quality top soil and a loamy mix of mulch, bark, sand, and vermiculite obtained from AG Mart in Chico. They were ready to plug in their esoteric mix of super nova clones come mid-May. This time there would be no stupid disasters. This time it would be done right.

Luz and Wes installed an eight foot American wire fence, along with the alarms and motion sensors. There would be no more 'Ronnies' to fall asleep on duty. Now, there was a twenty foot guard tower, which was reached by ladder and equipped with a television to keep the guard company. Down below, a fire pit kept alive all night by a second guard who would patrol the grounds when the buds began to develop. Both guards had guns.

Fourteen varieties of marijuana were planted on May 15. Cush, Sour Diesel, Blueberry, Northern Lights, and Mazar-i-Sharif were the star crops, while the hybrid mixes of Indica and Sativa filled in the rest. Within two months, five foot specimens reached to the skies and swayed in the warm summer breezes.

The weed man needed to tend to his flock in Prescott, so he and the wife drove to Arizona to arrange a bale and meet with Harbor about the big Beltrans job.

"You gotta be there when I am, Harbor," Lencho told him. "If you guys are late, you're outta luck. I won't wait." They weren't late and everyone met at the legendary Ghost Ranch Motel, built in Tucson decades earlier to host the many Hollywood actors, directors, and crews that visited the area to film westerns. The place was a warren of individual adobe bungalows, cactus gardens, and carports. It was the perfect location for a large transfer in the middle of the desert city. The actual risks in Tucson were small as regards to law enforcement, because the Beltrans had a lot of juice there. Lencho had made the game plan clear. He would order a twenty-five pound bale of high quality commercial weed and have it delivered to one of three bungalows he had rented. It would be inspected, and if found satisfactory, the boys would hand over the money to the suppliers who would take their pickup truck and fill it to capacity. Then it would be returned, and they would leave town to distribute their purchase back east. The Beltrans were big time, so you could expect honesty and efficiency when doing business with them. The cartels worked that way. They kept their end of the bargain. There were no rip-offs or funny business. And it was expected the customer would act the same, because if they didn't, lead might fly.

James Roberts, the lead man, was called 'Ponytail' because he had long, thick hair that extended to his waste. He was a dapper youngster who heralded from wealthy blue blood stock. He reminded Lencho of the equally self-confident Charlie he had known years before back in O.B. Smooth, self-assured, but impulsive and relatively inexperienced. Ponytail's partner was Mark Bush, called 'Peepers' for his thick eyeglasses. The two were out to conquer the world.

The Beltrans brought the pickup back stuffed to capacity, but they returned some of the money because there had not been enough room for the amount of money fronted. "Can we score some kilos of coke with the balance?" they asked.

"Not a chance in hell!" Lencho thundered. "I am a weed man. I don't do cocaine. Don't ask again."

The whole operation took only two hours. After transferring the weed into large naugahyde satchels, Bush and Roberts had their driver take off for home while they stayed behind a couple more days to party in town. They managed to score a quarter ounce of perico—thrown in by Ignacio Beltran as a party favor. Lencho took his bale and fee back to Prescott with relief all had gone okay. He took some satisfaction knowing that the Mexicans didn't totally own the pot distribution business in the U.S. There were still a few large domestic distributors in the trade, although they were vanishing daily.

Returning to Prescott for a couple more days, the weed man left his bale in the hands of trusted compatriots, visited one last time with family and friends down at the Lizards Lounge, and then headed back to Space Acres with his wife. There was a large plantation of domestic mota to be looked after. This year it would go right. This was the year he would realize the initial potential of the now wide open medical marijuana trade, a business that would soon gross over twenty billion dollars a year in California alone, as well as put a serious damper on cartel profitability in the marijuana trade nationally.

As the plants matured that season, Lencho, Connica, and some Mexican laborers made major infrastructural inroads on his six acres. They built a solid, six foot cedar fence facing their spread and cleared a pad for their dream home that was planned for the future. They also built a 20 x 36 foot studio shop, garden sheds, and a pump house. This was all built with lumber they milled themselves from trees that needed to be removed. An eight foot wire fence went up over four acres to discourage snoops and the occasional bear. A gravel driveway was laid. Down the hill at Space Acres, the plants were doubling in size every two weeks. They began to resemble orange trees, approaching ten feet in height and just as wide. Super nutritious fertilizers of secret ingredients developed by the legendary Ag Mart lads caressed the billowing root systems beneath the soft and loamy medium. The plants generated THC levels approaching fifteen percent. Then twenty. And then beyond!

Around mid-summer, Harbor came to visit once again. He gaped in amazement at the sight of these female behemoths. He also announced that Ponytail and Peepers wanted to do the Beltran shuffle once again. They were ready with their five hundred grand, and this time offered Lencho his bale plus thirty thousand dollars in cash as an incentive.

"Okay," the weed man answered. "Just like the last time, we do it the same way. I'll get a bale for inspection. You front your money and the truck, and the cartel will do the rest. Agreed?"

"Agreed," they replied.

Lencho decided to take care of Harbor-Beltrans deal while he was in Prescott for a huge family get together in celebration of his father's 86th birthday. A big crowd gathered at the home of Lencho's sister, Susie, and her husband, Arthur. A good time was had by all. Pop seemed moved by the attention, and one at a time he gave his five sons, four daughters, nieces, nephews, and grandchildren big hugs and kisses. Then it was Lencho's turn. "Happy birthday, dad," the weed man whispered into the old man's ear as he pressed a CD of Billie Joe Shaver into his freckled hands. His dad looked up from his chair quizzically and set the music aside on an end table.

"Oh, Lencho," he sighed. And he gave a gentle pat on the knee like he was some sort of wayward six-year-old. The weed man took it for what it was worth, and with a tear in his eye moved on.

The next day Lencho and Connica drove down to Tucson and took up residence once again at the Ghost Ranch Motel. And like the last time, a bale was delivered to the reviewing room on orders from Ignacio Beltran via his soldier Luis Vega and Harbor. Ponytail and Peepers declared it 'first rate,' so the money and keys to a large pick-up truck were handed over. Two hours later, the truck was returned full to the brim with bales of fragrant weed grown in the distant mountains of the Sierra Madre del Sur. The bales were slightly encrusted in a mud overcoat from having been dragged through a rather wetish new tunnel, no doubt one of many that crisscross the downward sloping geology of the Nogales area. The pot was shifted into more manageable naguahyde satchels and then driven off.

James Roberts asked, "Are you sure we can't buy some perico, Lencho? We got a potentially big market."

Flush with the rewards of success, the weed man stifled an inclination to bite the kid's head off and only said, "I do not sell cocaine. I will not facilitate that trade. My experience over many years has shown it to be down consciousness, as we old hippies used to say. If you value our business relationship, you'll drop the subject."

Just then, soldier Luis Vega showed up unexpectedly with another taste of cola from Señor Beltran. Lencho didn't disapprove of a snort or two when it was time to party—it was the trade itself that made Lencho so disagreeable. Lencho briefly flashed through his mind a small regret that the lads had now met a member of the Beltran cartel. Though brief, the flash would prove to be prophetic.

With the assignment finished, Lencho and Connica hurried back to Phoenix to catch the new up and coming outlaw of the country music scene, Shooter Jennings and his actress girlfriend, Drea de Matteo. Shooter was doing a gig at a club and outside amphitheater on the edge of town.

"Man, Lencho, I sure appreciate this bud," Shooter enthused. "It mixes well with whiskey."

A chip off the old block, Lencho left thinking. Just like his old man. It was time to head back. Harvest was not far off.

*****

In July, Lencho hired two experienced security guards to stand a serious watch over the 72 budding plants. Both were armed with pistols and rifles. They carried cell phones with quick dial directly to the sheriff's department.

"Hey, Tío, it's Harbor. How are the babies?"

"They're huge," Lencho answered. "Where are you?"

"I'm in Prescott, and was hoping you might be ready for another jaunt down to Tucson."

"The boys ready again?" Lencho asked.

This time there would be no inspection bale. No need, Ponytail and Peepers assured. The other times had been most satisfactory, so the boys trusted the Beltrans implicitly. They would just hand over two hundred thousand dollars and most assuredly be happy. "Only two hundred thousand this time?" Lencho asked.

"Apparently so," Harbor answered. "They still got product back home, but felt they wanted to score now for the upcoming holidays." The meet was arranged and, like the last two outings, the third was at the same place, the Ghost Ranch Motel. They only needed two rooms this time.

The load was arranged to be delivered to a house owned by Scotty, the Lizard Lounge bartender who also worked for a restaurant supply house and maintained the residence, because it was useful in his route through the southwest. Lencho had the run of the place, and Scotty never asked what he might need it for. The Beltran soldiers delivered three hundred pounds of high grade reefer there and left. Lencho looked it over and pronounced it fine. The next morning he got a call from Harbor as he was watching the news in his room at the Ghost Ranch. "They don't like the weed," Harbor said. "They want an exchange."

"Don't like it? What the fuck is that?" Lencho choked. "The weed is the same exact stuff they always get. It was good enough before and now it isn't?"

"Sorry, Tío," Harbor replied. "They say it ain't the same, and they want something better."

This can't be good, Lencho thought. He knew the Beltrans well, and he knew they weren't going to be happy about this turn of events. Picky little fucks! This could turn out badly, but he figured he had no choice but to pass the word.

"Well fuck, Lencho," Ignacio Beltran told him when they met, "this is a real bother. Are your friends trying to pull some kinda fast one?"

"I don't know what the problem is, Ignacio. I shoulda insisted on the inspection beforehand like the others. They said it would be okay. Now, this bullshit."

"Well, I gotta talk to Marco about this, and he's in the hospital."

"The hospital? What happened? Did someone shoot him? Was he in a car wreck?"

"Plastic surgery," Ignacio replied. "And I won't even be able to talk to him for a couple days." Lencho hoped Scotty wouldn't be coming home soon.

"They say, 'no problem,'" Harbor reported. "They say they'll be happy to chill and see the sights." Lencho couldn't help but feel this whole thing was on the strange side. Almost a week later, Marco knocked on his bungalow door. Lencho opened it to find a swarthy man with a bruised face, bandaged nose, and look of displeasure.

"What the fuck, Lencho?" The gangster said curtly. "I don't feel too fucking good right now. I don't need this grief. What was wrong with the mota?"

"I appreciate your help in this matter, Marco," Lencho answered. "But I haven't got a clue what the problem is. Seemed to me the product was fine. The weight was good, price right. But they want something else. Can it be done?"

"It can be done this time because you are a good friend and customer, but the next time we will be more thorough with these gringos."

"That's great. I'll tell them. And say, old pal, why the surgery? Your mug looked fine to me."

The bandaged nose crinkled as Marco managed a smile. "I wanted to be more handsome," he answered.

By noon the next day, three hundred pounds of reefer had been removed from the little cottage and replaced with three hundred pounds of a different batch. Lencho thought the quality was identical, although this bud had a few more red hairs in it. Ponytail and Peepers told Harbor they were happy with the new product. Now it was time to party.

"They say they are tired of the bars they've been going to," Harbor told Lencho. "Can you recommend a really good joint with a lot of action and hot broads?"

"I'll ask Ignacio and get back to you," the weed man replied.

"Tell them to go to the El Charro club," Ignacio advised. "The girls there are primo, and the place rocks." Late that night, Harbor called the Ghost Ranch just as Lencho and Connica were turning in. "What's so important you gotta call this time of night?" the weed man grumbled. Loud music and general hilarity blared from behind the payphone Harbor was calling from.

"Tío, we got trouble. I think those motherfuckers have been gaming us."

"Explain," Lencho barked.

"I'm here at the club with Mark and James. We're partying and all, and in walks Ignacio Beltran and his shadow Luis Vega. You remember Vega met those boys briefly the last trip? Well, he knew who to look for in this crowded ass joint, and now they're all getting sauced on Dom Pérignon, doing toots, and talking business. It's just like they were all old time buddies."

"Talking business?!" Lencho yelled. "We just did business. What kinda business would there be to talk about now?"

"Cocaine, boss. They're talking cocaine."

"Son of a bitch!"

"Yeah, it looks like they're gonna buy a couple hundred grand worth of keys from Beltran and send it along with their mota. I think they got tired of you saying 'no' to their requests about that stuff and went around your back. I think this whole we-don't-like-the-load-riff was bullshit. They were just stalling so they could make contact with the Beltrans and get the good perico."

"And cut me out of the loop," Lencho fumed.

"No, they say they don't want that. They say they love you and all that shit. It's just you wouldn't do coke. So, they did it themselves. They say you're still in the picture for the future on the weed, if you want."

"Well, I don't want," Lencho hissed. "Those little weasels can have the Beltrans and the perico. I wash my hands of them, Harbor, and you can tell them that. Nothing any good can come out of such treachery. The ungrateful little assholes." And he hung up. The next day the two met at a lonely old cemetery across from the Ghost Ranch. Sitting on tombstones, they discussed the situation at length. Pulling out a fat bundle of cash, Harbor handed it over. "Here's your fee. Thirty-five grand. This, plus your bale. Pretty good score."

"Not good enough, young man," Lencho whispered. "Mark my words. Trouble will come from all this. Weed is a blessing; cola is the devil's own handiwork. I don't understand how come these little Jew boys on the fucking make can never leave well enough alone. Making a fortune off weed is never enough. They think they gotta join in the big time and do coke. Very sad, very bad."

"Look at the profits in it," Harbor replied. "The Beltrans are going to take those ten kilos and cut them in half for a ten thousand dollar fee. The stuff is pure, uncut from Colombia. Ponytail and Peepers never had any so good. Now they'll have twenty keys. Hard to resist the numbers."

"Easy to resist once you're dead. In my forty years in this business, I have watched a lot of cats die. Nothing good will come outta this betrayal." And nothing good did come from it.

The cola was loaded into the boys' truck with their mota and the driver headed home. On the outskirts of Wichita, Kansas, a state trooper pulled him over for "driving too close" to the car ahead of him. The trooper profiled his vehicle: tinted windows camper shell, lone white boy driving with Virginia plates. When the trooper asked to inspect the vehicle, the driver said, "No, not without probably cause."

The cop said, "I'll get some," and called for a dope dog. Enough said. The DEA jumped all over the boy and his load. Three hours later he was back on the road, now a true believer in law enforcement's mandate to make America safe from the scourge of narcotics. It was either that or be ready to live the rest of his life in a USP or medium security federal joint. The DEA trailed the truck back to the drop house in old Virginia, and when Roberts, AKA Ponytail, showed up a few days later to oversee the distribution of his latest swag, they pounced. Three hours later, Ponytail had seen the error of his ways and was firmly in the camp of the federal drug enforcers himself. The DEA swooped on dozens of people in the next two weeks. When word finally reached Harbor, he called and delivered the bad news the weed man had predicted.

"I'm leaving for Europe," Harbor told him. "As far as I know, everything is cool out here. I don't think either one of us has anything to worry about. Ponytail says he will keep quiet. He realizes now how stupid he was not to listen to you. The pot load was bad enough, but the cola may be the end of the world. But he's got great, big time lawyers working on it, and he's out on bond. I'm gonna go visit some friends in France and Germany I met back in Costa Rica." Famous last words, the weed man thought to himself.

*****

His older son Luz had been caught up in the terrible scourage of meth addiction back when Lencho was working for 'One call does it all' but happily was currently free and clear of the habit and the weed man beamed with pride as they worked alongside each other among the towering colas. The irony was not lost on those hot and sunny days of all that had passed through the years. The epiphany of that first puff out at the quarry when he was twenty one had turned into his life's work and calling. Running from the badges and thieves of the law. Time in jails and prisons. Children born and raised in the marijuana trade. So long illegal, but now changing. Now, not so illegal. Almost legal. Quasi-legal? What the fuck would you call the pot game these days with all the recent twists and turns? What the heck, he thought as he looked at his boy sweating beside him up at Space Acres.

Still the helicopters flew over. At least once a week, a big Blackhawk from the C.A.M.P or a shiny, smaller white and black State Police chopper made its presence known. They flew, probably taking aerial photos, still spying. Only now they were unable to land and disgorge teams of heavily armed C.A.M.P soldiers to pillage and pull and stuff their own pockets with fragrant reefer. They were like big, impotent mosquitoes.

On October 10 the harvest began. First off were the large upper branches and flowering tips. Monster buds of red and yellow. Green and purple. Silver and blue. Fourteen strains of heaven. A few days more of sunlight for the middle regions and they were gathered in, leaving the lowest buds to the same process. Finally, the job was complete and a crew of manicurers set to work. Patty and Keith, old hippy friends from Shelter Cove of the 70's, came to town. Molly, the now retired post mistress from Prescott, lent a hand. Starlove Girl, the legendary pruner from Eugene, Oregon, brought her regular crew of seven ladies in to work. All at two hundred dollars per pound, and all paid in bud. The place hummed and Lencho calculated the weight would come in at about three hundred pounds. At the going rate of two hundred bucks an ounce, the total value could be as high as one and a half million. Less overhead and expenses, the weed man should glean about a third of that when all was said and done.

But once again a lesson in human nature was unfolding. As he had always said, a flowering marijuana plant is many things. Heaven to the consumer, medicine to the sick, and one hundred dollar bills to the greedy. Brother Joe finally went the extra mile in the avarice department. They hadn't been close since Joe married Pam, around the same time Lencho had married Connica. Joe smoked and drank to excess, but Pam was another matter altogether with a maniacal preference for methamphetamine and the behavioral maladjustments that went with it. Just plain rotten in Lencho's opinion, lost in a haze of paranoid covetousness. "I want one third of that crop," Joe suddenly announced. "It's ours, it's on our land and me and Pammy deserve it."

When the weed man caught his breath he replied, "All these years I took care of you and your family. When you didn't have money, I gave you money. I paid for everything including the hundred grand it took to set up this crop. Every year you tell me 'all I want is smoke, brother,' and then you stick me. Now this?"

"No, Lencho," Joe said, "there's more. From now on you gotta grow on someone else's property or grow on your own. Me and Pam want you out. We're gonna do our own thing exclusively here on Space Acres." So Lencho ended all close ties with Brother Joe. And Joe got his wish. The weed man wasn't going to fall prey to the urge for retribution, because he knew from years of experience that these things took care of themselves. He'd never grow weed on Space Acres again, and picked up the tab for all the expenses. Which came to an awful lot. He walked away with sixty pounds, much of which was sold to various dispensaries in California. By mid-December, the 2005 project was complete and wrapped up. Everything was done and stored, most already sold off, and the weed man turned his attention to the pot loving good old boy musicians of Nashville. Willy Nelson was the best known of the once booze swiggers turned stoners, but there were scads of others, all well-known and wealthy.

"I'm sending you ten pounds of the best weed you may have ever seen," Lencho told Sandy Rhymin over the phone. "I'll send it FedEx, and then fly down behind it. When I get to the Nashville Hilton, I'll call you, and your boys can come over to pick it up. Sound good? Right on, see you then."

The double package shipped via FedEx was disguised to look like recording gear, and had arrived smoothly by the time the weed man walked up to the desk in the lobby. "Your room is ready sir, and your instruments were delivered this morning. Would you like them brought up to your room?" The clerk asked.

"Please," Lencho replied. "We're gonna make some sweet music in some of the studios around town this week."

Over beers and smoke, he discussed a new plan he'd hatched to get a substantial pile of the mota across the country in time for a number of tours beginning in the spring. "When the next tour bus for those boys hits the west coast, what we want to do is stick sixty pounds on board for the trip back here," he told Rhymin. "Can you arrange this on your end? We must keep this close to the vest, so that the artists don't know it's on board, and especially the driver."

"I know a guy," Rhymin answered. "Consider it arranged."

Twitty Messenger headed up one of the premier tour outfits in town—in all the country and rock world actually. Rhymin went over to see him, and by mid-March when a tour bus for the Flying Fistfuls showed up in Reno at the tail end of a tour, the sixty pounds was crated up in innocuous packaging and placed in the front of the trailers that carried the band's staging, instruments, and gear. No one knew it was anything else besides equipment except the three conspirators, and a week later it was unloaded at a warehouse in Nashville. From there, the product was distributed to dozens of bands and individuals of great musical repute. The elite of country music went on their merry way enjoying the best of California's green product, and keeping their money in the United States instead of the coffers of some of the most vicious organized crime characters the world has ever known. The work of a weed man is never done, however, and it was time to prepare for the '06 crop.

Having been banished by his favorite brother, Lencho called his daughter Liz and asked if he could use her property and work a deal with her. The reason he dare not use his own were two fold. First and foremost, he had the proverbial record as long as his arm. And secondly, where he and Connica lived, it was simply too shady from the old growth forest that covered their land. Lumens are everything. Lots of light, lots of bud. The herb worships the sun.

"Sure, dad," Liz told him. "I heard about what Uncle Joe said. Just come over here. You're always welcome." That's daddy's little girl, Lencho enthused. He built round, above ground planters, and put in the esoteric soils and mediums that brought in some of the best clones he had ever seen.

Chapter Nineteen

"Working Without a Net"
Released 1985
Waylon Jennings

I used to depend on some things I did not need
I leaned on some crutches that kept me off my feet
Standing here without them now, well it scares me half to death
Your love helps me forget, I'm working without a net

DEA REDUX

Lencho's patience was wearing thin as the June 2006 legal marijuana crop got underway in the little town of Durham. A busy street ran past the effort which was prospering behind a tall wood fence. Across from it lived a broker and grower named Richard who was an ace. His own project was enormous, so Lencho didn't worry too much about rip offs. Anyway, he was only forty minutes away over on the mountain, and made it to work each day around 10:00 a.m.

But to soothe his mind of the tribulations, it was time for the annual Goose on the Lake concert back in Elkton, Kentucky.

For fifteen years, old Lloyd and his wife Donna had chased the cows out of the pasture and invited a small but loyal crowd of two thousand to listen to some musicians from the country and outlaw world of music. Bluegrass, hillbilly, folk, and rock echoed through pastoral settings while the crowd of old hippies and young acolytes moved and grooved, smoked the herb, and drank beer and moonshine. At night, fires burned around camp sites, and barbecues roasted hot dogs, burgers, steaks and chicken. In the sizeable lake-reservoir, hung over revelers came to in the morning from the night's revelries. Pretty young girls in skimpy bathing suits were abundant. It was also the setting for marijuana comparisons, Kentucky being a state well-known for its epicurean botanical efforts. Lencho had not missed a season led by the famous Charlie Gearheart and the Goose Creek Symphony since the festival began, and this year he brought along a pound of various selections from the fourteen he had cultivated the year before. His herb was not the prettiest, but it was by far and away the most potent.

"Lencho," old Lloyd enthused coughing fitfully as his lung expansions exploded into rapturous tears and wheezes, "this is some good shit."

"It's the difference between inside dope and outside, Lloyd," the weed man exclaimed. "You can grow pretty pot that's pretty good under lights, but if you want THE KIND buddy, you gotta go El Sol. Lumens are the name of the game." Lloyd's daughter Torry and friend Danny both agreed, and both begged to be inducted into the Northern California fraternity of mota wisdom.

"I'll do anything to help, man," Danny pleaded. "Pull weeds, kill gophers, trim water leaves."

"I could use some help," Lencho pondered. "Tell you what, young man. Pack up your stuff, bring your dog, and drive out west in a couple weeks. I'll have a trailer for you to live in and your main duty will be to guard the crop. Can you stay awake all night and sleep in the day? I've had serious problems with night watchmen falling asleep on duty. Can you do it?"

"I swear to god, man. I can do it. I won't fail you."

After the festival wrapped up, Lencho flew back home, and two weeks later Danny showed up full of vim and vigor and eager to learn how the Emerald Trianglers did it.

The buds at Liz's were just excellent by late August, and were a portent of fragrant wealth to come. A gnarly bud worm had invaded many crops in the area, including Brother Joe's at Space Acres. Richard, ace grower across the street, was the only cat who had a clue on how to get rid of it. He taught Lencho, and Lencho, putting aside his anger at his brother, passed the word, thus saving Joe's sorry ass from disintegrating colas.

During the day, Liz was on guard along with Lloyd's daughter Torry who had now showed up. Lencho joined them in the early morning. By mid-September, the flowering plants were sticky and fragrant with one more month to go that would make them fat and hard. This was the danger time, when the scum bag thieves came crawling out from under their meth and heroin rocks to do their rip offs. It is always a danger time for growers, a time of being alert, and sometimes of violence. Now, however, for the first time, you could call the cops. What a wonder that was! Still, the cops were of little use after the fact, as he had found out back in 2004.

On the drive to town, Lencho gave his daughter Liz a call. "How're you this morning, honey?" Lencho asked.

"Torry and I need to go to the D.M.V. this morning. She decided to stay here in California and wants to get a new license, and mine is also about to expire. Danny will be here, although he's been up all night; he should be able to hold down the fort till you get here, dad" Liz said.

"Okay, tell him I need to make a quick stop. I'll be there in about an hour."

When Lencho arrived at 10:00 a.m., he found Danny and his pit bull Jack snoring like a couple guys who had been up all night. The kid was instructed to stay awake until Lencho arrived, since Liz and Torry went into town to the D.M.V. He had hunkered into a comfy lawn chair and promptly nodded out. In the meantime, shortly after the phone call from Lencho, someone had climbed over the tall wood fence. Someone who knew Jack the pit bull and didn't set off his usually cacophonous barking. An inside job, Lencho sadly noted. The bulk of the weed was gone, stripped from the giant plants leaving only the lower boughs. At least fifty pounds stolen once again under the nose of the guard and his guard dog, and it was obvious who had done it. The weed man wept.

*****

The phone rang. Lencho answered and heard Harbor's mother on the other end sounding odd. "Are you okay?" she asked.

"Sure, I'm okay," Lencho replied.

"How are your people down in Tucson?" She asked.

"As far as I know, they're okay, too. What's this about?"

"They arrested Harbor, you asshole. He's in jail!"

The shoe had fallen, and Lencho knew instantly that it was time to lawyer up once again. The bobbsey twins from Virginia, James Roberts and Mark Bush, aka Ponytail and Peepers, had dropped the dime just as he had known they would. Harbor, who had been gone almost a year now in Europe, had come home only to be snared by the typical DEA 'ongoing investigation.' Naturally, he had been blamed for the whole thing. He thought the world of Harbor and his dad, and he considered his mother, Carol, a dear friend also. What the hell, nothing new.

Who could he turn to in his latest time of legal need? He would try to head the feds off at the pass—machinations began to form in his mind. From years of dodging bullets, he had come to understand the byzantine workings of the legal system. The treachery of the drug trade and the real crooks that ran it. When dealing with dealers and smugglers, gangsters and cartels, things were basically cut and dry. When dealing with federal agents, what was called for was cunningness. They watched from the sideline of the barrel at all the fish swimming within. Then they relied on their army of informers to set up the next fish. Hook the sucker, reel 'em in. Nothing much to it. Make busts, brag to the press, start over again. Swoop into houses and book the evidence. Dope, cash, property. Steal most of it, report the remainder. Divvy up the spoils among themselves and kick up the rest to HQ. A rapacious lot to be sure. Lencho knew them well, and knew it all meant nothing. Just a game. The so called 'big' bad guys played with the real bad guys, the narcs.

Tom Connelly came to mind. Years earlier in the eighties he had been the hot shot prosecutor who helped Lencho cut a deal to go after DEA agent Wayne Boyd and his partner in the Mexico City Bank robbery. Working with Connelly, Lencho had beaten a seventy-five year rap. Worked then, might work again.

Lencho dialed up his brother Ed in Prescott and explained the situation. "Find Tom Connelly if you can. Is he still an AUSA or is he in private practice now?" Ed got back in two days.

"Tom Connelly is in private practice over on Camelback Road in Phoenix. Big shot in a big building. Doing some kinda real estate law. Don't know if he will take a criminal case." One way to find out. Lencho called and made an appointment, so he and Connica drove down to Phoenix to see the great man.

"Well, you old crook," Connelly laughed. "Haven't seen you since the DEA got off the hook back when. How are ya?"

"I've been better, Tom," Lencho answered. "I got a problem once again. What's your fee?"

"I don't even talk to anyone who doesn't have at least one hundred and fifty thousand. But for you, I may make an exception. Tell me all about it."

Lencho was keen to make it clear that he did not sell coke, and was most indignant that he was going to be implicated in this cartel caper that was supposed to have been exclusively pot.

"Listen, I know you are a pot man, Lencho," Connelly said. "But the nature of conspiracy laws is pretty basic. It's just a grab bag. If cocaine came into the mix, then the government will nail you for that as well. Doesn't make any difference if it was news to you. What we need to do at once is arrange a self-surrender. I'll contact the AUSA in Virginia and you go there and tell him your story. You gotta offer to give the government useful information. Cut a deal for leniency. That's how it works." Lencho knew how it worked, so he began writing a script in his mind as to what he would tell them and what he would offer. Most or all of it would be fiction.

"Say, listen, Tim," Connelly said to the DEA ASAC in Virginia, "before we sign off here, let's set a date for a meet between your office, the Tucson office, and my client. Lencho is the real deal. He can set you straight on some juicy stuff. Next Thursday at the Scottsdale PD. Neutral territory. They'll loan us an office. Good for you? Fine, see you then." In September of 2006, Lencho and Tom Connelly met with Special Agent Michael Conway from the Tucson DEA—late thirties, lean, laconic—and Arlington, Virginia DEA G.T. (Tim) Becouvarakis-swarthy Italian, barrel chested, short, and rarin' to go.

"How was your flight out?" Connelly asked him shaking hands.

"They sent me on the Lear. Not too bad. Course you must have your own Gulf. If I had your money, I'd throw mine away." There were laughs all around, inside cop-lawyer stuff. Lencho studied his feet.

"Let's get down to it, Lencho. We've read your jacket. Weed man. You go way back. A regular OG. Say you don't do coke. We believe you. It doesn't matter, of course, because as Mr. Connelly may have explained, with a conspiracy anything that was sold is equally divided for indictment purposes. We noticed there was mud on the bales. Want to tell us where that came from?"

Where it came from?! They knew, and he knew they knew. Tunnels. How else would there be mud? And what the hell… he knew they had it all down pat because they had Ponytail and Peepers, the bobbsey snitches.

They already knew Beltran was long gone. More plastic surgery maybe. Ignacio Beltran was disappeared deep into Mexico where he'd pop up at some cartel assignment later.

And remember back in '02? Right after 9/11, the border closed up tight as a clam. Nothing moved in or out. Then the 'all clear' came down. Someone way up on the American side gave the word and all the pot stored on the Mexico side thundered across. What did that say? Pretty clear that DEA was well aware of the comings and goings of the cartels, especially DEA on the border. So he gave them a tunnel, so what? They no doubt already knew where every tunnel was anyway, and maybe even helped the Beltrans load the dope into their trucks after they dragged it across. Hell, DEA might have helped dig the things. This was a charade. So go with it. Be inventive.

"The dope was smuggled via a tunnel," Lencho told them deadpan. "Right under the noses—no make that feet—of Customs. I can give you the exact location of where it began and where it exits. One thousand meters."

"Do tell," Agent Conway mused, playing with a pencil.

"Sounds good," Agent Becouvarakis chimed in. "We'll need the location."

"Trouble is, Lencho," Conway continued, "although DEA considers you a reliable witness and that business a few years back about SA Boyd in Mexico City still sticks in some people's craw, there just ain't anybody left in the conspiracy we have before us to give up. You, Sir, are the end of the line. The Beltran boys are probably gone. We got Bush and Roberts and all their pals. So what new thing can you give us?"

Lencho knew Conway and the Tucson DEA were involved with the tunnel and he also knew they would do anything to protect it from agent Becouvarakis. The tunnel was located at the Hotel San Pablo, but Lencho's plan was to play this thing out to the end. Very risky stuff, but he had made up his mind and it was time to play his card.

"I've seen this tunnel with my own eyes. They showed it to me when I asked about bringing my Chinese friend into the U.S. illegally. It's over a thousand meters long, and it sits about one hundred feet from the fence in the basement of a pharmacy in downtown Nogales."

"Under a pharmacy?" asked Becouvarakis. Lencho looked deep into the narcs eyes and said "Yeah, beneath a pharmacy, right under one of the busiest parts of town. I'm not sure where it comes up, but it shouldn't be hard for you guys to figure this one out."

Becouvarakis sat up straight trying to stay calm while he wrapped his brain around what was being said. "If this is all true, Lencho, and we can bust a tunnel, I'm sure your time in jail will be brief, if at all. Agent Conway, what do you think about all this?" Becouvarakis asked.

Conway snapped himself out of his trance and said, "Well, we sure would like to take down a tunnel. So if what Lencho is telling us pans out, this could get some big media play and that's what it's all about. Of course, you will get the credit for this, Agent Becouvarakis." Becouvarakis smiled like a possum eating shit.

"Well Gentlemen, I think we can adjourn this meeting," Attorney Connelly announced. "Lencho, I'll leave you in the hands of the Tucson DEA. Does that work for you agent Conway?"

"Yes," Conway said. "I think Lencho and I will get along just fine."

That night Lencho and the DEA agent made the rounds to all the titty bars. "My boss thinks we're working the case tonight, so we have to at least make a show of it. That all right with you, Lencho?"

"Whatever pays the rent, Mike."

Lencho was not a titty bar kind of guy, but he also knew that these pigs were exactly what the name implies. "I'll show you the best flesh in town, and the good news is the government will pay for everything." Conway drooled.

Oh, goodie, thought Lencho. So they made the rounds, and the agent slammed drinks while Lencho held back saying his doctors had advised him to go easy on the alcohol. Soon enough Conway was getting loose lipped. "You're a pretty good guy, Lencho, and I'm going to do everything I can to get you out of this mess. I know you know how the game is played, so just stick with me and we'll both get through this."

"Well, Mike, as far as I'm concerned, I put you guys onto this so called tunnel and all I really care about is a letter sent to the AUSA in Virginia saying what a big help I've been and the risk I'm putting myself into. I'll hang out with you as long as you need me to as a matter of fact. The longer it takes, the better off I am."

"Yea, Yea, Lencho. Would you look at the tits on this babe?"

They gave him another two months which stretched into five, because DEA agent Conway was just in no particular rush.

"What is with these narcs?" Lencho asked his attorney. "You heard anything since the meeting?"

Tom Connelly stretched his considerable girth in his high back chair and pulled long legs up onto his desk. "Listen kid," he said, "these clowns are just as spooky as the CIA. Spooks one and all. Only they know what they're up to. Not to worry. It is axiomatic in the legal world that no news is good news. I talked to Agent Becouvarakis in Virginia the other day. He told me their SAC is happy with you. It's all good. Things are on track—whatever that means. But this yo-yo, Mike Conway, is another matter. It's very quiet from Tucson. Let it rest. When they decide to move they'll let us know. And they will move."

Finally Conway called.

"DEA considers you a co-operating witness, Lencho," he told the weed man at a Phoenix Starbucks. "Been real busy with other cases, but now it's time we get to work. Let's take a drive down to Tucson and make the rounds. Show me where Beltran lived. The stash house. The clubs where Bush and Roberts partied. This Ghost Ranch Motel. We'll take some pictures. I gotta fatten up my report."

They made the drive in a big, black Hummer right out of a showroom. "Pretty cool, huh?" Conway said shoving it into gear. "Confiscated from a drug lord over in Nogales. It's good to be king."

The two made the rounds of the dusty desert city, and the narc took photos and jotted notes as Lencho described the three trips and all the arrangements that had been made buying the hundreds of thousands of dollars worth of pot the previous year. Ignacio Beltran was long gone from the little clap board shack he had called home. An old white guy was outside raking up weeds and trash in the front yard. "Not much of a pad for a big shot cartel guy," Conway sneered.

"Well, this dump was just a hangout he used. Brought his putas here and made some arrangements. I'm not sure where he really lived. He has a wife and a bunch of kids like all those hombres," Lencho answered. "I think maybe he really lived in Mexico."

At the stash house that belonged to Lizard Lounge barkeep Scotty, Lencho lied. "This place also belongs to Beltran," saving Scotty's ass. DEA Agent Mike Conway made notes.

It was just as he had thought. When the first tunnel showed up a decade or so before in the Tijuana, Mexico and Otay Mesa, California area, it was a sensation. Since then, many more had come to light. In the Nogales region, natural tunnels caused by subterranean water flow were common and had been put to use by the cartels. But even so, what he could have given them had it been true was an engineering marvel used to funnel billions of dollars worth of contraband under the noses of Homeland Security. He knew what the truth was. It always hit him at times like this. The DEA was in on it. Cartel tunnel. DEA tunnel. No difference.

When he was summoned to a meeting in Phoenix three weeks later, he sat in front of three new DEA guys as well as Mike Conway. Time was moving on, they told him. DEA and U.S Attorney Putney were getting restless. Put up or shut up time was approaching. The case had to be filed within five years, and time was running out.

Once back home in California, Lencho's head was full of contemplation and disquiet. He knew his bullshit stories were nearing their useful end. If the narcs were buying it or not, it probably wouldn't matter. He figured he had earned some time off his ultimate fate, and that would be that. As for becoming a snitch to save his ass, was he really? He didn't see it that way. The world of drugs and drug dealing, dealer vs. cops, was a pit full of vipers. More than a couple times his attorney Tom Connelly had winced at being a party to all this sleaze, but Lencho reminded him of his previous endeavors in behalf of the federal government.

"Come on, man. You used to be knee deep in that snake pit. That's how it works. It's always how it worked. When I was a kid just starting out in this game, I didn't know. I had no idea. But I do now. To survive the occasional arrests and incarcerations, you do what you have to do. And considering how treacherous the government is, it's not too hard to string them along. Those guys are so used to fabrications and bullshit to make their cases, what do they care if what I tell them is true or not? And I haven't told them a whole lot that's true, for your information."

Lencho got back together with old pal Malcom to arrange a visit with young son Harbor who had much earlier pled out on his end and was incarcerated at Lompoc Federal Prison Camp in California. He had received ten years. Lencho was hoping he could convince Harbor to join in with him on his DEA scamming. Make some shit up, give them ghosts and get a reduction. It didn't look promising. Harbor didn't know the game like the old weed man did. He had given up. He was sick at heart over the whole episode, and having never been in the joint before was determined to do his time and let it go at that. But ten years was a long stretch for pot, even if it was quite a lot of it.

"So, I can't take a chance visiting your boy," Lencho told Malcom as they drove down the coast highway towards the Lompoc Federal Prison compounds. "The scam I'm working on precludes that because the DEA might check records and see I was there. They'll figure I was coaching him."

"What exactly do you want me to tell him then?" Malcom asked.

"I gave the feds a story about a tunnel. It was BS, but like I thought, they didn't give a shit anyway. Got credit for it anyhow. But I want more credit, and I want your son to get some also. He could get his sentence reduced to the point he might go home pretty soon. All he need say is that we had nothing to do with any cocaine in the Ponytail and Peepers bust. I'll tell the DEA Harbor wants to help also, and they'll come down and see him. He just needs to verify what I've already told them. We aren't giving anyone up. No one will go to jail because of what we're telling them. It's just important to appear to be playing their game. That's how this bullshit works, Malcom. It's how it has always worked."

The weed man and Malcom stayed at a motel in Lompoc for two days while Malcom visited Harbor and passed the plan along. Initially, Malcom was enthused. The young man had begun his sentence two and a half years earlier. He had been sent to a low security camp, but said he could dig seeing forty months or so knocked off. But when the DEA did show up to question him about 'assistance:' "Your young partner wouldn't sing," Agent Conway told Lencho afterwards. "We went all the way out there and he just dummied up. Told us to hit the highway, he had nothing to say. Fuck him, let him do his ten years."

"I'm sorry, Tío," Harbor wrote him shortly thereafter. "I don't have the heart for anymore of this sick bullshit. I think I'll just do the ten years and let it rest. Please do not contact me again. – Harbor"

The drug game is a dirty business, no question about it, and it's only after years of sloggin' through the filth does a person learn the harsh but true lessons. Despite the rebuke, Lencho loved the boy like his own sons, and told Malcom,

"I'm sorry but if that's the way he wants to play it, it's his decision."

Lencho raced to put the DEA off and hastened to finish up the 2007 crop he was allowed to grow with his nephew Hodi at Space Acres. He would try and get his affairs in order before they arrested him. Make as much money as possible for Connica.

"My old man burned me on last year's crop, Lencho," Hodi told the weed man. "Just like you, he clipped me of most of my cut. We got into it and I've disowned the dishonest son of a bitch. But since I'm on the deed to this property, I expelled him from Space Acres. He doesn't want a bad dust up over it, and he's rich anyway. He's got another grow place, so we can do our thing. The beds are in good shape and we'll grow a big one this year." And grow a big one they did.

As the crop prospered in the hot summer sun, Lencho's mind was racing. He wanted more protection from his impending imprisonment. He had only two choices, face the music and do the time or flee. He had been a fugitive before. He was sixty now. It wasn't much fun that last time and it didn't appeal to him now. Especially since Connica wasn't keen on it. So to bolster his situation, he called Kelly Kasun back in Prescott.

Back when the wild woman Susan Rogue had visited near disaster upon his head with her boyfriend Lalo, and the big weed deal that got out of hand, Lencho had turned to the cops in desperation. Kasun had been the leader of Prescott Area Narcotics Task Force (PANT). He wanted a letter from him to present to the Virginia U.S Attorney further establishing his history of substantial assistance to Uncle Sam. He called the number he still had and left a message. An hour later his call was returned, but it was not from Kasun. "This is GR Menara," the voice said. "Kelly Kasun is retired, now, but I remember the Susan Rogue case because I worked on it with Kelly, and I remember you. In fact, Lencho, we're family. Let's setup a meeting."

Racing back to Prescott, Lencho met Menara at the DPS office. The two men shook hands and the cop pushed the button on a tape recorder. "Lencho and I are acquainted from a previous case wherein he assisted the federal government and the State of Arizona in a matter regarding public safety. We are also related through marriage, as I am married to one of his relatives. I can attest from personal experience that Lencho is a well-regarded asset of federal law enforcement." So, trust was established and both agreed it was a small world indeed. The weed man now recalled seeing Agent Menara at a wedding in Las Vegas of his nephew Joey, but had not made the connection at the time. A cop now as an inlaw. What next?!

Lencho once again ran down the story of the Beltran connection, Ponytail and Peepers, Harbor and the DEA, and his predicament. "I gave those SOB's a tunnel, for god's sake, and they weren't interested. I need to bolster my creds as much as I can, so I was hoping PANT would write me a letter attesting to my past and continuing service to law and order. You know I'm a weed guy. Always was, always will be. I'm legal now in California. But I have no use for the serious scumbags that hurt the community. In the past, due to my lifestyle and work, I have been aware of evil doers, as President Bush might say. Evil doers, though they be murderous DEA agents or murderous tunnel diggers. If I can help, I will, and have. Now I'm getting sucked into a cocaine caper not of my doing and I won't hear it. I know I'm going to jail soon, but I want to mitigate the situation as much as possible. I ain't a young man anymore. I want to watch my grandkids grow up."

Agent Menara understood. "We're gonna do it, buddy. You'll owe us one, but we're gonna do it. In fact, I'm gonna let you write the letter through your attorney. Compose it and send it to me, and I'll retype it on department stationary."

A glowing letter was written and endorsed by the Prescott Area Narcotic Task Force (PANT) of Arizona and then sent to Assistant U.S. Attorney Putney in Virginia. Attorney Tom Connelly was delighted with the direction things were going and predicted DEA would be forced to show gratitude whether they liked it or not.

The 2007 harvest back in Space Acres was a good one. A bountiful yield resulting from excellent weather, careful cultivating, and tight security. That was a relief at least and the weed man netted fifty pounds as his share. At between two and four thousand dollars a pound, depending on where it was sold, his finances were once again solid. But it was back and forth to Tucson to see his DEA 'handlers' and constant communication with Attorney Tom Connelly in Phoenix. The stall was on. He promised them the moon. He would pull it off. "Looks good on this end," he would say. "I'm going down to Nogales and cross the border. Taking some pictures on Saturday. I'll be back at ya on Monday."

He wanted to establish what he was doing was risky so he and Connica traveled to the industrial section of town and while he held up a newspaper with a clear view of the date, had a few photos taken. DEA loved that kind of stuff for their bureaucratic reports. Lots of paper. They thrived on it. Brought in a paycheck, and as long as there was paperwork, that meant they were on the job. The investigation was 'ongoing'—blah, blah, blah. And though he didn't know exactly how, DEA always seemed to know shit. Eyes and ears everywhere. The best technology on earth although they couldn't seem to win their unending war on drugs. But regardless, they knew. All part of the game.

He would tell them the pharmacy he stood in front was the entry point for the tunnel he tried to give them. But they weren't interested. Didn't care. What the fuck, he played the game and dragged things out. Before leaving town, he bopped into a local Pharmacia and purchased some over the counter Viagra, the wonder dick drug. Mexico is easy as regards prescriptions.

That evening he and Connica dined at a nice Italian restaurant and drank some red cabernets and zinfandels. He smoked his usual bomber, and the two snorted some lines of sparkly Escobar's revenge. The two were rapturously involved in a coitus magnus when both his arms went numb. "Oh my god," he moaned. "Not now! This can't be happening." But it was. As his wife eased him back on the bed and wiped the beads of cold sweat from his brow, he groaned from the pain.

"We gotta get you to the hospital," she cried. "You're pale as a ghost."

"No, no. If I go, they'll test me for drugs. I can't have coke in my system. It'll fuck everything up with the narcs." They waited in fear until the next morning, and by then the chest pains and numbness had subsided. He knew he was hardly out of the woods, though. That had been another big one. They drove non-stop to northern California and rushed in to see Dr. Moffit, his favorite cardiologist.

"Call the narcs and tell 'em I ain't coming. Tell 'em I'll send the pics," he told his wife.

"You're a mess," the doc said after the attempted treadmill tests and the EKG. "I suspect we may have to do our work all over again. I'm sending you to see an excellent physician over in Sacramento. His name is Ingram."

"Five of the six bypasses from your previous surgery have collapsed," Ingram told him gravely. "What we must do is go back in and redo the damage from the backside of the heart. In this sort of surgery, it is not a matter of 'fixing things'. It's a matter of starting over. And by the way, if this happens again, you're screwed. We've run out of options."

Assistant U.S. Attorney Putney was informed of Lencho's status, but as luck would have it, his own father had just suffered a similar fate and was recuperating from multiple bypass surgery. He was sympathetic. Lencho was hoping he would be so sympathetic the feds just might let the whole thing slide. The five year statute was drawing ever nearer. If the government didn't get him charged and into the court system, he would be home free. Fat chance of that, however.

"They say they're giving you time to recover, but as soon as you do it's D-day," Tom Connelly told him over the phone. Lencho did some calculations as he lay in bed at home. "If I can drag this thing out until August of 2009, I'm safe. Hot dog, gotta get the docs to postpone my next operation until winter ends. Hope I don't die."

"End of winter?!" Dr. Ingram exclaimed. "Lencho, you're pushing your luck."

"I've always pushed my luck, Doc," the weed man replied. "But the snow is heavy where I live and getting in and out and back and forth will just be too much until the spring. I'll be okay. Can you fax a letter about all this to my lawyer in Phoenix? He'll send it forward to the feds."

"Lencho will have to wait until the spring at the earliest for his surgery due to technical difficulties and time restraints," Dr. Ingram wrote. "We will then do the surgery, and after that recuperation could take up to a year." The note was duly forwarded to Virginia.

On his way to major heart bypass surgery on March 25, Lencho smoked his last joint. "How many fingers am I holding up, Lencho?" the doc asked after surgery. "Eight," he replied. "Where's my wife? Cause I got me a serious woody." The assembled staff laughed, and nurse Tucker patted him on the shoulder gently.

"That's not a woody, Lencho, that's a catheter. You rest now. We'll tell your wife you seem fine."

Down the hall from the hospital room where he was recuperating after four hours of grueling slice and dice, the doctors and nurses were startled to hear the weed man singing loudly from the Waylon song Luckenbach: "The only two things in life that make it worth living—guitars are tuned good and firm feeling women!"

"I smoke pot myself, and even grow a few plants each year legally for medical purposes," nurse Virginia Tucker told him the next day. "So I am sympathetic. But I strongly advise you stop smoking. The smoke in marijuana is too much for your system to metabolize now and the coughing could very well burst sutures. I advise you to eat it from now on." Lencho never smoked weed again, but became a passionate advocate of pot oil capsules.

The weed man felt relatively terrific after the operation. It was never his heart that was the problem, but his arteries. Arteries plugged up with cholesterol, and now that they were once again unplugged, he felt his energies surging. "Let me outta here," he bellowed. "I'm fine. I wanna go home." They made him stay four more days.

Assistant U.S. Attorney Putney was chomping at the bit now. It would have been a devastating humiliation to any upstanding prosecutor to do the right thing and let someone off the hook if they could help it, but the faxes came hot and heavy from the weed man's lawyer and his doctors. "Lencho needs a full year to recover. Anything less may prove fatal!"

At home, Lencho was reading up on the manufacture of hash oil. His favorite of all doctors, Molly Fry, long time breast cancer patient, loved the stuff. Good enough for Molly, good enough for Lencho. You took a piece of two inch diameter PVC and capped it on each end. The upper cap had a small hole drilled so you could shoot butane gas into the tube, which was filled with super stash. The gas liquefied and acted much like heat does in breaking loose the THC. The stuff that ran out the bottom hole into a warm Pyrex dish was an oil. It was golden honey colored and once put into double 'OO' horse capsules was ready to eat. And then it was off to heaven minus the coughing and wheezing of a joint. Of course the dose could be very strong and psychedelic at times. Lencho, being well practiced, ate two at a time, twice a day. The oil being medicine, he felt no pain. More months passed.

"DEA in Tucson is still in no hurry with you," Tom Connelly reported. "Putney in Virginia is another matter."

"Tell them all I lost contact for the moment. But I'm back on it as of now." Now was June 2008. Last year's crop had been a great and profitable one. His inventory was sold and his bank account was flush, so even though he prayed the feds had forgotten about him, he knew they hadn't. When the day came, his wife was set for a few years of his incarceration. The new crop was planted.

Hodi and Luz were at Space Acres working on the new plants, and as usual, they were robust and beautiful. The phenomenon of northern California weed was racing around the world now, and the news was full of articles, stories, and controversy over medical marijuana. In Mexico, there was a new front on the War on Drugs. Mexican President Felipe Calderon had been pressured by the U.S. to ramp up the battle against the cartels. The American powers that be in the Justice Department and the DEA had to continually appear to be fighting the good fight against the evils of marijuana and the addictive drugs. It was part of the illusion being carried forward decade after decade.

The recent body count was now over ten thousand in Mexico and rising. The cartels were butchering politicians who opposed them on the side of another cartel. Policemen died and killed each other. Headless bodies were displayed from bridges and highway overpasses. Bombs exploded and the press was intimidated, kidnapped, and executed. But the pot growers of northern California were unfazed and largely oblivious, although rogue growers from Mexico worked side by side them in the national forests and on public lands. Sometimes threats and even bullets were exchanged up there between them, though it was little reported. Lencho was hoping the '08 crop would be finished up before they took him. Putney finally issued an ultimatum. "Finish up your dealings with the DEA or face immediate arrest. I'm holding Ponytail and Peepers in the can to testify against you. Can't complete our deal with them until you show up, God damnit. Quit milking that fucking heart attack!" But like Meyer Lansky and others before him, Lencho the weed man made the most of that heart condition.

Still, while down in Tucson, Connelly called and informed him: "It's over. Self-surrender or they'll come after ya." Fuck!

On Saturday, September 15, the weed man flew into Norfolk, Virginia and met his younger son Fred at the airport. They checked into a Holiday Inn for two nights. Father and son headed for the beach so the old man could watch his boy surf the choppy Atlantic for a couple hours and then they had a nice dinner. The next night they did the same, only this would be their farewell. On Monday morning they drove to the Federal building downtown and the tired and dispirited old pot smuggler self-surrendered for another go round in the menagerie known as the American Justice System. Breakfast that morning had been one large brownie laced with the equivalent of two fat joints of purple kush. He was very high, but off to face the music. That was a Lencho tradition. LSD in his youth, super pot now. It was the way he rolled. They stopped in the lobby, at the drinking fountain where he popped two pain pills prescribed after his heart surgery and steeled himself for the trip to the fifth floor where the Drug Enforcement Agency was expecting him. SAC Bob Kennedy came out to the lobby and greeted him with a handshake. "Lencho," he said, "I've read your jacket. Heard a lot about you. Take a seat, please, I'll get the warrant. Just formalities from here on." The room swayed. The room began to spin. Beads of sweat formed on the weed man's brow and he felt clammy.

"Are you all right?" Kennedy asked. Fred grabbed his father's left arm while Kennedy grabbed the other and Lencho slowly slid downward. Suddenly, he was staring blankly at the ceiling and moaning. "Maybe we'll hold off on the arrest," he heard Kennedy say. "Bill, call the medics. Lencho may be having a cardiac episode." The weed man lay there, but a slight smile played upon his lips.

He came to at Sentera Cardio Center Emergency Room in the depths of Norfolk. The place was a battle ground. Three gunshot wounds and one stabbing were ahead of him. The head narc had held off on the arrest, so the government didn't have to foot this bill. Bastards. "How many fingers?" Routine once again out of a black orderly. He could barely hear the man over the bedlam all around him. "Dad, dad," Fred was yelling. "Are you all right? Dad!"

The whole episode was not totally what it had appeared. The cagey old weed man had felt weird, but he had become a pretty good actor in the ongoing stage play known as the war on drugs. Since he was feeling woosey anyway, and he was sure his blood pressure was pretty high, why not go with the flow? Worked once, might work again. After tests and a call back to California to check on his insurance, he was admitted and placed in a room upstairs. Thank god, he thought. The cacophony had faded away. Fred called Connica and she called Attorney Connelly.

"Man," Connelly hooted, "that's terrific. He will live, though, won't he? He will? Well, this can't hurt. That crook might still drag this out over the line." Five days later he was released and his cardiologist had been persuaded to write Putney a letter stating Lencho was delicato. Very touchy situation here. Needed to be sent home and be put in the care of his own doctor. While they waited for an answer, Lencho and Fred went for a nice drive to see the sights. The answer came an hour later when a black and white pulled Fred's truck over with lights flashing.

"So long, son," Lencho told him. "I think the jig is up."

When the policeman came to the door, the weed man told him, "I know what you want officer, and I was on my way to turn myself in."

"That won't be necessary, sir," the cop said as he tucked him into the back seat in cuffs.

DEA Agent Tim Becouvarakis came down to the holding cell they had placed him in an hour later. Lencho did not recognize him at first. "Haven't seen you in a while, Tim. We missed ya."

Tim was pretty friendly, actually, and explained Lencho would be taken to Courtroom 7J at one p.m. for the purpose of being indicted formally and to discuss bond. Bond? Bond was something he had not even thought about, especially after Connelly had tut-tutted the possibility months earlier. He got fingerprinted and photographed up the ying yang while he waited, and at noon they gave him a bag lunch with baloney sandwich, two knock-off Oreo cookies, and a soggy carton of lukewarm juice. He was moved again, and shared his meal with five other gentlemen awaiting their time in front of a federal judge. One of them was a skinny black kid not quite thirty named Jaque Folks.

"Jaque?" Lencho asked. "That how you spell it? Sounds french."

"Cajun. You know when you said you was from Arizona just now, I thought I knew that name from someplace. And then it hit me. My cellie over at Tidewater is your fellow defendant. Mark Bush. White boy."

"Get outta here!" Lencho roared.

"Yeah, yeah. He told me all about it. We been in that cell over a month. He says he's real sorry he got you involved. You know the narcs. Scared the shit outta him. He feels sick about what he done."

"I'd like to make the motherfucker feel sick," Lencho groused. "There was absolutely no reason he had to involve me. I did that punk a lot of favors in California. He knows it. He went behind my back and got mixed up in a pile of coke and then rats me out!"

"Well, like I says," Folks replied meekly, "he knows he done wrong and sure would like to make it up to ya. Anything I can do?"

"Yeah," Lencho laughed looking at the others, "you can strangle the little prick for me." The cell roared with machismo merriment.

The court appointed attorney he got was a fat little guy named Steve Wiesbrough. Rumpled and sweaty, he did not instill confidence. Clearly a hack with not enough clients, so he had to beg for scraps from the courthouse table. "We're going to plead you innocent after the judge reads the indictment. Then the issue of bail will be brought up. Just sit tight and let me do the talking."

"So you have pled not guilty," the judge intoned. "Mr. Wiesbrough, do you wish to add anything?"

"Your Honor, I would like to ask that Lencho be released on a surety bond at this time. He flew all the way here from Arizona to self-surrender. He has been free for over two years on this case, and there is no reason to believe he would be a flight risk."

"What about it, Mr. Putney. Does the U.S. Attorney's office have a problem with bond being granted to the defendant?"

"Your Honor," Putney almost shouted, "this man has lived in Costa Rica. He is not without money, although he claims to be destitute. His record as a marijuana importer, grower, and dealer is very long. Yes, we believe him to be a flight risk and ask that bail be denied."

Lencho glowered at the man in astonishment. He had been in touch with him faithfully all this time, had assisted them (or at least acted like he had assisted them), and now here he was trying to hump him on bond.

"You know, Mr. Putney, as I look over all this, I get the feeling your case is not a strong one. This has been ongoing for a long time, right down to the wire. I am not convinced he does not deserve bond. What does probation have to say?"

A petite woman named Candice Meese who was sitting beside the prosecutor spoke up. "We have talked to his wife, Your Honor. She apparently has some collateral for the surety bond. We have no objection."

"Hmmmm," the judge said. "Well, I need some time to consider the request. What's my calendar, Mr. Smith?" He said to the bailiff.

"You're clear Friday afternoon, Judge, at three p.m."

"Fine. We'll continue this until Friday afternoon. I'm inclined to grant bail, if his wife can produce the necessary equity. See everyone then."

The weed man was elated as he was cuffed and led back to the Tidewater Regional Jail, a private edifice to the glory of law enforcement owned by three local Judges. Connica was in touch with the probation department arranging things on her end. She was elated her man would be coming home for what would certainly be the better part of a year. He needed a safe environment in which to heal from his recent surgery and away from the tension he was involved in. On the following Friday, they drove him in chains to his hearing around, noon and at three p.m. he once again stood before the judge.

"I have decided to grant you bond, sir. I'm going along with probation, and sorry Mr. Putney, I am not persuaded the defendant is a flight risk."

"I'm sorry to interrupt, judge," Bailiff Smith chimed in, "But there's a problem. We don't have time at this late hour on Friday to finish the paperwork on this. I think it will be Monday at the soonest we can conclude things."

"Oh my," the judge said, "I am sorry, Sir. Well, I guess then you will have to spend another weekend as guest of the federal government. I trust your accommodations are not too uncomfortable. Please return the defendant to this courtroom at eight a.m. to finish this matter up."

"Thank you, Your Honor. I understand, and don't mind. See you then," Lencho said.

It was unfortunate, but the weed man really couldn't bitch. He would survive one more weekend as a guest of the federal government. Then it would be back to home and hearth, just in time to help harvest the current crop of seventy two towering plants. He was placed this time in the hole at Western Tidewater, alone in a cell where the staff could monitor him because they had decided to administer a new round of pain medications related to his condition. Pill call was three times a day, the first being at three a.m.

But now he was incommunicado, since there were no phone privileges in the hole. He couldn't talk to Connica and keep abreast of the situation as he always liked to do. Sunday night the guards moved him back into the population in Pod A.

Western Tidewater Regional Jail was a nine hundred man, private facility. Big and fairly new, it was divided into numerous units all monitored via zoom cameras, audio boxes, and loudspeakers. Doors clanged open and shut remotely. Guards directed the inmates via walkie talkies. Lencho was placed in a double deck unit with twenty men topside and twenty at the bottom. A staircase separated the two. At three a.m., the pill call lady showed up and administered Vicodin and soma, a combination that was essentially hillbilly heroin. He fell into a stupor until five a.m. when the squawk box bellowed, "Lencho, time for court."

Startled awake in his upper bunk, he dropped clumsily to the floor in a daze and stumbled into his jumpsuit. Then he fell down the stairway doing one somersault and landing with a thud at the bottom.

"Man down, man down!" went a chorus from his fellow prisoners. The heavy steel door clanked open and guards with a stretcher marched in. They loaded him up and transported him to the hospital.

"You're pretty much okay," the doctor announced after looking him over. "Some bruising on the back, a bump on the head, but no trauma. No sign of concussion. Your biggest trouble is you missed court." Groan!

The new date was the following Wednesday and when he finally sat down in front of his lawyer, the sweaty fat man looked into his face with a grimace and demanded to know why he had threatened to commit murder.

"What are you talking about?" Lencho demanded. "Murder? Murder who?"

"The prosecutor has new information that you attempted to hire a hit man and kill the witnesses against you, Mr. Bush and Mr. Roberts. He will produce him in the courtroom in a few minutes. I gotta tell you, this is bad. There goes your bond and the government will have an additional witness against you on your case. A weak case just got a bit stronger, looks to me."

"Why in god's name would I try and hire a killer when I been out for two and a half years, and if I wanted to kill anyone, coulda done it then?" Attorney Wiesbrough just shrugged.

The weed man got his answer when he and his attorney entered the courtroom. In a seat next to the prosecutor and probation sat a skinny black man, the cajun Jaque Folks. He had a big grin on his face when he saw Lencho glaring at him.

"Your Honor," Assistant U.S. Attorney Putney began gravely. "It has come to the attention of the government that the defendant has made serious threats against the two witnesses against him in this case, Mr. Bush and Mr. Roberts. We allege, in fact, he attempted to hire a person to kill them. In light of this new evidence, we would ask that the bond issue be rescinded. This is a dangerous man."

The judge looked at Lencho over glasses perched on his nose. "Continue," he said.

Jaque Folks was sworn in and began his testimony.

"I was in a holding cell last week with Lencho. I was waiting to see my attorney. So, I says to him that my cellie back in jail is Mark Bush, and that I had heard all about his case from Bush. So, I says how sorry Bush is that Lencho got in hot water, and Lencho just laughed with scorn and hate all over his face and he says to me, 'I'll pay you ten thousand dollars if you kill de motherfucker!' Boy, was I shocked. And then he also says he give me ten thousand more if I kills the other white boy, Roberts. See, Lencho was real mad they told de truth about all that cocaine. The pot wasn't so bad, but he was real pissed off about the coke."

"What exactly did he tell you about the cocaine?" Putney asked.

"He told me he didn't make 'nuff money off that coke to be put to such trouble. That the white boys cheated him or somethin'. I guess Lencho is just real greedy."

It was fortunate the weed man was sitting down, because after that he would have fallen down. It was a stunning act of deceit from a punk snitch who was facing life for his seventh drug conviction. On cross exam, Attorney Steve Wiesbrough asked all of two questions.

"Mr. Folks, what makes you say my client was involved in the cocaine part of the case?"

"Cause he referred to his Mexican Amigos several times on de subject. When a man calls Mexicans amigo, dat mean dey tight."

"What did you do after my client told you all this, and why?"

"I went straight away to my DEA agent and told him. Couldn't let nothing happen to my cellie. And so's I get me some credit 'gainst my sentence."

"That's all, Your Honor," and fat boy sat down.

The judge shuffled some papers and looked once again at the weed man.

"Firstly, Sir, there is the issue of your stumbling down the stairs the other day at the jail. Let's have a look at the security footage. I have some thoughts on this."

The lights dimmed and video came up on a large television set on a table where all could see clearly. There he was all right, nearly falling out of his bunk, fumbling into his clothes, and then three long steps over to the stairs where he fell head over heels to the next level. What was the problem? His head still hurt a little.

"That looks fake to me," the judge said. "That was a pratfall, was it not Lencho?"

His lawyer said nothing, so the weed man took the initiative. "Your Honor, they over medicated me. I was stoned silly and almost killed myself on those steps. That was not a fake or a pratfall!"

"Well," the judge went on, "we have addressed the issue here in open court. I doubt now you will have much success in suing the institution claiming they over medicated you. Course you can if you want to try. Now regarding bond, I'm denying it. I was inclined to grant it the other day, Sir, but after listening to this disturbing testimony from Mr. Folks, I have changed my mind. I don't know if additional charges will be brought for soliciting a murder. I think perhaps they should be, but that's up to the prosecutor. You are remanded back to Tidewater Regional Jail until your next appearance. That will be on December 12. Court dismissed."

In the federal system, to go to trial is the kiss of death. It is simply de facto. Go to trial, you will lose and then get double, triple the sentence. Lencho pled guilty as charged in December and sentencing was scheduled for March 16, 2009. His two former associates and now informers against him, Mark Bush and James Roberts, had been already sentenced to one hundred and forty months each. But because of the American Justice System, they are now both free. It all fell on the old hippy with the big, but weak, heart.

The time spent at Tidewater Regional was dull. There was marijuana available as there is in all prisons and jails (especially private ones), but he couldn't and wouldn't smoke anymore. He made friends, especially with the Hispanics because he spoke passable español, and also with a young white guy named Wesly Allen. A man with an addictive personality, he was a methamphetamine addict who had come from a good and prosperous southern family. Lencho liked him and felt badly for him because he reminded him so much of his own son, Luz. Same age, handsome, hooked on speed. Wesly did him a great favor when he hooked Lencho's wife, Connica, up with his mom.

The faithful Connica flew all the way to Virginia several times to visit her man for all of fifteen minutes. It was killingly expensive and very depressing. Mrs. Gail Allen, a sweet, talkative lady, and her husband Neil took to Connica at once and opened up the top level of their sprawling antebellum home on three hundred acres on the outskirts of Suffolk to her for when she would fly down. The house was beyond spacious and furnished in southern antiques. They hooked up a telephone, installed a television, and gave her a key. It was with great sorrow Lencho learned a couple of years later, young Wesly, their only son, was killed in an auto wreck, wrapped around a tree on a lonely southern road.

So Connica would visit once or twice a month, and the weed man went through all the federal paperwork mumbo jumbo the bureaucracy so loves, such as the Pre-Sentencing Investigation wherein everything you ever did, all the dope you ever took, all friends and relatives and your relationship to them is compiled. It is very useful at your PSI interview with the Probation Department to accent your drug usage because that plays into getting accepted at the Residential Drug Abuse Program (RDAP) toward the end of your stay in prison. Everyone wants RDAP because it means a year off if you can run the hurdles, jump through the hoops, and grovel adequately. Attorney Tom Connelly flew down to make sure.

Then one day it happened again. This time would be the last as far as he was concerned. Rising from his bunk just before dinner, he went dizzy and clammy. He lost the feeling in his fingers and felt pains in his chest. Along with the depression he was feeling about his situation, and this being about the eighth attack, he decided then and there he would just let nature take its course. He would not push the panic button by the intercom. He would quietly die. Better call the wife and say goodbye. Tell her what a fine woman and partner she was. Tell her how much she had meant to him. When she answered in faraway California he just said, "Baby, I love you. Just called to say goodbye." His own voice sounded so far away to him. He slumped to his knees. The other inmates just figured he was trying to get comfortable if they noticed at all. After he got it across to Connica he was checking out, she demanded to speak to another inmate. Any other inmate. The weed man was puzzled, but was in no condition to argue. "Hey, shorty," he said to a small black man sitting at a table nearby, "mind talking to my wife? She has something she wants to tell you."

Shorty was confused as to why a white man would let him talk to his wife, or why the white man's wife wanted to talk to him for that matter, but he did as asked. "For god's sake," Connica yelled into the mouthpiece, "my husband's having a heart attack. Push the panic button!" As Lencho sunk to the floor again the guards came running.

"Not again, Lencho," they said pushing the gurney to sickbay. "I just wanna die. Leave me in peace," he moaned. Once again, he didn't die.

"The problem here, Lencho," Dr. Sullens told him, "is here. Literally, here. This is a poor environment for a man with your history of cardiology. You need a proper environment to heal. Good food, exercise, monitoring. This ain't the place, son." He went back to jail in the same condition knowing another episode was bound to follow. All pleas to Putney, Judge Davis, and God himself fell upon deaf ears. Once in the belly of the beast, one stays there until regurgitated out or carried away in a box.

His best pal there was a Mexican lad named Ceaser who was born and raised in Apatzingan, a region of Michocan, Mexico. Lencho knew the area well having done much business there decades earlier. They talked about weed prices and methamphetamine, which was the big money product from the area now manufactured and smuggled into the U.S. by the notorious cartel La Familia. He was amazed the prices of commercial marijuana were identical on the east coast of the U.S. as the west. It was clear to him the drug trade had become totally vertical over the decades since his youth. It was truly from 'the farm to the arm' now, and the days of the gringo independents were pretty much a thing of the past. You worked with the cartels or you didn't work at all. The cartels ran things totally now.

Then there was the sinister Noe Robles from Honduras. The killer.

"He's the angel de muerte, Lencho. Angel of death they say. A man that has killed hundreds. Guns, knives, his bare hands. Very dangerous," Ceaser whispered as they watched him standing at the mirror in front of everyone shaving every last hair from his short, stocky body. Bald head, chest, arms, legs. "He got no hairs on his balls, either," Ceaser went on. "I seen him in the shower. Very strange."

Noe Robles was forty years old and a product of the political strife and violence of his native land. As with all of Latin America, the CIA had been active and Noe was a man who sold his services to either the right or the left. Whoever would pay him. He was a member in good standing with the dreaded MS-13. To him, killing was fun. As the days dragged on at Western Tidewater, the killer with ice in his veins warmed to the weed man and began talking openly of his trade as an assassin. What especially interested him was the story of Ponytail and Peepers, the rats who were sending Lencho to jail for the next eight years. "You want them dead, amigo?" He hissed one day as they sat in front of the TV.

"Dead?" Lencho whispered back. "I had not thought of that," he lied. "What would that cost?"

"One hundred twenty thousand dollars. Five thousand dollars down, so we can buy a tool. A photograph and any information you may have such as names and addresses of their relatives. I will send this out to my son-in-law, and he will buy a high powered rifle with a scope and make all the arrangements. They can't keep me in here much longer. I got charged on a weapons beef, but it ain't nothing. They'll deport me pretty soon and I'll be back with a new identity within a month. Then will snuff the ratas. Are you interested?"

Further discussion in hushed tones yielded more data from this psychotic character. "I like blood. I feast on it," he said once when he cut himself shaving an ambient hair he found sprouting on his chest. He licked the burgundy drop from a sinuous finger. The guy gave Lencho serious creeps. "I personally killed six people in this country. One of them was a cop," he bragged another time.

"A cop?!" Lencho choked. "My god, man. Killing a cop is the kiss of death in America. All the other cops go ape shit over something like that."

"I smiled into his dying eyes just before I cut his fucking throat," Noe laughed. The wheels were turning in Lencho's head now. He had played games with the feds for almost three years giving them bullshit data and fake tunnels. It had resulted in a promise of forty months off for valuable cooperation. What would they give him for a cop killer? This wasn't a pretty picture, but the weed man had learned how the game was played. There was no alternative but to play it this way. Give the cops more data still or do the time—a long, long time. And it wasn't hard justifying this concept when it came to a man like Noe Robles, a sick and remorseless murderer. A man so vicious and calculating he would even kill an American policeman. He decided to see if the FBI might be interested.

"They're interested," his attorney Steve Wiesbrough told him breathlessly. "A couple agents will be here to debrief you tomorrow."

Special Agent John Sinclair and his partner Richard Warren opened a file folder on the table between themselves and Lencho. "Noe Robles is a very wanted man," Sinclair began. "Our data is largely gleaned from federal and state intelligence as well as Interpol. This is what we have on him. Suspected of involvement in the San Pedro Sula Honduras massacre of 23 December, 2004 in which 27 civilians were killed, many women and children. Suspected involvement in Battalion 316, a right wing death squad active throughout the 1980s, responsible for the deaths of teachers, leftist politicians, and union bosses. Suspect in fifteen murders in the United States in Arizona, California, Texas, and Kentucky. Member of the street gang MS-13. No hard evidence tying him to these killings, hence he has always been held but released. Just like now. He's in here for possession of a .380 which had been stolen. Like he told you, though, he'll be convicted and then deported. We know he'll be back shortly. How can we nail this monster?"

"First of all, I want immediate release and all charges dropped."

"If this is a success, you got it," Agent Warren answered.

"I'll set this up with Noe, then. He says he'll send a letter to his son-in-law on the outside. They don't check outgoing mail in here. You guys intercept the letter as proof, cause in it he'll tell the boy to buy a gun for the killings and to meet with my wife who'll give him photos and addresses for the hit. She'll give him ten thousand in cash as a down payment. Do you have a female agent that will fill the bill? Good. Then that should prove conspiracy, right? Get it all on video and tape and it's a done deal." The FBI was back the next day to confirm.

"We're ready on our end, Lencho," they told him. "Have him send the letter."

Noe Robles wrote the letter and mailed it out to his son-in-law. The FBI intercepted it and the race was on. Robles, the legendary killer, had stepped into a snare.

"Man," Attorney Wiesbrough enthused through visitor's glass, "you're the star, now. The feds are beside themselves with excitement on this. To bring down a bad guy this epic is a real big deal. We're all proud of you." But not everyone was so proud. The DEA was definitely not proud nor happy.

"You old cocksucker!" DEA agent Becouvarakis screamed a week later. "What the fuck are you trying to do here?"

The outburst stunned the weed man. He had been summoned from the pod to the conference room in the expectation of additional debriefing for a worthy cause. Instead he was being cursed.

"What are you talking about?" He stammered.

"I'm talking about this," Tim thundered, throwing down a photo of Noe Robles on the table in front of him. He recognized it as the same picture contained in the Interpol file.

"I'm working with the FBI on this guy. He's a ruthless killer. Killed hundreds of women and children, and an American cop for god's sake."

"Lencho, I don't care if he killed JFK. You are out of your league on this, you never asked DEA. You never asked me."

"I didn't know I had to ask DEA," he shot back.

"Well, you do. You gotta go through us for everything. You can't take a shit without asking, my friend. And you go to the fucking FBI? Famous, But Inept!"

"Whoa, whoa paco," Lencho said raising his hands to the heavens. "What's this all about? I been assisting you guys for two years. Why can't I assist the FBI? This is supposed to be about America. This is supposed to be a service to our country. You federal agencies are supposed to work together, but it sounds to me like a competition. Nobody owns this old man, not you or anybody!"

"That's where you're wrong, buddy boy. You think we don't know what you're up to? What you been up to all along for that last two years? You're a liar! You been feeding us bullshit, stringing us along. You gave us nothing. What else have you been lying about? You make this shit up about this beaner, Robles?

"Man, this guy's a killer. His record is hideous, I saw it. Worldwide murder. They want him bad."

"Well, they ain't gonna get him. You ain't buying your way outta this rap any longer. You're going down. You're going to jail. We been gunning for you for years."

"Oh, I see," he replied. "DEA still got a hard on over the Wayne Boyd case. That scumbag was a killer, too. A fed killer and you're still defending him. You guys are sick."

"'Us boys are in charge, Lencho," the narc said standing up. He glowered at the weed man and began to pace. "The others ain't shit," he snarled. "FBI, Secret Service, Customs, ATF. Ain't shit. These days it's DEA and CIA, kings of the hill. Pretty soon, it'll be just DEA."

"So, it is a competition," Lencho gasped. "I been in this game a long time. The first time a narc ripped me off, Tim, you weren't even born. I knew a customs man years ago that told me you DEA are just thieves and punks. You'd be gone in a few more years, put out to pasture by Congress. Guess he was wrong."

"Guess so, little man. The way the world is today, it's terrorism and dope. It's the spooks that get the glory and move over CIA. DEA is international and the terrorists have become narco-terrorists. And we're the narcs. America can't live without us. DEA gets the busts. DEA gets the ink in the news. DEA gets the money."

"Well, you ain't lying there," Lencho whistled. "I bet you're a millionaire yourself, ain't ya, Tim? Drive around in the big fancy cars you confiscate. Eat at the best restaurants. Fuck the prettiest girls. Oh, you're a credit to democracy, all right."

"Shut the fuck up. You're going down. I'm going straight to the prosecutor and the judge and we're gonna charge you with additional crimes. Soliciting murder for starters. You'll never see the light of day. And you will not get leniency on this Noe guy. Fuck you and the horse you rode in on if you think you will." The door slammed and the weed man sat there for a moment before he was led out. He was stunned, yet he was not surprised. He knew there would be no additional charges, because even though DEA was very powerful, they hid under a rock. If there were charges there would be word of how they squelched the takedown of a psychopathic cop killer just to get their pound of flesh out of him for pissing them off over the years. For beating them at their own game. But he knew Tim was right about this Noe guy. He'd be free to kill again. He went back to Tidewater with a heavy heart and never heard squat from the FBI again.

Chapter Twenty

"Will the Wolf Survive"
Released 1985
Waylon Jennings

Through the chill of winter
Running across a frozen lake
Hunters' hard right on his trail
All odds are against him
With a family to provide for
But one thing he must keep alive
Will the wolf survive?
Will the wolf survive?

CAMPING

At 4 a.m., the guard at Tidewater Regional Jail bellowed over the squawk box, "Lencho, get ready for court." He staggered to his feet and clamored into his jumpsuit. Another sentencing day had come in his long history of breaking the marijuana laws of the country. Two and a half years of machinations, maneuvers, and bullshit had come down to this day. He gobbled down his breakfast of grits, corn flakes, a bitter apple, and two cartons of skim milk and was led to the van waiting outside. Once shackled he was whisked downtown through the grim morning fog of Norfolk and placed in a holding cell to await his 1 p.m. appointment with Judge Davis.

"Your attorney is here to see you," a federal marshal told him. "This way."

"How you holding up, Chief?" Connelly asked through the thick screen that separated them in the lawyer's conference room.

"I feel crappy," the weed man replied. "This old heart will conk out yet. I hope they'll be happy when it does."

"I'll mention that to the judge," Connelly answered. "So Connica is here and we're all set to go. Now, don't go off on the judge if he says something you don't like. It won't help."

"Oh, you mean if I tell him how pitiful it is that the DEA lets cop killers and ruthless assassins go free to kill again when they coulda stopped it?"

"Exactly," Connelly said. "That's water under the bridge. Nothing we can do about that."

"So what's your guess as to what I'll get?"

"I think maybe no more than thirty six months. Can you live with that?"

"I guess I'll have to," the weed man said.

"On the other hand, you gotta be prepared for the worst. He could do an upward departure from the guidelines and give you twelve years. The guideline is 120 to 144 months. So there's no telling."

"Jeeeze," he whispered.

Connelly stood up, all six foot six, two hundred seventy pounds in his exquisite Brooks Brothers suit, and ran a hand through stately gray attorney hair. "See ya out there," he smiled. "I got a little speech prepared for the benefit of the court. I think you'll like it."

He was allowed to wear civilian clothes Connica had brought along, and after changing into them, was led down the long corridor, shuffling from the ankle bracelets and chains they had reattached. Then they were removed again and he was led in promptly at 1 p.m.

He smiled at his wife sitting in the front row of the visitors section. He couldn't wave or acknowledge her presence beyond that for fear of reprisals. In a sonorous voice, the bailiff called out, "All rise", and the judge made an imperious entrance.

"Please be seated," he instructed.

Judge Davis began the proceedings by explaining the government and the defendant had reached an agreement. A guilty plea had been proffered and accepted by both sides. There would be no trial, the weed man had admitted he was guilty as sin to the charge of conspiring to import a couple tons of marijuana and a couple dozen kilos of cocaine. Lencho winced when he heard the words.

The judge went over the PSI that had been prepared by Probation noting his long usage of marijuana, cocaine, and alcohol. "You are being recommended for the Residential Drug Abuse Program at an institution of the Bureau of Prisons," he said. "The plea you have agreed to carries a minimum sentence of 120 months, considering the dollar value of the drugs imported was ten million dollars. Do you have any witnesses to examine, Mr. Wiesbrough, before sentence is handed down?"

A thoroughly obsequious Wiesbrough grinned foolishly as he welcomed the great man to Virginia.

"Your Honor, this must be the first time I have had the pleasure of cross examining such an august figure of the American Bar as Mr. Connelly. He is a former Assistant U.S. Attorney and now a prominent attorney in private practice out of Arizona. Good morning to you, counselor."

"Good morning," Connelly replied. The bailiff asked him to raise his right hand and swear on the bible they produced to tell the truth and nothing but the truth. He did swear and proceeded to lay it on pretty thick, as far as Lencho was concerned.

"How long have you known the defendant?"

"I first met Lencho in 1987 when I was Assistant U.S. Attorney out of Phoenix, so that makes over twenty years."

"In what capacity was he before you then?"

"He had been arrested on charges of marijuana smuggling, but the government's main interest in him regarded a matter of great internal security which we were hoping he would assist us with."

"Can you tell the court about that matter?"

"I'm sorry, but that is still a classified matter. Of course, I can brief his honor on this in chambers, but it would be inadvisable to put it on the record."

"I see. I can infer, then, that it was of considerable importance to national security?"

"Oh, yes. It was matter of great national importance. Lencho did assist the government to the best of his ability and it was very valuable. As a result, charges against him were all but dropped."

"Wonderful. And tell us, sir, who is this man Lencho? This legendary pot smuggler and dealer, a man reputed to have been in the drug trade for most of his life, for over forty years?"

"Lencho is a paradox, I think. A man that does not see his vocation as a crime, but more a calling. He has told me many times from the day I met him that marijuana is medicine, not dope. Marijuana is a sacred herb, not a crutch. Marijuana is an alternative to alcohol, not a habit. I have come to believe that Lencho is sincere when he says these things and that he believes that it is only a matter of time before his 'sacred weed' becomes a legal commodity across the land.

"This man was brought up on a conspiracy charge," he continued. "There is an old layman's saying that goes, 'when they can't get you on anything else they charge you with conspiracy.' And the conspiracy was to also sell cocaine. Knowing Lencho for as long as I have, and knowing his aversion to the cocaine trade, I at first urged him to fight these charges. He is not a cocaine dealer and in fact is insulted by the accusation. But as I contemplated the nature of conspiracy charges and the fact that he was assisting the government to the best of his ability, telling the total truth to the DEA, I changed my mind. Your Honor, if this case was strictly a marijuana case, as it should be, the federal government would not have involved itself. It would have been left to the State of Arizona. So, Your Honor, if this is true, how does it and how should it affect your judgment here today as Lencho stands before you for sentencing under the federal guidelines? I think the court should consider the arc of history in this matter. Consider that all things pass, and as in the case of liquor prohibition of the nineteen twenties and early thirties, when the gavel of the will of the people came down upon the lectern of fate, all previous cases of involvement in that once illegal trade were moot. So too here. Legality is just around the corner, now, and to send Lencho to prison for a long term will serve no purpose, and in fact be meaningless."

"What kind of family man is Lencho?" Wiesbrough continued.

"I have had the pleasure of meeting his entire family. His wife is a wonderful woman, sitting today in this courtroom. His children are all fine upstanding members of the community, none involved in criminal pursuits. His mother has passed on to her reward, but his father is a pillar in his old age and has always been supportive of his son. He comes from a large family, eleven brothers and sisters, all of whom but one are still living, and they all love and support him. He has been in touch with me for all the years I have known him and there has never been a Christmas that I and my wife have not received a card. Not one birthday of mine that I have not received a long letter from him enumerating his civic efforts along with his best wishes. He is a true and loyal person. If the court were to show lenience, I would not hesitate to take him into my own home for supervision and I say that with conviction. That's the kind of man

Lencho is in my view."

Lencho about choked.

Tom Connelly stepped down and returned to his position beside the defendant and his court appointed attorney at the lectern in front of the judge. A nice looking woman tapped efficiently away on her stenography machine in between. The judge shuffled some papers and said, "Does the defendant wish to add anything? Do you have anything you would like to say, Lencho, before I pass sentence?" Both attorneys cast sideways glances at their client, and Connelly actually reached over and gave the weed man a sharp pinch on the thigh, a clear warning to keep his yap shut.

"Yes, Your Honor," Lencho replied. "I do have some remarks, if I may address the court."

"Proceed, Sir," the judge replied.

"As Mr. Connelly so eloquently attested, I agree that I am a good citizen. I have always been a good citizen with no malice directed at anyone. I am somewhat renowned for my line of work, apparently, but that is because I do consider it a calling. Marijuana began to become very popular decades ago during the turmoil of the counterculture. Before that time, it was virtually unknown to the main body of the public. If you review the congressional testimony of Harry Anslinger who was the chief of the Bureau of Narcotics during the 1930s, you will note he spoke of 'jazz musicians, Negroes, Mexicans, and Filipinos being the main users of what he called 'demon weed.' He also was worried that white women would fall victim to the influences of marijuana if they were in contact with those just mentioned and might even 'tap their feet' to the beat of jazz music. He said he saw this happen in bars he frequented while doing research on the banishment of marijuana in America. Now, isn't that a trifle ridiculous? Isn't that racist? Isn't that just plain stupid? Isn't that a lie? Many think it is and I certainly do."

"I won't deny it, Your Honor. I started to tap my own feet to the music of change back in the sixties, and I'm still tapping. I tried pot and I liked it. As Ginsberg said, 'pot is fun,' and that's about all it is. And millions of young people discovered that it was fun and millions continue to discover that to this day. Now millions are re-discovering that marijuana is a medicine, and its legal use is expanding to one state after the other. Once all the states allow it for medical purposes, it is only a matter of time before the federal government falls in line and the evil that Harry Anslinger accomplished in 1937 will be cast aside. We have been waiting for that day a long time. I have been waiting all my adult life and I don't deny I ignored the strictures against obtaining marijuana and provided it for those that wanted to use it. I have seen my share of grief as a result. The day will one day come when it is legal, so I marched to my own drum and got into airplane wrecks, boats that almost sank, Mexican jails where life was very cheap, and once into a car trunk on the orders of government agents. Oh, sorry about that one, Your Honor. That isn't supposed to be in the public record! But my point is that I am a weed man. Weed is a product like no other. We will never see bank robbery legalized. We will never see murder made legal or the over the counter sales of the atomic bomb or a million other restricted items or deeds. But we will see legal pot one day and that day is near, so I never stopped providing it. But in the meantime the federal government has never stopped pursuing me for doing it. I have been bluntly threatened by federal agents that they are out to get me and apparently they have finally succeeded. Even though I am involved in the marijuana industry on a legal basis, I still find myself standing before you about to go back to jail.

"I will not comment on the charges. They are well established. I will only say that the whole marijuana phenomenon is surreal and absurd. The people know it should not be illegal, but the government is determined to thwart the will of the people and keep it so. I ask you to show wisdom and shine a light on this fog of bullshit that envelops America. Strike a blow for common sense and what is right and give me a downward departure on this sentence because that is the right thing to do. Thank you."

There was silence for some moments while everyone contemplated the weed man's soliloquy as well as the use of the expletive 'bullshit' that just went into the public record. Then Judge Davis spoke.

"Very eloquent, Sir," he began. "I would applaud if we were in a theater. I have before me a very large pile of pro Lencho letters from all walks of life in the Prescott area and beyond. Very impressive stuff and I have read every one. Here's one from the local YMCA expressing their thanks for your past efforts at fundraising. Another from the mayor. Here's one from a drug and alcohol rehabilitation center. This is from Judge Blake, who has known you for years. Letters from business people and music luminaries down in Nashville. Very impressive indeed. I can't remember in my many years as a judge reading so many. I come away, Lencho, with the considered opinion you are a paradox and after listening to the honorable barristers testimony, I am truly puzzled."

"For you see, Sir, I must uphold the law. The law is what it is and that is immutable. Not changeable. At least not until it is changed—the laws regulating marijuana must ultimately be changed at the federal level. History has shown that the federal government trumps the states. And regardless that marijuana may or may not be quasi-legal in California or Colorado, or that medical marijuana may or may not become legal even here in Virginia, cocaine is definitely illegal and no doubt shall remain so in all the fifty states of the union. This is fact. Federal fact. The law says you have broken federal statutes, you have admitted to that, like it or not, and I must sentence you as such.

"But as I said, you seem to me to be almost schizophrenic in your lifestyle.

All those testimonials indicate you are held in high esteem while at the same time you have spent your life, over forty years, breaking the law of the land. You say it is a moral issue; that you have always sought the moral high ground, and that may be so. There have been many in America who have even laid down their lives in the pursuit of their convictions, and I believe you may be one of those who would do so. I do not believe at this point—you are 60 years old?—no, I don't think you will ever change your point of view. Fine. I do applaud you for your convictions. However, as I have just said, we are all dealing with an immutable law that even though may be in transition has not transitioned, yet. Under the guidelines and considering your guilty plea, you should consider yourself very lucky you are standing before this court without a RICO (Racketeer Influence and Corrupt Organization) charge or CCE (Continuing Criminal Enterprise) hanging over your head. Your criminal history is atrocious, Lencho. You dodged a bullet to the tune of seventy-five years previously, and the government could very well send you to jail for the remainder of your life today. However, that is not going to happen. The prosecutor has urged you be given a thirty percent reduction on the guideline of 120 to 144 months. I am not going to give you that long a sentence, but instead a term of eighty months. I will recommend you serve this time at the Federal Prison Camp in Herlong, California where you will be able to visit your wife and children. It is a medical facility where they have excellent medical staff for your heart condition. The Residential Drug Abuse Program, also. I will conclude these remarks by saying that you do remind me of one of those political dissidents we read about in China. You know the sort that challenge endlessly the government over their rights and then inevitably end up serving time in a reorientation camp of some sort. I am not saying I applaud your attitude, Sir, but I do grudgingly admire it for whatever good it ultimately does. Also, let me put into the record that my hands are tied as are all federal judges with regard to sentencing. I couldn't give you a downward departure if I wanted to. That is what the guidelines are all about. Perhaps they too will change, but they have not, yet. Good luck to you, Sir. Court is adjourned."

Two weeks later, Lencho and a group of others left Tidewater Jail on a bus to spend four weeks at the Great Neck Regional facility in Richmond, Virginia. It was the old federal two step again. The guests of Uncle Sam are given a sightseeing tour of a good many lockups around the country as they wind their way to their ultimate destination. They left ground transport when they arrived at the giant inmate staging facility of Con Air in Harrisburg. The weed man was agog at the sight as he counted thirty vans that could hold nine, twelve buses that held forty, ten cars and a hundred U.S. Marshals, all armed with nine millimeter sidearms and several with shotguns at the ready. A fleet of 727s and L1011s, and one Learjet, sat on the tarmac. After one government passenger liner offloaded its 175 inmates (several of whom were women), it was his turn to board and be on his way. After hours of stop and go he and the others in his group climbed quickly into the clouds and headed for Atlanta, Georgia, manacled from head to foot all the way. Stopping there to offload and pick up new prisoners, they winged towards the really huge and bustling Oklahoma routing center, El Reno, outside Oklahoma City. Just like at LAX, an accordion gateway rolled to the plane's door and all the men cumbersomely disembarked into a long hallway that led into the bowels of the facility. After an all day effort, everyone was tired and even though they had been fed a sack lunch earlier, very hungry.

Years previously, Lencho had flown Con Air from Oakland when he was finally nabbed as a fugitive. But since then the federal government had greatly expanded their operations. Then it had been big; now it was huge. The war on drugs had certainly created infrastructure and job opportunity for a lot of people. It was also an equal opportunity employer as the staff from one end to the other in this vast bureaucracy were both men and women. The pay was good, starting at forty thousand dollars a year on the low end. God only knew what these air marshals were making.

At Oklahoma City, he and the others were rushed through one line after another. First to get changed out of the jail clothes they had arrived in to light Oklahoma gray. Then a medical checkup, photograph, chow, and finally to some guy who looked everyone up on his computer and confirmed their final destination.

"Lencho," he mumbled searching his database. "Let's see Yeah, you're going to Lompoc Federal Prison Camp."

"The judge said I was going to Herlong, but I guess that didn't mean anything."

"No worries bud. I hear Lompoc is truly lovely," the guard laughed. "Next!"

The quarters, like the food at Oklahoma, were pretty good, especially compared to a year or so in various jails. The bunks were warm and comfortable, but it didn't last long. On the second morning there he heard his name boom out on the intercom. "Lencho, door five." It was time to go to Lompoc.

He recognized some of the guys he had flown in with, but others were long gone. Everyone was being shipped hither and yon in the vast federal prison system that was the land of the free's pride and joy. He found himself lined up, once again shackled along benches in the same corridor he had disembarked from two days earlier. A guard with a clipboard called out names and the one hundred seventy-five men about to board their continuing journey west obediently complied. Feeling weary and ragged, he looked around at the hustle and bustle wondering just how much all this cost. The old guy behind him with the goatee and long grey hair seemed just as bemused. "This must cost a fuck of a lot of money," he said to Lencho.

"Man, I guess," he replied.

"What's your beef?" The old hippie asked. "I'm a weed guy."

"Oh yeah? Me too. Weed. Been a weed man for a very long time. Lencho's the name."

"It's a pleasure, Lencho. I'm Kelley. Mike Kelley."

The bewildered always seek company. It's reassuring in a disorienting world, and prisoners on the march are always disoriented. The two men were near the same age, Lencho now sixty-one and Kelley sixty-three, sat next to each other the entire journey. It took two more days.

From Oklahoma the plane flew across the Texas panhandle into New Mexico and from there into Arizona. As he looked down on the badlands below, all bleached oranges and browns, dry lakes and arroyos, the weed man pointed out spots he recognized and had landed many times before in pot laden aircraft. "That's where Doc and I stopped to refuel," he would say. "Yeah, I think that's the spot. Nothing but rattlesnakes and brimstone down there in the summer. They call that pile of boulders 'the cemetery' because so many were buried there over the years. Mexicans, Americans, Indians. A lot of history."

Kelley would ask, "Did you ever know anybody up in Berkeley?"

"Does a bear shit in the woods?" he replied. "The whole Bay Area beckons to me from the mists of time. I live up in Butte County, but I come from all over." And the more Kelley listened to the endless stories, the more he believed this old bird was on the level. Kelley was a listener and student of all things. The history of the counterculture and the drug trade, of which he himself had been a long participant, were near and dear. Somewhere around Victorville, Lencho told him about being tossed into the trunk of a Mexican police car by American DEA agents, robbed of a fortune, and almost murdered. Kelley knew then he had met a man who had been a witness to history.

The Con Air flight landed on the perimeter of the federal prison at Victorville. The area is high desert and bleak, the prison the same. The group would be separated as to directions, and the twenty or so men headed for the coastal city of Lompoc would spend the night there before boarding a bus for the final leg. Everyone looked forward to settling in at the Camp because after spending a year or two confined in county or contract jails, locked down for twenty-three hours a day in two man cells with open toilets and obscenely bad food, settling anyplace was like dying and going to heaven. They rose early the next morning and headed out.

"I've had a million people tell me I should write a book," Lencho said to Kelley. "Almost ten years ago Lew Stieger and I sat down with some pot, beer, and coke and recorded tapes. I told him the story of my life. You know, outlined it from the day I smoked that first doobie up until 2002 when I was gonna move to California and get into the medical marijuana business. I got seventeen sets of those tapes transcribed. I thought at first they might read well enough for a book or that I would go back and write the book myself. Lew is a film maker and a screenwriter, and he wanted to write it, but he never did. Not yet, at least."

"I write," Kelley told him. "I can't say I been published very often, usually self published. Oh yeah, once actually, in the San Diego Reader. Got paid fifteen hundred dollars for a story on my adventures with the feds and Tom Metzger."

"The White supremacist?" Lencho asked.

"The very one. Yours is a fascinating story, my friend. You are the real deal, for sure. I have known my share of colorful characters and the last couple days shooting the shit convinces me you take the cake. You're my kinda guy. Let me write your bio. What else we got to do, anyway, for the next few years?" And so it was decided. They discussed the Camp and what it might be like. Was it a barracks setup or two or three man rooms? Would there be computers?

"We sure could use a computer," Kelley said. "Plug the draft into word processing files and go back and make corrections and changes as needed. I hear the fed joints have the best equipment, conditions, and food. I hope it's true. Especially the food. I've been starving for the past year in those Arkansas jails."

When Lencho had his first taste of federal detention after his return from Mexico at La Tuna, the place was spacious. In the entire system, there could not have been twenty-five thousand inmates. When they pulled into Lompoc on May 8, 2009 there were over two hundred ten thousand men and women in over one hundred ten federal and contract prisons. The food back in the 1980s as he had remembered it had been pretty good. "They asked you how you liked your eggs in the morning. Over easy or medium." In 2009, they seldom served eggs at all except on Sundays when it was the mass produced, powdered variety. "Not since my Navy days on the USS Galveston have I seen food as bad as in jail. At the federal level it goes from adequate to awful," Lencho said later. Six out of ten inmates were there for drugs, nine out of ten had plead guilty. The feds brag of a ninety-six percent conviction rate. No one with any sense argues with the feds. If you did, you went to trial. There you lost. The feds cheat and then give you three times the years for making them mad.

The bus pulled in late that afternoon after a circuitous route that skirted Los Angeles to the coast, but had to turn around just outside Santa Paula because of a fierce brush fire whipped up by sundowners, the cold cousins to the Santa Ana winds. All the way the two geriatric delinquents yacked and hooted over doper war stories and past days of glory and terror. As is so common with old guys from the counterculture, they learned they had mutual acquaintances and shared experiences with protests and confrontations in the old days of the sixties and seventies. Not to mention the drugs. Certain loads and types of marijuana were legendary such as the renowned Thai stick, the Colombian reds and golds, the red Lebanese hash. These were guideposts to their history, what they held in common. The concept, the vision of Lencho's story began to coalesce.

"Yes, my friend," Kelley said. "This is some heavy stuff. The public needs to hear this. Get your notes sent soon as possible and we shall begin."

"First I would like to have one of these jailhouse lawyers draw up a contract between you and I. I'll pay you for your help, but I don't want you or anyone else trying to put their claim on my story. But we gotta be careful," Lencho whispered conspiratorially. "I have things to say that can still come back and bite people on the ass. Stuff about the cartels, the mafias, and especially the dirty cops. Some people aren't going to like what I have to say. Yeah, we gotta be real quiet about this." Easier said than done, as it would turn out.

Lompoc Prison Camp South was six acres of compound where three hundred and fifty men were cramped asshole to elbow in two barracks. The whole prison system sat on the coast midway between Santa Barbara and San Luis Obispo. It was an outpost of windy vistas owned by the U.S. Air Force at Vandenberg and in fact unlike the Oklahoma guards joke, was not particularly lovely.

It was a green place, but cold. Everywhere else in California in the summer is hot, it seems, except Lompoc where the winds howl daily and the heavy fog and marine layer keep the sun at bay. The land once belonged to the Indians and Lompoc means 'Lake' or 'Lagoon' in the Chumash tongue.

Infrastructure at the camp was primitive compared to the two behind the fence prisons that sat alongside. The Low and the Medium both had better amenities such as computers, recreation, and classes for rehabilitation, but the camp had no fences. This seems (to many people) like a sign that it is a 'club fed,' and while it was less stringent to some degree, the boys found this to be disingenuous. The place was a work camp, which struck them as similar in many ways to southern plantation type prisons. Everyone had a job at the camp. Lencho was sent to grounds maintenance where in short order he was in charge, barking orders and doling out jobs to the new A and O's much as he had done when he was on the landscaping crew out of Phoenix in his halfway house days. Kelley was sent to food service with his vast skills at dish washing. Soon, due to his diligence and old age, he was put on the line dishing out chow for the hungry rabble. As time passed, both men found their jobs getting easier until they became virtual sinecures.

At the chapel, Lencho organized what he euphemistically called 'geezer yoga' led by the spiritual smuggler Gordon Shuster. The old guys grunted and groaned to cosmic stretches and balancing positions. Kelley pounded the piano and regaled them all to his 1968 composition , "Pocket (got a hole in it and my joint fell out)." The library was full of books of all description and they read voraciously. The New York Times was provided by Juan Tortuga. The Wall Street Journal from Will the Pharmacist. The Economist came up from Dr. Bob Jones, DDS emeritus and Kelley's oldest and truest pal from grade school. Conversation and anecdotes and observations, and experiences came in abundance from the treasure trove that lived at the camp: the inmates.

Connica sent Lencho his seventeen volume collection of notes numbering around four hundred pages and the two old weed men began the task at hand. Kelley flopped in his bunk for over a month reading the notes that had been transcribed from tape recordings to paper by Lencho's niece, Jessica, and marveled at the story being told.

South of the border, in many places where Lencho had traipsed with impunity years before, the battles between the cartels and the government saw historic peaks of gore and violence. In the border city of Ciudad-Juarez, a place he had witnessed wild orgies between the mafia and the police, now had become the most dangerous city on earth. A place where hundreds were murdered each week over the drug trade. Decapitated corpses were hung from bridges in Tijuana, policemen and mayors of towns great and small disappeared or were found dead along the roadsides. The U.S. government itself was laying contingency plans to invade Mexico with troops to defend the third war it was involved in worldwide or so said the Wall Street Journal. And in California, the voting public was about to say yes or no to legalizing marijuana for purely recreational use. And the weed men sat in a federal prison for weed while in the state itself, it was virtually legal. Such was now the conundrum of the war on drugs. And the vaunted DEA and Justice Department were threatening the voters if they voted 'yes' to legalization. The war must go on, they intoned ominously. These issues were discussed daily by the two, and on August 17, 2009 they began the first chapter of 'Lencho.'

Two weeks later, Lencho got paranoid. One of the inmates took him aside and solemnly warned him the word was getting around about the big pot dealer smuggler and all his colorful stories. This would no doubt end badly when the prison got wind. Typing all this was hard enough on 1980's vintage IBM electric typewriters (there were no computers), but suddenly the momentum came to a screeching halt while Lencho contemplated his next move. Should he continue or not? Would the authorities at the camp toss him and Kelley in the hole? Finally, they agreed it should be continued albeit cautiously and that meant as little chit chat as possible.

"I just got done editing the first chapter, rough though it be," Kelley said to the weed man one Monday morning. But the weed man seemed troubled again. "What's wrong now?" Kelley asked.

"My daughter had a stroke," Lencho said. "Little Callie. I delivered her myself. She's only thirty-four."

"My god!" Kelley exclaimed. "How is that possible?"

"She's in the hospital in Chico. The prison won't give me a furlough to go see her."

A month later, on September 12, 2009, Callie died from heart failure. The weed man was stunned. He had called home and his wife had to deliver the news. Instead of a gradual recovery, his little girl was gone. "My life will never be the same," he told Kelley with tears welling. "The prison is refusing me a furlough to attend her funeral, of course. They might even toss me in the hole over depression. I will hold my grief until I am a free man. Then I can weep for her memory. But I don't think I will ever be the same."

*****

Lencho's bunkie was a black fellow named Dee. Not quite forty, he was spending twenty five years in federal prison for selling fifty-two grams of rock cocaine. His stories of procuring crack to sell as a youth from Hispanic sources in South Central Los Angeles caused the weed man to reflect back in time to the days of Jerry the spook down in Mexico City. He had put those scary memories largely out of his mind and they weren't even included in his notes done with Lew. Now they returned and he made the rounds of the black inmates collecting their anecdotes of the mid-eighties. Thousands of black men were incarcerated for decades under the draconian crack cocaine laws enacted by Congress in the wake of the crack epidemic. Many in the black community thought then that the CIA had a hand in this tragedy. Crack dealers from those days had become legendary among the black crews in the prisons of America. Men and organizations like Motor Head Bo Bennet, Michael Harris (aka Harry O), Big Dave, Du-cee, Young Tommy, Big Pat, the Whitey Enterprise, 3rd World Brother, Mark Ozone, and of course Freeway Ricky Ross. These men were revered for the money they made and the money was truly epic. Millions a week. But who had introduced the crack they all were now serving decades for selling? Who was really behind it? Lencho and Kelley agreed with the blacks that it was the CIA, despite that agency's denials and 'the witness to history' had his own insights, of course. Lompoc prison camp was not only a warehouse of men, it was a storehouse of knowledge. An awful lot of that contradicted the official line.

Was a prison a storehouse or more a microcosm? A world unto its own? Lompoc was populated by a vast cross section of races, creeds, and cultures. Take a look around and see the multitudes drawn together by crime.

Besides the native born, the population consisted of English, Irish, Russian,

Ukrainian, Israeli, Syrian, Palestinian, Greek, Mexican, Colombian, Nicaraguan, and Panamanian. All the Asians were there, including Chinese from the mainland and Taiwan, South Korea, Thailand, Viet Nam, Cambodia, Malaysia, Japan, Laos, Burma, and the Philippines. Micronesia was represented. Guam and Samoa and naturally the Hawaiians. And everybody pretty much got along, even the Jews and various Arabs.

And all the crimes the men were charged with were held in common. Mostly drugs, but also a bunch of pretty clever and determined white collar types. The more forthright of those would tell you they were the real crooks, not the dopers. They had consciously set out to steal, and steal they did. One favorite, Juan Tortuga, was embarrassed periodically when his story showed up on a popular television show reminding the world he had beat the Scientologist religion out of over half a billion dollars with his cagey pyramid. The man was also a scholar and a savvy economist. But most of the others had engaged in garden variety scams such as bank embezzlements, security and identity theft, credit card and mail fraud, forgery, and counterfeiting. There was also cell phone and communications capers and computer fraud. A favorite typist was actually sentenced on obscenity charges for spamming members of adult web sites with ads during that period when everyone was bitching about that. You didn't actually have to be guilty to come to Lompoc.

The dopers were the most plentiful, however. From smuggling to street dealing on a fairly epic scale, most of these lads never knew what had hit them. Some were hardened vets, but many more were just kids caught up in the Miami Vice, Hollywood, Gangsta Rap syndrome and eager to go back out and hustle again. They'd be back and maybe become more circumspect the next time. And, of course, the marijuana cultivators including many, many medical marijuana entrepreneurs like Eddy Lepp. Nothing was irritating the DEA more than they.

And in the chapel, they all bowed their heads or bowed to Mecca or crossed their legs and meditated or genuflected one way or another. A lot of religion in jail. And this was the world Lencho found himself in at the age of sixty-three when he had a visit from some old pals.

On November 8, 2009, G.R. Menera, the narc from PANT, accompanied by a detective out of the Prescott, Arizona police department came to Lompoc. They had a proposition for the weed man that didn't involve weed.

"Lencho you crook," Menera began, "you owe us a favor for that letter I wrote on your behalf. I should say the letter I let you write for yourself. My buddy here, Detective McClain, has a problem. Tell him about it, Mark."

Mark McClain was forty, an up and coming cop who was almost related to Lencho as was Menera. Lencho's sister Suzi had been a second mom who had helped raise him. He had been a de facto brother in that family along with Jim, Joe, and Tommy. Tommy had sunk into the cesspool of methamphetamine addiction, and he was the reason the two cops had come that day.

"My dad and Art were best friends all their lives, Lencho," the detective began. "Your sister and Art mean an awful lot to me. They were very decent to me when I was a kid and I know the family situation very well. That louse Tommy is a hop head maniac and he's ruining those folks' golden years. He's running all over town high as a kite all the time causing grief and trouble. He ain't dealing exactly cause he don't have to. Mom and dad are well off and they have always taken care of him. Buy him a new car every year, let him live with them and give him money. Frankly, they clearly enable his dreadful lifestyle, but I guess they love him. We think he's a menace and needs to be put down like the rabid dog he is."

"You got that right," Lencho answered. "I can still see the bullets in that revolver when he stuck it to my forehead years ago. He was out of his mind and coulda killed me. I see nothing has changed."

"Not a damn thing," agreed Menara.

"Not just me," McClain continued, "but someone else in the family wants the police to do something. Trouble is, he ain't a dealer so we haven't been able to do much except run him in now and then for being under the influence. Little by little though, he's just killing his folks. One day he will manage to kill some innocent bystander. Those meth freaks all love their guns."

"What do you want me to do about it?" Lencho asked.

"We want you to set him up, bud. You know everybody in Arizona. We want to bust him with an involvement in a meth deal. At least two pounds. Then we'll kick him over to the feds and he'll get twenty years minimum. His folks will be rid of him. The city will be rid of him. We can all breathe a sigh of relief. But it's gotta look real and it's gotta stay quiet. Can you help us?"

The wheels began to turn in the weed man's head. He had received a sentence reduction of forty months for valuable assistance to the federal government over nothing once. Maybe it could work again. But he knew at that very moment he could do little to assist with this half-baked plot the two cops had hatched, but that would not stop him from saying he would. "Sure, I'll help. I'll do everything I can. But I'll need a letter for my judge. I still got five years to go on this bogus charge. This could earn me a reduction under Rule 35. Do we have a deal?" They had a deal. If you can't join 'em, beat 'em.

When he passed the news to Tom Connelly in Phoenix, the big man whistled. "Son, you are a pistol. Still got your hand in the game! Well, just the fact the cops came to see you gives you the right to claim privilege due to endangerment. You as an inmate in the joint are put at risk when the police pull you out of your cell for any sort of a chat. It's been upheld in the courts that this activity can be dangerous to the health of a prisoner, and hence he can request consideration. Also, if you can be of assistance to them, we can ask. What are your thoughts on that?"

"I can't do squat for them, Tom," Lencho answered. "Firstly, I'm in prison. Secondly, I don't associate with any low life meth dealer. Of course, the cartel could do it, but all the guys I knew there are in hiding. No, not much I can offer except sympathy for Suzie and Art. Like they think putting Tommy in prison would end his parents' problems. Still, I want you to petition the court on my behalf. Tell them I'm helping. It's the old 'ongoing investigation' thing again. I seriously don't believe Menara and McClain will pursue this for long anyway. This is just wishful thinking on their part cause they love Suzie and Arthur. But once they get back home they'll think twice about it all. They could get in serious doo-doo over this. They'll chicken out." And they did chicken out.

*****

Lencho was originally placed in VT Meats to learn to be a butcher at camp snoopy. But he had already been a butcher way back in the stockyard days of his youth and was not very enthused with his assignment.

"This guy named Harbor got busted for growing pot out in the far corner of the corn field last year," Paul Kelsner told him. "It was hilarious."

"Did you say Harbor?" Lencho blanched. "One of my oldest pals has a son named Harbor. He was in here."

"How many Harbors can there be?" Paul went on. "Him and two other guards cooked up a caper to grow the herb. May have done it successfully the year before even. But last year, 08, they were well along with the crop and an inmate cowboy came upon it out riding the range. The bastard turned them in. This camp is full of rats."

The pot growing incident was a big embarrassment to the prison, and Harbor had been transferred to Safford, Arizona while the two guards took early retirement. Just goes to show a weed man never sleeps, Lencho thought with a grin.

*****

At Lompoc Federal Prison Camp, the men worked out at the weight pile and ran the track that winds around the ball field. They played bocce ball and tossed horse shoes, snuck smokes behind the out buildings and watched the TVs in the chapel, rec room and kiosk. They shot pool and ate microwave, homemade meals in the dorms. They all felt the food stunk. Everyone worked for pennies an hour. Now and then, they watched an Atlas ICBM launch from afar at Vandenberg Air Base.

Tall eucalyptus trees were everywhere and marked the boundaries. Once upon a time, the camp was a more easygoing place some say. In his book, 'Stormriders', Jimmy Freeman tells of climbing up in the branches and smoking hash. Dropping LSD and tossing frisbees. He had been sent here on a smuggling rap. Fifteen tons of red Lebanese hashish. Three years! What a hoot. Jimmy and his friends had been a part of the legendary Brotherhood of Eternal Love out of Laguna Beach. Little George, Lencho's buddy with whom he had driven the northern loop years earlier selling bennies and weed had been a Brother. Now, almost forgotten. So much had changed. The super severe federal guidelines had come down the pike in the eighties. That fifteen tons of hash Jimmy served three years for would have netted him a life sentence today. That's how it went with the war on drugs. This invention of the DEA and the crooked politicians. All on the take but with no fed ever going to jail for their involvement.

The prison camp at Lompoc was quite the enterprise with over 1800 acres in cultivation. Corn and vegetables. A huge dairy farm producing enough milk for the inmates at several prisons. VT Meats slicing and dicing hamburger and the federally chartered UNICORP plants cranking out defense department wiring and other goods. The inmates earned from six dollars per month to a princely one dollar an hour. A crew of cowboys rode the range on their horses rounding up herds of Angus cattle that were sold to beef processors.

Over at the tool shed, Lencho did his duty, obeyed all the orders given to him, and directed the new A and O's he oversaw painting and mending fences and raking up the mountains of eucalyptus leaves that endlessly littered the ground.

In his tool shed office, he had as many comforts as he could procure from around the compound. A coffee maker with coffee stolen out of the kitchen, a fridge, microwave, typewriter and a small floor heater to remove the chill in the air. A large table with six chairs for him and the boys to sit around and discuss current affairs of this ever changing world. The subjects were vast, ranging from social changes to political turmoil. Information came in from all over the world via this diverse society contained within the Lompoc Prison Camp. Doctors, lawyers, college professors, cartel big wigs, Chinese, Russian, Italian, Greek, Armenian and Hawaiian mafias, all of whom sat around the table throwing in their two cents worth. The Hells Angels through religious zealots and assorted political sleaze bags all came and went through this ersatz war room tool shed. One day, Nick Bacala, goomba, political analyst, campaign fundraiser, and former associate of corrupt lobbyist Jack Abramoffa came in all excited, "Look at this Lencho," he shouted.

"Sit down and rest your neck," one of the H.A.'s barked.

"What have you got?" Lencho asked.

"Hot off the press, the feds have finally stepped on their own dicks. Let me read this to you." Bacala read from the New York Times:

Today, Attorney General Eric Holder was held in contempt by Congress, which has been requesting documents concerning "Fast & Furious," an operation carried out by the ATF, which resulted in thousands of guns "walking" into the hands of the Mexican drug cartels. Two American border guards were killed with these weapons. 'Since the documents were asked to be turned over, the Justice department has engaged in stalling tactics and has failed to deliver,' said a house staffer. 'This has deep implications regarding the current administration's involvement with the most dangerous elements we have ever faced on our borders.'

To that Lencho replied, "Well, you've come out of that trance you've been in for the last thirty months. I've been saying this all along. The U.S. is up to no good down there and it's just going to get worse. What do you think about this, señor Mendosa?"

"It's like we been agreeing, Lencho, the United States has been infiltrating Mexico for some years now. It ramped up with the DEA involvement back in the early eighties, helping to get drugs passed through the border to build the resources of various La Familia members building their power through money and influence. Then they move to another area and do the same thing. In time, they have divided the players into different camps around Mexico made up of the Tijuana cartel, Juarez cartel, Gulf cartel, Sinaloa cartel, Familia Michoacán, Zeta's Cartel de Millenio, and the now new Generation cartel.

"Then come the guns and the shooting begins with one area trying to take control of another area," he continued. "It's worked out well for your feds. Over fifty thousand people have been murdered over the past five years. Now the Mexican government cannot control any of this. All we need next is for some international incident to take place, like an American airline to be shot down or a hostage situation at some beach resort full of Americans, and here come the troops. You know," he laughed. "CIA 101! They'll be all over Mexico in a matter of hours."

"We're going to take that country or at least its resources. Of course it makes sense now. I've been trying to figure this drug war out for years," Bacala stammered.

"And it all started with a little weed in some backpacks," Lencho sighed remembering so long ago.

"You gonna give up this crazy weed stuff?" Kelley asked him. "When you get out, you gonna bend to the iron heel at long last? Was everything you went through worth it?"

"I'm a weed man," Lencho replied serenely. "I was born a weed man…. and I'll die a weed man."

Epilogue

The other day I asked a fellow inmate, what is your favorite federal agency? After thinking about this for some time he answered, "I don't have one." There are a lot of us that feel this way. It seems we have become comfortable in our lives and have forgotten just exactly what it is that the federal government is hired to do for us.

Shouldn't they be providing us with national infrastructure, education, health care, and protection against invasion from other countries? We give huge amounts of our income to them only to see them waste our tax dollars in bad planning, budget overrides, and constant fighting in our nation's capital, never getting anything accomplished. Wasting billions to get elected only to fight over the spoils when it's time to do the work.

Of course, I am a simple man. Not knowing a lot of the ins and outs of government, but even a simple man can see when something is not working. In my own humble opinion, I believe that it is we the people who have let this happen. Those in power know that as long as there are enough of us who are comfortable, or "fat" if you will, the rest can just get fucked. Our leaders have sold us out. The national debt is projected to be fourteen trillion dollars, economic chaos is upon us. We've outsourced our jobs and have allowed illegal immigrants to take over the workforce that at one time was the mainstay of our own family security. We are going bankrupt both morally and financially.

Social Security and Medicare are slowly sinking, and going down with them is the promise we made to those that deserve to be taken care of in their retirement. Politicians and government employees have set things up so they are covered in this respect. Spend twenty years in government and you're on the gravy train.

They build huge bureaucracies that suck tax dollars beyond belief, most of which is wasted with no results. The war on drugs is the perfect government black hole. Created sixty years ago, politicians have used it to get themselves elected using special interest groups like law enforcement and religious zealots thumping a moral tune that is such bullshit that millions of us are no longer listening.

Thirty to fifty million people in this country enjoy using marijuana (illegally) in their lives without causing any damage to themselves or others. Certainly compared to alcohol or tobacco, which even a fool can see is not only allowed, but through advertisement it is encouraged. How many people look forward to having a drink after a long day at work despite the fact that four hundred thousand die in this country alone from alcohol related deaths. Cigarettes are easily obtainable by our youth without any kind of deterrent. They are not arrested. They are not sent to prison. Yet four hundred thousand die each year from related diseases. In contrast, illegal drug use kills less than fifteen thousand annually. What's wrong with this picture?

When I was a young man back in the late sixties, I was passed a little corn cob pipe and tried my first hit of weed. The effect changed my life. It's not like all at once I became a saint, but it did put me to thinking. Can you imagine what things would be like if we all started to think things over and acted accordingly? It happened to a lot of us at that time. All of a sudden young people across America were in the streets protesting all things wrong in our society. War became unacceptable. Men burned their draft cards. Women burned their bras. Capitalist exploitation of the world was not cool. Material possessions were considered a real bummer. Communes popped up all over the place. One no longer need be hungry or homeless. Seldom was anyone turned away. I myself visited many places such as this. We were looking for peace and happiness. The fortunate helped the unfortunate. The unfortunate did the best they could. Skeptics will say that government assistance fed most of these people; but in the long run, the concept of communal living could have been a balance between capitalist greed and poverty.

Of course, the government is in itself a sort of commune, living off of the tax dollars under a big red, white, and blue teepee. The only difference is we didn't waste much or want much. Now, we will all agree that mankind has an obsession with all kinds of vices. We abuse all kinds of food and drink, literally killing ourselves on too much bad food, alcohol, and drugs both illegal and legal—the legal ones killing more people than the illegal.

Through law enforcement we have created a multi-billion dollar drug market where we have lost control of our borders as well as our streets. Whole communities are under siege by ruthless drug dealers that are so bent on controlling the drug market, they care not who gets in the way. They have control of so much money, absolutely nothing is going to stop them. Law enforcement from cities, counties, state, and the federal government have not come close to even hampering their efforts. Drugs are easy to obtain, accessible to anyone interested. This would not be true if drugs were not in demand.

But that is not the case. We like our vices, and as long as we are not harming others, the only real victims are those that choose to use and abuse. A crime needs to have a victim. When we steal, vandalize, abuse, rape, or terrorize, others suffer. These types of crimes receive shorter sentences than non-violent drug offences. The reason for this is that law enforcement and prosecutors like to lead us to believe they are out there protecting us from evil. Drugs are cheap to manufacture or grow. The money involved in drug trafficking is all about law enforcement, lawyers, and incarceration. What a scam they have created.

In 1973, when arrested for thirteen hundred pounds of marijuana in San Diego, large bonds were paid and lawyers' fees were astronomical. I had the feeling that everyone was enjoying the new economic trend involved with prosecuting such a large group of easy marks that we were. Even Judge Walker commented that he had never had a group of such nice young men in his courtroom with the price tag we had attached to our case. He ended up giving the leader of our bunch nine months. I myself only served three and a half months. This was before they had learned how to capitalize on this new phenomenon. Today, this same offence would cost you your property. Your children would go to the state. Your bank accounts would be confiscated. Your career would be over and you would be sent to prison for as much as ten years or more, while the lawyers, prosecutors, judges, and jails are happier than a pig knee deep in shit.

What is currently going on in California is mind boggling, but no one seems to get it. In 2004, State bill 420 was passed legalizing the cultivation and sales of medical marijuana. What the common man didn't know was that it would turn into California's number one agricultural product. Valued at a stunning twenty billion dollars annually compared to one billion for oranges and three billion for grapes. Twenty Billion!

So the government (President Obama) announces that they will not interfere with what Californians voted into law. Eight years later, after billions of dollars have been made and spent on all sorts of different properties, homes, businesses, vehicles, and everything that you can imagine, the federal government began in the summer of 2012 to shut it all down seizing bank accounts and confiscating everything that was acquired over the past eight years. Pretty smooth way to do business. Go ahead and let it happen, then come in and take it all back. This was the plan all along. They take what we have and put us in jail, and then take more tax dollars from us to pay for it all. Ouch!

We know damn well this is not going to change as long as the government has us scared into submission, hiding in our closets afraid of being destroyed by the very tactics previously mentioned. The people of this nation need to join together like the good old days and get back on the streets to fight these bastards with peaceful protests. We must stand up for the return of freedom and our right to our own pursuit of happiness, like the Declaration of Independence clearly states. Thomas Jefferson said that the citizens of this country have the obligation to police our government and overthrow them when we see them out of control.

You know they would shoot us down like dogs. The ones left would be locked up in prison camps until they were ready to kiss the government's fat asses and promise to be good little citizens and return to their station in life. Fuck you very much.

I hope you found some enjoyment in reading my story. More than that, I hope you enjoyed my weed. I wish there was something I could say that would return us to the days when Americans had the balls to stand up against oppression and fear.

Good luck in the future. I'm taking my grandchildren to the beach. Love it or Leave it~~ Lencho

Photo: Gary Quiring

L.L. Kellerman was born May 15th, 1947 and grew up in Prescott, Arizona. Long-time activist, distributor, and connoisseur of the sacred herb. Could never figure what the problem was. Has won no achievement awards, merit-badges, or civic recognition. Lives in parts unknown, mostly tropical beaches, rodeo grounds, and trout streams. More info at: www.facebook.com/LLKellerman.